Collaborative Innovation Mechanism of GBA in China

AF902928

Shusong Ba · Peng Shen · Xinning Liang

Collaborative Innovation Mechanism of GBA in China

A Free Port Approach

厦门大学出版社 XIAMEN UNIVERSITY PRESS | 国家一级出版社 全国百佳图书出版单位

Springer

Shusong Ba
Chief China Economist Office
HKEx
Hong Kong, Hong Kong

Peng Shen
Greater Bay Area Financial Institute
Shenzhen, China

Xinning Liang
Shenzhen SOEs Innovation and Reform Institute
Shenzhen, China

Translated by
Feng Yue
College of Foreign languages
Fujian Normal University
Fuzhou, China

Huali Wu
College of Foreign Languages
Fujian Normal University
Fuzhou, China

Hanxiong Zhu
College of Foreign Languages
Wuhan University of Technology
Wuhan, China

Yan Jiang
College of Foreign Languages
Wuhan University of Technology
Wuhan, China

ISBN 978-981-19-2253-4 ISBN 978-981-19-2251-0 (eBook)
https://doi.org/10.1007/978-981-19-2251-0

Jointly published with Xiamen University Press
The print edition is not for sale in China (Mainland). Customers from China (Mainland) please order the print book from: Xiamen University Press.

Translation from the Chinese language edition: "粤港澳大湾区协同创新机制研究——基于自由贸易组合港模式" by Shusong Ba et al., © Xiamen University Press 2019. Published by Xiamen University Press. All Rights Reserved.
© Xiamen University Press 2022
This work is subject to copyright. All rights are solely and exclusively licensed by the Publisher, whether the whole or part of the material is concerned, specifically the rights of translation, reprinting, reuse of illustrations, recitation, broadcasting, reproduction on microfilms or in any other physical way, and transmission or information storage and retrieval, electronic adaptation, computer software, or by similar or dissimilar methodology now known or hereafter developed.
The use of general descriptive names, registered names, trademarks, service marks, etc. in this publication does not imply, even in the absence of a specific statement, that such names are exempt from the relevant protective laws and regulations and therefore free for general use.
The publishers, the authors, and the editors are safe to assume that the advice and information in this book are believed to be true and accurate at the date of publication. Neither the publishers nor the authors or the editors give a warranty, expressed or implied, with respect to the material contained herein or for any errors or omissions that may have been made. The publishers remain neutral with regard to jurisdictional claims in published maps and institutional affiliations.

This Springer imprint is published by the registered company Springer Nature Singapore Pte Ltd.
The registered company address is: 152 Beach Road, #21-01/04 Gateway East, Singapore 189721, Singapore

Preface

Theoretical Exploration and Institutional Design of Combined Free Trade Ports of Guangdong-Hong Kong-Macao Greater Bay Area

In tracking and studying the development process of the Great Bay Areas globally, especially that of China's Guangdong-Hong Kong-Macao Greater Bay Area (GBA), we have come to see huge potential of the GBA in institutional innovation due to its unique diversity and compatibility of differentiated institutional mechanisms. We believe that GBA practice will provide valuable reference for China's regional development and institutional innovation, among which, we regard the exploration of GBA synergy innovation and combined free trade ports most valuable. We offer the present book as a milestone in our phased research and thinking.

Great changes are taking place in the current international economic and financial environment as has never happened in the past 100years. Taking Sino-US trade frictions as an example, we see the rise of global trade protectionism and emergence of deglobalization after four decades of high speed globalization in the world. Certain extreme forces in the United States are setting the stage for decoupling Sino-US relations in certain areas. Against this background, China continues to promote reform and opening-up and globalization, and its impact on China's future development and the evolution of the global landscape deserves attention. Specifically, it is important for China to conduct multi-level platform design and path innovation in the process of promoting globalization. Learning from the experience of the third generation of global free trade port construction, China can lead the innovation and exploration in positioning, mechanism, and functionality of free trade port construction. In the next development phase, it is possible for THE GBA to take the lead in the design and construction of free trade ports to promote regional industrial chain coordination, form international production capacity cooperation with countries and regions along the Belt and the Road, build an integrated international Belt and Road public service platform, enable organic integration of Belt and Road and free trade port construction, resulting in internal and external spillover functional value, serving China to participate in and promote a new round of globalization and supporting the provision of new international public goods.

On June 20, 2018, the document *Suggestions for Accelerated Development of Shenzhen Port* was released by the Shenzhen Municipal People's Government. It has set out the development goal of "*turning Shenzhen Port into a global green and intelligent hub port and building an international shipping center together with Hong Kong Port.*" To achieve this goal, it is necessary to improve the infrastructure of port and navigation, improve the system of collection and distribution, upgrade the greenness and intelligence of ports, and accelerate the concentration of shipping services. We are thus inspired to explore the model of combined free trade ports in the collaborative innovation mechanism of the Greater Bay Area. A combined ports model is not only a regional development strategy, but also the product of the deepening of regional cooperative governance and the development of free trade theory. At the same time, the emergence of combined ports may further promote economic globalization and the progress of free trade theory.

The book starts from the background of the construction of combined free trade ports of GBA and adopts a global perspective. We have carried out a systematic survey of the theoretical research and development practice of free trade ports and regional synergy in the world. After analyzing the conditions for building the combined ports of GBA, we have come up with preliminary conceptions for its collaboration from various aspects, including space, industry, finance, science and technology, institution, governance, human resources, and so on. On top of this, through the value simulation analysis of the combined ports model, we find that the coordinated policy of the combined ports will significantly enhance the economic, trade, and financial strength of the Greater Bay Area, and strengthen the effect of population agglomeration.

In the research and writing process of this book, I have been in charge of the research framework and research focus while a huge amount of foundational work has been undertaken by researchers from Shenzhen Qianhai Institute for Innovative Research and HSBC Institute of Finance of Peking University, including writing the first draft and literature sorting. Here is a list of scholars in charge of the main chapters: Chapter 1, Li Ruan and Li Ke; Chapter 2, Song Jing and Cui Xuegang; Chapter 3, Wang Xi and Song Mingying; Chapter 4, Cai Tiancheng and Wei Yujun; Chapter 5, Song Jing and Li Wei; Chapter 6, Xu Jianbin and Song Mingying ; Chapter 7, Cui Xuegang and Li Ke; and Chapter 8, Liang Xinning. Multiple revisions and adjustments have been made on the basis of the first draft and great improvements have been achieved by enriching the contents of key chapters.

From the theoretical logic and historical experience, the function design of the combined ports of GBA should take GBA Synergy Innovation as its core function. At the same time, we should take into consideration that the combined ports model corresponds to the current restructuring of the pattern and rules of global trade, China's supply-side structural reform and industrial upgrading process, and the Belt and Road construction framework. It answers the call for China to build a platform for international cooperation and actively participate in a new round of globalization. Therefore, on the basis of synergy innovation, it is bound to be a process of continuous evolution and innovation to design and build a new integrated value chain of combined ports of GBA. To this end, we have made meticulous survey on the past experience and policies. Despite our efforts in covering many angles, there is no absolute safeguard for perfect trend judgment and forecast. We are more than happy to accept criticisms and suggestions from our readers.

November 2019 Shusong Ba

Contents

About the Authors

Shusong Ba Ph.D. Researcher. Chief China Economist, Hong Kong Exchanges and Clearing (HKEX). Professor Ba is the Managing Director and Chief China Economist of Hong Kong Exchanges and Clearing Limited (HKEX), Chief Economist of the China Banking Association (CBA), and Executive Director of the HSBC Financial Research Institute at Peking University. He is also a member of the Mainland Opportunities Committee of the Financial Services Development Council (FSDC) of Hong Kong, Vice President of the China Society of Macroeconomics, a member of Ministry of Commerce's Economic and Trade Policy Advisory Committee, a member of China Banking and Insurance Regulatory Commission's Expert Guidance Committee for the banking industry's implementation of the new Basel capital accord, a member of China Securities Regulatory Commission's M&A Specialists Committee, and a member of China's 13th Five-Year Plan National Development and Planning Specialists Committee. Professor Ba is a fellow of experts who receive the State Council's special allowance. He was previously Deputy General Manager of the Bank of China Hangzhou Branch, Assistant General Manager of Bank of China (Hong Kong), Director-General of the Strategy and Development Committee of the Securities Association of China, Deputy Director of the Economics Department of the Liaison Office of the Central People's Government in the Hong Kong Special Administrative Region, and Deputy Director-General of the Financial Research Institute of the State Council's Development Research Centre. He also served as the chief expert in the basic research field of "International Economic and Financial Structure" in Development Research Center of the State Council. He was engaged in post-doctoral research in the China Center for Economic Research at Peking University and was a senior visiting scholar at Columbia Business School. He is an expert in the business operations of the Chinese financial market, in the making of financial policies, and in the theoretical research on finance. In recent years, he has taken part in major financial reform projects including Bond Connect and Shenzhen-Hong Kong Stock Connect. His publications include *Research on New Basel Capital Accord*, *Basel II in Financial Crisis: Challenges and Improvements*, *Study on Basel Capital Accord III*, *Annual Reports on the Development of Chinese Assets Management Industry*, and *The Financial Perspective of the Urbanization Transformation in China.*

Author's blog: http://weibo.com/bashusong
Author's WeChat account: bashusongonfinance
Author's Email: bashusong@163.com

Dr. Peng Shen is Secretary-General of the Shenzhen Qianhai Institute for Innovative Research. He is also a member of advisory committee on policymaking of many local governments, including that of the Shenzhen Municipal Government. He is a guest postgraduate supervisor at Huazhong University of Science and Technology. He has been involved with policy formulation and reform research on FTZs in China. He has published multiple research papers, including the ones in the journal of *Macroeconomics*. He has been awarded the national second prize in Business Management Modernization Innovation Competition.

Dr. Xinning Liang graduated from the University of Hong Kong and was a postdoctoral fellow at China Merchants Group (HK). Currently, Dr. Liang is Executive Director of the Office of Future City Innovation Research, recognized as a top-level overseas talent by the Shenzhen municipal government. Being a Level 1 Certified Constructor, Dr. Liang has working experience in large enterprises such as China Merchants Group and China Vanke Co., Ltd and a solid foundation in research areas covering synergetic innovation, regional development, and engineering management. Dr. Liang has published English and Chinese papers in top international journals including *Research Policy*.

Chapter 1
Background of the Construction of Combined Free Trade Ports of the GBA

Starting from the background and connotation of the concept of *Combined Free Trade Ports of the GBA*, this chapter demonstrates in detail that building combined ports in the Guangdong-Hong Kong-Macao Greater Bay Area is an inevitable choice for China to respond to domestic and international challenges such as the restructuring of the global economic and trade patterns, the support and advocacy to carry out China's Belt and Road Initiative, and the promotion of domestic supply-side structural reforms. On this basis, the target is set to construct the combined ports of the GBA against the highest international standards and level, thus promoting the integrated development of factors through institutional innovation and building a world-class bay area suitable for living, working, and traveling.

1.1 Conception of Combined Free Trade Ports of the GBA

The concept of Combined Free Trade Ports of GBA includes three different levels and key words, namely, the Guangdong-Hong Kong-Macao Greater Bay Area, free trade port, and combined ports.

To begin with, the concept of GBA is derived from the *Outline of Development Plan for the Guangdong-Hong Kong-Macao Greater Bay Area* issued by the Central Committee of the CPC and the State Council on February 18, 2019. The *Outline* upgrades the concept of GBA to a national strategy, benchmarking GBA against the top bay areas in the world. On the basis of strengthening cooperation between Guangdong, Hong Kong and Macao, the *Outline* is aimed to enhance the economic strength and regional competitiveness of the entire GBA. The GBA comprises nine cities in Guangdong Province, Hong Kong SAR and Macao SAR. The nine cities are leading the country in terms of economic development, opening to the outside world, and innovative vitality. Hong Kong is the world's most successful free trade port and Macao is a world tourism and leisure center as well as a world free trade port. The

© Xiamen University Press 2022

S. Ba et al., *Collaborative Innovation Mechanism of GBA in China*,
https://doi.org/10.1007/978-981-19-2251-0_1

pattern of *Two Ports plus One Area* has laid an unparalleled natural advantage for GBA to meet the standards of more open economies in the future.

Next, the free trade port is currently the most open special economic zone in the world. It is a specific area located within the borders of a country (region) where goods, capital, and personnel are free to enter and exit, and most goods are exempt from tariffs. Hong Kong, Singapore, Rotterdam and Dubai are all successful and typical free trade ports in the world. In addition to the free trade port of Hong Kong SAR, the Chinese government first proposed the establishment of a free trade port in the report of the 19th National Congress of the Communist Party of China. President Xi Jinping said, "*We will grant the pilot free trade zones greater autonomy in reform and explore ways to construct free trade ports.*" On April 13, 2018, President Xi Jinping delivered an important speech at the celebration of the 30th anniversary of the establishment of Hainan provincial special economic zone. He emphasized the resolution of the CPC Central Committee to support the establishment of a free trade pilot zone to cover the whole Hainan Province and encourage Hainan to explore and steadily advance the construction of free trade ports with Chinese characteristics. Subsequently, on April 15, 2018, *Guidelines of the CPC Central Committee and the State Council on Supporting Hainan in Comprehensively Deepening Reform and Opening Up* was issued, which outlined the development positioning and specific timetable for the construction of Hainan free trade port. So far, building a free trade port with Chinese characteristics has become an important national strategy for China to deepen its reform and opening up.

Finally, as a coordinated development model among regional ports, the combined ports model is based on the integrated interconnection of port facility construction and shipping-related fields. For example, as early as 1997, in order to strengthen the construction of the Shanghai International Shipping Center, the State Council issued the *Reply of the State Council on Approval of the Construction Plan of Shanghai Combined Ports* (Document of the State Council [1997] No. 87) and stipulated that the Combined Ports of Shanghai take Shanghai as the center and the two provinces of Jiangsu and Zhejiang as two wings, and the corresponding ports are combined without changing the original administrative affiliation. In addition, the *Suggestions on Promoting the Rapid Development of Shenzhen Port* on June 20, 2018 (Shenzhen Government [2018] No. 48) was issued by Shenzhen Municipal People's Government. It stipulates "*accelerating the construction of combined Shenzhen-Hong Kong ports, and promoting the establishment of a combined ports system in the Greater Bay Area*", "*exploring the model of Shenzhen-Hong Kong combined ports, and realizing the integration of port logistics services between the two regions*", and "*building a combined ports system in Greater Bay Area, strengthening the business links between Shenzhen Port with the rest of GBA and surrounding ports, as well as encouraging Shenzhen enterprises to enhance cooperation with ports in Humen, Zhongshan, Shunde, Huizhou, Shantou, Shanwei and Zhanjiang through technology and capital and constructing a GBA combined ports system with the combined ports of Shenzhen and Hong Kong as the core.*" In China, similar ports include combined ports of Suzhou[1] and the Ningbo-Zhoushan Port.[2]

The construction of GBA combined ports is a regional development strategy, a product of the advancement in regional coordinated governance and free trade theory. Such practice will contribute to the promotion of further economic globalization and theoretical progress on free trade. Of the "9 + 2" city cluster of GBA, free trade ports already exist in Hong Kong and Macao.

1.2 Necessity of the Construction of Combined Free Trade Ports of the GBA

1.2.1 Time to Construct Combined Ports as the Test Field for High Level Opening Up as the Global Economic and Trade Is Facing Change of Rules

President Xi Jinping pointed out that the global economy has shown a stable and positive trend since 2017, but the world economic growth is still weak. Trade protectionism, isolationism, populism and other thought trends continue to rise, and world peace and development are facing grimmer challenges. On June 28, 2019, President Xi Jinping delivered a speech on the world economic situation and trade issues with the title of *Joining Hands to Build a High-quality World Economy* at the G20 Summit. Xi said: "*We must grasp the general development trend. Throughout the ages, human beings have moved from isolation to openness and integration, which is an unstoppable trend of the times. We must embrace development opportunities with greater openness and seek mutual benefit through better cooperation to guide economic globalization in the right direction.*"

1.2.1.1 The Rise of Deglobalization and Trade Protectionism

In the world today, the slowing down of global economic growth and the rise of trade protectionism will aggravate the uncertainty of the future. The current protectionism and unilateralism led by the United States continue to spread. Meanwhile, trade and investment disputes have intensified. As a typical businessman, former US President

[1] A new port alliance formed by the integration of Zhangjiagang Port, Changshu Port and Taicang Port, and the former three ports are now Zhangjiagang Port Area of Suzhou Port, Changshu Port Area and Taicang Port Area.

[2] According to *Ningbo-Zhoushan Port Master Plan* (2014–2030), Ningbo-Zhoushan Port is divided into 19 port areas, of which there are nine main port areas (Beilun, Yangshan, Liuheng, Qushan, Chuanshan, Jintang, Daxie, Cenggang and Meishan), five key port areas (Shengsi, Daishan, Zhenhai, Baiquan, and Ma 'ao) and five general port areas (Dinghai, Shipu, Xiangshan Port, Yongjiang, and Shenjiamen).

Trump had a different understanding of international free trade and the concept of free trade lost favor. Douglas A. Irwin, an American trade historian, observed that the trade agreements made in the 1930s were referred to as *free trade agreements* in the 1980s but in recent years the agreements were signed as cooperative relations. An example is the *North American Free Trade Agreement* (NAFTA) signed by the United States, Canada, and Mexico, which was enforced on January 1, 1994. After President Trump took office, he made the three countries to resign the agreement which is called *The United States-Mexico-Canada Agreement* (USMCA).The term free trade was deleted.

From the perspective of international economic development trends, since the 2008 global financial crisis, aggregate demand has been shrinking. Global trade in goods has slowed down. Global trade has entered the stage of stock game. Total factor productivity has fallen and the international economy is experiencing deglobalization. As the world's major economies slowly recover from the 2008 crisis, the global economy will resume growth despite great difficulties. Most of the world's major economies will underperform for a while, leading to weak global GDP growth in the short term (as shown in Fig. 1.1).

In addition, the global population continues to grow, while the growth rate has slowed down. It is estimated that the world population will increase from about 7.3 billion to 8.8 billion in 2035. By the end of the twenty-first century, the total population will have reached an equilibrium point, remaining at about 11 billion. At the same time, the proportion of working-age population in various regions tends to decline, especially in developed countries. It is estimated that the proportion of the global population of working age will remain between 45 and 55% in 2040. The global population continues to age, i.e., the proportion of people over 65 years old is gradually increasing, while the proportion of people under 14 years old is decreasing.

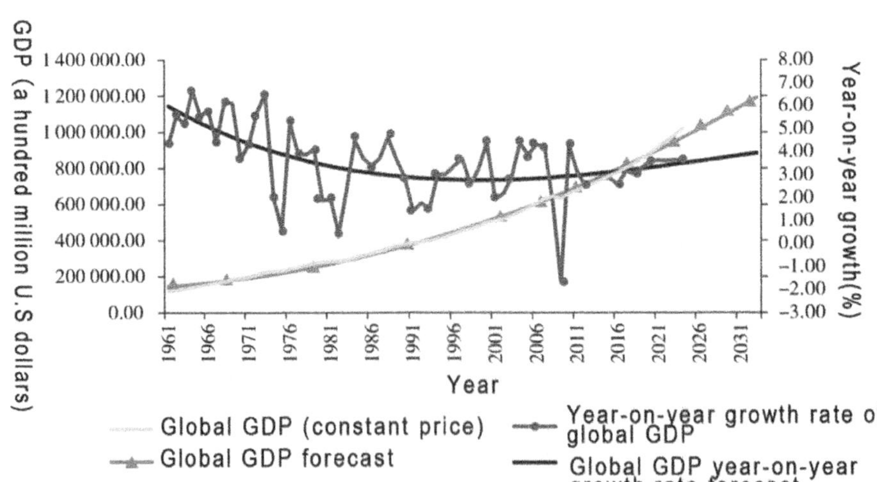

Fig. 1.1 Forecast of global GDP and its growth rate (*Source* United Nations website)

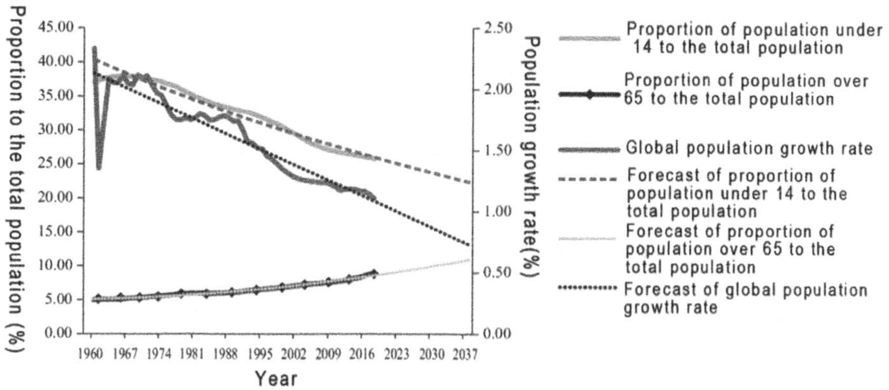

Fig. 1.2 Forecast of the age structure of the global population and its growth rate (*Source* Population Division, the United Nations)

It is expected to remain at 24% in 2035, as shown in Fig. 1.2. The gradual decline in fertility rates in various regions has led to a decline in global population growth rates. In Africa, it has declined rapidly from high levels. Fertility rates in Africa are declining rapidly, with women expected to have about 1.5 births per capita after 2020.

Apart from the challenges brought by economy and population to the international community, especially to the developed countries, the rise of developing countries in economic globalization has also led to political protectionism in some major developed countries in a way of deglobalization. For example, since the twentieth century, the economies of developing countries represented by China have developed rapidly. Taking the global GDP as an example, in 1990, China's GDP accounted for 1.7% of the global economy, while the United States accounted for 25.5%. But in 2018, China's GDP accounted for more than 16% of the global economy, while the United States accounted for 24.2%. China's rapid growth has made some developed countries believe that developing countries are the greatest beneficiary of economic globalization and developed countries, on the other hand, are increasingly becoming the biggest victims of globalization. A typical case is the United States' attempt to shape international rules. For example, the United States withdrew from the *Kyoto Protocol to the United Nations Framework Convention on Climate Change* in 2001, which was designed to address climate change issues, on the grounds that "*reducing greenhouse gas emissions will affect the US economy*". For another example, when in office, the former US President Barack Obama bypassed World Trade Organization (WTO) but participated in and organized the negotiations of the *Trans-Pacific Partnership Agreement* (TPP), trying to reshape the high-standard regional economic and trade rules to replace the international multilateral trade agreements.

1.2.1.2 Accelerated Adjustments of International Economic and Trade Rules

Since the WTO Doha Round entered an impasse, the United States has begun to exert its discourse power on global governance rules by actively introducing TPP, TTIP (*Transatlantic Trade and Investment Partnership*), TiSA (*Trade in Service Agreement*) and other trade agreement negotiations, in order to proactively adjust the layout of global trade rules. Since Trump became president, the U.S. has pulled out of the TPP negotiations, but has pushed for the USMCA. The TPP without the US came into effect and became the *Comprehensive Progressive Trans-Pacific Partnership* (CPTPP), but its main framework continues what it was when the United States was leading. These latest international high-standard rule systems have stipulated higher requirements for market openness and standards than the WTO framework, which reflect the advantages of developed countries. From the implementation of comprehensive market opening to better investor protection, from the regulation of the behavior of state-owned enterprises to the introduction of new issues such as environment and labor protection, these will have a profound impact on international trade and the international economic system.

Compared with the original agreements, the new high standards of international economic and trade rules pay more attention to the "intra-border" areas behind tariffs, with the main focus on the sharp reduction of tariff barriers, non-tariff barriers and industrial subsidies to create a fair competition between all types of enterprises. Therefore, rules and standards related to market access, Intellectual Property Protection (IPR), technical standard, environmental protection, dispute settlement mechanism (DSB), regulatory consistency, and service trade, cross-border e-commerce, free flow of cross-border data and other aspects are becoming the main content of negotiations on free trade agreements led by developed countries.

In addition, trade in services and digital trade are the focus in the areas highlighted by high standards of economic and trade rules. Especially with the rapid development of the global new technology revolution, trade in knowledge-intensive services such as telecommunications and IT services, business services and intellectual property rights has increased significantly. Promoting the opening up of services markets and the need for free movement are becoming increasingly important in global negotiations on both regional and bilateral FTAs.

Next, the rapid development of global digital trade has put forward urgent demand for the formulation of digital trade rules, but global digital trade has not yet formed a unified rule. Currently, more than 50% of global service trade has been digitized, and more than 12% of cross-border goods trade is realized through digital platforms. It is estimated that world trade will be dominated by trade in goods, trade in services and digital trade, a "tri-party" pattern. As an important digital trade mode, cross-border e-commerce is developing rapidly. It is calculated that global cross-border e-commerce B2C will maintain an average annual growth rate of 27% from 2016 to 2020.[3]

In contrast, the reform of WTO still faces numerous obstacles even though many countries are actively promoting it. At the end of 2018, WTO Director-General Azevedo emphasized the two major tasks of WTO reform. On the one hand, the current trading system should be maintained strong enough to continue to provide a stable basis for global trade cooperation; on the other hand, the WTO system should be flexible enough to help countries meet challenges and seize opportunities.[4] A new global trade rule system with regional high-standard trade agreements as the main form is quietly taking shape. Developing countries, in particular, are under pressure to compete under new rules.

1.2.1.3 Developing Countries in Asia Providing a Strong and Stable Impetus to World Economic Growth

The Spring Meetings of the World Bank and the International Monetary Fund was held in Washington, USA on April 12, 2019. IMF predicts that economic growth rate of the Asia–Pacific region will be 5.4% in both 2019 and 2020, contributing more than 60% to global economic growth, of which China contributing more than 30%. The stability of China's economic growth is higher than that of major developed countries. In 2018, China's GDP reached 90,030.9 billion yuan by an increase of 6.6% at comparable prices, achieving the expected development goal of about 6.5%. The growth rates in the four quarters of 2018 are 6.8, 6.7, 6.5, and 6.4% respectively. It has been operating within a narrow range of 6.4% to 7.0% for 16 consecutive quarters, showing high stability and resilience.

The economic growth has slowed down in major developed countries in the world. *World Economic Outlook* issued by IMF in 2019 predicts: "*Developed economies will continue to expand at a rate exceeding their potential growth rate this year and next, followed by a slowdown in economic growth; however, the growth of emerging markets and developing economies will be accelerated, and then stabilized.*" IMF even issued such warnings and predictions: "*The escalation of trade restrictions and retaliation is a risk. The first shot in a potential trade war has already been fired. If U.S. fiscal policy leads to a widening of its trade deficit and Europe and Asia do not shrink their surpluses, the conflict could intensify. The rules-based multilateral trading system needs to be further strengthened. This trading system was developed after World War II and has promoted unprecedented growth in the world economy, but it is currently in danger of collapse.*"[5]

[3] Wang Xiaohong. *Building High Standards of International Economic and Trade Rules to Promote Higher Level of Opening to the Outside World*. Guangming Daily, August 20, 2019, 11th Edition.

[4] General Director of WTO visits China and Japan to solve WTO deadlock dilemma [EB/OL]. The First Finance and Economics, November 9, 2018, https://www.yicai.com/news/10005660.html, last access time: October 1, 2019.

[5] IMF. World Economic Outlook [EB/OL]. https://www.imf.org/zh/Publications/WEO/Issues/2019/07/18WeoupdateJuly2019, last access time: October 15, 2019.

1.2.1.4 The General Trend of Economic Globalization and Regional Integration

Economic globalization has reached a new height since World War II. From the establishment of the IMF in 1994 to the signing of GATT (*General Agreement on Tariffs and Trade*)in 1946 and then to the establishment of the WTO, orderly systems are created inglobal trade, investment, and finance in the form of international multilateral agreements, constantly promoting the global flow of economic factors and resource allocation. For example, in 1980 FDI (Foreign Direct Investment) was US$54.396 billion and in 2018 it increased to US$1.2 trillion.[6] In 1990, the number of immigrants worldwide was 153 million, and the number is expected to reach 272 million in 2019, accounting for 3.5% of the global population.[7] The global flow of production factors promotes the global distribution of industrial chains and supply chains, which provides strong momentum for world economic growth. It is the consensus of economists such as David Hume, Adam Smith and many others that a free international trade is in the interest of consumers and the vast majority of the population.

The developing countries represented by emerging economies are the beneficiaries of economic globalization and hope to further enhance their position in the global industrial chain. Therefore, they support the promotion of economic globalization in a higher quality and more balanced direction. Meanwhile, the comparative advantage of developed countries is still concentrated at the high end of the industrial chain, which contributes to a large part of the GDP. Employees in these fields, middle- and senior-level managers and some grass-roots personnel of various institutions remain strong supporters of economic globalization.

The developing countries, represented by China, urgently need to align high-standard international economic and trade rules with regional opening-up. On the one hand, they adapt to changes in the international rules system with a higher level of opening-up. On the other hand, they compel the transformation and upgrading of the domestic economic structure and push forward incremental reform to form a new pattern of comprehensively deepening reform and opening up.

The Guangdong-Hong Kong-Macao Greater Bay Area is the region with the highest export-orientation, the deepest marketization and the earliest opening up in China. At the same time, assisted by the openness of Hong Kong and Macao, it is the best choice for China to carry out a new round of high-standard opening up and explore economic transformation and upgrading. However, institutional innovation aimed at regional synergy is vital to cope with the existing barriers to the flow of factors brought by the status quo of *One Country, Two Systems, Three Tariff Zones, and Four Central Cities* in GBA. The construction of the GBA combined ports can be a breakthrough and serve as a *testing ground* for driving a new round of reform and opening up in China.

---

[6] The Data from the United Nations Conference on Trade and Development (UNCTAD).

[7] The Data from Global Migrant Population Data Report of the United Nations for 1990 and 2019.

1.2.2 Combined Ports as the Support Point for China's Belt and Road Initiative

At present, China is actively promoting the implementation of Belt and Road Initiative (BRI), urging China's global industrial chain layout to extend to both ends. At the same time, through the diversified use of huge foreign exchange reserves, it will exert a significant impact on global energy and mineral resources allocation and pricing mechanisms. Economic upgrading in China is becoming an important force to change the global industrial competition pattern, asset pricing mechanism and offshore market structure.

In the implementation of BRI, on the one hand, we should take the FTZ pilot as the main breakthrough point, combined with the dynamic trend of the global FTA network to build a global network around China's own "axle-spoke" FTZ. What BRI strives for is to build a community of shared future for mankind by *three togethers for five connectivities*. Based on these strategic measures and relying on a high degree of economic complementarity between China and OBOR (One Belt One Road) countries, we can carry out FTA negotiations with top-level design, forming a self-reinforcing ability with "magnet effect" and "hub effect", as well as mutual benefit and win–win development pattern. The ultimate purpose is to form the effective combination promoted by the joint efforts of the global FTA network, the BRI and the FTZ test zones.

The GBA is one of the most open and economically dynamic regions in China and occupies an important strategic position in the overall development of the country. As China has entered a stage of high-quality development, it is necessary to unite Hong Kong, Shenzhen, and Guangzhou ports together with other ports at the Pearl River Estuary to form a world-class port cluster. The combined free trade ports, together with the Pearl River Delta airport group, high-speed rail network, and expressway network together, will form a much needed grand transportation system in the Greater Bay Area.

Furthermore, the practice of constructing GBA combined ports can be a sample case for the further advancement of BRI. There are great regional differences in GBA The level of economic development varies greatly in different regions. Capitalism and socialism coexist in GBA. Therefore, the promotion of institutional innovation through combined ports in GBA is of great significance for the interconnection practices of China's BRI policy, facilities, trade, capital and people. On the one hand, it will vigorously promote the development of regional integration, and explore new models for the joint connection of new markets and new businesses in the OBOR countries, making GBA an important supporting zone. On the other hand, it will also provide theoretical and practical experience for regional economic cooperation and coordinated development of different countries and regions through institutional innovation, so that GBA may serve as the source of policy innovation for China's BRI.

1.2.3 Combined Ports Serving as a Growth Pole for China's Transformational Growth Facing Supply-Side Structural Reforms

On November 10, 2015, President Xi Jinping mentioned "*economic supply-side reform*" for the first time in his speech at the 11th meeting of the Central Financial and Economic Leading Group, emphasizing that "*promoting economic structural reform is an important measure to implement the spirit of the Fifth Plenary Session of the 18th CPC Central Committee...... We should persist in seeking progress while maintaining stability, adhere to reform and opening up, and implement policies that require stable macroeconomic policies, accurate industrial policies, flexible microeconomic policies, practical reform policies, and support for social policies...... We must focus on strengthening the supply-side structural reform, improving the quality and efficiency of the supply system, strengthening the momentum of sustained economic growth to promote the overall leap of China's social productivity.*" He further pointed out: "*To carry out the supply-side structural reform, we need to focus on liberating and developing social productive forces, promoting structural adjustment by reforms, reducing ineffective and low-end supply, expanding effective and mid-to-high-end supply, enhancing the adaptability and flexibility of the supply structure to changes in demand, and improving TFP*".

The GBA strategy is an important institutional innovation for China to respond to the new economic normal. The combined ports model is an exploratory and forward-looking attempt for China's transformational development. The emphasis of supply-side structural reform measures has been gradually shifted from macro-level and industrial level to micro-level and regional level. China has accumulated rich experience in the 40 plus years of reform and opening up by carrying out pilot progressive reforms in regions. Now, China's reform has entered the deep water zone and supply-side structural reform has entered a critical stage. Innovation cannot stop at mere *sample significance*. Allowing the market to play a decisive role in the allocation of resources is a major principle for the effectiveness of supply-side structural reforms. More innovative trials are needed in a region where there is a substantial overall impetus to reform, from the amount of economy to the level of efficiency and effectiveness.

Internationally, the Bay Area model is proved to be a form of urban cluster development. Tokyo Bay Area, New York Bay Area, and San Francisco Bay Area are the world's most recognized city clusters with the best development conditions and the strongest competitiveness. Their core competitiveness is manifested in cross-regional industrial integration within a certain physical space, achieving the best industrial structure layout. Free trade ports are internationally recognized open zones. In a way, when a bay area meets a free port, significant effects can be achieved. In terms of economic size, the Guangdong-Hong Kong-Macao Greater Bay Area is crucial to China's deepening of supply-side structural reforms. The urban population density is high. All 9 + 2 regions are highly developed, possessing comprehensive technological development elements, strong in high-tech as well as traditional manufacturing and service industries. GBA cities are most endowed with international features, and are bound to become the most developed urban cluster in the world with strong innovation and high openness. The GDP of the Guangdong-Hong Kong-Macao Greater Bay Area has grown exponentially since 1994, from about 1.3 trillion yuan to about 11 trillion yuan. Starting in 2020, the GDP growth rate is expected to gradually slow down, from about 5.6% in 2020 to about 3% by 2035, which is expected to reach 23 trillion yuan in 2035. A two-wheel drive production system supported by an advanced manufacturing and modern service industry is founded, laying a good foundation for the structural adjustment. Further learning from the experience of opening up free trade ports is bound to have a substantial effect on deepening the supply-side structural reform in an all-round way.

1.3 Construction Goals of Combined Free Trade Ports of the GBA

As the forerunner and pilot zone of reform and opening-up, GBA plays a very important role in the overall situation of China's reform and opening-up and socialist modernization. In the new era, the exploration and construction of the GBA combined ports should follow the national strategic development requirements and integrate the construction of GBA with the construction of the Belt and Road.

Firstly, the construction of GBA has provided a major strategic opportunity for the construction of free trade ports in Guangdong province. On July 1, 2017, the *Framework Agreement on Deepening Guangdong, Hong Kong and Macao Cooperation in the Development of the Greater Bay Area* was signed in Hong Kong. The agreement aims to give full play to the comprehensive advantages of GBA, deepen cooperation between Guangdong, HongKong and Macao, promote the construction of GBA, participate in high-level international cooperation, enhance its leading role in national economic development and all-round opening up, inject new momentum into the development of Hong Kong and Macao and maintain the long-term prosperity and stability of Hong Kong and Macao.

Next, Guangdong has entered a crucial stage to break new ground at a new starting point after the 19th National Congress. At a new historical moment, GBA should look up to the best practices and most advanced standards to achieve integrated development. GBA will serve as an important window and demonstration zone representing president Xi's thoughts on Socialism with Chinese characteristics. Therefore, it is necessary for GBA to fully benchmark against the highest international standards and levels, and actively explore the construction of combined free trade ports.

Finally, new requirements for Guangdong's work were made by President Xi during the deliberations of the Guangdong delegation on 7 March 2018 during the annual two sessions. Xi required that Guangdong "*promote full opening with a broader vision, higher target, and stronger measures to accelerate the development of a higher-level open economy and the cultivation of new trade formats and models, with actively participating in the construction of BRI, and strengthening open cooperation in innovation capabilities. We must seize the major opportunity of building the Guangdong-Hong Kong-Macao Greater Bay Area, joining hands with Hong Kong and Macau to accelerate related work to build a world-class bay area and a world-class city cluster.*" Therefore, Guangdong should take the requirements into consideration while exploring the construction of combined ports. The goal is to turn Guangdong into a core shipping engine, trade engine, financial engine, and S&T innovation engine for GBA and a portal hub for BRI, thus becoming a major strategic platform for China to participate in international competition.

Therefore, the goal of GBA combined ports is to seize the major opportunity of GBA construction, fully benchmark against the highest international standards and level, promote the integrated development factors through institutional innovation, build the core engine for GBA and a portal hub for BRI, and create a world-class bay area suitable for living, working and traveling through the joint efforts of Guangdong, Hong Kong and Macao.

Chapter 2
Advanced Theories on Combined Free Trade Ports

The necessity for China to construct combined free trade ports of GBA is discussed in the last chapter. It is China's inevitable choice when facing domestic and international challenges such as the restructuring of the global economic and trade patterns, the implementation of the Belt and Road Initiative and the promotion of supply-side structural reform. This chapter will look into the development path of FTZs and review literature on synergy theory in order to summarize the areas and directions for future research on combined free trade ports and prove in theory that it is an inevitable choice for the GBA to build combined free trade ports through dislocation development, mutual supplement and coordinated development in order to make a breakthrough in regional development and enhance its international competitiveness.

2.1 Literature Review of Research on Free Trade Ports

2.1.1 Connotation of Free Trade Ports

Free trade ports are the outcome of economic globalization and the development of free trade theories. At the same time, the emergence of free trade ports has also facilitated the deepening of economic globalization and the progress of free trade theories. The first free trade port was born in the Gulf of Genoa in Italy in 1547 and was named Livorno Port. In seventeenth century, Hamburg Port in Germany, Dunkirk Port in France and Copenhagen Port in Denmark became major free trade ports one after another in Europe. With the growing of global economic and trade exchanges and the recovery of economy after World War II, free trade ports have been constructed all over the world whose functions have also evolved from single trade to diversified ones like processing and manufacturing, financial services, and modern service industry. The major global free trade ports include New York Port in the United States, Rotterdam Port in Netherlands, Jurong Port in Singapore, Busan Port in South Korea and Hong Kong Port in China. The development of free trade

© Xiamen University Press 2022

S. Ba et al., *Collaborative Innovation Mechanism of GBA in China*,
https://doi.org/10.1007/978-981-19-2251-0_2

ports produced radiation effects facilitating the development of relevant industries. According to the *25th Global Financial Center Index* (GFCI) ranking in 2019, the top five international financial hubs are New York, London, Hong Kong, Singapore, and Shanghai. Among them, New York, Hong Kong and Singapore are free trade ports with high standards which set examples for other ports in the world, and Shanghai is actively exploring the construction of free trade zone. The construction of free trade ports can not only attract foreign investment and advanced technology by virtue of its own policy advantages, and create freer and more open economic environment in domestic market but also reduce trade resistance and promote the development of economic globalization and multilateralism in international cooperation.

2.1.1.1 Connotation of Free Trade Port in the World

The interpretation of *free trade port* began with an entry of *free port* in *Terms of Trade: Glossary of International Economics (the second edition)*[1] created by Deardorff of Michigan University. It refers to an area within a country where imported goods can be stored or processed without being subject to import duty, also called a *free zone*, *free port*, or *bonded warehouse*. In addition, the description of *free trade port* in *Concise Encyclopedia Britannica*[2] points out that the free trade port is an area within which goods may be landed, handled, and re-exported freely. The purpose is to remove obstacles to trade and to permit quick turnaround of ships and plans. Only when the goods are moved to consumers within the country in which the zone is located do they become subject to tariffs and customs regulation. Internationally, these were no strict distinctions in relevant policies or literatures between these words, such as free port, free zone and foreign trade zone. Usually, these terms bear similar connotations though born in different periods of various regions or countries according to the laws, policy documents or customs at that time. In conclusion, *free trade port* refers to "*an area within a country or a region but outside of the customs control checkpoints, where foreign goods, capital, and personnel are allowed to enter and exit freely. Duties are exempted for all or most of the goods entering or leaving the port area. Business activities such as free-storage, exhibition, dismantling, modification, repackaging, sorting, processing and manufacturing are allowed in the free trade port*".

2.1.1.2 Connotation of Free Trade Ports in China

The official formulation of free trade port has four versions in China.

[1] Deardorff. Terms of Trade: Glossary of International Economics. Singapore: World Scientific Publishers, 2014.

[2] Concise Encyclopedia Britannica (Volume Nine). Encyclopedia of China Publishing House, 1985:577.

First, on March 31st, 2017, the concept of *free trade port area* was put forward in Item 16 of *Notice of the State Council on Issuing the Plan for Further Deepening the Reform and Opening-up of China (Shanghai) Pilot Free Trade Zone* (Guofa [2017] No. 23), which points out that the construction of free trade port areas should benchmark against top international level and set up a regulatory system that allows full opening of the front line and safe and effective control of the second line.

Secondly, on October 18th, 2017, the concept of free trade port was put forward by President Xi Jinping in Part 5 Item 6 of his report to the 19th National Congress of the CPC titled *Secure a Decisive Victory in Building a Moderately Prosperous Society in All Respects and Strive for the Great Success of Socialism with Chinese Characteristics in a New Era.* Xi points out that more power will be granted to pilot free trade zones to conduct reform, and explore the opening of free trade ports. For the first time, the report proposes the term of *free trade port* and identifies its main subject as the free trade test area.

Thirdly, on November 10th, 2017, Wang Yang, then Vice Premier of the State Council, published an article on *People's Daily* which explained the connotation of *free trade port.* It specifies that *free port* refers to area within a country or region but outside the customs where goods and capital personnel are free to enter and exit, and most commodities are exempt from tariff. It clearly indicates the necessity of building free trade port with Chinese characteristics and its construction objectives of higher levels of openness, better business environment and larger radiation effect for the openness of China and the further innovative development of China's open economy.

Fourthly, in April 2018, the Central Committee of the CPC initially unveiled the concept of *free trade port* and decided to fully support the development of a free trade port throughout the whole island of Hainan. Free trade ports are different from free ports and free trade pilot zones, and the degree of openness has been further enhanced. All or most of the goods entering or leaving the ports are exempted from tariff and business activities such as free-storage, exhibition, dismantling, modification, repackaging, sorting, processing and manufacturing are permitted in the free ports.

In a way, the connotation of *free trade port* is closer to *free port* but different from *free trade pilot zone* in the Chinese context. The main difference lies in the degree of openness. Free trade port can refer to an area within a country or region but outside the customs where goods, capital and personnel are free to enter and exit, and most commodities are exempt from tariff. Broadly speaking, it is not necessarily located adjacent to the seaport. It can also be an inland airport or a land port which is essentially a customs exclusion zone with Chinese characteristics under the regulation of free port policies.

In conclusion, China has adjusted the internationally accepted standards of free trade ports, added elements of Chinese characteristics which are more in line with China's actual national conditions of development and related policies and strategies. It is an important step for China to deepen reform and opening-up, and one of the important measures to firmly support multilateral trade. Free trade port is a test field for a new round of high level opening strategy, a forerunner for the realization of China's industrial transformation and upgrading, and an important platform for China to actively participate in the formulation of international economic and trade rules and strive for the institutional power of global economic governance.

2.1.2 Development and Future Trend of Free Trade Ports

As a vital node in the development of trade, free trade port is the earliest special economic zone model with a history of more than 470 years among all kinds of free zones and special economic zones, whose emergence cannot be separated from the joint role of politics and technology. The functions and forms of free trade port have also been expanded due to the diversification of trade demand. Apart from original single re-export trade, it boasts other functions or responsibilities like processing and manufacturing, financial services and modern service industry. It plays an increasingly important role in the development of a country and becomes a window to open up to the outside world and an innovation test field to introduce technology and capital.

2.1.2.1 Development of Free Trade Ports

From the perspective of geography, the free trade zone is a product in pursuit of trade facilitation in the development of international trade. The European regions become the birthplace of free trade zone due to certain economic foundations and geographical advantages. On the one hand, feudalism gradually collapsed in Western Europe at the end of fifteenth century, and the seeds of capitalism sprouted up. With the process of great geographical discovery, European market began to go global. The flourishing of commerce, navigation and industry gave a strong impetus to foreign trade. On the other hand, the European continent, which is surrounded by sea on three sides and has a tortuous coastline, has the natural advantage of developing ports. The first free trade port was born in the Livorno Port in Genoa in 1547, becoming the world's first special economic zone officially named as a *free trade port*. Shannon in Ireland also took the lead in the exploration of on free trade zones. As an important base for refueling on European and American routes, it lost its advantage after the aircraft's flying range was greatly extended. The local government, seeking transformation, decided to establish the world's first export-processing-oriented free trade zone near the airport, attracting foreign investment, especially from the United States, on the basis of tax-exempt advantages. The initiative was a major success, transforming Shannon from a remote airport to be the first FTZ in the world.

Later, with the development of European navigation, more and more free ports have been opened in Europe. The development of the Rotterdam Port began in the second half of the thirteenth century when it was just a small fishing village. The first ports were built in the period between 1600 and 1620 and gradually developed into a prosperous commercial port. During the French occupation of Rotterdam from 1795 to 1813, it went through the decline of trade volume and the disappearance of industry. It only recovered after the war. In 1938, it become the largest port in Europe followed by London, achieving its first milestone. In 1962, its freight volume reached 96 million tons, surpassing New York for the first time. This seaport from the Netherlands has since become the largest in the world. In 2004, it was exceeded by Shanghai Port in scale, and followed closely behind by more Asian ports. However, it remains the largest port in Europe. Later, Antwerp Port in Belgium and Marseille Port in France also emerged in Europe.

The development of European free trade port has a long history. However, with the advancement of the EU's economic integration, it has lost some advantages such as the inherent tax preferences and trade convenience. Take the rise and fall of the Freeport of Hamburg as an example. It was founded on October 15, 1888 in Germany and was one of the largest free economic zones in the world at its peak, but its more than 100-year history ended in on the first day of 2013.Because of the EU's internal uniform tariff standards and tariffs dropped significantly, Hamburg Freeport lost its preferential policy advantages. The rest of the EU dispersed its cargo volume, reducing total cargo volume of non-EU member states by 1/3 and its former glory has been lost.

Free trade ports and free trade zones appeared relatively late in the Americas but developed rapidly. New York Port in the United States was founded in 1614 and occupied the top throughput list in the United States in 1800. Until now, it is still one of the largest free trade ports. The ports of San Francisco, Seattle, and Los Angeles have played important roles in the development of free tradeports in the United States. In addition to North America, free trade ports and free trade zones were constructed in Central and South America such as Chile and Honduras. Cologne FTZ was established in 1948 at the Atlantic estuary of the Panama Canal. Since then, it has become the largest FTZ in the Western Hemisphere. It is listed as the transit center of Central and South America together with the Miami FTZ in the United States. It is also the world's second largest transit station after Hong Kong with cargo distribution as its main function. It had been in operation since 1953. By the 1970s, its development was in a bottleneck due to adverse political environmental influences at home and abroad and the establishment of free trade zones in Central and South America to compete for business. By the end of the twentieth century, Cologne was actively seeking transformation by adding retail businesses to diversify its development. At the same time, the formulation of the *Makira Plan*[3] brought new opportunities for its development.

Free trade ports started relatively late but developed rapidly in Asia, especially in Southeast Asia. Singapore has been an important international trading port since the thirteenth century by virtue of its special location on the shipping route between the Pacific and Indian Oceans. The Jurong Port in Singapore, officially put into operation in 1965, is one of the most important free trade ports in Southeast Asia. The port is located in the west of Singapore and on the south bank of Jurong Industrial Zone. It is the largest re-export port in the Asia–Pacific region and one of the largest

[3] Meng Guangwen, Liu Han, Zhao Yuanyuan et al. Development and Enlightenment of Cologne Free Trade Zone in Panama, Scientia Geographica Sinica, 2017, 37(6); 876–884.

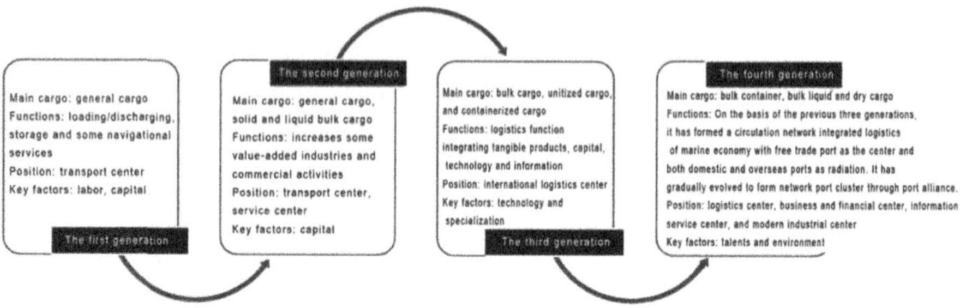

Fig. 2.1 The development of four generations of ports (*Source* sorted by the authors)

container ports in the world. Hong Kong Port in China is a hub for Far East trade and one of the important free trade ports in East Asia due to its superior geographical location. On June 7th, 1841, the representative of the British government, Charlie Elys, announced that Hong Kong had become a free trade port. After 178 years, it had gradually developed from a single entrepot to an international trade and financial center and even one of the most open free trade ports in the world. Other essential free trade ports in Asia include Jebel Ali Port in Dubai, Busan Port in South Korea, Tokyo Port in Japan, and Kelang Port in Singapore. In 2016–2018, top 10 of the list of global top 20 ports are in Asia. The rapid development in Asian provided fertile ground for the establishment of free trade ports.

In conclusion, from a geographical point of view, free trade port originated in Europe, developed in the Americas and flourished in Asia. The development of Asian economy promoted demands on free trade ports while the booming of free trade ports provided a gateway for Asia to open up.

In 1992, United Nations Conference on Trade and Development (UNCTAD) put forward the theory of "port generation division" (See Fig. 2.1)[4] based on port functions. According to this theory modern ports can be classified into three different generations or categories and the concept of the fourth generation port was proposed.[5] The theory has the characteristics of conciseness and universality, and is generally accepted by the industry and academic circles. Therefore, this book analyzes the development of free trade ports based on port functions mentioned in this theoretical framework.

The first generation of ports function as seaports, which are different from ordinary ports in that they are closely integrated with transport and trade. Ordinary ports usually connect only maritime and inland transport, and seaports are a major link between local and overseas markets and an effective tool for the global expansion of capital. The main type of cargo is general cargo. Functions include the transportation, temporary storage and delivery of seaborne goods. In this period, seaports are regarded as transportation center with labor and capital as key factors of development.

[4] UNCTAD. Development and improvement of ports: the principles of modern port management and organization. Geneva: UNCTAD, 1992.

[5] UNCTAD. Technical note: the fourth generation port. UNCTAD Ports Newsletter, 1999, 19: 9–10.

The second generation ports emerged in the late 1950s. After World War II, international trade began to develop in the direction of liberalization and facilitation with the development of economic globalization and the third technological revolution, thus forming the second generation ports. Breaking through the limitation of space, ports developed and expanded towards the hinterland consisting of inland areas and neighboring airports. At the same time, ports were allowed to undertake and offer industrial or commercial services with higher added value to their users. Industrial free ports represented by export processing have emerged. Apart from general cargo, solid and liquid bulk cargo were added to transport lists. In addition to transport activities, some value-added industries and commercial activities were added, turning the ports into a service center. In this period, capital is the key development factor of free trade ports, which is used for the construction of modern ports and the development of modern service industries.

The third generation ports emerged in the 1980s in virtue of the development of information technology. The spatial scope of ports has been expanded with ports as the core and port cities as the main body. Equipped with functions of international trade and logistics, they began to show the characteristics of free trade ports such as the high-level openness and remarkable international trade. At this time, it operated more complicated cargo such as bulk cargo, unitized cargo, and containerized cargo requiring higher transportation technology. With the increase in global trade volume and the global extension of value chains and industrial chains, it has become increasingly important. At this time, it has become a transport center and logistic platform for international trade with diversified functions integrating tangible products, capital, technology and information. In this period, the key factors for port development are technological progress, specialization and regional preferential policies.

The fourth generation ports started at the beginning of the twenty-first century. The ports have higher degree of openness, which can be called *combined free trade ports* and can represent the development trend. Different from the narrow concept of port, their spatial scope has been further expanded which breaks through the limitations of individual ports and develops into a harbor city integrating functions of port, port industry and urban cities or a network port cluster jointly formed by multiple ports. They enjoy a higher degree of economic openness and internationalization than previous three-generation ports and have become the pacesetter and explorer in the evolution of port functions.

From the perspective of function, free trade ports mainly serve as ports due to their geographical advantage and play the role of port and trade. Later, with the development of technology and trade, the diversified demand for the function of free trade port increased and free trade processing zones appeared, serving processing and manufacturing, logistics and transportation functions. The scope of free trade port also expanded. By the time of the fourth generation, modern free trade ports have gradually shown the characteristics of city-ports integration and increased value-added services. On the basis of the previous three generations, ports have formed a circulation network of integrated logistics of marine economy with free trade port as the core and both domestic and overseas ports as radiation. The modern free ports also become a center of logistics, business and finance, information service, and modern industry. Talents and environment have become two important conditions for the development of the free trade ports. As a multi-functional integrated platform, policies in ports range from the logistics industry to finance, insurance, tourism, and information services. The integrated development of the free trade ports and relative industries forms industrial cluster bases. For example, in Dubai, the Dubai Motor City and the Dubai Jewelry City have been created with the support of Jebel Ali Free Port and Dubai Airport.

The special customs supervision zones are the predecessor of China's free trade ports. China's special customs supervision zone refers to a specific enclosed area in the territory of China upon the approval of the State Council. Under the supervision of customs authorities, it connects domestic and foreign markets, enjoys a free and convenient customs clearance environment and preferential policies, and has a special economic function. The development of bonded processing trade is a key incentive for the formation and development of China's special customs surveillance zone. With its rising, rapid development and transformation, China's special customs special customs supervision zone has grown from scratch and its types and quantities also grow from small to large and gradually become mature. Free trade ports have gradually taken shape with special customs supervision zones developing from bonded areas, export processing zones, bonded logistics parks, bonded port areas, comprehensive bonded areas to pilot free trade zones.

China's free trade ports were built during the construction of pilot FTZs. Previously, the development of China's FTZs has gone through three stages. In the first stage, in September 2013, Shanghai Pilot Free Trade Zone—China's first FTZ was officially established. As a pioneer of pilot free trade, Shanghai established four customs surveillance zones and at the same time set up Shanghai Yangshan Port as a pilot FTZ to explore reforms in the transformation of government functions, trade services, financial systems, tax policies, and foreign investment. In the second stage, in April 2015, three FTZs were officially established one after another in Guangdong, Tianjin, and Fujian. The structure of China's FTZs has evolved from one to four. The free trade pilot area is no longer limited to the geographical scope of the special customs supervision area, but adopts the "inside plus outside" approach. At the same time, the construction of FTZ is not limited to the scope of the port. For example, Guangzhou Nansha Port supports Guangdong Nansha FTZ; Shekou Port supports Guangdong Qianhai FTZ; and Xiamen Port supports Fujian Xiamen FTZ. But these FTZs cover a larger geographical area than the original customs special supervision area. In the third stage, in March 2017, the State Council approved the establishment of Liaoning Pilot FTZ, Zhejiang Pilot FTZ, Henan Pilot FTZ, Hubei Pilot FTZ, Chongqing Pilot FTZ, Sichuan Pilot FTZ, and Shanxi Pilot FTZ. They help China to further match up with high standard international economic and trade rules and create pilot zones with distinct characteristics in a wider area and on a larger scale to promote the comprehensive deepening of reform and opening up. On April 13, 2018, Xi Jinping solemnly announced at the 30th anniversary of the establishment of Hainan special economic zone that "*the Party Central Committee has decided to support the construction of pilot free trade zone on the whole island of*

Hainan, to support Hainan to gradually explore and steadily promote the construction of a free trade port with Chinese characteristics as well as establish free trade port policies and system systems step by step and phase by phase". This signifies a milestone in the construction of China's pilot free trade ports. Hainan Free Trade Port will be given greater autonomy for reform, break down the constraints and obstacles of institutional mechanisms through the highest opening-up in the world, connect with the new rules of international economy and trade, speed up the establishment of a new system of open economy, and promote the formation of a new system of China's comprehensive opening up. On August 26, 2019, the State Council issued the *Overall Plan of China's (Shandong), (Jiangsu), (Guangxi), (Hebei), (Yunnan), and (Heilongjiang) Pilot Free Trade Zone*. With the establishment of the fifth group of FTZs, now FTZs have been established in more than half of the provinces, cities and regions in China. It formed an open pattern of "1 + 3 + 7 + 1 + 6" east–west-north–south-central coordination and land and sea interaction. From a strategic point of view, the construction of free trade zone can not only serve major strategies, such as the Belt and Road initiative, the Beijing-Tianjin-Hebei integration initiative, the Yangtze Economic Belt initiative, and the Guangdong-Hong Kong-Macao Greater Bay Area initiative, but also support some regional development strategies, such as the Great West Development, rejuvenation of the old industrial bases in northeast China, the Rise of Central China and the leading development of the eastern region. A new round of reform and opening up will be promoted vigorously in China.

2.1.2.2 The Development Trend of Free Trade Ports

Free trade ports are developing in the direction of functional diversification. Driven by the integration of international economy and technological development, the free trade port with a single function of re-export cannot meet the demands of individualized and diversified customers. Urgent changes are required to transform from single to diversified function. With the change of international economy and the downward trend of smile curve, productive services have become important in the competition of international market, forcing free trade ports to derive productive services, such as financial, communications, and modern logistics, to enhance their international competitiveness. In 2016, FDI magazine ranked 600 FTZs in 120 countries and regions around the world, which indicated that diversified FTZs are highly competitive. Seven of the top ten successful zones are large diversified FTZs. It shows that functional diversification has become the trend in the development of FTZs.

Free trade ports are developing towards the high-end internal industry. From the 1970s to the early 1980s, developed countries moved labor-intensive manufacturing industries out of their own countries, and at the same time, developing countries began to implement export-oriented policies, which promoted the combination of the capital in developed countries with the low-cost labor in developing countries, turning the export processing zones into the main form of free trade ports in developing countries and regions. With the development of economy and technology in developing countries, scientific industrial parks with foreign high-tech equipment and talents have emerged. Some ports have undertaken technology and equipment from developed countries, mainly participate in business related to technology innovation and knowledge-intensive products and develop towards specialization and advanced technology. Secondly, the economic exchanges arising from goods exchange leads to higher requirements on its degree of financial openness. It attaches great importance to financial openness. The modern financial industry has become an embodiment of the development advantages of the global free trade port. It also justifies why financial centers are normally the most successful free trade ports in the world, such as Hong Kong, New York, and Singapore. By now, free trade ports have entered the new development stage of high-end industries.

Free trade ports are booming in developing countries and regions. They were born in developed countries with prosperous economy like Europe and America because of their locations in important international channels and trade distribution centers. After the end of World War II, the number of free trade ports continued to grow globally, and free trade ports represented by relevant countries in Asia played an important role in the global trading system. From a quantitative perspective, according to the statistics of the International Labor Organization, among the nearly 1,000 free economic zones at the end of the 1990s, the vast majority of the newly added were in developing countries and regions. Developing countries and regions are creating an appropriate environment for the development of free trade ports, with a more adequate development hinterland. Some trade advantages of developed countries and regions, such as the disappearance of the EU tariff integration, have restricted the further development of free trade ports in Europe and the United States. The process of economic globalization has been hovering between moving forward and running backwards. Trade frictions and disputes are manifestations of deglobalization. Economic globalization and trade liberalization is bound to squeeze the development space of free trade ports, which has an important impact on the development of free trade ports. However, free trade ports are still an important platform for many countries and regions to open up to the outside world as long as the customs systems remain here.

Free trade port is still in the stage of dynamic development as a concrete representation of the evolution of trade at different stages and as the result of the interaction of international relations and national economic system. Its development not only reflects the deepening of the international division of labor and the improvement of the international trading system but also promotes the development of economic globalization and the extension of value chains. In the future, free trade ports will continue to play an important role in international economic and trade relations and export-oriented economy.

2.2 Literature Review of Research on Regional Synergy Development

2.2.1 Research Objects of Regional Synergy Development

Regional synergy development usually is concerned with urban agglomeration or city cluster. The concept of urban agglomeration evolved from the megalopolis theory first proposed by a French geographer Gottmann (Gottmann 1957). According to this theory, the new metropolis is no longer a single city but a closely linked regional community. In the late 1990s, Chinese scholars began to conduct researches on urban agglomeration and related issues. Yao Shimou (1992) defines urban agglomerations as an aggregate of cities within certain geographic areas. These cities often vary in size, function and characteristics. There are one or two large cities acting as the core and connecting to the other peripheral cities via highly developed transportation and information networks to form an integrated "aggregate" or urban agglomeration. With the in-depth study of urban agglomerations by scholars, Zhou Yixing and Shi Yulong (1995) have proposed to build the concept of physical area of Chinese cities and named the large area of urban agglomerations as metropolis interlocking regions. Based on previous definitions, Xue Dongqian (2000) proposes that urban agglomeration is an organism composed of factors such as regional space, nature and social economy. The spatial difference of the economic and social development factors in the region leads to the inter-city connection and becomes one of the dynamic mechanisms for the evolution of urban agglomerations. Later, Guan Weihua and Yao Shimou (2003) have upgraded their original research and claimed that the essential feature of urban agglomerations is the network between cities in the region. Fang Chuanglin (2011) proposes that urban agglomeration is an urban entity, centered on one megacity or megalopolis and based on at least three large cities. These cities ultimately achieve integration with closely linked economy and compact spatial organization via a highly developed transport and telecommunication infrastructure. Gu Chaolin (2011) points out that urban agglomerations are an all-round integrated organic network composed of central cities exerting their own unique economic functions by their own special structures and different allocation resources. Chen Shouqiang and Huang Jinchuan (2015) have summarized the basic characteristics of urban agglomerations and clarified the identification means of urban agglomerations' spatial development range. They point out that the gravitational model has become the mainstream of the development range of urban agglomerations in China. Mao Ling (2019), on the basis of previous studies, identifies the relationship between urban agglomerations and the level of urbanization and indicates that industrialization and urbanization are the main factors for the generation of urban agglomerations. The concept of urban agglomerations gradually converged even through scholars expressed them in different ways. Urban agglomerations are usually composed of multiple cities. From the perspective of city size, they are usually composed of one megacity, multiple large cities and small peripheral cities. From the perspective of inter-city connectivity, they are often closely linked with huge agglomeration benefits, and have an impact on regional economy. It can be said that the urban group is an advanced regional urban spatial form in the process of urbanization, and it is an important symbol of the level of regional modernization.

The domestic research on urban agglomeration has gone through four stages. Scholars still disagree on the division of stages, but they also have clear consensus. Zhang Jingxiang (2000) proposes that the formation and expansion of urban agglomeration has experienced the following four stages in China. They are the expansion stage of independent and multi-centered urban areas; the stage of oriented expansion of urban space; the stage of inter-city centrifugal and centrifugal expansion; and the stage of compound expansion in metropolis interlocking region. Guan Weihua and Yao Shimou (2003) propose the four stages as the stage of urban area; the stage of urban agglomeration; the stage of metropolitan complex; and the stage of megalopolis. Despite the differences in division, there are also similarities. Scholars agree that urban agglomeration have undergone a gradual development process from low-level to high-level, an evolution of the interconnectivity within urban agglomerations from looseness to tightness, a gradual shift of cooperation and division between cities from being simple to maturing. Finally, a high degree of coordination in the geographical space of the urban agglomeration is formed with its structure and function much improved.

The Greater Bay Area is such an urban agglomeration consisting of nine cities including Guangzhou, Shenzhen, Foshan, Dongguan, Huizhou, Zhuhai, Zhongshan, Jiangmen, Zhaoqing and the two special administrative regions of Hong Kong and Macao. Together with Songshan Lake High-tech Zone, Foshan Sino-German Industrial Service Zone, Lok Ma Chau River Set New Area, Tsuiheng New Area and Luhu Eco-Smart Zone, GBA aims to become the largest urban agglomeration in China. Du Weixi (2018) points out that the economy of the Greater Bay Area is an important form of global economic development. After reviewing global researches on urban agglomerations and industrial structures, Du analyzes the spatial relevancy mechanism of the industrial structure optimization within the urban agglomeration in the Greater Bay Area and points out that there is an insignificant spatial spillover effect of the industrial structure optimization in GBA. The driving force of industrial structure optimization is still the gathering of elements. Technology can significantly promote the upgrading and rationalization of urban industrial structure. Qin Yanhua and Cao Xiyu (2019) have applied the analytic hierarchy process to analyze the innovation capabilities and ranking of 11 cities in GBA based on the statistical analysis of their technological elements. They have identified the problems of technological collaborative innovation faced by urban agglomerations in GBA and provided corresponding suggestions. By calculating the competitiveness of GBA cities, Wang Liangwei (2018) finds that cooperation has been established among the cities. Competition is found in some cities which is detrimental to the development of other cities in the urban agglomeration, while cooperation is beneficial. Zhao Xiang (2019) points out that one important strategic positioning of China is to build world-class urban agglomerations. Therefore it is imperative to promote research on urban agglomeration in GBA. His research shows that the urban scale distribution structure, urban industrial division of labor and cross-regional public goods supply are the three important aspects of urban agglomeration construction in GBA whose development will greatly affect the urban agglomeration effect,externality and comparative advantage, thus exerting a great impact on the overall economic development efficiency and people's quality of life in the area. Therefore, much emphasis should be placed on them in the process of building a world-class urban agglomeration in the GBA. The aim is to optimize the scale distribution structure of urban clusters in GBA, promote the formation of efficient industrial division of labor between different cities, and realize the coordination and supply of public goods of urban agglomeration through deepening reform and continuously promoting institutional innovation.

The existing literature on GBA shows that the basis of coordinated development among the GBA cities is good, but there are some problems. It is necessary to carry out researches on the path and strategy of regional synergy development in GBA.

2.2.2 Theoretical Basis of Regional Synergy Development

Scholars at home and abroad have done a lot of theoretical research on regional synergy, among which the most famous theories include synergetic theory, the gradient theory, the symbiosis theory, the comparative advantage theory and the game theory.

Synergetic theory, first proposed by German physicist Harken, emphasizes the process of elements gradually changing from a state of dispersion and disorder to an orderly and unified stable structure under their interaction, correlation and interference. Synergistics in regional studies refers that urban agglomeration, as an open system far from equilibrium, promotes the generation of synergistic effect between the cities within this area and spontaneous formation of ordered structure in time, space and function through the exchange of mass or energy with outside world (Fang Chuanglin 2017). Synergy, occurring in a complex and open system, is a process of qualitative change from disorder to order. New structures and functions are formed through the interaction between its internal subsystems (Liu Min 2018).

The Gradient theory is another theory of regional synergy, whose development has gone through three main stages—the traditional gradient theory, the inverse grads process theory and the generalized gradient theory. The traditional gradient theory, also known as the restricted gradient theory, means that the difference of economic levels leads to the formation of different gradient areas within a certain region. High-tech industries are mostly generated in high grads areas and then gradually move to low grads areas in accordance with their development. On this theoretical basis, inverse grads process theory was put forward. Some scholars found the obvious defects in traditional gradient theory in their practice and research. They pointed out that the development of low grads areas would not always lag behind even though economy and technology were transferred from high grads areas to low grads areas. Because some low grads areas could introduce capital and technology with their abundant resources and then achieve leapfrog development (Li Guoping and Xu Yang 2002). The generalized gradient theory is a theory of regional synergy put forward on the basis of China's reality. The most famous generalized gradient theory is proposed by Li Juheng and Li Guoping (2004). They point out that it is a comprehensive theory integrating economics, politics, and sociology. It mainly includes three aspects: first, it recognizes that there is a natural and objective gradient for all the matter and energy in nature; second, there is a natural gradient in the development level of cities in economy, society, and culture; third, there is a gradient in the degree of ecological environment (Li Guheng and Li Guoping 2004). The spatial combination of these three aspects is often different, that is, regions with rich resources may have a poor ecological environment, and regions with better economy may not enjoy the coordinated development of society, economy, and culture. The true high grads areas are where elements, such as resources, culture, economy, society, and environment, gradually flow between areas and develop in a coordinated way (Xia Yulong et al. 1983). Therefore, if we take urban agglomerations as our research object, we can find that gradient distributions in both between and within cities are complex. There is a specific ratio relationship between distance and the quantity or characteristics of space, industry and infrastructure. The process of human evolution is also a process of comprehensive use, continuous generation and disappearance of gradient distributions. The development of human society is also closely related to these gradients. Take the reality of city agglomeration into consideration, we need to adjust measures to local conditions to achieve a balance between different gradients and promote the integrated development of a certain area.

The symbiosis theory was put forward by German microbiologist Anton de Barry in 1879 and applied to biological research at first. It is a biological phenomenon which refers that different organisms live together and achieve mutualistic symbiosis through their cooperation and complementation (Wu Wenjuan et al. 2019). Different organisms live together to achieve a harmonious state of complementarity, cooperation, coordination and sharing (Wu Wenjuan etc. 2019). The basic unit of the symbiotic relationship is symbiotic unit; the basic environment is symbiotic environment; and the basic model is called the symbiotic model. The symbiotic unit provides basic materials for symbiosis; the symbiotic environment provides external conditions for the exchange of material, energy and information; the symbiotic mode is the form or state of interaction or fusion between symbiotic units, reflecting the process and intensity of the interaction between different units (Zhang Meiqing et al. 2012). Symbiosis theory refers to the state of interdependence between different symbiotic units in a region. These units learn from each other, share common benefits, and promote the healthy development of symbionts (Wang Qingsheng et al. 2018).

The development of comparative advantage theory has mainly experienced two processes: traditional static comparative advantage theory and dynamic comparative advantage theory. In economics, especially in the field of international trade, the traditional static comparative advantage theory is based on David Ricardo's theory of comparative cost and unequal exchange theory. The essence of this theory is that t comparative advantages come from a single difference in labor productivity assuming that all factors flow freely in the process of trade. With the deepening of human's understanding and the increase of relative researches, many scholars raised doubts on Ricardo's theory of single factor of labor and proposed dynamic comparative advantage theory. This theory claims that the endowments of factors and resources in every country can change with the accumulation of factors and the advancement of technology. That is, the comparative advantages among countries are not static, and the industrial structure and comparative advantage industries are also changeable. In addition, with the international prevalence of "national overtaking", Chinese scholars have put forward the theory of endogenous comparative advantage based on the current condition of China. It emphasizes that some countries and regions find their comparative advantages from the division of labor and even achieve overtaking because of the higher level openness, the refinement and specialization of international labor dividing, the reduction of learning costs and production costs–-this is the basic principle of endogenous comparative advantage. It provides a solid theoretical foundation for researches on regional synergy with urban agglomerations as the research object, explains the reasons for industrial cooperation and labor dividing within this region, and also accounts for the circulation direction of industrial production factors and the reasons of their agglomeration to some extent.

The game theory is used to study the interaction between the behavior of decision-makers and ultimately make their decisions reach a state of equilibrium. It consists of four basic elements—player, action or strategy, payoff and information set. Players mainly refer to decision-makers within the context of the game. In regional researches, the major players include governments, enterprises, institutions, and people. Action or strategy refers to the final one among a series of different strategies that players choose within their power based on facts, their judgments on problems and expectations on future development. Payoff refers to the fact that players "pays" for their actions, that is, they take these action at the price of resources or some materials—they use their own resources to pay for their action. In this process, different players need to ponder over and over again to reach the ultimate equilibrium through the compromise of multi-party. Information set means that the information obtained by different players may be completely equivalent or totally non-equivalent in this process. The former means that all information is open and transparent; the latter means that some players have more information than others. In the case of asymmetric information, it is hard for different players to reach agreement on judgments or decisions. Under the influence of these four elements in game theory, multiple players need to reach common consensus on the same problem after their careful thinking, closer inspection and effective communication. In this process, some players may give up some resources while some players may get some resources, so this process is called game. Generally speaking, players with higher power pay less, and players with more information gain more. The process of regional development is full of games. Different cities play different roles. Multi-party often takes different actions on the same decision, which is the determinant of the difficulty and transaction cost in coordinated governance and a crucial element restricting the coordinated development between cities.

These theories extend to regional economic research based on their respective disciplines, forming regional synergy development theories. Regional synergy development refers to the interdependence and mutual opening of the regions in policy, industry and environment under the established environment, forming a relatively harmonious state in which development is more consistent and interests can be shared.

2.2.3 Research Contents of Regional Synergy Development

Summarizing the current research on regional synergy development, we find that most relevant researches are centered on economic collaboration, social collaboration, resource and environment collaboration, and collaborative governance.

The economic collaboration mainly refers to the integrated development of industry, finance, market and space. The industrial synergy can be regarded as a composite system coupled by the interaction of the location, layout, structure and subsystem clusters of industries (Chu Zhaopeng et al. 2018). The financial synergy demands to establish risk prevention systems and construct a safe, efficient, and unified system of financial interconnection within urban agglomerations to ensure the interconnection between central bank and other financial institutions (Fang Chuanglin 2017). The market synergy requires a unified market, a standardized market operation model, a regional market system with order competition, multiple functions, unify, openness, and prosperity, as well as a unified market access and exit mechanism in the city. On the basis of coordination, we will unify the conditions and standards of market access, eliminate market barriers, maintain a fair market environment, and finally realize the integration of market construction (Fang Chuanglin 2017). The coordinated development of space is to narrow the gap of economic development between regions and realize the integrated development of the regional economy. Therefore, coordinated development of space can be realized when the coordinated development of industries and markets reach a certain level (Wang Xueying 2016).

The social collaboration is embodied as narrowing the gap between different cities in basic public services, such as transportation, education, and medical care, improving social equality and the life quality of residents (Wang Xueying 2016). In 2014, President Xi Jinping pointed out that we should regard transportation integration as the pioneer to promote the integration of the Beijing-Tianjin-Hebei and accelerate the construction of an integrated transportation network with high-speed, convenience, efficiency, safety, large-capacity, low-cost and interconnectivity (Sun Mingzheng et al. 2016). Integrated development can be realized through the driving force of transportation integration and the interconnectivity of infrastructure.

The resource and environment collaboration aims at building a harmonious relationship between human beings and nature by improving overall regional resource utilization rate, controlling atmospheric pollution, and improving the regional ecological environment (Wang Xueying 2016). Collaborative protection of ecological environment is a major breakthrough of integrated development. Environmental problems, such as air pollution and atmospheric pollution, do not bare a territorial nature.

It is necessary to continuously improve the joint control mechanism, break through the localized management, build a unified governance team, conduct grid management to achieve ecological inter-construction and share of this region, which are realistic and meaningful measures to promote regional integration (Lu Dadao 2015).

Collaborative governance is a top design to ensure regional synergy development. There are lots of participants in collaborative governance including governments, enterprises, non-governmental organizations, and the public. It is a process of common governance with multiple roles. Through the mutual interchange of their respective resources, they can achieve the effect of mutual coordination, interaction, and mutual support, and finally realize an operation mode with well-organized and sustainable development. The advantage of collaborative governance lies in multiple participants, which can protect the interest of each participants to the maximum extent and promote the development of public interests (Zheng Qiao and Xiao Wentao 2008). Collaborative governance happens in public life, with the participants of multi-parties including the government, enterprises, non-governmental organizations, and individuals. Through the exchange, coordination and interaction of respective resources, they adjust the strategic language and structure of the system with well-organized and sustainable operation, generate new energy unavailable in some parts or subsystems, realize the increase of power, enable the entire system to jointly govern social public affairs while maintain higher order parameters, and ultimately achieve the purpose of safeguarding and enhancing public interests to the maximum (Ji Zhaoliang et al. 2013). The following five criteria can be used to make judgements on collaborative governance model. First, its governance subject is multiple, which includes not only the government but also enterprises, non-governmental organizations, and citizens. Second, it is characterized by decentralization and non-centralized power. Third, the relationship between behavior and subjects is relatively equal instead of a simple relation of managers and the managed in the previous mode. Each subject has equivalent speaking right in common governance and goal achievement instead of blind obedience or submitting to the privileged. Fourth, it is marked by self-organized coordination for it is organized by its internal system. Consensus are reached through various forms of information feedback and negotiation. With the characteristics of flexibility and adaptability, it aims to conduct reach consensus through positive negotiation, make up for the deficiency of government regulation and market exchange, and achieve coordination of various resources. Fifth, the goal is the common vision of all participants. The contributions of all parties are no longer unilateral or self-responsible, but coordinated and interdependent, or even encouraged and compensatory (Ji Zhaoliang et al. 2013).

Scholars at home and abroad have made valuable explorations on the relationship between industry, city and port. However, few studies focus on the integration of industry clusters, city agglomeration and port group. Therefore, this book proposes the concept of combined free trade ports in GBA and advocates to take combined free trade ports as a spatial carrier linking these three groups and an effective means facilitating the synergy development of urban agglomerations.

2.2.4 Measurement of Regional Synergy Development

It is generally accepted by scholars that central cities have positive or negative effects on the economy of the surrounding hinterland (Sun Dongqi et al. 2013). During certain periods in certain regions, cities (or counties, towns) near the fringe of central cities often enjoy the priority of development than other cities (or counties, towns), such as the Guangdong-Hong Kong-Macao Greater Bay Area with Guangzhou and Shenzhen as the center; or The Yangtze River Delta region with Shanghai as the center (Chen Chen and Zhao Min 2010); while in other regions, the development of hinterland may be restricted to a relatively backward degree, such as the poverty belt around Beijing and Tianjin, which can result in the formation of "metropolitan shadow area" (Zhang Jingxiang and Zhuang Linde 2000).

International Scholars have conducted researches on the measuring of regional linkages, including Berkeley, E. Ravenstein, Carey, Herbert Spencer, and Riley. They have explored the degree of connection between regions from the perspective of immigration or trade (Chen Ruishan et al. 2013). Chinese scholars mostly study the relationship between central city and surrounding hinterland from the aspects of spatial logistics, spatial transportation linkage, and the spatial structure of economic linkage (Li Luqi and Ma Xueguang 2019; Zhou Yixing 1998). Early quantitative methods of regional linkages are relatively simple. Reilly proposes that the flow of population between cities is proportional to the product of population and inversely proportional to the square of the distance between two cities (Reilly 1929). Later, based on this idea, Converseaims to find the breakpoint of the equilibrium point to describe the linkage between regions (Converse et al. 1958).

On the basis of Converse's research on the breaking point, social physicist Stewart of Princeton proposes a gravity model to measure linkages between regions (Haynes and Fotheringham 1984).The gravity model is used to predict the force of relation between the central city and its surrounding cities to establish a matrix. Based on the concept of "magnetic field", the connection between "influence" and "spatial linkage" has been established. The greater the potential energy of the nodal "magnetic field", the stronger the force between the nodes. At the same time, it is negatively related to the distance, so the relation force needs to be expressed with the assistance of "gravity model" (Sun Dongqi et al. 2013). This model is widely used in the empirical research of "distance decay effect" and "spatial interaction" (Gould 1967; Miao Changhong and Wang Haijiang 2006). Since 1990s, scholars in China have also widely used the gravity model of spatial interaction in the quantitative study of regional economic linkages, such as Wang Dezhong (Wang Dezhong and Zhuang Renxing 1996), Li Guoping (Li Guoping and Wang Liming 2001), Meng Deyou, etc. (Meng Deyou and Lu Yuqi 2009), Zhou Yixing (Yi Xing 1998), and Chen Yanguang (Chen Yanguang and Liu Jisheng 2002).

Subsequently, computer simulation technology has been applied to the study of regional connections, and the coupling coordination model is produced. This model can measure the degree of coordinated development of various subsystems in urbanization by quantifying coupling degree (Liu Hao et al. 2011; Wang Qi and Chen Cai

2008). It believes that the key to the transition of systems from disorder to order lies in the synergistic effect of internal parameters within the system. This synergy has great influence on the characteristics and laws of system change with the coupling degree as a measurement (Cao Wen Li et al. 2012; Sun Pingjun et al. 2012).

System dynamics model (SD), as a branch of system theory and management theory, is a systematic science which combines system theory and computer simulation theory to study the feedback structure and behavior of the system. This method is often used to measure the degree of integrated development and predict its future development level in relative research.

With the booming of research on the spatial pattern of future land use, a large number of models have been used to predict this pattern, such as the cellular automata (CA) model (Li Xia and Liu Xiaoping 2007), CLUE (conversion of land Use and its effects model)/CLUE-S (conversion of land use and its effects at small region extent) (Lu Wentao et al. 2015), multi-agent system (MAS) model (Fu Rong et al. 2012), etc., all of which provide basic models for the prediction of integrated development. At present, the forecasting integration model, considered as the latest method for prediction and analysis, uses a variety of data acquisition methods, such as big data, artificial intelligence, 3S technology (global positioning system, remote sensing and geographic information system). Combined with the simulation model, it improves the accuracy of prediction on urbanization level which will provide a basic database for the analysis of integrated development.

Accessibility analysis is one of the major methods to analyze regional connections. This method, firstly proposed by W. G. Hansen, usually uses gravity model to explore the interaction opportunities and interaction force of nodes in transportation network (Gu Mingdong and Yin Haiwei 2010). Mainly based on the current status of the regional transportation network as well as the grade and scale of line, it calculates the traffic time from a certain place to other place in the area, the length of which reflects the closeness of subsystems in this region (Fang Junzhi and Wen Shuhui 2017; Sheng Yanchao and Zhou Yujiao 2018).

In addition, such methods as social network analysis and cluster analysis are also effective to analyze regional connections. Social network analysis, a complex method integrating multiple methods, explores the relationship between network nodes and the overall network and requires knowledge of graph theory and mathematical models as basis. In this method, network nodes can be individuals, groups, organizations, or even countries. It is possible to explore the position of individuals in network structure from an individual perspective and its characteristics from an overall perspective. Through the analysis between the whole and the individual, the micro network is combined with the macro structure of the large-scale social system. The focus of social network analysis is the relationship and relationship patterns between nodes. It requires quantification of the phenomena reflected in their relationships and relationship patterns and description of interactive structural relationships between nodes through the study of quantitative indicators. By establishing an index system, the variation coefficient can be obtained after cluster analysis on the basis of this system, which can also reflect the degree of regional connection and then be used to make inference on integrated development.

In addition to quantitative models, qualitative methods are also very popular in the study of integrated development. Integrated development is a complex process which is difficult to simulate or predict with one or even several models. Qualitative research is an ideal auxiliary method to gain a deep understanding on the process and effect of collaboration. Existing relative researches mostly adopt case study method to select the concerning dimensions, such as integration of industrial transfer and development, integration of transport infrastructure, integration of ecological construction and environmental protection, integration of public service construction, and counterpart assistance, and predict the trend, difficulties, and key points of integrated development based on depth interview and relevant government documents in order to portray the process and effect of integrated development.

2.2.5 Researches on the Effect of Regional Synergy Development

In the past decade, urbanization has been a significant global trend. However, the speed of urbanization is not the same in all regions. This unequal development model is especially reflected in the development of urban agglomerations. The experience of the past decade has predicted the obvious trend that people tend to get together around city agglomeration. According to statistics and satellite imagery analysis, during the nearly 70 years from 1950 to 2019, the total number of global cities has increased from 300 to about 14,000. The phenomena of population agglomeration in large cities is obvious, for example, the three major urban agglomerations in China gather 75% of the population with 25% of the land. And the development speed of urban agglomeration is much higher than the overall speed of the world. Population agglomeration brings about the concentration of economic output and technological innovation. At present, urban agglomerations have become an important economy in the world. Globally, more than 40 urban agglomerations contribute to nearly 50% of the GDP with 20% of the population (Zhou Yuan et al. 2017). The combined economy formed by urban agglomeration has become the key to enhancing competitiveness. If the coordinated development of urban agglomerations is realized, the city can enjoy the dividends brought by the synergy of factors and industries, realize the overall improvement of regional vitality and innovation, promote regional development, and participate in global competition as a unity.

First of all, one of the most obvious effects of integrated development is the improvement of the ecological environment. Environmental problems, such as environmental pollution, are often a regional problem with temporality, spatiality and cross-region spillover effects. They will occur not merely within a city because of the existence of administrative boundaries. Instead, they are often manifested by the accumulation and interaction of multiple pollution sources (Wang Zhenbo etc. 2017). Therefore, in order to achieve better results in environmental governance, it is necessary to integrate regional development, jointly manage environmental problems, build a unified monitoring platform, improve the regional forecast and warning system, and improve the regional environment. In other words, one of the effects of coordinated development is to effectively solve regional environmental problems by constructing a collaborative governance model (Ning Miao et al. 2012).

Secondly, another effect of integrated development is social effect. Regional integration will bring about huge social effects including the benefits brought by population mobility and the increase of medical and educational carrying capacity. Zhang Zhidong et al. (2018) simplified the economic model in two regions: labor flows from area A to area B, which results in an increase of potential labor in area Band a decrease of labor in area A. Based on the analysis of neoclassical model, we found that the supply level of labor factors in area A has greatly decreased, which will increase the overall wage in area A; the influx of labor factors in area B leads to an increase of labor supply and a decline in wage. The decline of cost will help labor-intensive enterprises to expand their reproduction and make their transformation and upgrading. In addition, a large number of scholars have demonstrated that the regional integration of medical and educational service system will greatly improve the happiness of residents and reduce the inequality of social resource (Wu Xiaorong et al. 2018; Zhang Zhidong et al. 2018).

Finally, the obvious effect of integrated development is economic effect. Integrated development will facilitate the increase of trade value in import and export, growth of GDP and innovation of technology and the effective reduction of the proportion of traditional manufacturing. Lin Yifu et al. (1999) believes that integrated development promotes the flow of production factors which is positively correlated with the efficiency of resource allocation, and becomes an important affecting factor of economic growth. From the perspective of transportation costs, Chen Wen et al. (2019) believe that it is conducive to reducing cross-regional transportation costs, significantly improving the efficiency of factor allocation and thereby promoting economic growth. Deng Wenbo et al. (2019) has estimated the effect of regional coordination on the economic growth of underdeveloped areas in the Yangtze River Delta based on the DID (Double Difference) model. According to his statistics, since the implementation of the regional coordination policy in 2009, the average per capita GDP of the seven underdeveloped cities in the Yangtze River Delta has shown an obvious increase of 30%in 2016. At this time, the per capita GDP of these cities is equivalent to 108.08% of the national GDP per capita. Thus these seven cities have become relatively developed prefecture-level cities.

2.3 Literature Review of Research on Combined Free Trade Ports

2.3.1 *The Relationship Between Ports and Regional Development*

Cities are the products of the highly developed human civilization, in which transportation is an important location factor and the main basis for the selection of city sites. Waterway is one of the most important means of transportation because cities have been built around mountains and rivers since ancient times. Therefore, ports come into being and strive to develop. With the development of social economy, shipment of products has increased rapidly, which has promoted the development of ports. With the advance of social technology, the port facilities have been gradually improved thus leading to the further expansion of trade transport. In the world, many port cities have gradually developed by virtue of advanced waterway, such as New York and San Francisco in the United States, Busan in South Korea, Hong Kong and Shanghai in China. It can be said that the development of ports and cities bares a symbiotic and mutually beneficial relationship. Especially, the development of ports and trade is directly related, both of which promote each other and share a common development. With the process of global economic integration, international trade is becoming increasingly important in world economic development. Therefore, ports are playing an increasingly important role in promoting the development of urban and regional economy.

Theories of growth pole and port growing point provide solid foundation for the relationship between port and urban development (Wang Zhenzhen and Huang Maoxing 2013). The growth pole theory was initially proposed by French economist Francois Perroux in the 1950s, and then supplemented and completed by economists in the UK and the US. The theory emphasizes that economic development is unbalanced in geographic space. In some nodal regions, labor and capital gather together. At the same time, the effect of technological innovation and diffusion output result in the concentration and output of capital, economies of scale and external economic effects. Therefore, these nodal regions are called growth pole. The generation of growth poles is extremely dependent on "demand" to some extent, including internal demand within cities and the demand of factor exchanges between cities. Trade is the driving force of this demand. Transportation capacity directly affects trades between regions, especially in modern times, shipping industry brought about by port development is the main channel for urban trade. Therefore, cities with dense waterways, busy shipping and large throughput enjoy faster economic growth than other port cities and inland cities, which indicated the theory of "port growing point".

The relationship between ports and urban development can be basically divided into four types: the prosperity of the port and the city, the decline of the port and the prosperity of the city, the prosperity of the port and the decline of the city, and the decline of the city and port. Unlike inland cities, port cities are mostly developed on the basis of ports. Ports with better transportation are often the ideal place for large amount of trade whose generation requires the support of other factors, such as labor, daily necessities. In this case, the port often expands to form an urban economic circle with a set of facilities of production, society, and culture serving for the development of its industry. The first type of this relationship is the common prosperity of the port and the city. This is an interdependent relationship between ports and cities among which ports are regarded as links. These ports play an vital role in the transport network, urban agglomeration and diffusion, and the formation of growth pole based on port trade and bring about economic spillover; while cities enjoy this kind of economic spillover and gain rapid development in all aspects including the service industry whose development further promotes the development of the port and shipping industries. Thus, they are interdependent and coordinated. As for the development model of port decline and city prosperity, port resources play a major role in the early stage of urban development, but with the rapid development of cities, the functions of ports are degraded under natural and human effects. When the driving force of port economy is lower than that of urban economy, the city annexes the port land. For example, Venice and London relied solely on port in their early development, but now the development of other industries far exceeds port industries in these two cities. The prosperity of the port and the decline of the city is the main mode in the early development of port cities. At that time, cities are built on the basis of ports and the function of ports is far beyond that of cities. Over-emphasis on ports while neglect of the life quality of urban residents, especially their living environment and public demands, came into a situation where the port is prospering while urban declining because urban will develop from bad to worse while port function will be highlighted, for example, Rotterdam in Netherlands. The decline of port and city is the result of their uncoordinated development. This kind of port cities was once famous for a while, such as Liuhe, also called Liujiagang, in the Ming Dynasty of China. In the historical torrent and the changes of natural environment, development priorities in this city did not change in time with the continuously degradation of its port functions. Heavily depending on the development of the port lead to the loss of its former glory in the end. It can be seen that cities generated under the coordinated development model are often closely related to the development of ports. It can be said that "the city is built upon the port, and the city and port share the common prosperity." Once the strong linkage between cities and ports are destroyed, everything will fall apart.

2.3.2 Diversified Functions of Modern Ports

The main functions of modern ports are port and trade. On this basis, other functions have been gradually generated, such as processing and manufacturing, financing, logistics, transport, and modern services. Generally, different free trade ports have different functional orientations according to their geographical conditions, infrastructure construction, and industrial advantages and disadvantages. And even the same port will develop different key functions at different times.

Port function is basic for modern ports. It is highly complex including functions of openness, foreign trade, port operations and customs clearance service. Openness refers that all countries have equal trading rights and opportunities within the free trade ports—all foreign business people and enterprises enjoy national treatment, and citizens at home and abroad have access to this area in accordance with the law. As a traditional function of free trade port, foreign trade mainly refers to activities like import, export and re-export. Port operation is a basic function of free trade ports, which includes activities like dispatching, handing, stacking, storage, and other port services of vehicles, ships, airplanes, containers and bulk cargo. The customs clearance service refers to the customs declaration of goods and carriers as well as the inspection and quarantine of import and export commodities.

Processing and manufacturing is an extensional function of modern ports. Many export-oriented processing and manufacturing industries gather in the free trade port because of the huge business opportunities and export-oriented economy, forming a port-centered industrial zone. Thus the free trade port derives processing and manufacturing function. Different from developed countries, developing countries have not only formed port-centered industrial zone in free trade ports but also created scientific industrial parks on this basis under the changes of international trade and international division of labor. The sufficient and low-cost human resources and special preferential policies in developing countries attract many international capitals and high-tech enterprises to settle in the free trade port, which promotes the derivation of the science and industrial park. Therefore, the processing and manufacturing industry in China's free trade ports has gone through three development stages: the first stage is represented by labor-intensive industries like foods, textiles, and home appliances; the second stage is characterized by capital and technology-intensive industries like mechatronics and petrochemicals; the third stage is represented by knowledge and information-intensive industries with highly added value, for example, high-tech products. The ports, combined with high-efficient air transportation, attract many high-tech talents to get together, form a good interactive relationship with the Academy of Sciences, and generate an engine of development in the information economy era.

Finance is also a derivative function of modern ports. The rapid development of the free trade port determines its urgent demand for financial services. Financial institutions play an important role in the development of ports. The integration of financial services, port business and demands of the relevant industrial chain in upstream and downstream is carried out based on institutional innovation so as to provide diversified services and create greater value (Hu Fengqiao and Li Jinshan 2016; Wang Cunyu 2008). Financial function needs to be highly emphasized. First, we need to explore how to enhance the risk prevention capabilities of free trade ports; second, we need to figure out how to provide ports with personalized financial services, such as banking, foreign exchange, securities, credit, futures, trusts, funds-in or funds-out, and funds transfer (Hu Fengqiao and Li Jinshan 2016).

Logistics transportation is another derivative function of modern ports. Bonded warehousing is a basic service function of free trade ports, which aims to deal with the time difference of goods between import and export as well as between storage and processing. Transportation connection and distribution, as expansions on the basis of the bonded logistics function, are the basic functions of logistics. The logistics function has extremely high requirements for traffic: it is usually located in the main traffic thoroughfares of water-land-air transportation, and requires excellence transfer functions of water-land, land-land and air-ground. It is an important distribution center for international transit and domestic export. This function requires the free trade port to play the role of distribution center of bulk commodity, transporting goods from the wharf to the warehouse and then to the customer so as to promote the release of space and the circulation of goods.

The modern service is an extensional function of the modern port with comprehensive features, such as industrial services, cross-border e-commerce services, international communication and information services. Industrial services, derived from the development of industry, include catering, accommodation, insurance, taxation, accounting, law, tourism, education, medical treatment, ship management. Cross-border e-commerce service, derived from the development of cross-border e-commerce, bares a function of free trade port which includes international logistics, web design, and English description of products. International communication is an economic modality with coordinated regional cooperation and optimized resource collocation, which is generated based on the development of free trade ports. It facilitates the agglomeration of multinational companies and high-growth enterprises to form a polarization effect on the basis of the inter-connectivity of finance, trade, information, and transportation. It also forms a "headquarter economy",[6] which, with its "headquarter- manufacturing base" functional chain radiating further ahead and thus driving up the regional development (Chen Xuehui and Sun Xuan 2014). Information service is a free trade port function derived from the development of modern logistics. It enables the development from static nodes to dynamic networks. Informatization is a strategic development of free trade ports rather than a purely technological upgrade (Hu Fengqiao and Li Jinshan 2016).

Free trade ports are evolved from modern ports which have developed to a certain stage under the influence of certain economy, politics and technology. They are also direct reflections of economic globalization, the evolution of global industrial structures, the reorganization of global value chains, and technological changes. With a history of hundreds of years, free trade ports have experienced a process from gradual development to accelerated development, from quantitative change to qualitative change. Their development shows these three characteristics: the increasing of diversified value-added functions, the significant trend of high-end industries, and the rapid development in developing countries and regions. The driving force of the functional evolution of free trade ports lies in promoting the greatest economic

[6] Headquarter economy is defined as being sufficiently resource-rich to attract a cluster of corporate headquarters which set their manufacturing bases in regions with comparative advantages to achieve the optimal integration of corporate value chains and regional resources.

benefits with the least barriers through the simplification of trade and logistics. Free trade ports with sufficient competitiveness and developing impetus are those meeting the above conditions. The key to meeting the above conditions is to find their own accurate positions in global integrated transportation and logistics industry chain and improve their value and status in the industrial chain of transportation and logistics.

2.3.3 Integrated Development of Ports Promoted by Their Diversified Functions

With the integration of global economy and the rapid development of trade in service, modern ports have evolved to the third generation with integrated logistics and trade distribution as their main functions. Some developed countries have even begun to explore the construction of fourth-generation ports with modern logistics as the major function and development breakthrough to establish an effective and efficient economic cycle model which has enabled the transformation from "port-to-port" to "door-to-door" service with the development of port logistics. It is equipped with a comprehensive transportation network and hinterland market system that matches the development of modern port logistics. Therefore, to realize integrated development, modern ports must break free from the geographical concept of administrative divisions, integrate different port resources to form a regional combined model, integrate markets to achieve regional development and then generate an agglomeration effect to facilitate the economic development of hinterlands.

Combined ports are the products of the fourth-generation ports. International researches on combined ports started early with diversified contents and relatively advanced methods. But similar researches started late in China and are on the initial stage, especially in China's mainland. However, the regional linkage effect and promotion effect of combined ports on the coordinated development of domestic ports have given rise to the importance of relevant researches (Zhang Baoqing and Sheng Jinlu 2018). Internationally, with the development of economic globalization and shipping alliances, port industry has undergone global reforms resulting in the emergence of transnational port operation groups such as Port of Singapore Authority, Peninsular and Oriental Limited in Britain and Hutchison Whampoa Ltd in Hong Kong. Those groups build or operate ports around the world in a professional and well-planned way, expand their port business to the rest of the world, and form a new trend of cooperation in ports between different regions (Pan Shu and Chai Zhigang 2008). As early as 1996, China proposed the combined free trade ports model and called for closer cooperation among ports to achieve a win–win result. In 2001, China proposed to delegate all ports to local governments, which greatly mobilized the enthusiasm of local entities in port construction. While promoting the large-scale growth and rapid development of ports, it inevitably caused the problem of resource contention and market grabbing. Therefore, in 2014, to solve such internal conflicts, the Ministry of Transport issued the *Guiding Opinions of the Ministry of Transport on Promoting the Transformation and Upgrading of Ports* and set up Jiangsu and Guangxi as pilots to explore the model of integrated development. Subsequently, exploration on the integration of regional ports were conducted one after another in the Bohai Rim region, the Yangtze River Delta, and the Pearl River Delta (Pan Wenda 2019b). The report of the 19th National Congress of the Communist Party of China has put forward buzzwords such as "free trade port", "Guangdong-Hong Kong-Macao Greater Bay Area", "Belt & Road initiative", and "supply-side structural reform". These policies not only provide opportunities for the coordinated development of ports but also promote the integration of regional resources and functions in a direct or indirect manner. The construction of combined ports is conducive to promoting complementary advantages and reasonable layout of regional ports, avoiding duplication in construction, and achieving reasonable resource allocation (Jiang Yubo 2015).

In conclusion, combined ports refer to the port organization or union sharing the same hinterland, development goals, and operating specifications for unified planning, construction, use, and management of port resources and assets (Pan Wenda 2019c). The above port resources include resources like land, shoreline, waters and information, facilities like wharfs, harbor basins, storage yards, warehouses, logistics, public infrastructure such as breakwaters, waterways, anchorages, railways, highways, and pipelines, and even hinterland airports, logistics parks, bonded zones, free trade zones, and commercial facilities (Pan Wenda 2019a).

2.3.4 Connotation of Combined Free Trade Ports

Combined free trade ports model, with the wharf as the core element and the combination as the core concept, aims to integrate the development of ports and the cities and promote the coordinated development of regional economy with combined ports as the foothold.

Free trade port is the core element of combined free trade ports. As mentioned earlier, a free trade port refers to a specific port or port zone enjoying preferential policies, such as the exemption of almost all of the tariffs and the free access to border. It is a FTZ with high thresholds including highly open environment and efficient and convenient working environment. It is usually established in a specific area where the economy has developed to a certain stage. The most typical feature of free trade port is the diversified functions ranging from traditional port functions to supporting service industries including finance, modern logistics, catering and accommodation (Qu Dongsheng 2014).

From the perspective of overall regional strategy, combined ports integrate each port's advantages, scale, product ranges, transport conditions and other factors and make overall planning and reasonable labor division for the ports to form an organically integrated port network with clear levels, specific functions, and complementary advantages (Chen Qiuzhen 2019). In order to avoid vicious competition among ports and enhance overall competitiveness, the most effective way is to select several adjacent ports and give them accurate positioning in industries and functions according to their own characteristics and advantages to realize their differentiated development and joint participation in global competition. For example, a combined ports model has been formed in Western Europe, with the hub port of Rotterdam as the center, the Antwerp port and Hamburg port as two wings, and a series of specialized ports and small ports as supplements. All ports have achieved rapid growth of throughput due to their virtuous competition and cooperation (Liu Luojun and Huang Zhuo 2008).

Combined free trade ports model is not a simple superposition of FTZs and combined ports. On the basis of the theory and practice of the fourth-generation ports, more focuses need to be paid on the integration of industry and city, the coordinated development of ports and cities within this region, the breakthrough of the city Borders, the emphasis of dislocation development and openness, and the group competition with others.

Combining the existing research of ports alliance, the concept of free trade ports, the research purpose of regional synergy development, and China's opening-up strategy and national policies, this book proposes the concept of "free trade ports" with Chinese characteristics, whose essential connotation is port groups composed of several ports in a region or large port clusters composed of several small port groups, which share the inter-connectivity, mutual cooperation and common development. It is not necessarily to be adjacent to the seaport, that is to say, it could be an inland area. Actually, as a customs exclusion zone with free port policy, it allows free access of foreign goods, funds, and people, adopts tax exemption on almost all of the goods entering or leaving this area, permits the operation of business activities in the area, such as free storage, exhibition, dismantling, modification, repackaging, sorting, processing and manufacturing.

Integrating existing researches, we can find that researches on combined free trade ports are still insufficient and related research with the goal of synergy development is even scarcer. However, China's national strategy has clearly proposed the coordinated development of the Greater Bay Area and the acceleration of free trade port development. Combining these two factors, in-depth analysis of the connotation, model, and coordinated development of free trade ports in GBA is of great academic significance and practical value.

References

Cao WL, Zhang XL, Pan YY et al (2012) Research on the coordinated development degree of population, land and economic urbanization in developed regions. China Popul Resour Environ 22(2):141–146

Chen QZ (2019) A study on the efficiency and optimization of China's major ports from the perspective of the maritime silk road. Huaqiao University

Chen SQ, Huang JC (2015) Review of methods for identifying the spatial development range of city cluster. Prog Geogr Sci 34(3):313–320

Chen YG, Liu JS (2002) Analysis of urban spatial cross-correlation and power spectrum based on gravity model. Geogr Res 21(6):742–751
Chen XH, Sun X (2014) Founder of headquarter economic theory: opposing attires without industrial basis. Economic Daily, 2014-08-11
Chen W, Wang J, Sun W (2019) A case study of regional cooperative behavior mechanism of local governments in the Yangtze River Delta based on cost-benefit. Acta Geogr Sin 74(2):312–322
Chen RS, Ye C, Cai YL (2013) Review on the measurement methods of regional economic ties. Hum Geogr 28(1):43–47
Chen C, Zhao M (2010) "Rationality" and "alienation" in the spatial development of central cities and outer regions: the surrounding areas of Shanghai "Connecting with Shanghai". Urban Plan Rev 12:42–50
Chu ZP, Wang Z, Bian C (2018) Theoretical understanding and practical selection of coordinated development of Beijing-Tianjin-Hebei Industry. J Northeast Norm Univ (Philos Soc Sci Ed) 296(6):183–189
Converse PD, Huegy HW, Mitchell RV (1958) Elements of marketing. Prentice-Hall
Deng WB, Song Y, Chen XX (2019) Evaluation of the effect of regional integration on economic growth in the less developed areas of the Yangtze River Delta: based on an empirical study on DID model. East China Econ Manag 33(7):14–20
Du WX (2018) Optimization path of industrial structure of city cluster in the GBA from the perspective of spatial correlation. Guangdong University of Finance and Economics Science
Fang CL (2011) China city cluster development report. Science Press
Fang CL (2017) Theoretical basis and regularity analysis of the coordinated development of Beijing-Tianjin-Hebei City Cluster. Prog Geogr 36(1):15–24
Fang JZ, Wen SH (2017) Analysis on spatial economic connections of city clusters in the Greater Mekong Sub-region. RegNal Res Dev 36(6):50–53
Fu R, Pu LJ, Qian M et al (2012) Scenario simulation design and empirical analysis of regional land use change: based on multi-agent. Resour Sci 34(3):468–474
Gottmann J (1957) Megalopolis or the urbanization of the northeastern seaboard. Econ Geogr 33(3):189–200
Gould P, Haggett P (1967) Locational analysis in human geography. Geogr Rev 57(2):292
Gu CL (2011) Research progress and prospect of city cluster. Geogr Res 30(5):771–784
Gu MD, Yin HW (2010) Research overview on spatial accessibility and equity of public facilities. Urban Probl 5:25–29
Guan WH, Yao SM (2003) Study on the trend of spatial development and evolution of city cluster: a case study of Fuxia-Xiamen city cluster. Res Mod Cities Res 18(2):82–86
Haynes KE, Fotheringham AS (1984) Gravity and spatial interaction models (Vol. 2). Sage Beverly Hills, CA
Hu FQ, Li JS (2016) The development trend of the fourth generation of free ports under the "belt and road" initiative from the perspective of intergenerational evolution of free ports. Soc Sci (5):95–99
Ji ZL, Dai YX, Hu W (2013) Government collaborative governance: implementing path of collaborative governance for regional coordinated development in China. In West J Peking Univ (Philos Soc Sci) 43(2):122–126
Jiang YB (2015) Necessity of Anhui Province to join Shanghai combined ports. Water Transp Manag 37(10):24–25
Li X, Liu XP (2007) Cellular automata based on cse-based reasoning and simulation of urban evolution in large regions. J Geogr 62(10):1097–1109
Li LQ, Ma XG (2019) Pattern, structure and function of express logistics network in China based on waybill data: Taking residential express delivery as the example. Sci Geogr Sin 1:89–97
Li GP, Wang LM (2001) Measurement and analysis of the regional economic connections between Shenzhen and the PRD. Econ Geogr 21(1):33–37
Li GP, Xu Y (2002) Development and significance of gradient theory. Economist 4(4):69–75

Li JH, Li GP (2004) Integration and innovation of regional economic development theories: an extended analysis of the mechanisms underlying gradient pushing theory. Shaanxi Normal Univ (Philos and Soc Sci Ed) 2004(7):94–98
Lin YF, Cai F, Li Z (1999) Comparative advantage and development strategy: a review of the East Asian Miracle. Chin Soc Sci (5):4–20
Liu LJ, Huang Z (2008) Exploring the energy impact of urban planning: a model of urban transport energy consumption in a planning perspective. China Urban Planning Annual Conference
Liu M (2018) Research on the generative mechanism of urban park green space pattern based on synergetic theory. Anhui Agricultural University
Liu H, Zhang Y, Zheng WS (2011) Evaluation of spatio-temporal coupling and coordinated development of urban land intensive use and regional urbanization: a case study of cities around the Bohai Sea. Geogr Res 30(10):1805–1817
Lu DD (2015) Functional orientation and coordinated development of Beijing-Tianjin-Hebei city cluster. Prog Geogr 34(3):265–270
Mao L (2019) Study on the measurement of new-type urbanization level and spatio-temporal evolution of Cheng-Chongqing city cluster. Chongqing Normal University
Meng D, Lu Y (2009) The strength and direction of regional economic connections in Jiangsu Province based on gravity model. Prog Geogr 28(5):697–704
Miao CH, Wang HJ (2006) The direction and intensity of economic connections of cities in Henan Province. Geogr Res 25(2):222–232
Ning M, Sun YM, Yang JT (2012) Analysis of regional air pollution joint prevention and control management mode at home and abroad. Environ Sustain Dev 37(5):11–18
Pan WD (2019a) Differentiation analysis of port portfolio and port enterprise portfolio. J Dalian MaritE Univ (Soc Sci Ed) 18(2):59–64
Pan WD (2019b) On the development mode of regional port integration. China Port 5:1–5
Pan WD (2019c) The integrated development of China's regional ports from the perspective of combined ports. Water Transp Manag 2019(1):1–5, 12
Pan S, Chai ZG (2008) Research on the combination and development strategy of port groups in Liaoning Province. Commun North 6:208–210
Qin YH, Cao XY (2019) Research on the collaborative innovation of science and technology in the GBA. J CentL China Norm Univ (nat Sci Ed) 53(2):96–103
Qu DS (2014) Study on the development and construction of Tianjin Dongjiang free trade port area. Dalian Maritime University
Reilly WJ (1929) Methods for the study of retail relationships. University of Texas Press
Sheng YC, Zhou YJ (2018) Appropriate human capital and coordinated development of regional economy. Geogr Res 37(4):797–813
Sun PJ, Ding SB, Xiu CL et al (2012) Research on the coordination of "population-economy-space" urbanization in Northeast China. Sci Geogr Sin 32(4):450–457
Sun MZ, Yu L, Guo JF et al (2016) Research on problems and countermeasures of integrated transport development in Beijing-Tianjin-Hebei Region. Urban Transp 3:61–66
Sun DQ, Zhang JX, Hu Y et al (2013) "Metropolitan Shadow Area" based on industrial spatial connection formation mechanism analysis: a comparative study of Yangtze River Delta city cluster and Beijing-Tianjin-Hebei city cluster. Sci Geogr Sin 33(9):1043–1050
Wang CY (2008) The concept of strengthening port financial service function. Port Econ 8:34–37
Wang XY (2016) Research on Beijing-Tianjin-Hebei collaborative development mechanism based on collaborative theory. Capital University of Economics and Business
Wang LW (2018) The intercity competition and cooperation relationship within city cluster and its impact on urban competitiveness. Jinan University
Wang Q, Chen C (2008) Coupling degree analysis of industrial cluster and regional economic space. Sci Geogr Sin 28(2):145–149
Wang ZB, Liang LW, Lin XB et al (2017) Summary of air pollution model and evaluation of control effect in Beijing-Tianjin-Hebei city cluster. Environ Sci 38(10):4005–4014

Wang QS, Zhang XF, Guo J (2018) Discussion on improving rural governance capacity from the perspective of targeted poverty alleviation: thinking based on symbiosis theory. J Jinling Univ Sci Technol (Soc Sci Ed) 32(3):56–59
Wang DZ, Zhuang RX (1996) Quantitative analysis of regional economic connections: a case study of economic connections between Shanghai and Suzhou-Xizhou-Changzhou. Sci Geogr Sin 16(1):51–57
Wang ZZ, Huang MX (2013) Theoretical evolution and coordination mechanism of "Industry-port-city" linkage development. J of Manag 26(4):43–48
Wu WJ, Kang YH, Qiu HQ (2019) Research on regional collaborative development of logistics industry based on symbiosis theory: a case study of collaborative development zone in southwest Fujian. Logist Sci Technol 2019(6):32
Wu XR, Zhao YF, Yang JM et al (2018) Modular vertical collaboration to build a new regional integrated medical service system. Jiangsu Health Serv Manag 29(2):150–152
Xia YL et al (1983) Gradient theory and regional economies. Sci and Sci and Technol Manage 1983(2):2
Xue DQ, Yao SM, Zhang H (2000) Functional connection and structural optimization of Guanzhong city cluster. Econ Geogr 6:52–55
Yao SM (1992) Characteristics, types and spatial distribution of city cluster in China. Urban Probl 1:10–15
Zhang JX (2000) Urban group space combination. Southeast University Press
Zhang BQ, Sheng JL (2018) Research review of combined port. Transp Financ Account 2018(5)
Zhang ZD, Wu D, Zhou SD (2018) Flow of production factors, regional coordination and integration and economic growth. Ind Technol Econ 37(11):58–66
Zhang MQ, Zhou Y, Zhou CL (2012) Research on coordinated development of logistics industry and regional economy based on symbiosis theory. J Nanjing Univ (nat Sci Ed) 11(1):27–34
Zhang JX, Zhuang L (2000) Study on the evolution mechanism and countermeasures of metropolitan shadow area. J Nanjing Univ (nat Sci Ed) 36(6):687–692
Zhao X (2019) A strategic approach to the coordinated development of the Guangdong-Hong Kong-Macao Greater Bay Area urban agglomeration—a literature-based review. Dev Stud (3):9
Zheng Q, Xiao WT (2008) Collaborative governance: the governance logic of service-oriented government. Chin Adm 7:48–53
Zhou YX (1998) On the direction of main economic relations. City Plan Rev 2:22–25
Zhou YX, Shi YL (1995) The concept of physical region in Chinese cities. Acta Geogra Sin 62(4):289–301
Zhou Y et al (2017) Building a first-class city cluster requires four major synergies. Sci and Technol China (6):6

Chapter 3
Research on the Development of Global Free Trade Ports

Since the 1980s, China has started to conduct research and exploration on free trade ports. However, due to relative short time for development, there are still insufficient efforts to improve awareness on its policy systems and function orientation of free trade port. There are many well-known free trade ports in the world, such as Singapore, Dubai and Hong Kong of China. They have rendered precious development experience and unique advantages for China to learn, and set new ideas and directions for China to explore the construction of free trade ports in the mainland, integrate the development of Hong Kong and Macao, and explore a model of combined free trade ports in the GBA.

3.1 Research on Free Trade Port of Hong Kong

3.1.1 An Overview

Hong Kong Free Trade Port originated in the First Opium War. On June 7, 1841, the British government officially announced that Hong Kong was its first "free trade port" in the Far East where free trade policies were adopted, mainly to British companies. It was not until after the Second World War that Hong Kong gradually developed into an international free port with a diversified economic structure. Table 3.1 provides an overview of Hong Kong Free Trade Port.

Hong Kong is endowed with superior geographical advantages. It is located at the center of shipping and international trade in Asia. It is a maritime transportation hub connecting Europe, Africa, South Asia and Southeast Asia. It is also an important window for Chinese mainland to conduct economic exchanges with the world. The Hong Kong Free Trade Port consists of Hong Kong Island, the Kowloon Peninsula, the New Territories, and Outlying Islands of Hong Kong, with a total area of approximately 1,106 km^2. Hong Kong's excellent location adjacent to the Chinese mainland offers great advantages to its port development. Chinese mainland supporting trade

© Xiamen University Press 2022

S. Ba et al., *Collaborative Innovation Mechanism of GBA in China*,
https://doi.org/10.1007/978-981-19-2251-0_3

Table 3.1 Introduction of Hong Kong Free Trade Region

Name	Hong Kong Free Port
Location	Hong Kong Special Administrative Region, the People's Republic of China
Date of establishment	1841
Area ①	Hong Kong Special Administrative Region (HKSAR) consists of Hong Kong Island, the Kowloon Peninsula, the New Territories, Lantau Island, and 262 other islands
	Its total land area includes 1,106.3 km^2, namely Hong Kong Island of 80.7 km^2, the Kowloon Peninsula of 46.9 km^2 and the New Territories of 978.7 km^2
	Except its land area, its water land extends 1648.7 km^2
Ownership	The Government of the Hong Kong Special Administrative Region
Administrator	Trade and Industry Department (TID), Customs and Excise Department, Hong Kong Port Development Council, Hong Kong Maritime Industry Council, Committee on Logistics Services Development, Hong Kong Logistics Development Council, Immigration Department (Hong Kong), etc.
Types of functions	It is responsible for handling foreign trade relations and implementing various trade policies and agreements; responsible for the implementation of taxation of dutiable commodities, inspection of goods, and statutory work of safeguarding dutiable commodities; providing discussion mechanisms for private organizations and governments; responsible for providing policy guidance; responsible for immigration control and law enforcement, etc.
Key law	No special legal provisions
Key policy	Freedom of trade, exchange and business management
Achievements	It has ranked first in the "World's Freest Economy" for 24 consecutive years; it has become an international center for finance, trade, industry, shipping, tourism, and information
Future trend	The function develops from singularity to diversification; its patterns transfer from commercial to comprehensive development

services and a free and open financial system have made up for Hong Kong's limited land space and lack of natural resources.

From the perspective of economic openness, Hong Kong, as one of the most open economies in the world, has been rated as the world's freest economy by the American Heritage Foundation for 24 consecutive years. According to data released by WTO in 2016, Hong Kong, as the world's eighth largest trading economy, has become one of the main export destinations for international ready-to-wear garments, watches, jewelry, toys, games, electronics and some light industrial products. Meanwhile, in the *Doing Business 2017 Report* released by the World Bank, Hong Kong ranks third in "starting a business" in the world owing to its free business environment and streamlined procedures for business registration.

As shown in Fig. 3.1, in 2016, Hong Kong's total trade in goods reached 7.6 trillion Hong Kong dollars, of which goods exports (including domestic product trade exports and re-exports) were 3.6 trillion Hong Kong dollars and imports were 4.0 trillion Hong Kong dollars. The total value of trade in services is approximately HK$1.3 trillion, HK$0.76 trillion of which comes from service export, and HK$0.58 trillion of which is dedicated by service import. Hong Kong is an important maritime transport hub in Asia. For example, the container throughput in 2016 was 19.81 million TEU, ranking fifth in the world's container ports. Hong Kong International Airport is one of the world's top ten busiest passenger airports as well as one of the world's busiest cargo hubs. There are 1,100 daily flights to about 190 international destinations (including 42 Chinese mainland cities). In 2016, Hong Kong Airport handled 4.52 million tons of air cargo, ranking first in the world, and 70.5 million passengers, ranking eighth in the world.[1]

Chinese mainland and Hong Kong are important trading partners. According to data from the Ministry of Commerce, from January to December 2018, the trade volume of goods between the Mainland and Hong Kong was US$310.56 billion, with a year-on-year increase of 8.4%, accounting for 6.7% of the total external trade in goods in the Mainland; Mainland exports to Hong Kong was US$302.07 billion yuan, with a year-on-year increase of 8.2%, and imports from Hong Kong amounted to US$8.49 billion, with a year-on-year increase of 16%. The trade surplus was $293.58 billion.[2] Hong Kong is the Mainland's sixth largest trading partner, fourth largest export market and the largest source of foreign investment. From January to December 2018, Hong Kong set up 39,868 enterprises in the Mainland with a year-on-year increase of 120.68%. Actual use of Hong Kong capital was US$89.92 billion, accounting for 66.6% of the US$134.97 billion actually used by the Mainland, down 4.86% year-on-year. By the end of December 2018, the Mainland has approved a total of 456,900 Hong Kong-funded projects, with the actual use of Hong Kong-funded projects amounting to US$1,099.2 billion. Hong Kong capital accounted for 54.03% of the total overseas investment absorbed by the Mainland. In recent years, as a series of pilot policies such as "Shanghai-Hong Kong Stock Connect", "Shenzhen-Hong Kong Stock Connect", and "Bond Connect" have come into effect, there has been further progress made on capital market exchange channels and cooperation mechanisms between the Mainland and Hong Kong.

The main functions of the Hong Kong Free Port can be summarized in two aspects. One is the use of free port functions to promote transit trade, maritime resupply and ship repair and other related industries. The other is tariff exemption. Having the function of export processing zone and exempting the import tax on goods can form a relatively low-priced international shopping center and promote the development of international trade and international tourism. These functions and economic activities

[1] Source from Census and Statistics Department, HKSAR Government. Hong Kong Statistical Yearbook 2018 Edition. https://www.statistics.gov.hk/pub/B10100032018AN18B0100.pdf.last, access time: March 13, 2019.

[2] Department of Taiwan, Hong Kong and Macao Affairs, Ministry of Commerce. The economic and trade exchanges between the Mainland and Hong Kong from January to December 2018. http://tga.mofcom.gov.cn/article/sjzl/hk/201903/20190302844193.shtml, February 28, 2019.

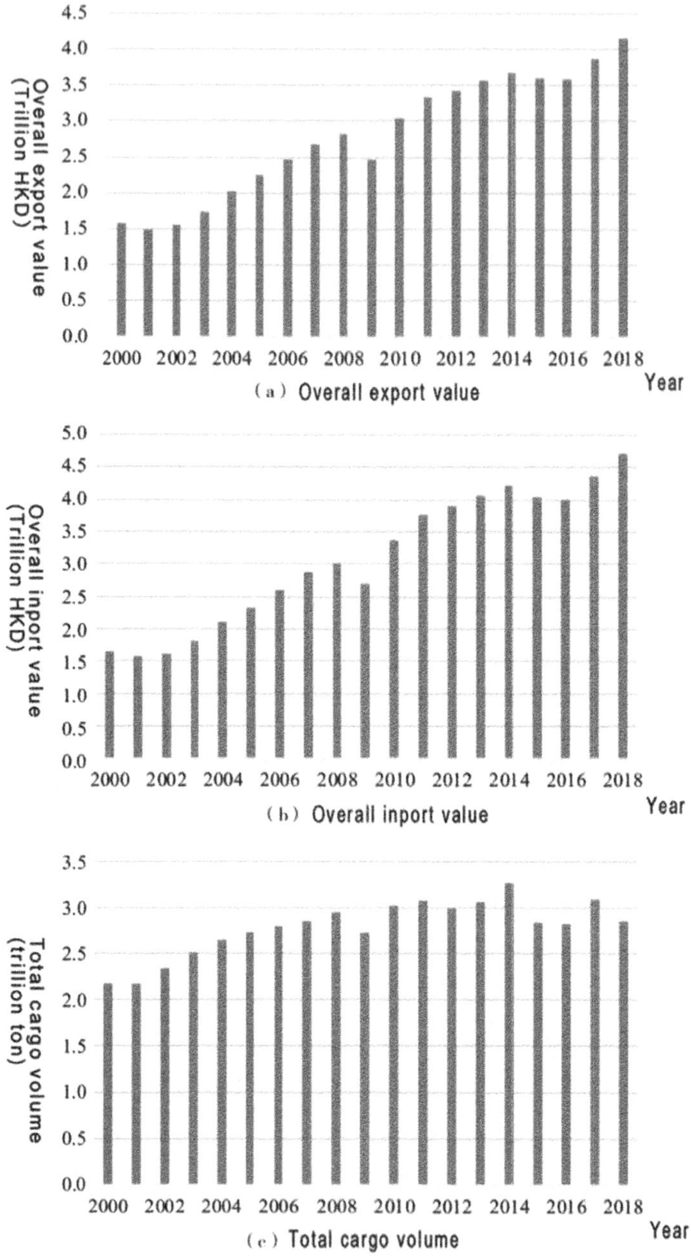

Fig. 3.1 Overall cargo volume of Hongkong (*Source* Hong Kong Statistical Yearbook 2018 Edition)

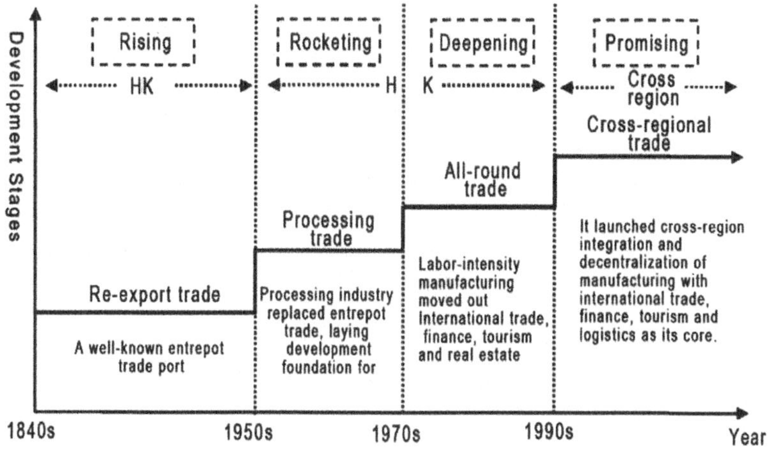

Fig. 3.2 The development history of Hong Kong Free Port (*Source* Chen Huizhu et al. 2015)

are mutually reinforcing and organically connected, playing a significant role in promoting Hong Kong's economic development.

3.1.2 *The Course of Development*

The development course of Hong Kong free port can be broadly divided into four stages: re-export trade, processing trade, integrated and cross-regional (see Fig. 3.2).[3]

3.1.2.1 Re-export Free Port (1841–1950)

From 1841 to 1946, re-export trade was very important to Hong Kong's economy, which was dependent on the social and economic foundation, natural conditions and history of Hong Kong at that time. Before the Opium War, due to narrow territory, inadequate natural resources, and small population, fishery had become Hong Kong's pillar industry. However, thanks to its favorable position as it is backed by the Chinese mainland and faces the Pacific Ocean with the natural deep-water port of Victoria Harbor, Hong Kong has a significant location advantage as an entrepot. Since the administration of British colonial government, with its own geographical advantages, Hong Kong has gradually transformed into a city supported by re-export trade, and its economic structure has directly changed from fishery to service trade. This single economic structure, dominated by entrepot trade, lasted until the 1950s.

[3] Chen Huizhu et al. On the Evolution of Hong Kong Free Trade Port Model. Tropical Geography, 2015(1).

From 1946 to 1950, Hong Kong's economic development mainly benefited from its role as an entrepot trade port in the triangular trade of Britain, India, and mainland China. And then a free and open economic system, free entry and exit of commodities, preferential tariff policies, and superior location conditions provide important foundations for Hong Kong to develop its re-export trade. What's more, all other industries in Hong Kong have direct or indirect relations with re-export trade. The entire economic system prioritizes the re-export trade, leading to sluggish development of processing and manufacturing industries and laying hidden dangers for hollowing out of manufacturing in the future.

3.1.2.2 Processing Trade Free Port (1951–1978)

In 1951, the United Nations' embargo on China manipulated by the United States put the trade between Chinese mainland and Hong Kong to a stop, resulting in Hong Kong's re-export trade to plummet. Hong Kong took a turn to processing trade. It is difficult to develop an independent industrial system in Hong Kong since it does not have a natural resource base for the development of heavy industry. Because of the narrow market and other obstacles, Hong Kong sought to accept the capital, technology, equipment and labor transferred from the Mainland by virtue of the "low labor cost and low land price mode of production". It actively explored the European and American markets to form a labor-intensive industry with textile and garment industries as its pillar. At the same time, a number of industrial areas, such as Chai Wan, Sha Tin, Tai Po, San Po Kong, Tsuen Wan and Kwun Tong have come into being, which are supported by various services such as film, television, entertainment, education and logistics.

In addition, the containerization of terminals has promoted the development of the manufacturing industry. By 1959, the share of industrial exports in Hong Kong's export trade had risen to 69.6%. By 1969, Hong Kong had implemented an export-oriented strategy, focusing on promoting the development of light industry and the export of its products, and had gradually replaced the re-export trade with processing industry, so that it has completely reversed the traditional pattern of re-export trade and has marked Hong Kong's formal entry into a processing trade-based free port stage.

3.1.2.3 Integrated Free Port (1979–1990)

Since China's reform and opening up, the economic integration of Guangdong and Hong Kong has taken a huge turn. Hong Kong has taken advantage of the shift to a labor-intensive processing and manufacturing industry in the Pearl River Delta region with lower labor costs. Combined with its advantages in capital, management, technology and marketing, Hong Kong has implemented industrial upgrading and product upgrading to promote the expansion of the manufacturing industry and the continuous optimization of its structure and products. In addition, the service industry, which is compatible with the manufacturing sector, has developed rapidly, with the financial, real estate, tourism and information industries becoming pillar industries, Hong Kong's international economic status was enhanced and became one of the "Four Asian Tigers".

Hong Kong's "active non-intervention policy" has created a free environment for it to become an international trading center, international shipping center and international financial center in the Asia–Pacific region. The services sectors such as wholesale and retail, hotel, restaurant, insurance, finance and real estate have gradually become pillar industries, with GDP increasing from 34.5% in 1970 to 39.5% in 1986. Among them, the development of financial insurance and real estate is particularly significant (Chen Huizhu et al. 2015).

The time difference in the world also creates convenient conditions for Hong Kong to become an international financial center. East 8th time zone of Hong Kong stands at the midpoint of Europe, Asia and America. It is located between the two major global financial centers of London and New York. Since there is 8 h and 13 h away from London and New York (winter time) respectively, it naturally bridges opening and closing vacancies of two major international markets in Europe and America, having been an important node for ensuring the all-weather operation of global financial transactions.

3.1.2.4 Cross-Regional Integrated Free Port (1991–Present)

Since the 1990s, world economic cooperation has become increasingly close. The cross-border growth triangle between Guangdong, Hong Kong and Macao has significant potential in terms of information flow, technology diffusion, investment and infrastructure improvement. Since the reunification in 1997, Hong Kong has benefited from the preferential co-operation policy brought about by the "one country, two systems" policy, in-depth division of labor and cooperation with the Pearl River Delta region, and has maintained stable economic growth through economic vitality, eventually becoming an important re-export port and offshore fund-raising center for mainland enterprises in line with international standards. However, Hong Kong's economic development has also encountered many difficulties, such as the lack of industrial structure which led to slowing economic growth. Therefore, there is an urgent need for Hong Kong to enter a new stage of cross-regional cooperation.

Firstly, the trend of service of industrial structure is becoming more and more obvious, and the contribution rate of service industry is increasing steadily. According to the 2019 edition of the *Service Industry Statistics Summary* compiled by the Hong Kong SAR Statistics Department, the output value of Hong Kong's service industry accounted for 93.1%[4] of GDP in 2018, and it has developed more outwardly and

[4] The data comes from the 2019 edition of Statistical Digest of the Services Sector compiled by the Census and Statistics Department of the Hong Kong Special Administrative Region Government, https://www.statistics.gov.hk/pub/B10800072018AN18B0100.pdf, April 11, 2019.

productively.[5] In terms of financial services, Hong Kong's economy has continued to develop steadily, with sound laws and regulations, and a free economic environment, making it the first overseas RMB settlement center. At the same time, the accession of RMB to SDR (Special Drawing Right) marked an important step towards RMB internationalization, and international capital's demand for RMB exchange has increased. Relying on its geographical advantage of being close to the mainland, Hong Kong has accumulated a large amount of RMB, laying a monetary foundation for an offshore RMB center. In 2014, the establishment of the "Shanghai-Hong Kong Stock Connect" laid the foundation for realizing the interconnection of the mainland and Hong Kong stock markets and also safeguarded Hong Kong's status as an international financial center. If Hong Kong builds a RMB cross-border settlement center and an offshore bond market, it will expand the RMB overseas application channels, promote the diversification of overseas RMB-denominated products, and accelerate the internationalization process of the RMB.

Secondly, emerging industries are developing rapidly. In the early 1990s, a global wave of knowledge economy led to a new industrial revolution and a change in the division of labor system. However, Hong Kong's economy has long relied on import and export trade, finance, real estate and tourism, with manufacturing accounting for less than 3% of GDP. Structural unemployment is serious because the service sector is mostly capital-intensive and unable to absorb the surplus labor released by the transfer of manufacturing. The Hong Kong government continues to make the cultivation of innovative industries a long-term economic plan, proposing to nurture six new pillar industries of environmental protection, testing and certification, medical services, education services, cultural and creative industries and innovation and technology, as well as the Hong Kong Science and Technology Park, which is the international technology development platform, and to provide productive services to technology-intensive enterprises (Chen Huizhu et al. 2015).

Thirdly, Hong Kong free port has developed in depth with the signing of policy frameworks. Hong Kong's free trade policy is based on the multilateral trading system. In accordance with multilateral trade and related regulations, Hong Kong carries out activities such as safeguarding its rights, fulfilling its obligations and maintaining and enhancing its own exports and market access. Since 1995 when Hong Kong became a founding member of the WTO, Hong Kong has actively participated in a series of regional economic cooperation organizations such as APEC, and has become a full member of the Asian Development Bank as well as the World Customs Organization (Chen Huizhu et al. 2015). In addition, under the principle of *one country, two systems*, Hong Kong has successively signed the *Hong Kong and New Zealand Close Economic and Trade Cooperation Agreement*, the *Hong Kong and EU Free Trade Agreement* and the *Hong Kong and Chile Free Trade Agreement*, creating a favorable external environment for the free development of economy.

[5] Productive service refers to service industries that directly or indirectly provide intermediate services for the production process, mainly including finance, insurance, warehouses, communications, wholesale, retail, transportation, and intermediary services.

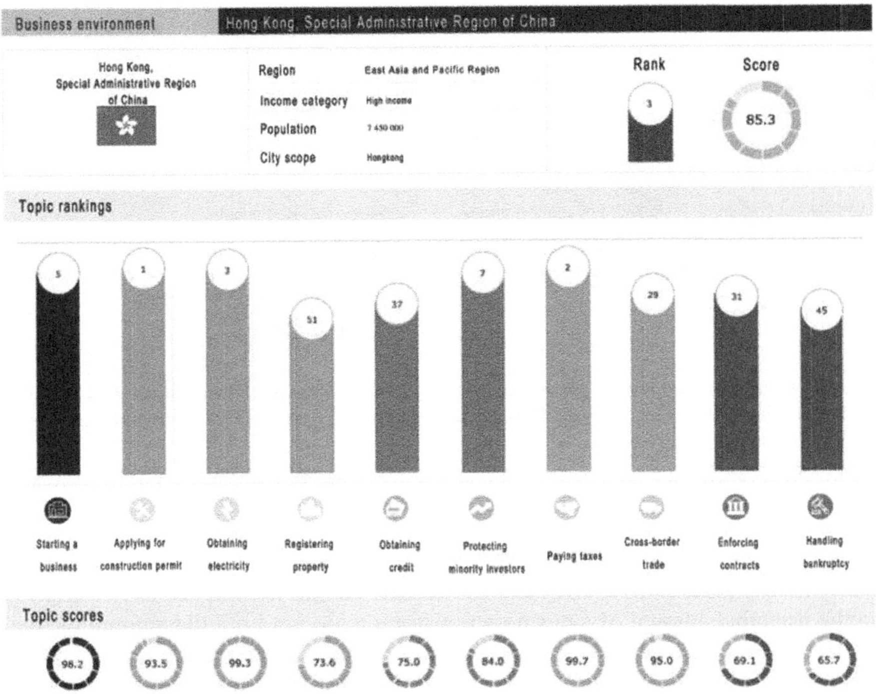

Fig. 3.3 Assessment of business environment in Hong Kong (*Source* World Bank Business Environment Assessment [https://chinese.doingbusiness.org/zh/data/exploreeconomies/hong-kong-china])

3.1.3 Construction Experience

The Hong Kong SAR government implements an "active non-intervention policy" to streamline government functions and delegate powers to ensure the free operation of the market. In terms of market access, it has achieved outstanding service efficiency and standardized management to run a free and orderly market. The overall business environment is assessed by the World Bank to be the third in the ease of doing business in the world (see Fig. 3.3[6]).

3.1.3.1 Efficient Government Services and Convenient Enterprise Registration Process

As shown in Fig. 3.4, it only takes three steps for an enterprise to obtain a business license. Through online business registration application, the relevant certificate will

[6] World Bank. Doing Business 2020. October 25, 2019.

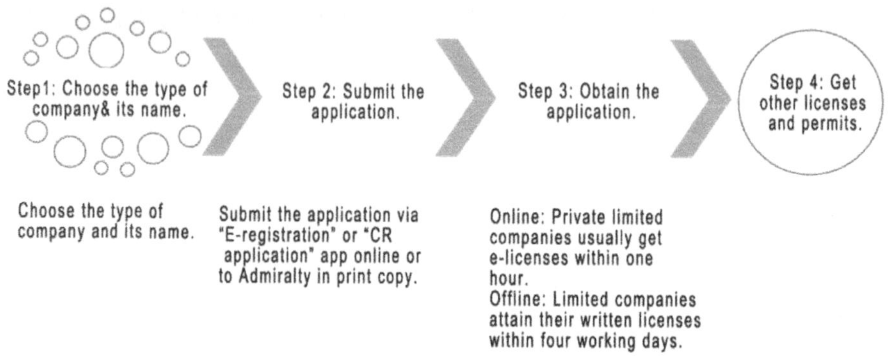

Fig. 3.4 Hong Kong Enterprise registration process (*Source* The official website of the Companies Registry of the Hong Kong Special Administrative Region Government [https://www.cr.gov.hk/sc/services/register-company.htm])

generally be issued within one hour. If the application is submitted on paper, it only takes four working days to obtain the relevant certificate.

First, easy registration. The laws of the HKSAR do not impose any restrictions on the principal amount of a business registration, do not limit the amount of funds in place, and do not require capital verification. Only a 0.1% stamp tax is required. After the establishment of an enterprise, as long as the shareholders unanimously approve the resolution on the addition of registered capital, the registered capital can be arbitrarily increased and the resolution and related forms will be submitted to the Hong Kong Companies Registry together with the appropriate fees. As a result, Hong Kong has attracted companies from many countries around the world (see Fig. 3.5).

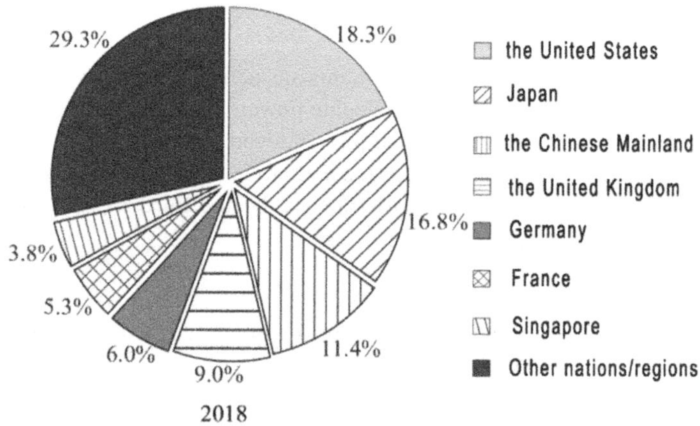

Fig. 3.5 Percentage of the location of the parent company of the regional headquarters and offices in Hong Kong in 2018 (*Source* Hong Kong Trade Development Council)

Second, standardized supervision of investment enterprises. The HKSAR shall exercise "national treatment" for foreign capital, supervise investment enterprises in accordance with laws and regulations such as the Companies Act and the Regulations on the Silver Industry, and regulate and restrain the conduct of enterprises. In addition to the rule of law, civil society organizations such as trade associations and chambers of commerce also play an effective role in supervising industry self-regulation.

3.1.3.2 Open Investment Sector

Hong Kong's investment system is open and treats all investors equally and does not discriminate against them. The Government shall not interfere or subsidize any investment activity to the extent permitted by the laws and regulations of Hong Kong.

Firstly, the industry entry barriers are low. Theoretically, in all business activities permitted by the existing laws of the HKSAR, no industry is completely prohibited from private and foreign investors, nor is there a limit on the proportion of holdings, and both domestic and foreign investors can take 100% control. However, the gambling industry is tightly regulated. There are entry conditions for telecommunications and broadcasting. In industries such as telecommunications, broadcasting, transportation, energy, liquor sales, catering, medicine and finance, in addition to the formalities required to register a general enterprise, they are required to apply for a HKSAR Government license before they can operate legally. With the exception of a few industries such as banking and insurance, the HKSAR Government does not, in general, impose entry thresholds for business licensing. The stock and inflow of foreign direct investment in Hong Kong are shown in Figs. 3.6 and 3.7.

Secondly, HKSAR actively seeks outbound investment opportunities. An important reason why the HKSAR has become an international financial center is that it is home to large financial institutions from all over the world, providing investors with

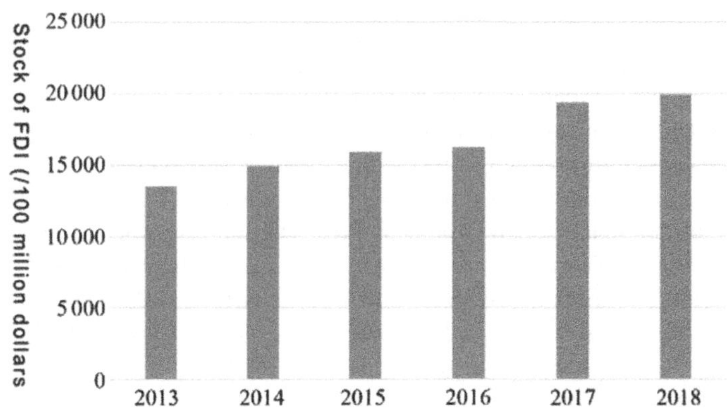

Fig. 3.6 Stock of foreign direct investment in Hong Kong (*Source* Hong Kong Trade Development Council)

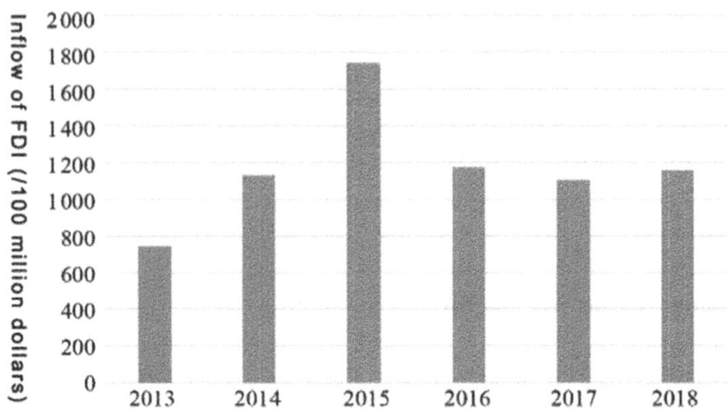

Fig. 3.7 Inflow of foreign direct investment in Hong Kong (*Source* Hong Kong Trade Development Council)

a wide range of services such as credit, financing and capital settlement. Not only are there few restrictions on investment in Hong Kong, Hong Kong government is also actively encouraging local investors to invest abroad. The Investment Promotion Agency was established in 2007 to provide information consultation, investment negotiation and other public services for overseas investment cooperation between local and mainland enterprises.

3.1.3.3 Powerful Financial Openness

Hong Kong's financial openness is reflected in its open money market. Hong Kong has achieved full openness under the capital account and implemented a free exchange system. At present, Hong Kong is the only integration center in Asia that has no distinction between offshore business and local business. The details are as follows.

First, freedom of investment and finance. Hong Kong has a sound legal system and regulatory body in line with international accounting standards. Second, with the development of science and technology, Hong Kong has been increasingly less affected by the flow of information and capital, and has been entitled with complete financial service facilities such as transaction, settlement and settlement, which has facilitated the provision of investment and finance services for overseas investors.

Second, a completely open capital market. There are no special restrictions on the Hong Kong stock market for foreign enterprises, where overseas enterprises and individuals can trade at any time with legal securities trading accounts. What's more, Hong Kong also has very few restrictions on bond investors. International investors can freely trade debt instruments issued by Hong Kong. Therefore, Hong Kong is known as the world's most open bond market. Overseas borrowers can also raise funds in Hong Kong by issuing various debt instruments, and bonds are extremely liquid on the market. Hong Kong has not only gained greater freedom in its domestic market but also in external financing. First of all, Hong Kong boasts a well-developed financial system and sound external financing channels, and its financial institutions have no limits on borrowing. The longer the cooperation lasts, the more benefits they will obtain. Small and medium-sized enterprise customers also enjoy preferential treatment. Some financial institutions have started small and medium-sized enterprise business departments to help enterprises with comprehensive and distinctive financing services.

Third, free flow of cross-border funds. Hong Kong has reduced restrictions on cross-border capital flows to a minimum, so that there are no restrictions on foreign investors' repatriation of profits or principals to their home countries. At the same time, Hong Kong abolished foreign exchange and gold controls in 1973 and 1974, respectively. International funds can freely enter and exit Hong Kong's capital market under various exchange rate regimes, which has brought great convenience to the development of Hong Kong's financial industry.

Fourth, a financial supervision system in place. Hong Kong's financial market is highly free. In order to reduce event risks and take pre-regulation and control as the core, Hong Kong has established special laws and regulations and regulatory agencies to handle financial issues. In Hong Kong, regulatory authorities are free from government intervention with a high degree of independence and freedom, and industry associations have a prominent role and focus on self-discipline mechanisms.

3.1.3.4 Trade Liberalization

First, freedom of international shipping. Hong Kong is a world-famous free port and its transport is not subject to customs restrictions. Ships entering and leaving ports by sea are not required to clear customs and goods entering and leaving ports, trans-shipment and storage are not subject to customs restrictions. In addition, customs, inspection and quarantine and border control departments do not require additional inspections of ships and crews. The total merchandise trade for the calendar year is shown in Fig. 3.8.

Second, freedom of international trade settlement. As a mature foreign exchange market, Hong Kong is one of the cities with the densest banking institutions in the world. It is closely connected with many international financial centers and can meet the needs of various settlement methods. Any currency can be used for trade settlement. As the RMB plays an increasingly important role in international business, Hong Kong's offshore RMB business has developed rapidly, and the total RMB settlement has continued to rise.

3.1.3.5 Relaxed Regulatory Environment

First, convenient customs clearance. Hong Kong's goods customs clearance procedures are very simple, with fewer quotas and trade controls and no import and export quotas. Except for goods exempted from customs declaration, the carrier only needs

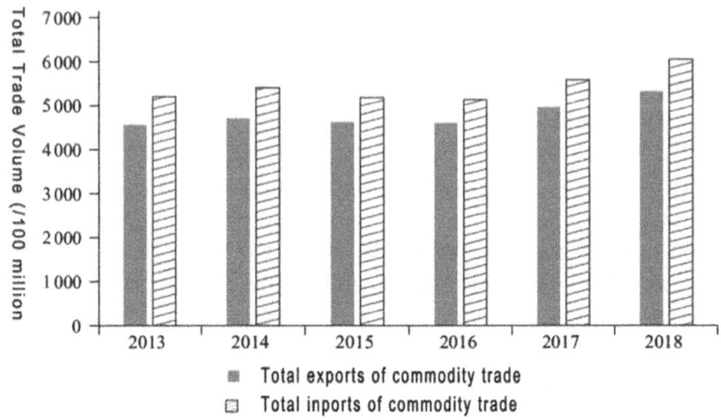

Fig. 3.8 The total amount of commodity trade in Hong Kong over the years (*Source* Hong Kong Trade Development Council)

to submit all the transport information and declaration form of the goods to the customs within 14 days after the entry and exit of the goods. The goods exempted from customs declaration in Hong Kong include transshipment goods, transit goods, ship supplies (including fuel tanks), aircraft supplies (including flight fuel), personal luggage other than cars, and any postal parcels with a value of less than US$4,000. In addition, the Hong Kong government has joined the *Istanbul Convention* and issued temporary import licenses for certain commodities (excluding postal commodities). These commodities include: commodities displayed or used in exhibitions, fairs or similar events, professional equipment, personal sporting goods or passenger goods.

Second, easy customs clearance. Hong Kong's customs clearance is varied and convenient. In addition to the conventional methods, customs clearance measures also include: Those measures adhere to the principle of voluntary and agreement as well as the *Hong Kong Approved Economic Operator Scheme* based on voluntary and trust management.

The purpose of the Haiyitong Project is to eliminate the issuance of the *Notice of Prohibited Removal of Items* (commonly known as "CV deduction"), simplify the current procedures for submission of subdivision data, and improve the efficiency of customs and carriers; it facilitates customs to obtain relevant data, carries out risk assessment, and enhances the efficiency of goods sorting. There is neither registration fees and other fees, nor any increase on information technology investment and the inspection rate, which greatly helps cargo clearance.

Hong Kong's *Accredited Economic Operator Program*, as a concept under the World Customs Organization's *Standard Framework for Safeguarding and Facilitating International Trade* (Hereinafter referred to as the "Framework"), has set its aims to ensure the safety of international supply chain and promote the circulation of legal goods through customs and industry partnerships. Currently, it has been carried out by the major members of the World Customs Organization, which has won wide recognition from Hong Kong's major trading partners. The *Hong*

Kong Accredited Economic Operator Program, as an open and voluntary certification system launched in 2010, has achieved remarkable results and is under the responsibility of the Customs and Excise Department. According to the requirements of the plan, local enterprises can be certified as recognized economic operators with reference to the established safety standards, enjoy the convenience of customs clearance without paying any fees (Xing Houyuan 2014). Accredited economic operators are regarded as strategic partners of the Customs and Excise Department with priority or reduction in customs inspection. After the full implementation of the Accredited Economic Operator Program, the Hong Kong Customs is actively striving to reach a mutual recognition agreement with overseas customs to provide overseas preferential treatment for accredited economic operators.

Third, fewer quotas. The Hong Kong Special Administrative Region has fewer quotas and trade controls. Studies have shown that Hong Kong only imposes total import control on live chickens for food safety; certain ozone-depleting substances should be subject to quota and licensing control; comprehensive and strict import and export controls are implemented on strategic commodities, including munitions, some electronic telecommunication and navigation equipment, etc. (Yang Ming et al. 2019). In addition, Hong Kong does not take the initiative to manage import and export quotas, except for passive quota controls on national textile exports. Hong Kong implements import and export licensing control on tobacco, alcohol, methanol, alcohol, automobile gasoline and diesel oil, which are very few commodities, in order to reduce trade control.

Fourth, trade facilitation in the inspection and quarantine process. The Customs and Excise Department conducts selective inspection or inspection of imports and exports, actively protects legitimate trade activities, prioritizes a sound business environment, and adopts risk management measures to select selected goods to minimize interference at immigration control stations. Hong Kong does not conduct inspection and quarantine on imported and exported agricultural products. It ensures food safety through the market mechanism and implements a "two-way check and intermediate verification" system for industrial and agricultural products, in which relevant authorities exercise strict quality supervision over imported goods from the three perspectives of procurement, entry and supply.

3.1.3.6 Relaxed Corporate Taxation

At present, the global competition among multinational companies is fierce, so the taxation greatly affects the profits of multinational companies. Hong Kong is entitled with loose taxation, having attracted global multinational companies to start business in Hong Kong.

Hong Kong implements a zero-tariff policy. Except for alcohol, tobacco, hydrocarbon oil and methanol, there is no need to pay any tariff on general import and export goods.

Hong Kong has carried out a simple low-tariff policy with few types of taxes and low tax rates. The taxes in Hong Kong include profits tax, salaries tax and property

Table 3.2 Overview of Hong Kong economic laws and regulations

Types	Law
Investment and trade	*The Companies Ordinance (Chapter 32, the Laws of Hong Kong)*
	Business Registration Ordinance (Chapter 310, the Laws of Hong Kong)
	Import and Export Ordinance (Chapter 60, the Laws of Hong Kong)
	Dutiable Commodities Ordinance (Chapter 109, the Laws of Hong Kong)
Financial sector	*Banking Ordinance*
	Securities Ordinance
Labor and capital	*Employment Ordinance*
	Labor Relations Ordinance
Intellectual property	*Trademark Ordinance*
	Trademark Rules
	Registered Designs Ordinance
	Copyright Ordinance

tax. There is no value-added tax or business tax. Profits earned outside Hong Kong are not taxable. Individuals are not required to pay interests, dividends, dividends, stocks and other investment income taxes except for business operations. From the perspective of the main tax categories, the profits tax rates are 16.5% (for limited companies) and 15.0% (for non-limited companies) respectively. Individual income tax is levied in different proportions after exceeding the allowance, up to a maximum of 17.0%

3.1.3.7 Sound Legal System

Hong Kong has a sound legal system as well as a fair, open and just business environment. Hong Kong's free port policy lays its foundation on a highly mature market legal system. There are more than 1,000 regulations and subsidiary legislation in Hong Kong, and economic laws and regulations account for about 45% of the total, having laid the basis of the "rules of the game" for free competition (see Table 3.2). Hong Kong has strict laws and regulations. Any economic activity has a legal basis and is subject to legal supervision. With economic development, some economic laws and regulations have been continuously supplemented, revised and improved.

3.1.3.8 Free Movement for Natural Persons

As a free port, Hong Kong has greater freedom and international mobility in population and labor.

First, the freedom of Entry and Exit Policy. The Hong Kong Immigration Department facilitates the entry and exit of business visitors, tourists and Hong Kong residents. Many citizens of other countries can even stay visa-free in Hong Kong for short periods.

Second, convenient international mobility of talents. There are many multinational companies in Hong Kong, and highly educated talents from many nations. Hong Kong provides the greatest convenience for international talent mobility, as long as companies apply for work endorsements from the government.

Third, flexible allocation of labor resources. Hong Kong enterprises can hire local or mainland employees, and mainland enterprises can also employ mainland professionals or local workers in accordance with the regulations after the establishment of Hong Kong. There are no restrictions on the flow of labor between industries and enterprises in Hong Kong. The allocation of labor resources in the private sector is affected by the market and is highly mobile.

3.1.4 Referential Significance

3.1.4.1 Adopting Appropriate Paths Based on Stage of Development and Foundation

Affected by a variety of internal and external factors, Hong Kong has developed different development paths at different times. As the construction of a free trade pilot zone in the Chinese Mainland is still in the initial stage, much can be learnt from Hong Kong and combine the actual situation in the Mainland to set up pilot free trade zones based on national strategies and local advantages, such as those for processing trade, and those for combined cross-border or trans-regional trade. Based on the reality of the Mainland, trade-oriented, processing trade-oriented, integrated and cross-border or cross-regional free trade pilot zones can be established in accordance with national strategies and local advantages.

3.1.4.2 Selecting a Favorable Location

Firstly, as a hub for communication between Chinese mainland and the main shipping lanes in Southeast Asia, Oceania, Europe and Africa, Hong Kong strengthens the network of external economic links of Chinese mainland. Secondly, as one of the most developed regions in China, GBA is able to provide sufficient goods, raw materials, market and labor force for Hong Kong's re-export, processing and service trade. Thirdly, Hong Kong, located between New York and London, is an important node in the world's round-the-clock financial services system, cementing its position as an international financial center. Similarly, China should choose the appropriate location to build its free trade pilot zones.

3.1.4.3 Fully Free Economic System and Sound Legal System

A fully free economic system and a sound legal system can guarantee the full development of free ports. After its return, Hong Kong, as a special administrative region with relatively independent legislative and administrative powers, can maintain its long-term and stable development. Therefore, if we want to establish a free trade area based on the model of Hong Kong, it is imperative to give it a stable and perfect legal status and administrative and economic management power, rather than reduce it to a conventional bonded area or development zone. Hong Kong's economic law accounts for about 45% of the statutory law. It constitutes a complete set of free competition rules in the market, guaranteeing free and fair competition and efficient operation of the market.

3.1.4.4 Appropriate Interventions

In the development of modern market economy, the government should give full freedom to the market and play an invisible role of the market, but it should also actively provide institutional guarantee for the steady operation of the market The Hong Kong Special Administrative Region government expects to build a free trade port in the entire territory, without special areas or special laws. The Hong Kong government exercises complete control over land, publicizes subway facilities, etc., and directly operates ports, airports, roads, Kowloon-Canton Railway and postal services. For private public service enterprises, the Hong Kong Special Administrative Region government uses contract methods to monitor and intervene in prices and service quality; it provides interest-free, low-interest loans or general assistance to agriculture, fisheries, residential buildings, and some quasi-governmental organizations and service organizations.

3.1.5 Development Trend

The Hong Kong free port was established with a single initial function, mainly re-export trade, mainly to facilitate the transfer of goods between both parties involved in international trade. It was not until the 1950s that Hong Kong took advantages of capital, technology, equipment, and labor transferred from the Mainland to establish a part of its export-oriented light industry and realized the transition from re-export trade to processing trade. Since then, Hong Kong free port has fully utilized its own unique advantages and made full use of the capital, technology and management experience provided by developed countries such as the United States and Japan, and further expanded its functions, from processing trade to foreign trade, transportation, and real estate, finance and tourism. Hence, it has achieved gradual transformation from a trade-oriented to a comprehensive business. At present, Hong Kong free port has become a model of international free trade port, as well as a famous international trade center, financial center, information center, shipping center and tourism center.

Since the reform and opening up, China, as an important global economy, has a higher dependence on foreign trade than other large economies. In 2006, China's total imports and exports accounted for 64% of GDP. Even though foreign trade dependence fell to 33% by 2016, trade remains an important engine of China's economic growth. According to statistics, in 2017, the proportions of the Mainland's trade with Southeast Asia, South Asia, West Asia, Central and Eastern Europe and other countries and regions re-exported through Hong Kong were about 10%, 9%, 2% and 4%, respectively, all of which are on the rise.

The Belt and Road Initiative (BRI) has injected new vitality into the development of Hong Kong Free Port. Hong Kong has high-end logistics services such as global supply chain management. Many port companies handle business in nearly 100 ports in dozens of countries around the world. As China has enhanced its trade among the countries along the Belt and Road, especially with Southeast Asia and South Asia, Hong Kong will fully play a core role of the Hong Kong International Trade Centre as well as the International Shipping Centre. In addition, China has established a network of multilateral or bilateral free trade zones with countries along the Belt and Road. As a world-renowned free trade port and separate customs zone, Hong Kong's free market has a complete legal system that can give full play to its software, hardware, and location advantages to facilitate trade.

China's export of industrial products has a huge production capacity, a complete industrial chain, and greater flexibility in foreign trade. The recovery in global demand may bring a huge boost to the Chinese economy. Thanks to its geographical location and policies, and favorable location adjacent to the mainland, the future of Hong Kong free trade port is bright.

3.2 Research on Singapore Free Trade Port

3.2.1 An Overview

With its unique geographical position and preferential natural conditions, Singapore guards the Strait of Malacca and works as the main link between the Pacific and the Indian Ocean. The Singapore government implements a free economic system characterized by freedom of finance, trade, company registration and navigation. It is a world-renowned free trade port. The basic information of Singapore free trade port is shown in Table 3.3.

In 1969, Singapore enacted the *Free Trade Zone Act* and set up the first free trade port area at Jurong Terminal. Up to now, Singapore has seven FTZs. In terms of functions, Changi Airport Free Trade Zone focuses on the development of aviation logistics, which is in the charge of the Civil Aviation Authority of Singapore; other free trade zones have prioritized the development of maritime logistics. Jurong Pier

Table 3.3 An overview of Singapore Free Port

Project	Introduction	
Operation and management organization	Port of Singapore Authority (PSA)	Brani FTZ
		Keppel FTZ
		Sembawang FTZ
		Tanjong Pagar FTZ
		Pasir Panjang FTZ
	Civil Aviation Authority of Singapore	Changi Airport
	Jurong Harbor Pte Ltd	Port of Jurong, Singapore
Investment	The Singapore Economic Development Board is responsible for attracting investment	
Customs clearance time	24-h	
Warehousing service	It provides 72-h free storage service for bulk cargo import and export, and 28-day free storage service for goods waiting for re-shipment or re-export	
Information networks	Trade Net, Port Net and Dock Operating System	
Liberalization of financial investment	We will completely remove foreign exchange controls; We will fully liberalize foreign investment in commercial, foreign trade, leasing, direct selling, advertising, telecommunications and other fields	
Legal environment	*Free Trade Zone Act; Singapore Customs Act; Goods and Services Tax (GST)*	
Business taxes and fees	With the exception of alcohol, tobacco products, petroleum products and vehicles, all goods are free to enter and leave Singapore without customs duties, whereas taxable and non-taxable goods are subject to a 7% value-added tax on imports into Singapore	
Enterprise tax and fees	The corporate income tax rate is 17%, and the corporate income tax rate for shipping companies and regional headquarters is 10%. Shipping companies are exempt from foreign currency ship income tax, etc.	

is managed by Jurong Port Pte Ltd, while all other free trade zones are operated by Singapore International Port Group. The Singapore Free Trade Area is subject to fence management and customs is responsible for monitoring entry and exit.

According to statistics from the Singapore International Enterprise Development Board, the total value of Singapore's imports and exports of goods in 2018 reached US$782.26 billion, an increase of 11.6% over the previous year. Among them, the export value was US$411.76 billion, an increase of 10.3%; the import value was US$370.50 billion, an increase of 13.0%; the trade surplus was US$41.25 billion, a decrease of 9.5%.

According to country (region) analysis, in 2018, Singapore's exports to Mainland China, Hong Kong, Malaysia and Indonesia were 50.41 billion, 48.63 billion, 44.87 billion and 32.97 billion US dollars, respectively, with an increase of −6.8%, 5.6%, and 13.2 and 17.9%, accounting for 12.2%, 11.8%, 10.9% and 8.0% of total exports; Mainland China, Malaysia, the United States and Taiwan's imports were 49.66 billion, 42.80 billion, 41.88 billion and 31.40 billion US dollars, increasing by 9.5%, 10.1%, 21.5% and 15.6%, accounting for 13.4%, 11.6%, 11.3% and 8.5% of total imports. The top five sources of Singapore's trade surplus are Hong Kong, Indonesia, Vietnam, Thailand and Australia. In 2018, the surpluses were 44.99 billion, 17.74 billion, 8.56 billion, 7.26 billion and 7.23 billion US dollars, respectively. The trade deficit mainly comes from Taiwan, Saudi Arabia and the United States. In 2018, the deficit was 14.45 billion, 11.87 billion and 11.24 billion US dollars, respectively, with an increase of 36.6%, 42.3% and 2.1%。

According to product analysis, electromechanical, mineral and chemical products are Singapore's major export products. In 2018, exports were 187.47 billion, 54.15 billion and 43.63 billion U.S. dollars, respectively, with an increase of 45.5%, 13.2% and 10.6%, accounting for 45.5%, 13.2% and 10.6% of total exports. Electromechanical, electrical and mineral products were the top two imports of Singapore, with imports of $154.66 billion and $88.83 billion in 2018, an increase of 11.8% and 21.0%, respectively, accounting for 41.7% and 24.0% of the total imports.

3.2.2 Development History

3.2.2.1 Complete Free Port Mainly for Re-export Trade (1819–1958)

In 1819, Sir Thomas Raffles of the British East India Company discovered that Singapore was a naturally sheltered deep-water port. He made full use of Singapore's special geographical advantages to establish the first freight terminal (trading station) here. The UK acquired a lease on Singapore and announced that it would open the whole of Singapore to a free port. In 1820, Singapore free port began to make a profit. Three years later, its trade volume surpassed that of Penang, Malaysia, a free port opened in 1786. After becoming a British colony in 1824, Singapore became a truly free port, with developed re-export trade and free entry and exit of foreign ships. Except for tobacco, alcohol, and opium which were monopolized by the colonial government, all other goods were exempt from tariffs. Until 1960, Singapore had always been a trade transit point, with a single economic structure and only basic industries such as processing and assembly.

3.2.2.2 Limited Free Port with Integrated Functions (1959–Present)

There are three stages of Singapore's transition from a complete free port to a limited one: transition period, development period and sustained prosperity period, as shown in Fig. 3.9.

First, transition to a limited free port (1959–1969). In 1959, Singapore attained self-government. To get rid of high dependence of re-export trade, it began to implement an "import substitution" strategy to protect local industries by restricting commodity imports. After that, Singapore has started a limited free port policy. To mitigate the impact of tariff protection on transit trade, the Singapore Parliament enacted the *Free Trade Zone Regulations* in 1966 and established the first Jurong Port FTZ at Jurong Wharf in 1969. The Singapore Free Trade Zone, a tax-free zone in essence, does not rely on preferential policies to attract foreign investment. At that time, Singapore's free trade port zones at the port terminals include Brani FTZ, Keppel FTZ, Tanjong Pagar FTZ, Pasir Panjang FTZ, Sembawang FTZ and Jurong Port FTZ.

Second, development period of manufacturing and service industries (1970–1989). The import substitution strategy promotes the manufacturing industry to become Singapore's pillar industry and stimulates the development of trade exports, transportation, finance and tourism. In 1967, Singapore began to implement an export-oriented industrialization strategy and successively established more than thirty industrial zones including Jurong. Since the 1980s, Singapore has focused on the development of high-tech industries, promoted the upgrading of traditional industries, and vigorously promoted the development of modern service industries such as logistics, finance and commerce. As far as port free trade is concerned, in addition to retaining some basic incentives, such as tax concessions and incentives

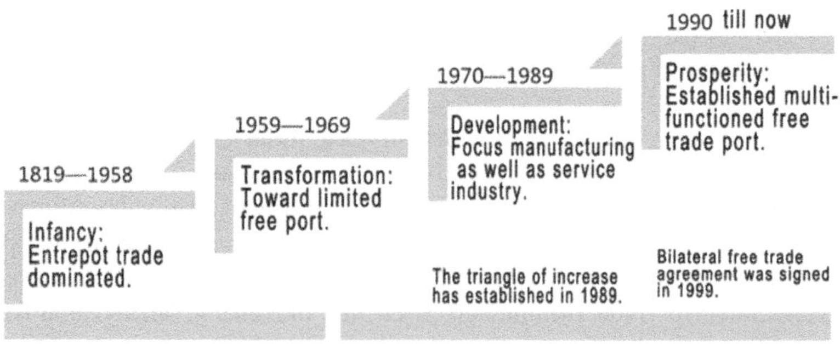

Fig. 3.9 The development of Singapore Free Port

to allow the free flow of capital, Singapore has formulated preferential policies for different industries and sectors.

Third, prosperous period of multifunctional free port (1990–present). Singapore's free trade port area has made greater efforts in its construction. In 1990, Singapore's port container throughput was the highest in the world. As an important shipping center in the Asia–Pacific region, Singapore has more than 500 routes connecting more than 600 ports around the world, whose ports are well-equipped and have extremely high cargo handling efficiency. It can provide services for ocean liners, cruise ships, container ships and other ships. At present, more than 90% of the world's goods can freely enter and exit Singapore without customs duties. Taxable goods include only four categories: alcohol, tobacco, petroleum and vehicles. Both taxable and non-taxable goods imported into Singapore are levied on a 7% consumption tax. In addition to improving infrastructure and developing financial services, Singapore is also committed to the development of strategic industries such as science and technology, tourism, and international exhibitions. The development history of Singapore free port is shown in Fig. 3.9.

To sum up, Singapore Free Port has gone through two stages of development: full free port and limited free port, and now it has become a new multi-functional free port.

3.2.3 Operational Modes

Jurong Port adopts a private management model. In 1997, the Port of Singapore implemented the separation of management and operation rights, and carried out port shareholding reform. The original port authority was divided into Singapore Maritime and Port Authority (MPA) and Singapore Port Group (PSA), and has undergone shareholding and privatization reforms on PSA.

MPA is responsible for handling port and maritime control and technical issues, while PSA has taken responsibilities for port investment and operation. After the reform, the government's service awareness and service quality have been improved significantly. It has achieved high operating efficiency and low operating costs, attracted a large amount of investment, and promoted the development of ports such as Jurong Port.

Singapore is a global free trade port. We will analyze the advantages of the "port-industry-city" linkage model on Jurong Port: first, the port runs efficiently; second, there are favorable business environment, local industry supporting capabilities, high labor quality and environmental quality and so on. "Port-industry-city" linkage model: it is driven by the government and prioritizes modern information technology as the core competitiveness; it has made Singapore a successful shift from a single-function port into a global supply chain management center of container as well as an important node in the global economic network.

3.2.4 *Operation Mechanism*

3.2.4.1 Two-Tier FTZ Market Management Model

The Singapore Free Trade Port utilizes a two-tier FTZ management model, where the central government guides urban planning and specific enterprises in the area engage in business activities. This is the main manifestation of the mature market operation of the free trade port. The implementation of the market mechanism is conducive to getting rid of the shackles of the traditional system and fully releasing the inherent advantages of freedom, autonomy and openness. It has learned from company's practice and understanding of operational activities and management, so as to ensure that the management system conforms to market laws.

3.2.4.2 Special International Commercial Court to Deal with International Commercial Disputes

In 2015, Singapore established an International Business Tribunal to deal exclusively with foreign-related business cases in the country and to facilitate the resolution of international disputes. The International Commercial Tribunal is part of Singapore's High Court system as well as the highest judicial bodies. And its decisions are of the highest force and their legal effect. At the same time, the relevant judges have rich experience in the trial of foreign-related economic cases, which also ensures the professionalism of the trial procedure and the fairness of the results. A relatively independent trial status minimizes undue interference by the Singapore International Commercial Tribunal in the process of accepting and hearing cases and ensures the fairness and justice of the trial process.

3.2.4.3 Greater Financial Supervision Model in Port Area

At present, the financial supervision of the Singapore Free Trade Port is mainly handled by the Financial Supervision Authority of Singapore, which has two responsibilities of central bank, namely, financial regulation and financial supervision. After the 2008 global financial crisis, in order to strengthen risk prevention and control, Singapore expanded the scope of authority of the Financial Supervisory Authority. In addition to the function of issuing money as the responsibility of the central bank, the Financial Supervisory Authority also has the power to carry out unified and standardized management over domestic banks, securities, insurance, other financial institutions and financial markets. The greater financial supervision model has the characteristics of centralization, efficiency and unity, which is conducive to improving the efficiency of financial supervision and providing safer and more reliable financial services for free trade ports.

3.2.5 Construction Experience

3.2.5.1 Favorable Policies

Singapore has a stable political environment, a favorable geographical location, sound infrastructure and a superior comprehensive business environment. In addition, the government also gives great policy support to enterprise registration, which is embodied in the following three aspects.

First, simple business registration process. A citizen of any nationality (aged 18 or above) only needs to offer a Singapore registered address, appoints a Singapore director and a local secretary, and provides the name of the company, the articles of association and by-laws, the certificate of identity, the registered address of the company and the report of office hours to accomplish registration. In another word, for an applicant, it only takes no more than three working days to register a company. For a registered representative office or office, it is advisable to register online on the Singapore International Enterprise Development Agency website. Industries in banking, finance, insurance, securities, communications and other industries and environmental pollution are required to apply for permits from other administrative departments, while other companies are supposed to apply for registration with the Commercial Registration Bureau. Those measures have facilitated the construction of an enabling business environment, attracting a large number of foreign companies to settle in Singapore, and finally have formed a headquarters economy.

Second, relaxed requirements for registered capital. According to the Company Law of Singapore, the minimum registered capital is 100,000 Singapore dollars, and a subscription system is implemented. The shareholders can increase the registered capital and pay the full capital at any time, and they only need to fill in the form and pay the fee at Singapore Business Registration Authority.

Third, relax restrictions on daily activities. There is an all-round legal and regulatory system. The enterprise has the ability to implement self-discipline management on labor rights, intellectual property rights, and environmental protection. Thus, it is no need to carry out real-time government supervision. Singapore implements an annual report system. Companies are demanded to submit annual statements and audit financial reports within 4 weeks after the general meeting of shareholders, so that the government can use this method to know the company's operating conditions.

3.2.5.2 High Degree of Openness in the Investment Sector

First, open foreign investment. Singapore does not restrict foreign investment, but there are restrictions on the investment sector. Except for the defense industry and a few specific industries, markets such as commerce, foreign trade, leasing, marketing, and telecommunications are completely open. However, the entry of foreign capital into special fields such as finance, insurance and securities shall be filed with the administrators. In Singapore, foreign banks are banned from entering the domestic retail market and foreign ownership of local banks is restricted. At the same time, the proportion of foreign investment in journalism cannot exceed 30%, and the proportion of investment in broadcasting cannot surpass 49%.

Second, no limit on the proportion of equity of foreign capital. There is no restriction on the proportion of foreign capital. Singapore encourages foreign companies to set up headquarters or regional headquarters in Singapore. For those reasons, a number of measures have been introduced, such as the franchise international trade plan, business headquarters awards, business headquarters awards, and transnational business headquarters awards. By the end of 2016, 4,200 multinational companies had established regional headquarters in Singapore. There is no restriction on the scope of business of enterprise. The enterprise may operate freely as long as the laws of Singapore permit, and may change the scope of business according to the market situation and its own operating conditions without approval.

Third, outbound investment encouraged. Singapore is not only highly open to foreign capital, but also encourages domestic companies to invest overseas and expand international markets. In terms of policies, Singapore provides support for domestic enterprises' overseas investment in two aspects: in terms of capital and credit, Singapore has formulated an incentive plan for overseas enterprises, an internationalization roadmap plan, and a double tax deduction plan for overseas investment; in terms of funding and credit, the International Enterprise Development Board of Singapore provides financial services such as credit, commercial and credit insurance to overseas investment enterprises, and also encourages local enterprises to go global. For overseas investment companies, Singapore financial institutions have designed an "insurance + loan" financing model.

3.2.5.3 Comprehensive Financial Service

First, freedom of financing and exchange. Singapore Enterprise Development Council, Economic Development Council and other institutions provide financial incentives to foreign-funded enterprises, such as new enterprise development plans, entrepreneur incentive programs, etc. In addition, the Singapore Stock Exchange can provide stocks or bonds insurance services to eligible foreign companies. Singapore's mature financial leasing and project financing market enables business to enjoy more comprehensive financing services. Different types of enterprises should have different financing business models. For example, petroleum trading companies use back-to-back letter of credit financing, and small and medium-sized trading companies will adopt various trade loans such as start-up financing and growth financing respectively according to their different development stages.

Second, relaxation of capital flow. Singapore's financial markets were internally and externally separated prior to the 1997 financial crisis, whereby commercial banks and other financial institutions were able to operate offshore under conditions of separate management and account opening. After the financial crisis, Singapore shifted the focus of regulation from mandatory regulation to information disclosure, risk prevention to financial innovation. The separate internal and external markets no longer exist. The internal and external markets have gradually merged into an integrated market, and the capital circulation control has been lifted, laying a solid foundation for an international financial center.

3.2.5.4 Trade Liberalization

Singapore's trade liberalization is mainly embodied in the following three aspects:

First, free settlement of international trade. There is no exchange control in Singapore and funds can flow out freely. Corporate profits are remitted without restrictions or special taxes. Companies can just set up an account in accordance with the relevant banking processes. Companies can independently determine the settlement of currency types, and usually open accounts in Singapore dollars, U.S. dollars, Hong Kong dollars, Euros, and Australian dollars.

Second, freedom of trading entities. Applications for import and export and transshipment licenses can be approved by registering with the Accounting and Enterprise Authority and applying for a central registration number free of charge from the Singapore Customs Service.

Third, advanced shipping services. Singapore's licensed international shipping scheme and maritime financial concession scheme can significantly reduce or even exempt shipping companies and shipping services from taxes and fees. Shipping chains such as shipping transactions, ship discipline, shipping information, ship maintenance and maritime training in Singapore provide important support for international trade.

3.2.5.5 Technological Innovation and Effective Regulation

First, convenient customs declaration. According to relevant laws and regulations, the owner of import and export goods or the agent only needs to fill in and submit relevant documents for inspection. For the import and export of goods that must be approved by the relevant authorities (such as medicines, cosmetics and dangerous goods, etc.), an approval license shall be issued at the time of customs declaration.

Second, high clearance efficiency. Singapore customs trade network system leads the world in terms of efficiency, and all procedures related to import and export (including transit) trade, such as application, examination and licensing control, can be carried out through the whole system. It only takes 10 s for importers and exporters to complete all the declaration procedures through the computer terminal and 10 min for the approval result. The import and export approval, inspection and quarantine, customs clearance and other procedures can be carried out in an orderly and efficient manner on the unified platform, which is completely aided by the trade network system connected with the relevant import and export departments.

Third, no quota limit. Except for special goods such as dangerous goods, weapons, medicines and cosmetics, and the import and export of specific areas, Singapore does not impose quota restrictions on the import and export of general goods. There are also no quota restrictions.

Four, expedient inspection and quarantine. Imported food, medicine and flora and fauna can apply to the inspection and quarantine department through the Customs Trade Network for inspection and permit which is highly efficient.

3.2.5.6 Loose Taxation

Singapore implements a unified corporate income tax policy for domestic and foreign companies. Taxpayers include Singapore-incorporated enterprises, foreign enterprises incorporated in Singapore in accordance with the laws of Singapore, and foreign enterprises not incorporated in Singapore but having taxable income from Singapore in accordance with the Singapore's territorial principle (except partnership enterprises and sole proprietorship enterprises). Since 2010, the corporate income tax rate in Singapore has been 17%, and all companies can enjoy partial tax exemption for the first S$300,000 taxable income; general corporates are exempt from 75% for the first S$10,000 income and exempt 50% for the last S$290,000 income; the first S$100,000 income of eligible companies is exempt from tax, and the second S$200,000 income is exempted from 50%. Except for alcohol, tobacco (including cigarettes) and petroleum vehicles, Singapore exempts all imported goods from customs duties, including international transport services and transport services related to import and export, as well as cargo handling, insurance, and other services related to import and export.

3.2.5.7 Sound Legal System

Singapore has inherited the British legal system and formed a complete legal system based on the Constitution, parliamentary decrees and subsidiary regulations, judicial precedents and legal practices. At the same time, Singapore has its own complete system of economic laws and regulations. As the core law for the operation of Singapore's free trade port, the *Free Trade Zones Act* comprehensively stipulates institutional arrangements, including positioning, functions, management systems, preferential systems, and regulatory systems. The preferential system mainly involves tax exemption, income tax and other tax relief, investment, customs system, labor policy, land system and so on. The routine administrative management of enterprises in industry and commerce, health, environmental protection and other aspects is not supervised by the Singapore government, but law enforcement agencies in accordance with the legal system.

3.2.5.8 Mobility Freedom of Natural Persons

There are many kinds of work visas in Singapore, which can be granted to people in different industries. According to the *Employment of Foreign Manpower Act*, Singapore has a quota system for foreign workers, under which there are different quotas for different industries, such as manufacturing and services, at 60% and 45% respectively. According to different industries, different skill levels, and the proportion of foreign workers employed by employers, labor taxes must be paid by the employers who hire foreign workers. In order to encourage the recruitment of foreign talents, the Singapore government has put forward some preferential policies. For example, companies should pay for recruiting and training foreign talents, and provide foreign talents with high salaries, housing tax reductions and preferential policies. At the same time, they have also attracted talents by lowering personal income tax and providing training opportunities to foreign talents.

3.2.6 Development Trend

3.2.6.1 Strengthening Infrastructure Construction

Singapore's infrastructure investment is not a blind expansion on the original basis, but a part of its strategy to facilitate the future development. This investment is not to respond to domestic demand, but to consolidate Singapore's existing regional and world major transportation and transportation hub status, further strengthen Singapore's connectivity with the world, and maintain its future competitive advantage. These huge investments in infrastructure development show that Singapore has great confidence in its future development and there is sufficient room for Singapore development, making well preparation for future development.

3.2.6.2 Strengthening Bilateral or Multilateral Trade Development

Singapore's state building relies on port trade. Faced with a volatile global trade environment, Singapore has been able to maintain an advantage in the competition owing to the fact that at different stages, Singapore can always adjust and optimize business based on different types of trade products, foreign trade policies, and industrial structure. Since the 1960s, Singapore has established a unilateral FTZ to develop re-export trade and labor-intensive processing and manufacturing industries. With the deepening of the international division of labor, Singapore has gradually shifted from simple processing manufacturing to high value-added, high-tech manufacturing, and changed its trade focus to service trade. At the same time, Singapore allows foreign business to directly invest and operate industry and commerce within the country, exempts most import and export commodities from tariffs, and provides great freedom to foreign investors, including financial services, personnel, capital, and materials in and out. Thanks to these measures, Singapore has gradually become one of the world's three major centers, namely a global trade center, a global financial center and a global R&D center.

From the analysis of the current trend, the mainstream form of global trade cooperation in the future will gradually transform into a bilateral or multilateral free trade area (FTA). According to WTO statistics, there are currently 259 free trade zones signed and implemented, a considerable amount of which have been completed in recent years. More than half of global trade is conducted in FTZs. Facing the future, Singapore urgently needs to sign different free trade agreements to promote economic and trade cooperation with the world. Currently, Singapore has signed bilateral FTA agreements with more than ten countries or economies including New Zealand, Japan, Australia, the United States, Jordan, India, South Korea, China, and the European Union. In bilateral negotiations, negotiations on service trade can be more flexible to lay the foundation for another upsurge of Singapore.

3.3 Research on Dubai Free Trade Port

3.3.1 An Overview

Dubai Free Port is located 50 km southwest of Downtown Dubai, with a total area of 48 km^2. It is the largest free port in the United Arab Emirates, the largest free port in the Middle East, and the world's famous economic and financial center. The trade volume of Dubai Free Trade Port accounts for more than 25% of Dubai's total non-oil trade. The basic information of Dubai Free Trade Port is shown in Table 3.4.

Table 3.4 Overview of Dubai Free Trade Port

Name	Dubai Free Port
Location	Dubai City, United Arab Emirates, Asia
Date of establishment	1985
Area	48,000 km^2
Ownership	Dubai government
Administrator	Dubai Port Authority and Free Trade Port Authority
Types of functions	Free Trade
Key law	Business Companies Act, Business Agency Act and Labor Law
Key policy	Customs policy, tax policy
Achievements	It ranks first among the world's 1,200 free trade zones
Future trend	Global shipping hub

At the beginning of the twentieth century, Dubai was just a seaside town with less than 10,000 people at the mouth of the Dubai Creek. In 1985, the Dubai government initiated the establishment of the Dubai Free Trade Port, becoming the world's first free trade zone to pass the ISO 9000 international certification. At present, Dubai Free Trade Port has grown from a small and micro free port area with only 19 enterprises in its initial stage to a super transit station with more than 7,000 enterprises. It has a set of effective measures in terms of facilities policy management and other aspects, and has become one of the most popular investment destinations in the UAE.

The Dubai Free Port was originally established to encourage foreign trade and investment. It is divided into two components-Rashid Port Area and Jebel Ali Port Area. The Rashid port area is a traditional port area and a ship repair center in the Gulf region; the Jebel Ali port area is a typical artificial port and a free trade port area, focusing on the development of trade, logistics and information industries. In the master plan of Dubai, the planned area of the Jebel Ali Industrial Zone is close to 80 km^2, with 120 km^2 reserved for long-term development (including 20 km^2 reserved for the future international new airport). The Dubai government has granted a number of preferential policies to settled companies, attracting global multinational companies to set up production and logistics centers, and realize the joint development of ports and industries.

Dubai has set up more than thirty FTZs, over ten of which are active, including Jebel Ali Free Trade Zone (JAFZA), Dubai Dragon City Free Zone, Dubai Airport Free Zone, Dubai Internet City, Dubai Media City, Dubai Jewelry City, Dubai Motor City, Dubai Hardware City, Dubai Knowledge Village and Dubai Multi-Commodity Exchange Center (DMCC) and Dubai International Financial Center (DIFC). Among them, the Jebel Ali Free Trade Zone has the largest area, covering an area of 48 km^2. And it is the most mature free trade zone in the world and even passed the ISO9000 international standard certification. The annual cargo throughput of Dubai Airport in the UAE is shown in Fig. 3.10, and the passenger throughput is shown in Fig. 3.11.

The FTZ is the growth engine of Dubai's economy, making great contributions to the most of Dubai's national income and jobs. In terms of GDP, JAFZA contributes more than 20%, DMCC about 10% and Dubai Airport Free zone about 7%. DIFC was established in September 2004, covering an area of only 1.1 km^2, but has nearly 1,000 listed companies, half of which are financial companies. DIFC has become the most important modern Islamic financial center in the Middle East and North Africa, contributing 12% of Dubai's total GDP in 2016.

Unlike Singapore's commitment to domestic industrial development, the vast majority of Dubai FTZs aim to promote global traders via Dubai as their trading hub, and therefore exhibit obvious characteristics of financial and commerce agglomeration. The industries concentrated here have become major contributors to Dubai's GDP. In its 2018 GDP structure, wholesale and retail trade ranked first with a share of 26.6%, followed by transportation and storage (11.8%), finance and insurance (10.4%).

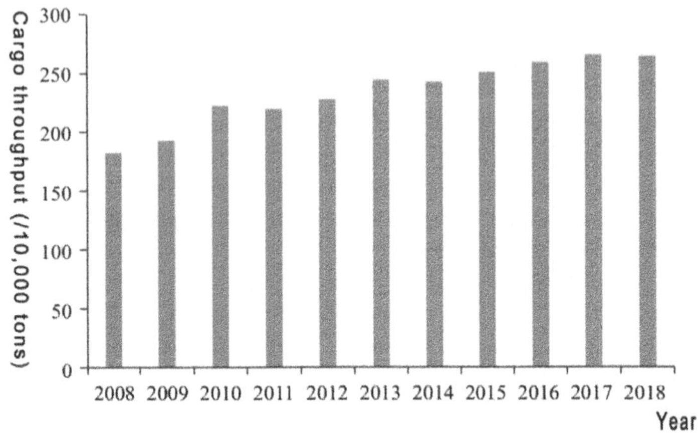

Fig. 3.10 Cargo throughput of Dubai Airport, UAE over the years (*Source* Dubai Airports [https://www.dubaiairports.ae/corporate/media-centre/factsheets-list/detail/dubai-airports])

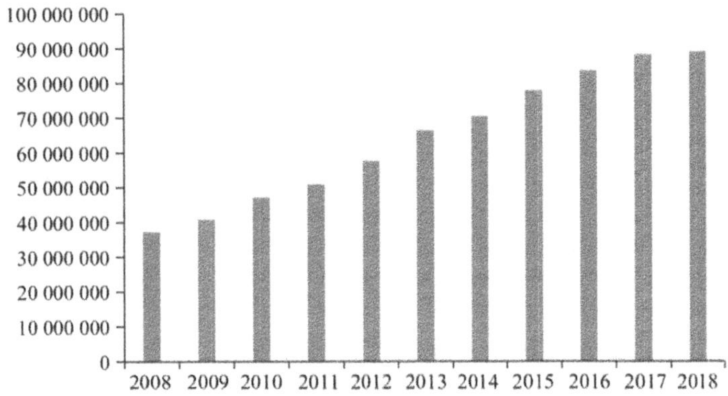

Fig. 3.11 Passenger throughput of Dubai Airport, UAE (person-time) (*Source* Dubai Airports [https://www.dubaiairports.ae/corporate/media-centre/factsheets-list/detail/dubai-airports])

3.3.2 Course of Development

The Dubai FTZ is part of Dubai World, one of the Dubai government's three sovereign investment groups. Since the start of construction in 1977, after more than 40 years of continuous development, the Dubai FTZ has formed complete supporting facilities. Currently, the expansion of the Dubai Free Port is on the way.

The Dubai FTZ originates from the Guarantor system commonly implemented in the Gulf countries. Guarantor means that: foreign investors must find local partners; the company establishment costs are fully borne by foreign investors, but the local "guarantor" must hold at least 51% of the shares. With the development of the free economy, this system caused a lot of dissatisfaction among foreign investors, which gradually became an obstacle to the development of Arab countries. Thus, the concept of FTZ emerged. Each emirate designated a zone within its territory as a free trade zone, in which foreign investors could enjoy 100% shareholding, but their goods and services could only be transferred within the zone. Those measures not only protected the local market, but also gave foreign investors greater freedom. In this context, in 1979, Jebel Ali Port, the world's largest man-made harbor, was put into use. In 1985, the Dubai government established the first FTZ: the Jebel Ali FTZ. The core advantage of Dubai FTZ is that overseas enterprises can hold 100% shares. Jebel Ali Port integrates logistics and warehousing, import and export trade, production and processing, etc., and Dubai International Airport is built next to it. Currently, Dubai has formed a logistics operation model of "airport + seaport + free trade zone".

The government of Dubai attaches great importance to the development of high-tech industry. In 1995, Internet City was built in Jebel Ali Port, which became the landmark project of Dubai's network economy. There are more than 30 world-renowned high-tech enterprises such as Microsoft, Siemens and IBM in Internet City. The projects under construction include: Internet University, software development center, network communication center, e-commerce free zone, electronic products industrial park, computer parts assembly plant, etc. Dubai is investing $800million in Media City at Port Jebel Ali. Once completed, it will become the exclusive "press and media free zone" in the Middle East. Dubai legislation stipulates that journalists are given "absolute freedom of the press" without violating laws and social norms, ethnic and religious precepts. According to reports, 85% of the office space in the media city under planning and construction has been reserved by world-renowned news organizations.

3.3.3 Operational Modes

Dubai's Jebel Ali Free Trade Port is a typical extended version of the free trade port, namely the "1 + N" free trade port. "1" means the Jebel Ali Free Trade Port, and "N" refers to several surrounding industries cities (Dubai Financial City, Dubai Internet City, Dubai Media City, etc.).

First, to build a free port with low investment and low operating cost. Jebel Ali port's main business is logistics trade supply chain management and processing and manufacturing re-export. Jebel Ali Port has a physical fence, which is mainly for regional supervision (Special Customs Supervision Zone). Special industries around the port area enjoy free policies in terms of talent capital and technology, providing preferential policies to promote the agglomeration of special industries. Each characteristic industrial city does not have a physical fence, and mainly implements industrial policy supervision and independent operation of enterprises.

Second, to rent but not to sell land. The land policy of Jebel Ali Free Trade Port is the same as that of other free trade areas in Dubai. The lease term of the land ranges from 15 to 50 years, and renewal is allowed. During the lease period, the enterprise may apply for subletting and the management authority is free to determine the approval of subletting, including the number of sub-tenants and subleases. When the leasing enterprise withdraws, the ground facilities such as the original plant are handled in the form of rent or auction, and the site requires restoration. For rent only not for sale, the free trade port also sets up a phase-out mechanism, under which an enterprise will be suspended lease if the leasing enterprises do not meet a certain port annual cargo volume requirement.

3.3.4 Operation Mechanism

Dubai Port adopts the operation and management system integrating government with enterprise. The Dubai Free Trade Port is owned by the local government of Dubai, which invests in the construction of port terminal and port area infrastructure, carries out overall planning and coordinates the development relationship between the port and the home city. With the advantage of port, local governments develop and operate port industrial zones and FTZs by leasing land.

3.3.4.1 Dubai Ports Authority

The Dubai Ports Authority (DPA) was established in 1991 under the local government of Dubai to administer the Dubai Free Port. At the same time, DPA is also an independent port operation organization, as an independent legal person, with an independent accounting system. Therefore, DPA has two characteristics at the same time: the functions of local government agencies and the nature of business operations. The operation and the management of Port Rushde and Jebel Ali are coordinated by the DPA, which also needs to build the functional area, infrastructure and port-related projects. To sum up, DPA needs to perform governmental functions externally and supervise and manage all affairs of the EPZ internally. The port shall implement unified management of customs, banks, post and telecommunications, transportation, public security, etc., unified office, and abolish parallel multi-head institutions.

3.3.4.2 Free Zone Authority

As a governmental service agency, the Free Zone Authority is a consortium composed of port customs and free zones, responsible for all investment services and management. The Free Zone Authority can directly issue business licenses to investors and provide one-stop services such as administrative management, engineering, energy supply and investment consulting. The Free Zone Authority provides a series of auxiliary services, including: (1) In the early stage, offer customers with future development and investment advice, and help customers find suitable investment sites and provide a list of necessary facilities for operation. (2) After the settlement of an enterprise, assist the enterprise to obtain business opportunities, including local business cooperation and joint venture opportunities in the international market. During this process, the Free Zone Authority will organize business delegations to visit and inspect, and provide customers with business consulting suggestions. The income of this management model mainly comes from land transfer, office lease and sale and warehouse lease.

3.3.5 Construction Experience

3.3.5.1 Expanding Geographical Advantages

Dubai port is convenient for sea, land and air transshipment, which can timely transport goods to the Middle East, Africa and Europe and other international consumer markets. In addition, the Dubai government is planning a logistics green channel connecting the port, free zone, logistics city and airport, which can transport goods from the port to the airport in just 10 min. Therefore, the location choice of a free trade port determines the starting point and future development space of a free trade port, and is an important foundation for the development of a free trade port.

3.3.5.2 Strengthening Infrastructure

In order to make better use of its geographical advantages, the Dubai government has been vigorously promoting the construction of transportation infrastructure since the 1970s, among which port development and airport construction are listed as the most important infrastructure projects. In addition, roads, communications, energy supply and high-speed data transmission, staff housing, supermarkets, pharmacies, banks, insurance and leisure facilities, and other supporting facilities. In addition to the vacant land for sale, the free trade zone can also rent the offices, factories and warehouses that have been built. The settlement of many large logistics companies also provides convenient logistics services for enterprises in the park.

3.3.5.3 Strengthening Port Management

DPA is the special authority for Dubai Port, which has unified management of Port Rashid and Jebel Ali. The Dubai Free Trade Port Authority can issue business licenses directly to investors and provide one-stop services such as administration, engineering, energy supply and investment consulting. Regularly organize business matching activities for enterprises in the area to create more business opportunities for enterprises. Dubai Port's favorable investment environment and customer service have attracted a large number of investors.

3.3.5.4 Convenient Port Usage

The cost of use of Dubai Port's ports and terminals is one of the lowest in the world, and it has been among the top ten container ports in the world since 2004. The main reason for the high-volume growth of Dubai Port is the increasing investment in improving terminal facilities and expanding container handling capacity. In addition, Dubai Port continues to simplify customs procedures and has launched an electronic platform to make it easier for customers to go through various procedures online. The approval and handling of import and export formalities can be completed within 24 h, while the approval of investment formalities only takes 7 days.

3.3.5.5 Preferential Policies

Dubai implements a free economic policy, no foreign exchange control, free exchange, less taxation. The three businesses in Dubai, such as trade, investment and contracted labor service, are all economic and trade activities, which shall be registered in accordance with the *Commercial Company Law*, *Commercial Agency Law* and *Labor Law of Dubai*. After an enterprise is registered, it joins the Chamber of Commerce for Industry and Commerce and becomes a legal person, enjoying the same rights and obligations as the domestic enterprises.

Foreign investors in the free trade port area can set up enterprises, and enjoy rich preferential policies. First, some products are exempted from customs duties and export taxes, including the equipment, equipment, spare parts and necessities that enterprises need to import for production. Second, companies can remit 100% of their profits abroad at any time without any financial or monetary restrictions. Third, employees of inside-area enterprises are exempt from individual income tax; Fourth, inside-area enterprises are exempt from corporate tax for 50 years. Fifth, there is no need to find a local partner or a guarantor. All enterprises have 100% of their own capital. Sixth, foreign employees can be admitted into the zone; Seventh, the procedures for handling affairs in the zone are simple and fast, and the enterprise registration can be completed within 15 working days; Eighth, the region has advanced communications facilities, adequate energy supply and low prices; Ninth, foreigners can own real estate through long-term leases. Foreign investors may set up FZE and FZE joint ventures in the Port of Dubai (FZCO). FZE and FZCO can be independent legal entities, and the difference between them is shown in Table 3.5.

Table 3.5 The difference between FZE and FZCO

Company type	Shareholder	Minimum registered capital
FZE	Only	1 million Dirhams ($280,000)
FZCO	2 ~ 5	Half a million dirhams (about $140,000); Each shareholder must have a registered capital of at least 100,000 dirhams (about $28,000)

For enterprises registered and licensed outside JAFZA, they do not need registered capital and can apply to open an office in FTA. For different types of customers, Dubai Port will issue different types of licenses according to the circumstances. Once the FTA enterprise project is approved and relevant legal documents are submitted, the FTA will sign the lease agreement with the investor. The authority of the Free Trade Area shall issue corresponding licenses according to the nature of the investors' business activities.

3.3.6 Development Trend

3.3.6.1 Building a Global Shipping Hub

In the long run, Dubai aims to become a global shipping hub, competing with China's Hong Kong and Singapore. Over the next decade, Dubai will focus on building its port infrastructure, opening a third artificial port. At the same time, Dubai also focuses on improving the technical level of port operation, introducing advanced technologies, including shipping systems and technologies for data processing, cargo monitoring, information transmission, terminal management and other functions, and striving to build Dubai into a comprehensive port, integrating "cargo handling port" and "logistics information port".

3.3.6.2 Market-Oriented Operation

In terms of the management system, Port Rushde and Port Jebel Ali in Dubai, which were formerly operated by the Dubai government, are now going to divest part of their businesses to the market for operation, and promote the privatization of some middle and lower reaches of the industry, such as dock loading and unloading business and warehouse leasing business, and turn them over to private enterprises for operation through bidding. This will facilitate the management, reduce the operation cost and enhance the market flexibility.

3.3.6.3 Innovative Management

On the basis of strengthening cooperation between port areas, the Dubai Government plans to merge three major agencies, namely Port Rushde, Dubai Customs and Jebel Ali, to promote intelligent and networked office work. At the same time, it will enhance the management capacity, service level and transport efficiency of ports, customs and free zones, reduce internal competition and better the investment environment.

3.4 Exemplary Cases of Advanced Free Trade Ports

Hong Kong Free Trade Port has long been ranked as the freest economy in the world due to its liberal economic policies such as the trading system, corporate system, financial system and immigration system. In addition, the HKSAR Government has provided various trade facilitation measures, making it a major aviation and shipping hub in the world and strengthening Hong Kong's status as a free port known as the "gateway to Europe", Rotterdam is one of the fastest and most efficient ports in the world. This port operates the PORTBASE system to exchange information in the port area. This has led to a high concentration of logistics at Rotterdam, which has spawned local oil refining, chemicals and shipbuilding industries. Relying on its advantages in modern service industry, Singapore has promulgated many preferential policies and attracted a large amount of foreign capital, which provides a foundation for its vigorous development of capital and technology-intensive industries. As a result, Singapore's free trade port has gradually developed into a high-tech free trade port. At the same time, Singapore free trade port also focuses on the construction of port and commercial information. The operation mode of Dubai Free Port is unique, which can be summarized as "1 + N": 1 free trade port (Jebel Ali Freeport) and N characteristic industrial cities (such as Dubai City of Finance, Dubai Internet City, Dubai Media City, etc.). This mode coordinates the development of free ports and characteristic industries and maximizes the advantages of free ports, namely "institutional dividend" and radiation effect.

A study of the development history of typical free trade ports in the world reveals that two attributes are essential for the success of free trade ports: a high degree of openness and a well-developed infrastructure. The development of each free trade port has its own characteristics and advantages, but their core is to attract capital, logistics, information, technology and talent to build the core hub of the regional value chain. The development process of these free trade ports can provide references for the combined ports of GBA in the following four aspects.

3.4.1 Diversification in Form

Free trade ports around the world come in many forms, ranging from port areas like New York and Cologne or multiple ports in Singapore and Hong Kong. Some free trade ports rely on seaports, such as Singapore Port. Some rely on aviation, such as Shannon Free Trade Port. Some free trade ports combine the two, such as Dubai World Trade Center. From the perspective of business form, GBA can focus on creating free and convenient trade just like the original Dubai port. It can also focus on trade in goods like the Dubai World Trade Center today, and gradually expand to a more complex form, developing trading, settlement, R&D and other services.

3.4.2 A High Degree of Openness and Freedom

Free trade port belongs to a special economic region within the territory of a country, and the principle of goods supervision and industry access is relatively relaxed. In cologne's Free Trade Port, for example, businesses can be registered even without a license and there are no minimum investment requirements. The board of Directors of Dubai Port has decision-making autonomy, adopts the "small special zone" mode of "integrating government and enterprise", and gives more space for foreign investment. It is not restricted by the proportion of "foreign investment is less than 49%" in the *Company Law of UAE*. Independent foreign investment and the establishment of wholly-owned enterprises are allowed. In terms of goods entry and exit, neither the Cologne Free Trade Port nor the New York Free Trade Port are subject to domestic quotas, and most goods are free to enter and leave the port area, excluding strictly controlled goods such as chemicals.

3.4.3 Convenient Customs Supervision

Generally, free trade ports are, or partly are, inside the territory but outside the customs boundary, so they are different from the strict supervision of "inside the territory and inside the customs boundary". This makes customs procedures easier at free trade ports. Customs declaration requirements are relatively relaxed, even without customs declaration. Import duties are only payable if you enter the domestic consumer market. Many free trade ports have such special arrangements including Cologne, New York, and Dubai. The introduction of advanced information technology and the simplification of customs procedures have greatly improved the convenience of free trade ports. At the Cologne Free Trade Port, customs use a uniform form in which import, export and re-export procedures are recorded. Singapore has introduced electronic procedures to handle applications, examination, licensing, control and so on in relation to import and export trade. Customs can log on to the computer terminal, using the customs trade network system, in 10 s can complete all the formalities. In order to avoid prohibited goods entering the port area, the customs strictly check the goods within the area at any time and strengthens supervision.

3.4.4 Popular Preferential Policies

One of the positionings of free trade port is the international logistics center. Ports competition helps to turn free trade ports into low taxation areas. Tax benefits for the world's major free trade ports are shown in Table 3.6.

Table 3.6 Comparison of tax preferences of major free trade ports in the world

Free trade port	Tax incentives
Shannon Free Trade Port	The corporate income tax rate is 12.5%; Eligible enterprises will be granted preferential treatment of "exempt from capital gains tax when making equity allocation", and employment subsidy, research and development subsidy, training subsidy and financial support
New York Harbor	When exporting to the "domestic customs", enterprises can choose to enjoy the preferential treatment fee of goods in the area according to the low tariff of finished products or parts
Cologne Free Trade Port Zone	Enterprises pay an income tax rate of less than 10%, less than a third of that "outside"
Jebel Ali Free Zone, Dubai	The enterprise shall be exempted from income tax within 50 years, and the staff in the area shall be exempted from individual income tax

3.5 Research on Free Trade Port Practice in Chinese Mainland

The construction of FTZ is a strategic measure taken by the CPC Central Committee and the State Council to comprehensively deepen reform and expand opening up in the new era. It aims to explore transferable and replicable experience for China's high-level opening up and deepening reform through institutional innovation of FTZ. From China's first pilot FTZ in Shanghai in September 2013 to the fifth expansion of FTZs in August 2019, there are now 18 (1 + 3 + 7 + 1 + 6) pilot FTZs across the country, covering all important regions and forming a new pattern of all-round and high-level regional opening up featuring coordination between East and West and coordinated development by land and sea. The China (Shanghai) Pilot Free Trade Zone (hereinafter referred to as the "Shanghai Pilot Free Trade Zone") has taken the lead in China, making bold explorations in areas such as freedom of investment, trade, capital, transportation and labor force, and achieved remarkable results. Since the 19th CPC National Congress when the CPC Central Committee proposed to grant pilot FTZs greater autonomy in reform and explore free trade ports, Hainan has been the first region to implement the free trade port policy, and has greater autonomy in the aspects of free trade port legislation, trade and investment liberalization and facilitation. Therefore, the summary of the construction practice of the Shanghai Pilot FTZ and the China (Hainan) Pilot FTZ (hereinafter referred to as "Hainan Pilot Free Trade Zone") can provide important reference experience for the exploration of the construction of the combined ports of GBA.

3.5.1 Exploration of the Shanghai Pilot Free Trade Zone

On September 29, 2013, the Shanghai Pilot FTZ was officially established. On December 12, 2014, the State Council executive meeting declared to deepen the reform and opening up, share pilot experience of Shanghai free trade area, and set up more free trade demonstration areas, which marks a new stage for the institutional innovation of China's pilot FTZs to popularize the experience of policy experiments and carry out multi-regional comparative policy experiments.

3.5.1.1 Construction Background

On February 13, 2017, Zhu Min, deputy director of the Shanghai Municipal Development and Reform Commission, said at a leaders' meeting of the Shanghai Port that the Shanghai Free Trade Pilot Zone will implement new regulatory policies and systems to build a high-level free port in parts of Yangshan Bonded Port Area and Pudong Airport Integrated Bonded Zone, as well as the FTZ or Freeport Zone, which have the highest degree of trade facilitation comparable to ports in Singapore and Dubai. Relevant preliminary work has been carried out, involving the adjustment of relevant laws and regulations, departmental rules and local regulations of Shanghai.

On May 15, 2017, the Information Office of Shanghai Municipal Government held a press conference. Relevant officials of Shanghai Development and Reform Commission, Shanghai Commerce Commission, Shanghai Finance Office and Shanghai Mouth Office introduced the latest progress of the Free Trade Zone. It is reported that the establishment of the FTZ is to meet the new requirements of China's trade transformation and upgrading and the new trend of international division of labor among multinational companies, and it is a new measure to facilitate trade at a higher level. According to the plan framework approved by the State Council, by the end of 2017, the Shanghai Pilot FTZ has formed a plan for the construction of a free port, to strengthen the integration of reform systems, and build a comprehensive reform pilot zone that integrates opening-up and innovation.

On October 18, 2017, in his report to the 19th National Congress of the Communist Party of China (CPC), President Xi Jinping proposed to "*grant pilot free trade zones greater autonomy in reform and explore the establishment of free trade ports*". By actively adjusting the structure of outbound investment, Shanghai has taken a firm step to further expand and open up to foreign trade. By now, the construction of Shanghai pilot FTZ has been further deepened.

On July 27, 2019, the State Council issued the *Overall Plan on China (Shanghai) Free Trade Area Lingang New Area*, aiming to set up the China (Shanghai) free trade area of Lingang New Area with an emphasis to carry out the "system innovation in eight domains" and "construction of the international market competitiveness of open industry system". This marks China's highest strategic positioning of FTZ as the core engine in leading globalization.

To sum up, the successful launch of the Shanghai Pilot FTZ in September 2013 can be regarded China's FTZ 1.0. In 2015, the Central Government approved the *Plan of Deepening the Pilot Free Trade Zone in Shanghai*, which became China's FTZ 2.0. In March 2017, the *Reform and Opening Plan of Comprehensively Deepening The China (Shanghai) Pilot Free Trade Zone* was approved by the Central Committee of the Communist Party of China (CCCPC), which became the China's FTZ 3.0. In July 2019, the State Council officially approved the *Overall Plan on China (Shanghai) Free Trade Area Lingang New Area*, marking China's FTZ 4.0.

3.5.1.2 Core Measures

The core measures of the *Overall Plan on China (Shanghai) Free Trade Area Lingang New Area* are summed up in Fig. 3.12.

3.5.2 Construction of Hainan Pilot Free Trade Zone

3.5.2.1 Construction Background

On April 13, 2018, to celebrate the 30th anniversary of the establishment of the Hainan Special Economic Zone, President Xi Jinping announced that the CPC Central Committee has decided to support the construction of a free trade pilot zone throughout Hainan Island, to support Hainan to gradually explore and steadily promote the construction of a free trade port with Chinese characteristics, and to establish a free trade port policy and institutional system in a step-by-step and phased manner.

On June 3, 2018, after in-depth research and overall planning, the Hainan provincial government decided to set up Haikou Jiangdong New Area as the key leading area for the construction of Hainan Free Trade Pilot Zone. On October 16, 2018, the State Council approved the establishment of the China (Hainan) Free Trade Pilot Zone and issued the *China (Hainan) Free Trade Pilot Zone Master Plan*.

On June 3, 2018, Hainan Provincial Party Committee and provincial government decided to set up Haikou Jiangdong New Area as a key and pioneering area in the construction of Hainan Pilot Free Trade Zone after in-depth investigation and overall planning. The highlight of Hainan FTA is the covering of the whole island, while other FTZ test zones are about 120 km^2. Hainan can give full play to the regional advantages of its independent geographical unit and the overall advantages of the island-wide pilot. The island-wide pilot project has a broader test space, a more diversified test basis and a more comprehensive test content. Through differentiated exploration, the national strategy can be better served and more systematic and integrated pilot experience can be formed.

On March 5, 2019, the *Government Work Report of the Second Session of the 13th National People's Congress* proposed to start the construction of Hainan Pilot Free

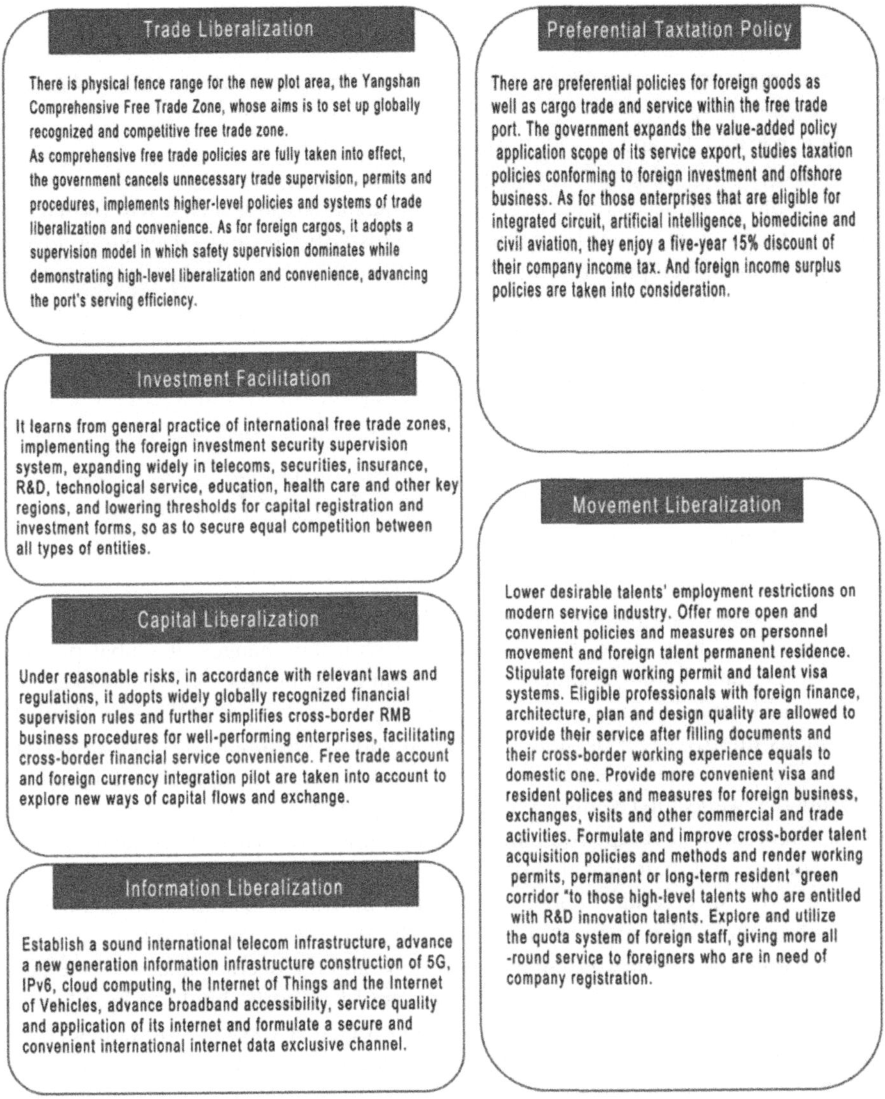

Fig. 3.12 Overall plan of port-neighboring new area of China (Shanghai) Pilot Free Trade Zone

Trade Area. According to the Statistics of the Ministry of Commerce, by April 2019, the implementation progress of various construction projects in Hainan Pilot Free Trade Zone has reached 60%. In terms of effectiveness, a "1 + N" policy framework has been formed, and 13 institutional innovation cases have been launched in two batches.

3.5.2.2 Main Contents

The core measures of the *China (Hainan) Free Trade Pilot Zone Master Plan* are summed up in Fig. 3.13.

Hainan Pilot FTZ and Free Port can be regarded as the outcome of a new national positioning strategy to guide the regional development in the next 10 or even 20 years. The Plan meets the needs of the national, regional and local levels. It will form a new path for the development of Haina's overall industry by means of deepening reform, innovation and development, military-civilian integration and industrial upgrading.

3.6 Research on the Development Trend of Free Trade Ports

3.6.1 On the Development Trend of Advanced Free Trade Ports

Firstly, the functional form of free ports shows the trend of integration and diversification. The functions of free ports evolve with the changes of global political environment and the development of science and technology. At an early stage of international trade, the main function of free ports was re-export trade. With the continuous improvement of the international supply chain and production system, production, processing and manufacturing business gradually appeared in free ports. Entering the twenty-first century, with more detailed social division of labor and more intense international competition, multinational enterprises have become the core of globalization, and their global supply chain networks have higher requirements in terms of cost, speed and efficiency. Free ports now serve as the network nodes of a global resource allocation optimization and linking corresponding functions with logistics functions, trade convenience functions and the overall linkage of the business environment as the core. The construction of free ports should be based on the establishment of comprehensive transport and logistics services. Modern services, including financial legal services, human resources management services, financial services, engineering services, cultural and creative services, educational and medical services, information services, intellectual property services, exhibition services and family services, should be vigorously developed.

The operation of free ports shows the trend of free development of various subjects operating on the platform provided by the government. According to the previous analysis, Hong Kong, Singapore and Dubai have all adopted diversification measures to liberalize and facilitate trade and investment. Hong Kong has created a non-interference free-trade system. Singapore has actively attracted business headquarters to reduce corporate compliance costs through technological innovation. Dubai has successfully attracted foreign investment through financial incentives. These are

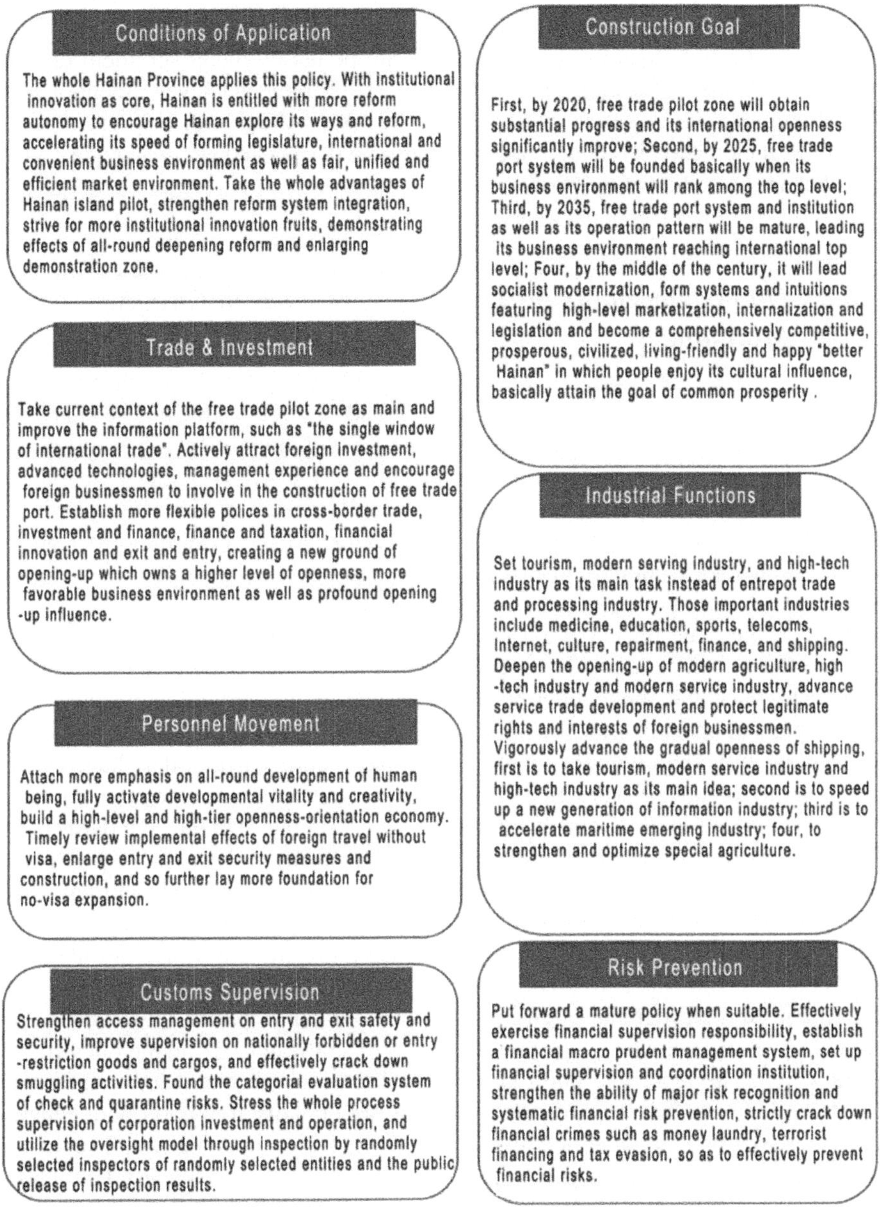

Fig. 3.13 Core measures of the general plan of Hainan Pilot FTZ

valuable references to the construction of free ports in Chinese mainland. In implementation, the construction of free ports should be led by the government to carry out top-level design, formulate practical target positioning and development plans to avoid unguided development of free ports. Free ports should not only promote the free flow of elements in the region, but also form a perfect and effective legal system to enhance the ability of risk prevention.

3.6.2 On the Development Trend of Free Ports in Chinese Mainland

In the process of development, an important trend of FTZs with Chinese characteristics is that they should not be limited to the development of specific regions, but should promote the development and innovation of the whole domestic market by radiating to the surrounding regions and gradually realize common development. To explore and build free ports with Chinese characteristics is an important step in China's transition from high growth to high-quality development. It is also of great significance in promoting innovative development of an open economy.

FTZ is the experimental field of reform and opening up that can be used to explore the establishment of differentiated multi-type free trade zones, to summarize the targeted and applicable reform experience and to carry out a wider range of reform promotion and expansion of opening up. China has established 18 pilot FTZs. According to the requirements of the respective overall scheme, they have carried out in-depth research and practice in various fields such as investment, trade, finance and government function transformation, and have set international standards in the fields of negative lists, commercial systems and overseas investment, so as to create a high level of business environment and gain a number of replicable and replicable practical experiences. At present, the global economy and trade are in an important period of transformation and reconstruction, and regional trade system arrangement has become the inevitable trend of global economic development. In the future, there is still a need to deepen the innovation practice of China's pilot FTZ system which should cover the following aspects. The first is to study and expand the open framework scheme in depth and build an open global economic rules and system with Chinese elements. The second is to construct high-quality free ports with Chinese characteristics and an integrated, gradient and multi-level open system. The third is to give greater reform autonomy to free ports build a few highly advanced pilot ports to lead and promote the country's general opening strategy. The fourth is to promote the construction of China's FTZs as the most advanced ones in the world, and build a new pattern of deeper levels, wider areas and greater openness.

China's pilot FTZs have shown a clear trend of all-round expansion, and the potential for making breakthroughs in China's west region has become clearer. The State Council has approved the establishment of pilot FTZs in 18 eastern coastal and inland areas, which has set an example in investment, trade, finance and other fields.

From the perspective of spatial planning, an all-round three-dimensional construction pattern has been formed in the east, west, south, north and middle of China.

China's BRI has brought new opportunities for the development and opening up of China's border regions, and it is expected that border FTZs with their own characteristics will continue to emerge. The border areas are rich in underground, surface and space resources. They should give full play to their unique advantages and set up pilot FTZs to turn the tail end of reform and opening up into the "vanguard" of reform and opening up, which bears on the overall interests of China's reform and development. China has a large number of border ports. Based on its basic advantages, China should give full play to the special customs clearance functions of ports, build more featured border FTZs based on the interaction between ports and other countries, and form a high-level pattern of communication and opening to Russia, Mongolia, North Korea, ASEAN, Central Asia, South Asia and other countries or regions.

References

Chen Huizhu et al (2015) On the evolution of Hong Kong Free Trade Port model. Trop Geogr (1)

Xing HY (2014) Comparison and reference of China (Shanghai) pilot free trade zone with Hong Kong and Singapore free port policy. Science 9:5–17

Yang M, Zhao M, Yuan F et al (2019) Policy analysis of Hong Kong and Singapore free port. New Econ 4:4–9

Chapter 4
Research on Regional Synergy Development in the World

The last chapter introduced the experience of advanced free trade port construction, with the emphasis placed on the analysis of the connotation of free trade. This chapter focuses on the study of regional synergy development of large-scale urban agglomerations in the word, offering an interpretation of the meaning of combination in the expression of *combined free trade port*. In terms of international experience, this chapter selects the San Francisco Bay Area, New York Bay Area, and Tokyo Bay Area, the world's three most famous bay areas as research cases. In terms of domestic practice, this chapter selects the Beijing-Tianjin-Hebei Urban Agglomeration and the Yangtze River Delta Urban Agglomeration as representative regions. It analyzes the selected collaborative innovation mechanism of various urban agglomerations at home and abroad from the perspectives of transportation infrastructure, economic and social governance, and industrial agglomeration development, in order to seek references for the synergy development of the Guangdong-Hong Kong-Macao Greater Bay Area.

4.1 Research on Synergy Development of the San Francisco Bay Area

4.1.1 Basic Situation and Development History of the San Francisco Bay Area

The San Francisco Bay Area (also directly referred to as the Bay Area) is a world-famous metropolitan area located in northern California, the United States, and around the San Francisco Bay and San Pablo Bay at the mouth of the lower Sacramento River. The specific scope of the San Francisco Bay Area is still controversial, but it is generally considered to include San Francisco on the west side, San Mateo on the south, Santa Clara (central city San Jose), Alameda County on the east (central

© Xiamen University Press 2022
S. Ba et al., *Collaborative Innovation Mechanism of GBA in China*,
https://doi.org/10.1007/978-981-19-2251-0_4

city Oakland), Contra Costa, Solano, and Marin, Napa and Sonoma counties to the north, a total of 9 counties and 101 cities with a population of 7.753 million (2018 data). These cities and counties have joined the Association of Bay Area Governments (ABAG). In a broad sense, the San Francisco Bay Area also includes the peripheral counties of San Benito, San Joaquin, Santa Cruz, and Stanislaus (joined in September 2018) and Merced (joined in September 2018). These 14 counties are collectively called the San Jose-San Francisco-Oakland, CA Combined Statistical Area, with a population of 9.666 million (2018 data), making it the second largest metropolitan area on the West Coast of the United States (after Los Angeles) and the fifth largest metropolitan area in the United States.

The Bay Area was originally a Spanish colony until Mexico's independence in 1821, which became part of Mexico's Alta California. In 1846, the Republic of California was established and declared independence from Mexico. In the same year, the US-Mexico war broke out. In 1848, James Marshall discovered gold in the American River, triggering the gold rush. By the end of 1849, news of the gold rush had spread all over the world. The Bay Area was the gateway to the hinterland of California. At that time, more than 1,000 new immigrants flocked in every day, including the first large-scale Chinese immigrants. At the same time, the California Constitutional Convention passed a resolution to add California to the United States as a state. The capital of the state of California (California) kept moving forward in the early days of its establishment, and it was finally settled in Sacramento in 1854. After the gold rush subsided, the Wells Fargo Bank and the Bank of California were established based on the wealth accumulated during the gold rush. The gold rush attracted many immigrants and profoundly changed the local population structure. In the 1870s, a large number of Chinese laborers entered the Bay Area in order to build the first longitudinal railway (starting at Long Wharf in Oakland). After the completion of the longitudinal railway, it will connect the Bay Area with other parts of the United States, making the Bay Area truly a commodity trading platform benefiting the entire United States and accelerating the urbanization process of the Bay Area.

However, just entering the twentieth century, the Bay Area was hit by an earthquake in April 1906 (the epicenter was near San Francisco). According to real-time estimates by the US military, the earthquake caused a total of about 700 deaths, including 498 in San Francisco, 64 in Santa Rosa, and 102 in San Jose and surrounding areas. However, modern research generally believes that the earthquake caused at least 3,000 deaths and destroyed more than 28,000 buildings. This earthquake caused very heavy losses, but it also provided an opportunity for the redevelopment of Bay Area. In the process of post-disaster reconstruction, the US Congress finally approved a plan to build a reservoir in the Hetch Hetchy Valley in Yosemite National Park. Today, the Hetch Reservoir provides drinking water for 2.4 million people in the Bay Area. Although Bay Area, which was hit hard by the earthquake, handed over the dominance of the California area to the Los Angeles metropolitan area, it had basically recovered its vitality by 1915 with showing the world its rebirth at Panama Pacific Fair that year.

Affected by the US stock market crash in 1929 and the subsequent Great Depression, the economy of the San Francisco Bay Area also fell into recession, and many San Francisco-based banks went bankrupt. In order to boost the local economy and create employment opportunities, two large-scale infrastructure construction projects were being promoted at the same time. The first is the Golden Bay Bridge project connecting San Francisco and Marin County, and the second is the Bay Bridge project connecting San Francisco and Oakland and the East Bay area. After the United States participated in World War II in 1941, the Bay Area became a very important military base and naval port in the United States. Many large docks were built in Sausalito of Marin County and East Bay to produce warships. Fort Mason became the primary port for US troops to send troops to the Asia–Pacific battlefield. After the war, a large number of veterans returned to the United States, and many chose to continue to live in the Bay Area. In addition, a large number of immigrants poured into the Bay Area during this period, causing a surge in population in the area. In the 1950s, San Francisco welcomed more than 100,000 new immigrants. The suburban population of the East Bay area doubled, the population of Daly City (in San Mateo County) quadrupled, and the population of Santa Clara has increased by 5 times.

In the early 1960s, the Bay Area and even the entire Northern California area became the core position of the counter-cultural movement. In the following years, it became the base for inspiring the New Left Movement, the Student Movement, the Anti-Vietnam War Movement, the Black Affirmative Action Movement, and Equal Rights Movement of Homosexual Groups. This has allowed the region to form a deep cultural identity with a liberal community. At the same time, the South Bay area where San Jose is located began to develop rapidly, from an area dominated by an agricultural economy to a hot spot for the development of high-tech industries. During World War II, Frederick Terman, who was in charge of a top-secret radio research project at Harvard University, returned to his Alma Mater Stanford University to help reorganize its engineering school. His students, including David Puckold and William Wheelett, later led the high-tech revolution in Bay Area–the first semiconductor company (Shockley Semiconductor Laboratory) in the Bay Area, which was established near Stanford University in 1955. Although it fell into a financial crisis causing bankrupt, the large number of high-tech talents it attracted became the backbone of high-tech companies in the region. These companies formed a high-tech industry cluster, which later became the world-renowned Silicon Valley.

In 1989, a magnitude 6.9 Loma Prieta earthquake occurred in the Bay Area. The earthquake damaged many infrastructures in the area, including the Bay Bridge. However, the high-tech industries in the Bay Area did not stop their pace of expansion. Instead, the development accelerated. According to the US Census, the population of San Jose surpassed San Francisco in that year. The commercialization of the Internet since the mid-1980s has caused the speculation of high-tech companies to continuously accumulate bubbles. At the beginning of the twenty-first century, the Internet bubble began to burst, and the entire industry fell into a continuous decline, almost suffering a devastating blow. Companies such as Amazon and Google finally managed to survive the downturn in the industry. As the development of the Internet economy related industries gradually returned to normal levels, the stock prices of these companies rose significantly. Having experienced the influence of the bursting of the Internet economy bubble, the high-tech industries in the entire Bay Area have paid more attention to investment risk management. At the same time, the entrepreneurial incentive mechanism of universities in the Bay Area, which began in the late 1980s, has continued, encouraging university teachers and students to transform scientific and technological achievements, seizing the opportunity of the development of the information industry, and finally, making the rapid development of the technology industry. On this basis, the San Francisco Bay Area presents an entrepreneurial ecosystem structure of "universities-venture capital-entrepreneurs". The technology industry and the financial service industry developed in a complementary way, realizing the coordinated development of the industry.

The "Two-Wheeled" structure supporting the emerging technology industry and the financial industry, as well as the seamless docking of industry, academia and research, have allowed the San Francisco Bay Area to keep pace with the era of information technology entrepreneurship. The San Francisco Bay Area has gathered the most creative scientific talents, the most ambitious creative entrepreneurs, and the most influential investors. There are about 9,000 venture capital companies in the world, while the San Francisco Bay Area occupies an important territory in the world's venture capital. In 2018, approximately $32.4 billion in venture capital flowed in the San Francisco Bay Area, accounting for 48% of the total US venture capital. International Internet giants such as Google, Apple, HP, eBay, and Facebook were all born in Silicon Valley. In 2017, 101 new unicorn companies chose to locate in Silicon Valley, accounting for 49.9% of the total number of unicorn companies in the world and 85.6% of the United States. They are mainly distributed in high-tech industries such as enterprise services, e-commerce, big data, and cloud computing. Internet-based industries accounted for 62.7% of the total.

In recent years, the vigorous development of industries in the Bay Area and the increase in jobs have led to a rapid rise in real estate prices in the area. In the face of increasing rent pressure, more and more people choose to live in cities and counties outside the Bay Area with commuting daily to and from work in the Bay Area and residences in the outer area. According to local media, SAN Jose Mercury News, there are 168,000 commuters in the Bay Area living in San Benito County, San Joaquin County, Stanislaus County, Merced County, Yuba County and Sacramento. The further expansion of the Bay Area has also increased the difficulty of regional coordinated governance.

4.1.2 Status of Economic and Social Development of the San Francisco Bay Area

Since the arrival of the first Spanish colonists in 1769, the San Francisco Bay Area has become a continuous strip of coastal cities with a population of nearly 8 million

Table 4.1 An overview of the 9 metropolitan areas in the San Jose-San Francisco-Oakland Grand Metropolitan Area

Metropolitan statistical area	Population in 2018 (person)	Land area (km^2)	Population density (people/km^2)	2017 GDP (a hundred million U.S. dollars)	GDP per capita in 2017 (U.S. dollars)
Merced	274,765	5,010	55	86	31,787
Modesto	549,815	3,870	142	207	37,888
Napa	139,417	1,940	72	114	81,193
San-Francisco-Oakland-Hayward	4,729,484	6,410	738	5,007	105,918
San Jose-Sunnyvale-Santa Clara	1,999,107	6,940	288	2,753	137,752
Santa Cruz-Watsonville	274,255	1,150	238	134	48,471
Santa Rosa -Petaluma	499,942	4,080	123	287	56,866
Stockton- Lodi	752,660	3,600	209	271	36,340
Vallejo- Fairfield	446,610	2,130	210	214	48,090
the whole metropolitan area	9,666,055	35,280	274	9,073	93,864

Source U.S. Bureau of Economic Analysis

after more than two hundred years of development. Together with the adjacent inland areas, it forms the San Jose-San Francisco-Oakland Grand Metropolitan Area. The metropolitan area is further composed of 9 metropolitan areas centered on the San Francisco-Oakland-Hayward Metropolitan Area and the San Jose-Sunnyvale-Santa Clara Metropolitan Area. The other 7 metropolitan areas are the Merced Metropolitan Area and the Modesto Metropolitan Area, Napa Metropolitan Area, Santa Cruz-Watsonville Metropolitan Area, Santa Rosa-Petaluma Metropolitan Area, Stockton-Lodi Metropolitan Area and Vallejo-Fairfield Metropolitan Area.

An overview of the 9 metropolitan areas is shown in Table 4.1.

Employment opportunities in the Bay Area are mainly concentrated in the coastal areas of the San Francisco Bay and San Pablo Bay, which makes the per capita output value gap of the various metropolitan areas in the Bay Area very obvious. The land scale, population size, population density, and per capita output value of the two core metropolitan areas are the highest in the metropolitan area. The San Francisco-Oakland-Hayward Metropolitan Area has a nominal GDP per capita of more than $100,000 in 2017. The San Jose-Sunnyvale-Santa Clara Metropolitan Area is closer to 140,000 US dollars. The Bay Area has formed an industrial structure with finance, real estate, professional and business service industries and information industries as the pillars. The output value of these three industries accounts for more than half of the total output value of the Bay Area's secondary and tertiary industries (see Fig. 4.1). Table 4.2 further presents the industrial agglomeration advantages of the nine counties in the San Francisco Bay Area in the United States.

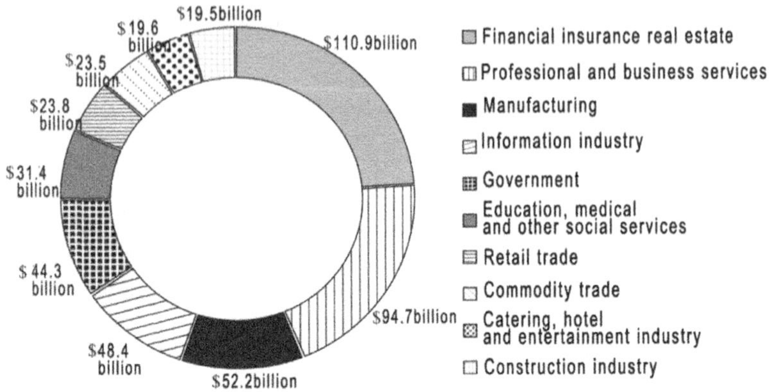

Fig. 4.1 The industry output value structure in the 9 counties of the Bay Area (excluding agriculture) (*Source* https://www.statista.com/statistics/591696/gdp-of-the-san-francisco-bay-area-by-industry/)

Table 4.2 The location quotient of the nine counties in the San Francisco Bay Area relative to each industry in the United States (in terms of the number of employees)

Industry type	Location entropy	Practitioners percentage	Contribute to employment (%)
Extractive industry, logging industry and construction industry	0.981 2	195,000	5.0
manufacturing	1.085 9	351,300	9.0
Trade, transportation and utilities	0.832 6	593,400	15.2
Information industry	2.664 9	194,900	5.0
Financial industry	0.884 1	194,300	5.0
Professional, service business services	1.394 4	743,700	19.1
Education, medical industry	0.974 8	587,900	15.1
Catering, hotel and Entertainment Industry	1.022 0	426,700	11.0
Government agency	0.822 4	480,900	12.3
Others	0.513 7	128,700	3.3

Source U.S. Census Bureau

In terms of the number of employees, location quotient[1] of the four industries in the San Francisco Bay Area is greater than 1, including manufacturing, information industry, professional and business service industries, catering, hotel and entertainment industries. The location quotient of professional and business service industries is close to 1.4, and the information industry is as high as 2.66 or more, showing that the Bay Area is a well-deserved gathering place for the information industry and modern producer service industries in the United States.

Although the booming of the information industry in the mid to late 1980s profoundly changed the economic structure of the Bay Area, the progressive cultural traditions of the Bay Area have continued to this day. The Bay Area today has inherited its position as the forefront of the twentieth century equal rights movement. Today, the Bay Area is the center of the affirmative movement for LGBT. In 2004, San Francisco began to issue marriage certificates to gay marriage groups, becoming the first city in the United States to issue legal certificates to gay marriage couples. In 2008, the *California Legislative Proposition 8* tried to prohibit same-sex marriage at the state constitutional level. Although the bill was passed in the state assembly at that time, most of the Bay Area lawmakers voted against the proposal. In addition, the Bay Area is also the center of the ongoing campaign against gender inequality and economic inequality. Communities in the Bay Area show distinctive features of diversity at the demographic level. Non-Hispanic whites are the main population of the United States, but around 2000, it accounted for less than half of the total population of the Bay Area. By 2018, less than 40% of the total population of the nine counties in the Bay Area were African Hispanic whites, while Asians accounted for more than a quarter, and Hispanic whites also accounted for 1/5 of the total population. See Table 4.3.

4.1.3 Regional Synergy Development in the San Francisco Bay Area

Restricted by the political system of the three levels "Federal-State-Local Government" and the deep-rooted tradition of regional autonomy in the United States, the

[1] Location quotient is a commonly used quantitative indicator to measure the degree of spatial agglomeration of certain regional elements, which can reflect the degree of specialization of a certain industrial sector. In the analysis of industrial structure, location quotient is mainly used to analyze the leading industry sector in a certain area. The higher the location quotient value, the more obvious the agglomeration advantage of the industry in the area. The location quotient value is greater than 1, indicating that the industry belongs to the "Export industry" of the area. For example, the location of industry *j* in region *i* is defined as LQ_{ij}, and q_{ij} is the relevant index of industry *j* in region *i* (industry output value or the number of employees, etc.). While q_i is the relevant index of the whole industry in region *i*, and q_j is industry *j* in the whole region. The relevant index of q is the relevant index of the whole domain and the whole industry, then the definition formula of LQ_{ij} is: $LQ_{ij} = \frac{\frac{q_{ij}}{q_i}}{\frac{q_j}{q}}$.

Table 4.3 Comparison of the ethnic composition of the population of the nine counties in the Bay Area and the situation in the United States

Area	Non-Hispanic white (%)	Hispanic whites (%)	African American (%)	Asian (%)
All America	60.4	16.1	13.4	5.9
Nine Counties in the Bay Area	38.9	20.2	6.6	27.8
Armida County	31.1	18.7	11.2	31.8
Contra-Costa County	43.2	22.2	9.5	18.0
Marin County	71.5	14.0	2.8	6.5
Napa County	52.0	31.8	2.5	8.8
San-Francisco County	40.3	12.6	5.6	35.9
San Mateo County	38.9	21.1	2.7	30.1
Santa Clara County	31.0	22.0	2.8	38.3
Solano County	37.6	22.1	14.8	16.2
Sonoma County	63.1	23.7	2.1	4.6

Source U.S. Census Bureau

Bay Area has exerted great efforts to actively seek regional synergy development. The complicated organization of local governments in the United States has resulted in 9 county governments and 101 city governments operating simultaneously on only 18,040 square kilometers of land in the Bay Area. This does not include single-function government agencies such as school districts. Due to the lack of a strong top-down management of the government covering the whole region, the synergy development of the Bay area is mainly realized by the establishment of consultation and cooperation platforms among the local governments, or promoted by the state government and even the federal government in the form of function specific funding.

4.1.3.1 Regional Coordination Planning and Governing

Association of Bay Area Governments (ABAG) is the most representative platform to meet local governments' need for coordination and cooperation in the Bay area. According to the basic governance structure of "Federal-State-Local government" in the United States, ABAG, as an advisory organization, has very limited statutory authority. Shortly after the end of World War II, the political and business elites in the Bay Area were aware that the Bay Area needed to be transformed from a wartime military base into a peacetime economy, requiring regional co-ordination and coordinated development. Many regional problems, including environmental governance (such as water pollution and serious smog in California at that time), transportation infrastructure construction and regional land use planning, cannot be solved by a local city or county government individually. It is imperative to carry out regional cooperation and unified layout planning.

As a result, in the early post-war period, a number of regional cooperation agencies focused on a single function were established. Regional Water Quality Control Board was established in 1949. Bay Area Air Pollution Control District (the predecessor of Bay Area Air Quality Management District) was established in 1955. Bay Area Rapid Transit District (BART) was established in 1957. In spite of the establishment of the above-mentioned special functional agencies, they lacked connections and integration. Therefore, a comprehensive regional planning agency was needed to coordinate the environmental, transport and land use policy objectives of common concern to local governments in the region. However, because of the deep tradition of local self-government in the United States, local legislators generally do not tolerate a strong regional governance quasi-government agency above the local governments under the state governments. Therefore, although ABAG was established at the initiative of the Bay Area Council in 1961, its function was still limited to constructive regional planning. In the 1960s and 1970s, California pro-regional politicians repeatedly proposed in the state legislature to establish a strong regional governance institution in the Bay Area. While such proposals were often supported in the State House of Representatives, they were often rejected in the Senate (the Senate is often considered more conducive to protecting the interests of relatively sparsely populated rural areas due to the way in which its members are generated). Because of the constraints of the legislature, ABAG has not been able to play its role in regional integrated planning for the past 20 years. It is widely believed that if the Bay area could effectively implement comprehensive regional planning in the 1960s and 1970s, the urban spread problem it showed in the 1980s and 1990s would not have been so serious.

Back in 1967, ABAG ushered in a turning point. In 1966, the federal government passed the *Demonstration Cities and Metropolitan Development Act of 1966*, which gave a large amount of financial support to regional planning organizations. But the good times did not last long. The economic crisis in the 1970s caused the federal government's funding to quickly dry up, and even large cities in the Bay Area were unable to afford the membership fees of ABAG due to the heavy financial burden of the major cities in the Bay Area. In order to cope with the persistent financial crisis, ABAG began to adjust its own functions, from a regional planning agency in the Bay area to the service agencies of the local governments in the Bay area. For example, ABAG introduced a credit pooling mechanism in 1983. Through the platform of ABAG, a group of cities can jointly issue bonds using mutual credit as the guarantee to reduce issuance costs. This credit sharing mechanism was later proved to be very successful with widely promoted. Today not only can the city and county governments join in the credit sharing, but also special function areas, hospitals, colleges, schools, and non-profit housing institutions, medical institutions and even private companies can join. Today, the mechanism has provided more than $1 billion in tax-free financing for these institutions, including the University of California's project to establish a system headquarters in downtown Oakland. Besides the credit sharing mechanism, the ABAG also set up various government purchasing consortia, which enhanced the bargaining power of local governments in procurement.

At this stage, the focus of the ABAG has shifted from a single regional planning function to promoting cooperation in financing and expenditure by local governments in the region, and cooperation with other special regional governance institutions such as Metropolitan Transportation Commission (MTC) to promote more efficiency in the region compact land development and utilization, and more effective environmental governance.

4.1.3.2 Transportation and Land Use

The core issue of regional synergy in the Bay Area is to build a complete, fast, and efficient regional transportation system. But in fact, because the job opportunities in the region are mainly concentrated in the coastal areas of San Francisco Bay and San Pablo Bay, there is a large commuter population. The problem of separation of jobs and residences is very serious, putting huge pressure on transportation. In view of this, the transportation and land use management agencies in the Bay Area vigorously promoted a transportation-oriented development (TOD). MTC and ABAG jointly delineated the urban growth boundary in the area, as well as priority development areas (PDAs) and priority conservation areas (PCAs). Priority development areas are concentrated in the communities where the rapid transit lines (expressways, rail transit) in the area have a certain development foundation, to encourage further infill development and increase development density. The strategy of the priority development zone is mainly realized by relying on financial subsidy incentives, which is largely dependent on the special appropriation of California Business Transportation and Housing Agency.

4.1.3.3 Housing

With the rapid development of the information technology industry and modern producer services in the Bay Area, as well as the gradual recovery of the macro economy from the downward cycle of the 2008 economic crisis, housing prices and rents in the area have risen significantly in recent years. The rapid increase in rents makes more people choose to live in the marginal rent depressions of the Bay Area or even the surrounding areas outside the Bay Area commuting daily. The severe separation of job and residence (Fig. 4.2) has caused serious traffic congestion and further aggravated air pollution.

In order to solve the housing problem in the district, a Regional Housing Need Allocation (RHNA) project was established under ABAG. Through the legislation of the state government, it is mandatory to stipulate the total amount of housing construction each year (including affordable housing), and each community must make corresponding plans in accordance with the law to implement the mandatory housing construction plan. California Department of Housing and Community

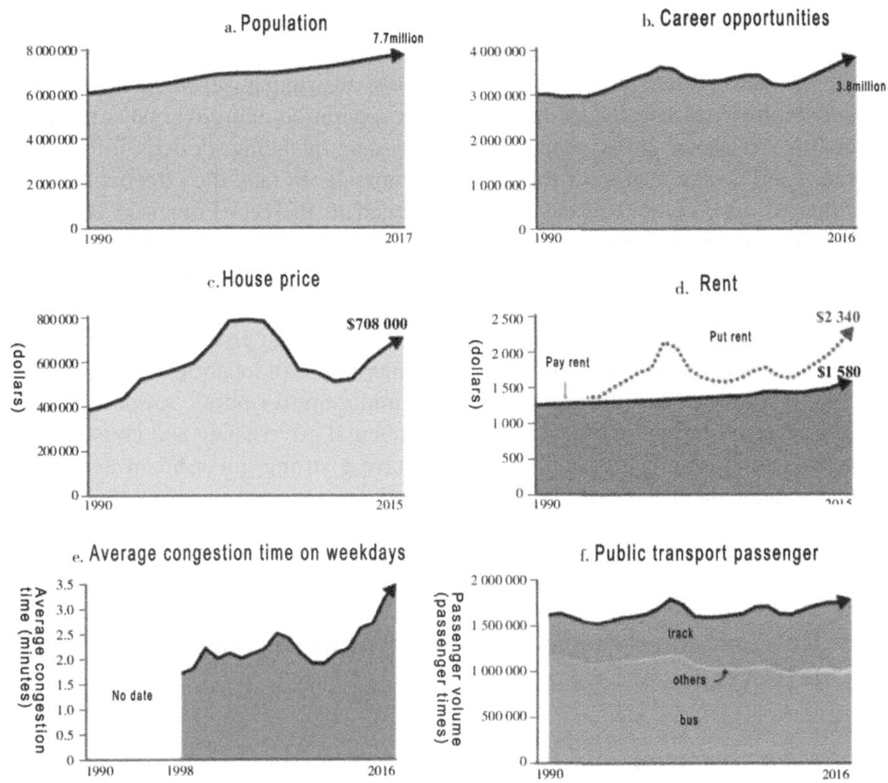

Fig. 4.2 The annual increase in housing prices and rents in the Bay Area and traffic congestion caused by long distance between job and residence (*Source People, Places, and Prosperity*, Association of Bay Area Governments)

Development determines the total housing supply scale of a region, and ABAG is responsible for coordinating the local governments in the region to further allocate these indicators according to the income level of each region in the Bay Area.

4.1.4 *Summary and Referential Significance of the Governance of the San Francisco Bay Area*

By reviewing the development history of the San Francisco Bay Area and analyzing its development status, it is not difficult to find that under the political tradition of the United States that emphasizes local autonomy, regional coordinated development has many constraints on the system and policy levels. In fact, the weaker regional coordinated governance model has become an important factor restricting the sustainable and coordinated development of the economy and society of the Bay

Area. Local government coordination platforms in the Bay Area mostly focus on a single hot issue, such as transportation planning, infrastructure construction, environmental conservation, and so on. In the absence of strong government agencies for unified deployment and leadership, regional cooperation and governance agencies in the Bay Area have shifted their focus to providing financing services, information services, and decision support for local governments. In fact, the effective regional coordinated development measures implemented in the San Francisco Bay Area often rely on unified arrangements (in the form of bills or administrative orders) and targeted financial support (such as special funding) from the superior government (state or even the federal government). Therefore, we can come to the conclusion that although the development of the Bay Area's economy must give full play to the role of the market in resource allocation with making full use of location advantages, and forming a competitive industrial cluster, it is important for public service products (such as transportation infrastructure, environmental governance and conservation, affordable housing construction, etc.) must have a strong government agency for unified management to form a solid guarantee for regional economic and social development.

4.2 Research on Synergy Development of the New York Bay Area

4.2.1 An Overview and History of the New York Metropolitan Area

The New York metropolitan area is a continuous metropolitan area on the Atlantic coast of the northeastern United States with New York City as its core. It is generally believed that its scope includes New York City, Long Island, the Lower Hudson Valley in New York State, and New Jersey's five largest cities-Newark, Jersey City, Paterson, Elizabeth and Edison and its surrounding areas, as well as the six largest cities in Connecticut-Bridgeport, New Haven, Stanford, Waterbury, Norwalk, Danbury and the surrounding areas.

The United States Census Bureau has a narrow and a broad definition of the New York metropolitan area. In a narrow sense, it is the New York-Newark-metropolitan statistical area. Broadly speaking, it is the New York Combined Statistical Area. The core of the New York Metropolitan Statistical Area is the New York-Jersey City-White Plains Metropolitan Division, including five districts (counties) in New York City, namely Kings (the borough of Brooklyn in New York City), Queens (the borough of Queens in New York City), New York (the borough of Manhattan in New York City), and Bronx (the borough of Bronx in New York City), Richmond (the borough of Staten Island in New York City), as well as Westchester, Rockland, Orange, and Bergen, Hudson, Middlesex, Memmoth, Ocean, and Passaic in New Jersey.

In addition to the New York-Jersey City-White Plains Division, the New York-Newark-Jersey City Metropolitan Statistical Area also has the Nassau-Suffolk Division (including Nassau County and Suffolk County), Dutchess-Putnam Division (including Dutchess and Putnam Counties of New Jersey) and Newark Division (it is composed of Essex in New Jersey, Union, Morris, Somerset, Sussex, Hunterdon, and Pike County in Pennsylvania).

The New York-Newark-Jersey City Metropolitan Statistical Area and its surrounding metropolitan areas that are more closely linked to economic activities constitute the New York-Newark Combined Statistical Area, which is generally considered to be the New York metropolitan area in the broadest sense. On the basis of the Metropolitan Statistical Area, the Union Statistical Area also includes the Bridgeport-Stamford-Norwalk-Danbury Metropolitan Statistical Area [geographically overlaps with Fairfield County in Connecticut], New Haven-Milford Metropolitan Statistical Area (geographically overlapping with New Haven County, in Connecticut), Allentown-Bethlehem-Easton Metropolitan Statistical Area (including Warren in New Jersey, and Carbon, Lehigh and Northampton counties in Pennsylvania), Trenton Metropolitan Area (Trenton, geographical range with Mercer County in New Jersey overlap), Torrington Small Metropolitan Statistical Area (Torrington, geographic area overlaps with Litchfield County in Connecticut), Kingston Metropolitan Statistical Area (Kingston, geographic area overlaps with Ulster County in New York overlap) and the East Stroudsburg metropolitan area (East Stroudsburg, geographic area overlaps with Monroe County in Pennsylvania). Except for the part that belongs to Pennsylvania, the area covered by the Union Statistical Area is also often referred to as the "tri-state area", i.e., New York, New Jersey, and Connecticut.

Table 4.4 summarizes the basic situation of the geographic scope and population of the counties in New York City, the New York Metropolitan Statistical Area, and the New York Unified Statistical Area. The New York metropolitan area, whether at the metropolitan statistical area level or the combined statistical area level, is the largest metropolitan area in the United States in terms of land area (Metropolitan Statistical Area 20,786.9 square kilometers, and Union Statistical Area 35,192.8 square kilometers) and total population (Metropolitan statistical area has close to 20 million people, and Union Statistical Area has more than 23.5 million people), which has obvious advantages. Even in the international arena, the size of the New York metropolitan area can be among the best, and most of them are included in the top 10 metropolitan areas in the world. However, unlike the Three-Center structure of the San Francisco Bay Area-"San Francisco-San Jose-Oakland", the New York metropolitan area presents a very obvious single-core structure. The land area of New York City only accounts for 3.77% of the entire Metropolitan Statistical Area and 2.23% of the Union Statistical Area, but its population has reached 42.04% of the entire Metropolitan Statistical Area and 35.07% of the Union Statistical Area.

Dutch colonists established the first settlement on the southern tip of today's Manhattan Island in 1609, and later named it New Amsterdam in 1626. The British won control of the area in 1664. Because King Charles II of England sealed the land to his brother, the Duke of York, the area was later renamed New York (Its Chinese

Table 4.4 The geographic scope and population of the counties in New York City, the New York Metropolitan Statistical Area, and the New York Unified Statistical Area

Area name	State	2018 population (people)	Land area (km^2)	Population density (people/km^2)
King County	New York	2,582,830	183.4	14,083.0
Queens County	New York	2,278,906	280.0	8,139.0
New York County	New York	1,628,701	59.1	27,558.4
Bronx County	New York	1,432,132	110.0	13,019.4
Richmond County	New York	476,179	152.0	3,132.8
New York City		8,398,748	784.5	10,705.9
Westchester County	New York	967,612	1,100.0	879.6
Bergen County	New Jersey	936,692	603.5	1,552.1
Hudson County	New Jersey	676,061	119.6	5,652.7
Middlesex County	New Jersey	829,685	800.1	1,037.0
Monmouth County	New Jersey	621,354	1,214.2	511.7
Ocean County	New Jersey	601,651	1,628.5	369.5
Passaic County	New Jersey	503,310	478.1	1,052.7
Rockland County	New York	325,695	449.5	724.6
Orange County	New York	381,951	2,100.0	181.9
New York Metropolitan Statistics Division		14,242,759	9,278.0	1,535.1
Suffolk County	New York	1,481,093	2,360.0	627.6
Nassau County	New York	1,358,343	740.0	1,835.6
Putnam County	New York	98,892	600.0	164.8
Duchess County	New York	293,718	2,060.0	142.6
Essex County	New Jersey	799,767	326.9	2,446.6
Union County	New Jersey	558,067	266.4	2,094.8
Morris County	New Jersey	494,228	1,191.9	414.7
Somerset County	New Jersey	331,164	781.7	423.6
Sussex County	New Jersey	140,799	1,344.2	104.7
Huntertown County	New Jersey	124,714	427.8	291.5

(continued)

Table 4.4 (continued)

Area name	State	2018 population (people)	Land area (km^2)	Population density (people/km^2)
Pike County	Pennsylvania	55,933	1,410.0	39.7
New York Metropolitan Statistical Area		19,979,477	20,786.9	961.2
Fairfield County	Connecticut	943,823	1,620.0	582.6
New Haven County	Connecticut	857,620	1,570.0	546.3
Warren County	New Jersey	105,779	924.4	114.4
Carbon County	Pennsylvania	64,227	986.8	65.1
Lehigh County	Pennsylvania	368,100	893.6	412.0
Northampton County	Pennsylvania	304,807	958.3	318.1
Mercer County	New Jersey	369,811	581.6	635.9
Northampton County	Connecticut	181,111	2,385.4	75.9
Ulster County	New York	178,599	2,911.2	61.3
Monroe County	Pennsylvania	169,507	1,574.7	107.6
New York Union Statistical Area		23,522,861	35,192.8	668.4

Source U.S. Census Bureau

translation is a transliteration of the sounds). As the region's fur trade gradually expanded northward, New York became the center of regional trade, attracting multi-ethnic immigrants to settle. The location advantage of Manhattan Island as a trade and shipping center is very obvious. It is a natural harbor as it is surrounded by New York Bay, East River and Hudson River on three sides. During the American Revolutionary War, New York became a battleground for military strategists because of its key strategic position. In 1785, New York became the first capital of the United States after independence. In 1790, the United States moved its capital to Philadelphia. In 1792, a group of businessmen signed the *Buttonwood Agreement*, which established the predecessor of today's New York Stock Exchange in Lower Manhattan.

New York ushered in a period of great development from the end of the nineteenth century to the beginning of the twentieth century. The strong labor demand in the New York area has attracted a large number of immigrants from all over the world (mainly Europe). A large number of immigrants from different backgrounds have made New York a rich and diverse immigrant culture, becoming the most culturally inclusive and ethnically diverse region in the United States. During this period, German, Irish and Italian immigrants formed the majority of immigrant groups. Foreign trade also expanded rapidly during this period. In 1884, more than 70% of American exports of goods were completed through the ports of New York and its surrounding towns. With the rapid development of regional economy and society, New York made its first major measure to integrate regional governance in 1898: five independently operated county and city governments, formerly known as the "Greater New York" area, merged into a single city government. This makes the New York City Government the first and so far only city government in the United States with a jurisdiction covering multiple counties.

After the merger, the New York City government began to encourage transportation links between the five districts, which further promoted the development of the "bedroom community" in the surrounding area of New York. More and more people choose to work in New York and live in the surrounding suburban counties. The New York City government bought the privately-owned Interborough Rapid Transit Company and established the New York City Subway in 1904. The construction of other rail transit infrastructure, represented by Grand Central Station and Pennsylvania Station, has strengthened the transportation links between New York City and the surrounding areas, which has also accelerated the suburbanization of the surrounding areas of New York.

The Great Depression that began in 1929 severely damaged the economy of the New York area, causing a large-scale unemployment and regional poverty problems. In order to stimulate employment growth, New York City began large-scale infrastructure construction. Represented by the proposal of the famous urban planner Robert Moses, a large number of bridges, avenues and highways were built, making New York's road system more suitable for large-scale applications of automobiles. During World War II, the economy of the New York area suffered huge losses due to the blockade of German U-boats, especially the sharp reduction in trade with Europe. During the post-war economic recovery period, the economic and social development of the New York metropolitan area entered a period of prosperity. However, after the population of New York City in New York City reached its historical peak in 1950, a significant process of suburbanization began. Over the next few decades, millions of people left New York City and moved to surrounding suburbs. Because most of the people who moved out of the city center were white middle class, this kind of suburbanization exacerbated the regional racial separation in space. This process of suburbanization inevitably led to the decline of industry and commerce in the central city, and many industries began to move to the suburbs.

Throughout the 1980s, the economy of the New York area developed rapidly. The injection of Wall Street capital has triggered the continued prosperity of the real estate market. After the end of the Cold War in the late 1980s and early 1990s, the economic development of the entire United States was very strong, so New York's position as the world's financial center and even the center of world capitalism was further consolidated. However, the September 11 attacks in the early twenty-first century severely affected to the development of the New York area and the United States. All walks of life in the New York area began to pay attention to and reflect on the security issues of cities and regions. Hurricane Sandy, which hit the New York area in late October 2012, caused serious losses, including extensive power outages, prolonged paralysis of public transportation in coastal areas, and damage to public and private properties in coastal areas. This severe natural disaster has received widespread social attention, meanwhile, it has also made urban and regional environmental governance and measures to improve disaster resistance have received more attention and support.

4.2.2 *Status of Economic Development of the New York Metropolis*

The economic strength of the New York Metropolis is very competitive in the United States and even the world. In 2015, the GDP in the New York Unified Statistical Area reached 1.83 trillion US dollars. If it were listed as a separate country, it would rank 8th in the world that year. In 2017, the GDP of the entire New York Metropolitan Statistical Area reached 1.72 trillion U.S. dollars, and the GDP of the New York Unified Statistical Area (except the Torrington Small Metropolitan Statistical Area) reached 1.85 trillion U.S. dollars. Many of the world's Fortune 500 companies have their headquarters in New York City which is also the first choice for many large foreign companies to invest and register in the United States. In New York City, 1/10 of non-public sector jobs are provided by foreign companies. From 2015 to 2018, New York ranked second in the Global Economic Power Index for four consecutive years (after London). The New York metropolitan area has a complete and diversified industrial system. Regional finance, international trade, traditional and new media, real estate, education, fashion and entertainment, tourism, biotechnology and manufacturing are all very competitive. While gathering a lot of wealth, New York has also become the most expensive place to live in the United States.

The two most important engines of New York's economy are Wall Street and Silicon Alley. Wall Street is the financial center of the United States and even the world, located in the financial district of Lower Manhattan. It is precisely because of Wall Street's huge economic and financial influence that New York is known as the world's major financial center and the most economically influential city. The New York Stock Exchange and the NASDAQ, the two stock exchange markets with the largest market capitalization in the world, are both located in the Wall Street Financial District of New York. In 2017, the pre-tax profit of the trust industry in New York City alone reached US$24.5 billion, and the average annual salary of the trust industry reached US$422,500. In the same year, the New York City trust industry contributed 7% of the city's tax revenue. It is worth noting that nearly 40% (38%) of the entire trust industry practitioners live outside of New York City, but work in New York City, and immigrants account for 1/3 of the entire trust industry practitioners.

Located in Midtown Manhattan, New York's Silicon Alley has rapidly grown into an important gathering place for the Internet, new media, financial technology, communications, digital media, software development, biotechnology, games and other information technology industries in the eastern United States. The development of Silicon Lane in New York is mainly due to New York's good entrepreneurial atmosphere and leading venture capital system. In 2015, Silicon Lane in New York received more than 7.3 billion U.S. dollars in venture capital. The companies that received investment are mainly located in Manhattan, Brooklyn, Queens and other areas in the metropolitan area. The development of biotechnology in the New York Metropolitan Area is mainly due to the scientific research capabilities of leading universities in the area and strong financial support. In December 2011, the then Mayor of New York, Michael Bloomberg, announced that Cornell University and the Technion-Israel Institute of Technology would jointly build Cornell Tech. It received a total investment of US$2 billion which is located on Roosevelt Island and positioned as a graduate school focusing on applied sciences. The New York City Economic Development Corporation established the Early Stage Life Sciences Funding Initiative, and in collaboration with other venture capital partners, injected at least US$100 million into 15–20 venture capital projects in life sciences and biotechnology.

Table 4.5 reflects the superior position of the New York Metropolitan Area in the industry in the United States. According to labor and employment data in 2017, the New York-Newark Joint Statistical Area (referred to as the Union Statistical Area in the table) contributes approximately 1/10 of the employment opportunities in the United States. Among them, more than a quarter of the employment opportunities in the financial, real estate and insurance industry in the United States are provided by the New York-Newark Unified Statistical Area. The information industry in the New York Metropolitan Area is now also important in the United States. In 2017, the United Statistical District contributed more than 13% of the information industry job opportunities in the United States, and the location entropy of the information industry has reached such a high level. In terms of jobs, the location quotient of most service industries in the New York-Newark Unified Statistical Area is greater than 1. Among them, the location quotient of the financial, real estate and insurance industry reached 2.47, and the professional and commercial service industry also reached 1.16, which further proves New York the status of the modern service industry cluster in the metropolitan area.

4.2.3 Regional Synergy Development of New York Metropolis

Similar to the San Francisco Bay Area, the regional collaborative governance of the New York Metropolitan Area is also subject to the strong tradition of local autonomy in the United States and the strict "federal government-state government-local government" three-level management system. The regional governance of the New York Metropolitan Area is even more complicated: First, the scale of the New York metropolitan area is even larger, which is not only reflected in the geographical space, but also in the scale of population and economy; Second, the New York Metropolitan Area also involves the issue of cross-regional governance. Its area is far more than a state and its regional governance involves 4 states including New York,

Table 4.5 A list of the industrial and economic status of the New York Metropolitan Area in the United States

Industry Type	No. of jobs in the U.S. in 2017	No. of jobs in the Union Statistical Area in 2017	Proportion of jobs in the Union Statistical Area (%)	Joint Statistical Area Location Entropy
Extractive industry, logging industry	678,000	15,234	2.2	0.22
Construction industry	6,956,000	689,179	9.9	0.97
manufacturing	12,420,000	534,579	4.3	0.42
Wholesale trade	5,813,100	528,334	9.1	0.89
Retail trade	15,821,400	1,331,910	8.4	0.82
Transportation and storage	5,183,800	–	–	–
Public utilities	555,200	51,522	9.3	0.91
Information Industry	2,809,000	377,553	13.4	1.31
Financial real estate insurance industry	8,447,000	2,136,728	25.3	2.47
Professional and business services	20,491,000	2,438,154	11.9	1.16
Education and medical services	23,170,000	2,576,884	11.1	1.09
Catering, Hotel and Entertainment Industry	16,061,000	1,398,267	8.7	0.85
Other service industries	5,771,000	867,207	15.0	1.47
Government department	22,356,000	1,541,697	6.9	0.67

Source U.S. Department of Labor

New Jersey, Connecticut, and even Pennsylvania, with more than 1,000 city government jurisdictions. However, the difference from the San Francisco Bay Area is that New York City has a very prominent dominance in the entire New York Metropolitan Area (New York City uses less than 4% of the metropolitan statistical area to create 45% of the employment opportunities in the region with 46% of industry value added). Regional development has also formed a very distinctive single-core circle structure in space. The reality of cross-state governance determines that it is difficult for the New York Metropolitan Area to establish quasi-governmental organizations to lead regional governance and make unified deployment and arrangements for regional development. The prominent central position of New York City in regional economic and social activities determines that New York City has an advantageous position in regional collaboration and governance, and it can seek effective regional governance by supporting non-governmental organizations and even corporate organizations.

4.2.3.1 Synergy of Transportation Infrastructure

Due to the single-core spatial structure of the New York Metropolitan Area, New York City, as the regional employment center, has a large number of commuters traveling between New York City and surrounding counties and cities every day. This large-scale mid-to-long-distance commuting is based on completed rapid public transportation (mainly rail transit). Within the New York Metropolitan Area, a network of different lines operated by a number of companies and agencies has been formed. These different lines are connected to each other and connected to the New York subway line network, becoming the backbone of inter-city and county public transportation in the region. Residents in the New York Metropolitan Statistical Area take a total of 4 billion public transportation trips every year, which is equivalent to an average of 184 bus, subway, commuter rail, or ferry rides per person per year. Table 4.6 and Fig. 4.3 further summarize the operation of rail transit lines in the New York Metropolitan Area. Table 4.6 shows that most of these rail transit lines are operated by the state government or even the authority established by the two state governments. This kind of authority mostly adopts a committee-based governance method, which provides a communication and coordination platform for cross-state transportation cooperation.

4.2.3.2 Regional Planning

As mentioned above, due to the complexity of interstate governance, the New York Metropolitan Area has not established a quasi-government agency like the Bay Area Government Association to lead the regional planning work in the metropolitan area. However, as early as 1922, the Regional Planning Association (RPA), which was based in the three states of New York, New Jersey, and Connecticut, was established. RPA is an independently operated non-profit regional planning agency that serves the so-called *Three-State Land* in the New York Metropolitan Area, covering 31 counties in New York, New Jersey, and Connecticut. Headquartered in New York, it also has branches in Princeton, New Jersey and Stanford, Connecticut. Moreover, it has made four editions of regional strategic plans for the New York Metropolitan Area in 1929, 1960s, 1996 and 2007.

In addition to overall regional strategic planning, RPA is also committed to promoting infrastructure projects that promote regional transportation links and economic development, as well as environmental conservation projects that improve regional environmental quality. Projects facilitated by RPA in the *Three-State Area*

Table 4.6 Overview of rail transit lines in the New York Metropolitan Area

Line	Affiliated institutions	Nature of Subordinate Organization	Service area
Long Island Railroad	Metropolitan Transportation Authority	New York State Legislative Body	Connecting Manhattan and Suffolk County on Long Island
Metro-north Railroad			Connecting Manhattan with Upstate New York and New Haven, Connecticut
Staten Island Railway			The only rail transit in Staten Island
NJ Transit Commuter Rail	New Jersey Department of Transportation	New Jersey State Agency	Connecting Manhattan with New Jersey and Pennsylvania
West of Hudson	New Jersey Department of Transportation and Metropolitan Transportation	New Jersey State Company	Connecting to Port Jervis, New Jersey (Port Jevis) and New Jersey Track
Port Authority Trans-Hudson	Port Authority of New York and New Jersey	New Jersey and New York state co-operate statutory bodies	Connecting Lower Midtown Manhattan and Jersey City
LaGuardia Airtrain			Connecting LaGuardia Airport and Jamaica Station (Jamaica Station)

Source Compiled by the authors

include: the location of the George Washington Bridge; the Palisades conservation project and the construction of the Palisades Interstate Highway; redevelopment of Governors Island, and the Governors Island Alliance established under the leadership of the Regional Planning Association; establishment of urban areas such as the Gateway National Recreation Area in Jamaica Bay National parks; renewal and development of regional centers such as downtown Brooklyn, Newark and Stanford, etc.

Many experts and scholars criticize RPA's guiding ideology and sum it up as *Cosmopolitanism* because it has been advocating large-scale industrial center projects and supporting population gathering rather than more decentralized development. Critics believe that planning under this guiding ideology will only benefit the owners of real estate assets in the city center. The key to the effectiveness of this planning model lies in whether the regional infrastructure and natural resource supply can support this kind of concentration. But there is no doubt that the Cosmopolitanism model is in line with the single-core circle development model of the New York Metropolitan Area promoting regional governance and collaboration with New York City as the core.

Line	Affiliated institutions	Nature of Subordinate Organization	Service area
Long Island Railroad			Connecting Manhattan and Suffolk County on Long Island
Metro-north Railroad	Metropolitan Transportation Authority	New York State Legislative Body	Connecting Manhattan with Upstate New York and New Haven, Connecticut
Staten Island Railway			The only rail transit in Staten Island
NJ Transit Commuter Rail	New Jersey Department of Transportation	New Jersey State Agency	Connecting Manhattan with New Jersey and Pennsylvania
West of Hudson	New Jersey Department of Transportation and Metropolitan Transportation	New Jersey State Company	Connecting to Port Jervis, New Jersey (Port Jevis) and New Jersey Track
Port Authority Trans-Hudson	Port Authority of New York and New Jersey	New Jersey and New York state co-operate statutory	Connecting Lower Midtown
LaGuardia Airtrain			Connecting LaGuardia Airport and Jamaica Station (Jamaica Station)

Fig. 4.3 The annual average daily passenger flow of rail transit (urban subway, commuter rail transit) in the New York metropolitan area (1972–2012) (*Source*: *One New York* [One NYC, New York City Government])

4.2.3.3 Large-Scale Regional Projects

A powerful tool for regional synergy development and governance in the New York Metropolitan Area is the large-scale regional projects invested by New York City and regional cooperative organizations. The *One NYC Plan* issued in 2014 lists important construction projects planned for the New York Metropolitan Area during the 12 years from 2014 to 2025. The total budget of these projects reached 266 billion U.S. dollars and was shared by New York City and regional cooperation organizations. These regional organizations include the Metropolitan Transportation Agency, the Port and Shipping Authority of New York and New Jersey, and other private utility companies. New York City's fiscal budget will cover 25% of the cost of these projects during the 12 years. Among the municipal agencies in New York City that have participated in these projects are the New York City Department of Transportation,

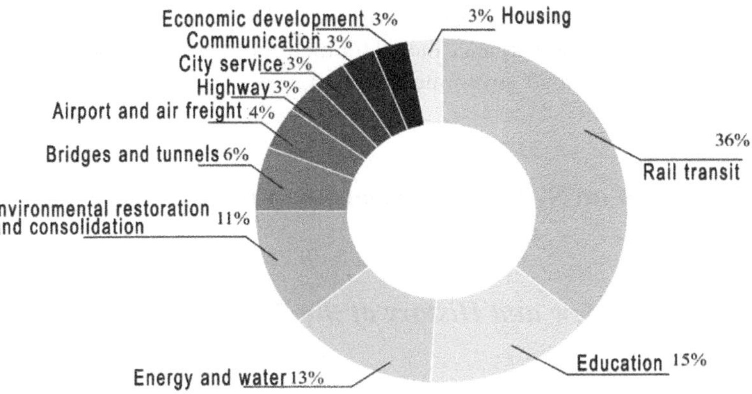

Fig. 4.4 The proportion of various types of investment in large-scale construction projects in the New York metropolitan area from 2014 to 2025 (*Source*: *One New York* [One NYC, New York City Government])

Department of Environmental Protection, the School Construction Authority and the City University of New York. Figure 4.4 analyzes the investment proportions of various projects. Among that, transportation infrastructure construction undoubtedly occupies the first place, and the budget of all transportation infrastructure projects exceeds half of the total budget.

4.2.4 Summary and Referential Significance of the Governance of New York Metropolis

Similar to the San Francisco Bay Area, the regional governance of the New York Metropolitan Area is restricted by the complicated political operating system of the United States. In addition, it spans over three states of New York, New Jersey, and Connecticut plus Pennsylvania. Due to the huge geographic scope and population size, the overall coordination will be impossible if it depends on local governments alone. It requires participation of organizations other than government departments such as statutory institutions, non-profit organizations, and corporate legal persons. Regional collaboration in the New York Metropolitan Area is more supported and driven by regional transportation infrastructure. For example, the establishment of the early New York metropolitan government was largely driven by the completion of the transportation infrastructure between the districts (for example, the Brooklyn Bridge made the economic and social ties between Manhattan and Brooklyn closer). New York City occupies an absolute core position in the New York Metropolitan Area, and regionally coordinated strategic planning and infrastructure construction have consolidated and even further strengthened this single-core structure at different levels. Correspondingly, New York City has also played a leading role in regional cooperation with the greatest investment. The New York Metropolitan Area provides a coordinated governance model for metropolitan areas that lack single-core development under unified government control.

4.3 Research on Synergy Development of the Tokyo Bay Area

4.3.1 An Overview and History of the Tokyo Metropolitan Area

Tokyo Bay Area, commonly known as Greater Tokyo in the world, refers to the urban agglomeration centered on Tokyo, the capital of Japan, also known as "Tokyo Area" or "Capital Area of Japan", generally including Tokyo Metropolis, Kanagawa(prefecture), Chiba(prefecture) and Saitama(prefecture). It is also called "one capital and three prefectures", which has the same scope as South Kanto. In order to integrate the development of Tokyo and its surrounding areas, the *National Capital Region Development Act* formulated by the Japanese government has extended the definition of the Capital Area to the whole Kanto Area (including Ibaraki, Tochigi, Gunma, Saitama, Chiba, the Tokyo Metropolis and Kanagawa), and Yamanashi. According to the United Nations statistics, the total population of the Tokyo Bay Area within the scope of "one capital and three prefectures" reached 38,140,000 in 2016, with a regional area of 13,500 square kilometers and a population density of 2,826 people/km^2. In term of the built-up area of metropolitan area (the built area of Tokyo Bay Area is 8,547 km^2), Tokyo Bay Area is the second largest metropolitan area in the world, second only to New York Metropolitan Area (11,642 km^2). In 2015, the total GDP (international exchange rate) of the Tokyo Bay Area is more than $1.9 trillion, ranking first among the urban agglomerations in the world. The economic scale of the Tokyo Bay Area would be second only to that of Italy if it has been regarded as a country. The population of Tokyo Bay Area (one capital and three prefectures) accounted for 1/3 of the whole Japan. Its total economic output accounts for close to half of that of Japan. Its urbanization rate is more than 90%.

Built on the orders of General Tokugawa Ieyasu in the early seventeenth century, Tokyo (then known as "Edo") was the site of the Tokugawa Shogunate and the de facto central government of Japan. In the eighteenth century, Tokyo had a population of over 1 million, making it one of the largest cities in the world at that time. After the Meiji Restoration (1868), Japan officially moved its capital from Kyoto to Tokyo. At the same time, through the measures of "*Abolishing the vassal state and establishing prefectures*", Japan established a prefecture system on the territory previously controlled by feudal lords (Daimyo and Syoumyo), and strengthened the central government's control over the local areas.

In the first half of the twentieth century, Tokyo suffered two major disasters. The Great Kanto Earthquake broke out in September, 1923 and the resulting fires, destroyed 44% land of downtown Tokyo, including the best part of city center, which was also the location of the major business centers. During the post-disaster reconstruction, Tokyo's built-up area took the opportunity to complete large-scale modernization by building many new main roads and completing the reconditioning of a total of 31 km^2 of land. A large number of people sought to move to the suburbs after the disaster. West Tokyo urbanized rapidly after new rail transit lines reached the area.

The second disaster occurred during World War II. Tokyo was hit by successive Allied air strikes until the end of the war in August 1945, resulting in the destruction of 710,000 houses on 159 km^2 (28% of the Tokyo Bay Area). Since then, Japan launched a land readjustment projects for post-war reconstruction, but only about 12.7 km^2 of land was redeveloped, mainly concentrated in the area along the Yamanote Line. The limited scale of the post-war reconstruction in Tokyo was mainly due to the fact that Japan experienced severe inflation in the early postwar period. In order to combat the inflation, the Japanese government adopted tight fiscal and monetary policies, which delayed and curtailed Tokyo's reconstruction plan.

Tokyo's development goal of becoming a modern capital was articulated as early as the *Tokyo Town Planning Ordinance* in 1888(the origin of city planning legislation in Japan), and a series of central-government regional construction projects that followed. From the late 19th to early twentieth century, with Japan's modernization and rapid development, the population of Tokyo continued to grow and urban areas were increasingly expanding into the surrounding countryside. In 1920s, multiple rail transit lines to the suburbs were built in Tokyo. Under the relatively loose Urban Planning system at that time, and affected by the 1923 Great Kanto Earthquake, Tokyo Area began a rapid sub-urbanization process. Until the 1950s, the development of Tokyo suburbs was still represented by typical low-density single-family houses. These sub-urbanized communities provided a decent living environment for the emerging middle class, although the infrastructure at that time was lagging, and many of these new houses had only self-sufficient well water and even no flush toilet.

In May 1947, a new *Constitution* and *Local Autonomy Law* came into effect. In August, 23 districts of Tokyo Area were officially established and continue to this day. By the 1950s, both Tokyo and Japan began to recover from the war. The outbreak of the Korean War in 1950 provided a great opportunity for the economic recovery and prosperity of Tokyo. The massive wartime purchasing of the United States provided a quantity of orders for Japanese companies. Thanks to the accumulation in the 1950s, Japan entered a period of rapid economic development in the 1960s. And thanks to technical innovation and Introduction of new technology industries, the mass production of synthetic fiber and household electrical equipment (e.g. TV, refrigerator, washing machine, etc.) grew rapidly in Tokyo. These had turned life in the Tokyo Area on its head. In 1962, the population of Tokyo had exceeded 10 million. In 1964, Tokyo successfully hosted the Olympic Games. Meanwhile, the operation of Shinkansen and the opening of capital expressway network set the stage for the continued prosperity of the Metropolitan.

In the 1970s, the problems brought by the rapid economic development gradually came to the surface. Environmental issues in Tokyo and across Japan were becoming more acute, including air pollution, river pollution and more severe noise pollution.

The oil crisis in 1973 also brought the economic development that lasted for many years to a standstill. In the 1980s, Tokyo gained new growth opportunities due to the prosperity of world economic and trade activities and the emerging information industry. Tokyo had become an internationally influential world city because of its leading position in frontier science and technology, information industry, cultural and creative industry, as well as high-level public security environment. But after 1986, real estate prices in Tokyo and stock prices of the Tokyo Stock Exchange both soared, forming a very typical bubble economy. After the bursting of the economic bubble in the late 1980s and early 1990s, and under the influence of the increasingly aging society, the economy of Tokyo and even Japan fell into a long-term stagnation and even recession, and did not see signs of recovery until recent years.

4.3.2 Development Status of Tokyo Bay Area

Entering the twenty-first century, the whole Japan has been faced with the serious problems of aging and sub-replacement fertility. As shown in Fig. 4.5, since 1975 the population of the Tokyo Area showed a slow growth trend on the whole. The natural growth rate has gradually declined, and even showed a negative growth trend around 2010. The population of Japan first showed a negative growth around 2005, and since then the compound growth rate of population has been maintained at or below 0. Although the national population growth has been negative, Tokyo has maintained the positive growth trend, indicating that the national population is concentrated there. Within the Capital Area, the population has been further concentrated in Tokyo Bay Area (one capital and three prefectures), with the four outer prefectures experiencing negative population growth since 2002 (see Fig. 4.6).

The proportion of the Capital Area's economic scale in Japan's economy has remained stable at 38% (Fig. 4.7), and its aggregate annual GDP is about 200 trillion yen. The Capital Area is not only the industrial center of Japan, but also the most active region of Japan's foreign economic exchanges. As shown in Fig. 4.8, in Japan

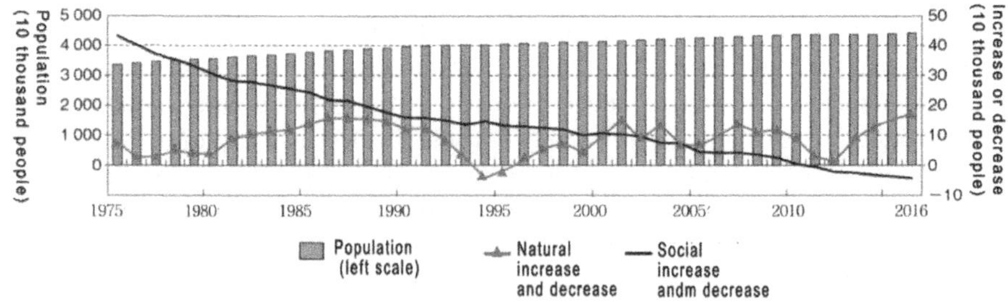

Fig. 4.5 Demographic changes of the Tokyo Capital Area (1975–2016) (*Source* 2016 Annual Report of the Capital Reconditioning Area [平成二十八年度首都圏整備に関する年次報告, Ministry of Land, Infrastructure, Transport and Tourism])

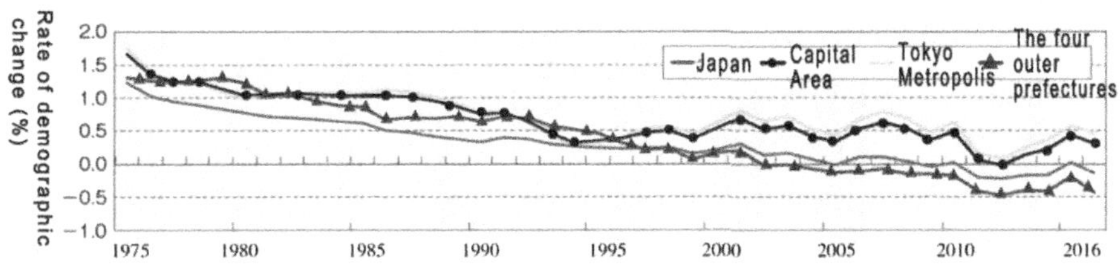

Fig. 4.6 Demographic changes of Japan, Capital Area, Tokyo Metropolis, and the four outer prefectures (Gunma-ken, Tochigi-ken, Ibaraki-ken and Yamanashi-ken) (1975–2016) (*Source* 2016 Annual Report of the Capital Reconditioning Area [平成二十八年度首都圏整備に関する年次報告, Ministry of Land, Infrastructure, Transport and Tourism])

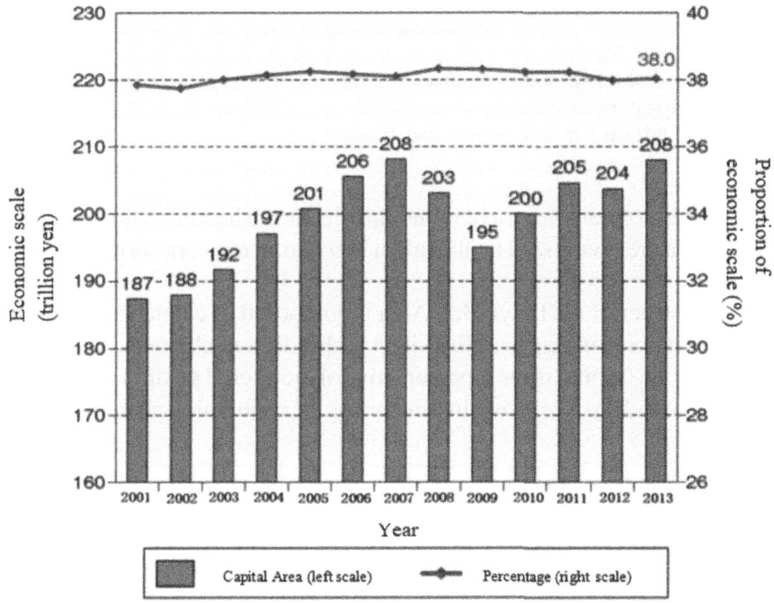

Fig. 4.7 Economic scale of the Tokyo Capital Area (*Source* 2016 Annual Report of the Capital Reconditioning Area [平成二十八年度首都圏整備に関する年次報告, Ministry of Land, Infrastructure, Transport and Tourism])

nearly 90% of foreign-funded companies with a registered capital of more than 50 million yen are concentrated in the Capital Area, which had formed an economic structure dominated by the tertiary industry. The added value of the tertiary industry accounts for nearly 80% of the industry's GDP, while the proportion of the first industry has dropped to about 0.5%.

As the financial and political center of Japan, Tokyo Metropolis is also responsible for education, information, industry and other functions. As a world-class city, Tokyo Metropolis has its own specialized departments to focus on the development of a wealth of related supporting industries, and through specialized division of labor

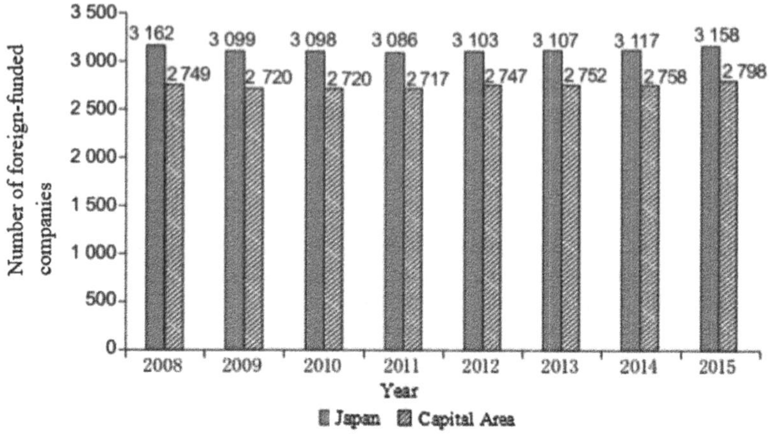

Fig. 4.8 Number of foreign-funded companies in the Tokyo Capital Area (*Source* 2016 Annual Report of the Capital Reconditioning Area [平成二十八年度首都圏整備に関する年次報告, Ministry of Land, Infrastructure, Transport and Tourism])

and cooperation to create intensive industrial clusters. The innovation and vitality of Tokyo Bay Area are revitalized by the urban innovation network formed by industrial integration.

The spatial structure of Tokyo Bay Area is composed of capital, sub-capital functional areas and surrounding satellite cities with different characteristics (see Table 4.7). Among them, Capital is the representative of the overall positioning and strategic planning of Tokyo Bay Area, owning the political, economic and cultural functions

Table 4.7 The main functional orientation of capital, sub-capital functional areas in Tokyo Bay Area

Capital/sub-capital functional areas	The main functional orientation
Tokyo Capital Area	Political and economic center, international financial center
Shinjuku	The first sub-capital, business office and entertainment center driving the development of Tokyo
Ikebukuro	The second sub-capital, business and shopping and entertainment center
Shibuya	Transportation hub, information center, business office, culture and entertainment center
Ueno-Asakusa	Traditional cultural tourism center
Osaki	High tech Research & Development center
Kinshicho-Kameido	Business, culture and entertainment center
Coastal sub-capital	Future oriented international cultural, technological and information exchange center

Source Sorted by the author

and driving the development of other cities. Sub-capitals are the result of the spillover of capital's functions. According to the different districts, they undertake part of the urban functions of the capital and also the comprehensive functions of some districts. Capital and sub-capitals jointly form a module that gathers industry, capital, population and comprehensive services to drive the rapid operation of Tokyo Bay Area, expand its the scale and economic aggregate, and strengthen its competitiveness. In Tokyo Bay Area, capital and sub-capital have clear division of work and complementary advantages, which promotes the development of multi-center network spatial pattern together with other towns.

Tokyo Capital refers to the central business district of Chiyoda-ku, Chuo-ku, Minato-ku. It is the political and financial core of Tokyo Bay Area and also the world-renowned financial center city. It is home to many financial headquarters and some of the densest and largest business activities in the world. As multi-functional and highly complex areas, the seven sub-capitals can not only carry out business activities, but also have other basic urban functions such as culture, residence, entertainment, etc.

Located in the outer ring of Tokyo Bay Area, many new cities are the main transportation, food and precision machinery manufacturing clusters in Japan, including Sagami Genji High-tech Industrial City, Yokohama Modern Port City, Chiba New Industrial City and Kisarazu Modern Port City. Saitama has shared the administrative functions of Tokyo, where many state institutions, residential and living areas were set up. It is also an important transportation hub in eastern Japan, and generally has taken on the functions of Japan's deputy capital. Among them, Urawa is the administrative center of Saitama, carrying out many international business exchange activities, while Omiya is the economic center of Saitama, focusing on commerce development. Kanagawa is one of the four major industrial bases in Japan, where industries and ports are gathered. It is also one of the places where enterprise headquarters and state administrative organs are located.

Yokohama in Kanagawa is Japan's second largest city by economic scale. Yokohama has developed and built the Keiyo Industrial Belt through sea reclamation since World War II, enhancing international competitiveness of Japanese industries. Meanwhile, Yokohama Port is the largest and the most important free port in Japan. It plays an important role in international exchanges. Kawasaki is one of Japan's centers of heavy industry. Kawasaki Port and Yokohama Port complement each other in functions, and jointly promote Kanagawa to become the concentration of industry and logistics in Tokyo Bay Area. Chiba is the gathering place of Japan's airport industry. It has Narita International Airport, international airport, seaport and other logistics centers. At the same time, it is also an important industrial prefecture in Japan. The development of Keiyo Industrial Belt promoted Chiba to play the role of international airport, seaport, commerce and international exchange. Tama Hill region is the gathering place of hi-tech industries, R&D institutions and universities. And the southern Ibaraki is home to a cluster of research universities and institutions with Scientific Town of Tsukuba as the main body.

On the whole, the tremendous economic strength of the Tokyo Bay Area is first reflected in its advanced manufacturing industry. It contributes 3/4 of Japan's industrial output value. The manufacturing bases of heavy industries such as Toyota,

Honda and Mitsubishi Heavy Industries are all located here, represented by household electrical appliances and electronics enterprises. The formation of industrial layout at the present stage benefits from the result of advanced planning and design, and precise implementation in the development process of Tokyo Bay Area. Initially, the strategy of *industrial decentralization* had been implemented in the Tokyo Bay Area in order to solve the problem of Tokyo being too large: manufacturing industries had been withdrawn from Tokyo, and modern service industries, mainly foreign trade and financial services, had been retained. This has driven the transformation and development of manufacturing industries left in Tokyo to high-end industries such as precision machinery and high and new technologies. The traditional manufacturing industry and heavy chemical industry moved to Yokohama, Kawasaki and other cities on both sides of Tokyo, forming two industrial zones, namely, Keihin and Keiyo industrial belts, surrounding the Tokyo Bay Port. In this way, the Tokyo Bay Urban Agglomeration had formed a two wing industrial belt around the port, which connected with the financial service industry with Tokyo as the core through the three-dimensional transportation of sea, land and air, forming an overlapping industrial form, gathering NEC, Mitsubishi Electric, Mitsubishi Heavy Industry, Mitsubishi Chemical, Toyota Research Institute, Sony, Toshiba, Canon, Fujitsu and other large-scale high-end manufacturing enterprises with the coexistence of technology R&D and manufacturing functions. The employed population of manufacturing industry in Tokyo Bay Area accounted for 1/4 of national total in Japan. Manufacturing industry, financial service industry and electronic information industry had become the main industries in the Tokyo Bay Area.

The Tokyo Bay Area also has a well-developed modern service industry. The foundation of service industry was derived from the industries which were extremely dependent on ports after Meiji Restoration, such as textile industry, mechanical processing industry and steel-making industry. A large amount of trade imports and exports in the port made Tokyo the first trade center. The demand for trade finance gave birth to the Tokyo Financial Center. To serve export-oriented industries, Japan had also introduced policies to strengthen financial industry regulation in addition to industrial policies, further enhancing the status of Tokyo Financial Center in the Bay Area. Meanwhile, for the purpose of effective utilization of the coastal land of Tokyo Bay, Disney and other entertainment facilities were built here on the basis of land reclamation, which strengthened the development of cultural and entertainment industries. At present, industries in the Tokyo Bay Area have moved to Keihin and Keiyo surrounding the port. As a result, Tokyo has become a highly concentrated place for financial, trade service and cultural industries. By 2017, the tertiary industry in Tokyo accounted for 82% of the city's total industrial value, among which the real estate industry, communications industry and modern service industry continued to grow.

In terms of financial industry, Tokyo is also one of the world's famous financial centers, which is closely related to the industrial development of Japan. The industrial policy implemented by Japan after World War II has made Tokyo a world-famous trade center, high-end manufacturing center. Banking, securities, insurance and other financial institutions serving trade and manufacturing industries have developed simultaneously. From the postwar to the end of the 1980s, a number of global high-tech enterprises with international competitiveness grew up in Tokyo, with solid support from the financial industry. The growth of Japan's manufacturing enterprises has also contributed to the boom of Japan's financial industry, which has entered the world capital market with the globalization of science and technology enterprises. The pattern of close development of finance and industry gives rise to the internal financial system of industry. This financial system highly integrated with industry and finance has formed a well-defined professional financial service system, effectively promoting the coordinated development of the industrial chain. For example, Toyota Group, based on automobile manufacturing, has formed banking, insurance and other financial systems. Its financial business only provides financial services around the upstream and downstream industries of Toyota, cooperating with Toyota's automobile R&D, manufacturing and sales.

4.3.3 Regional Synergy and Governance of Tokyo Metropolitan Area

4.3.3.1 Regional Planning

As mentioned earlier, although there was no large-scale battle in Japan during World War II, the huge consumption brought by the long-term war and the sustained bombing of the Allied Forces left Tokyo in ruins. After the war, Tokyo and even the whole of Japan experienced a long period of economic scarcity. The urban construction in Tokyo was very difficult. The supply of housing and transportation infrastructure was seriously insufficient, the housing shortage of residents was increasing, and the traffic congestion had not been improved. At the same time, severe inflation had further highlighted the shortage of basic living supplies. In order to cope with this situation, the Japanese government issued the *Comprehensive National Land Development Act* (enacted in 1950), with the purpose of leading the urban reconstruction and economic industry recovery through the land development planning.

The guiding ideology of the *Comprehensive National Land Development Act* was to solve various economic, social and environmental problems caused by excessive concentration of population and industry through the integration of Tokyo Metropolitan and surrounding areas. Specifically, the law on comprehensive land development proposes to build a political, economic and cultural urban circle in line with the functions of the capital. Comprehensive planning and construction of Tokyo Metropolitan and surrounding areas should be carried out to form an organic and unified "capital circle", while protecting green space and natural environment. Since 1956, five rounds of capital circle preparation basic planning (capital circle planning for short) have carried out in Japan according to *Capital Area Reconditioning Act*. According to the relevant provisions of the Act, the capital circle planning divides the capital circle into several policy areas in a top-down way, specifically, including built-up area, suburban green space, urban development zone and suburban preparation zone. Different policies have been applied to manage in different areas: the build-up area focused on the restriction of industrial development. The scope of the urban development zone is defined by the Minister of Land, Infrastructure, Transport and Tourism of the central government, and under the guidance of the Capital Circle Reconditioning Committee. The urban planning and zoning shall be formulated by Tokyo Metropolitan. Suburban green space and land remediation zones pay more attention to the protection of green space, and the relevant system is formulated by the Ministry of Land, Infrastructure, Transport and Tourism, with the purpose to limit the excessive urban expansion. Generally speaking, the land zoning of the Metropolitan Area reflects the strategic intention of the comprehensive land development law to alleviate the excessive concentration of industry and population, hoping to promote urban construction step by step and in a planned way.

However, with the economic and social development of Tokyo Metropolitan in recent decades, including the change of social structure, the change of social mainstream value orientation and the diversification of values, the capital circle planning has gradually been unable to adapt to the reality of social and economic development of Tokyo Metropolitan after five versions in different periods. Therefore, the Japanese government has made corresponding adjustments to the land planning policy, and has issued a series of guiding documents, such as *Prospects of Land Planning in the 21st Century* jointly proposed by the Japanese Committee of National Land Resources and the Land Policy Review Council in 2000. The Japanese Committee of National Land Resources began to set up a Ministry of Investigation and Reform in 2003, and carried out a comprehensive land survey in 2004. The results show that the period of high-speed urbanization in Japan has basically ended, and the pressure of land development has been fully eased. At the same time, some new problems have emerged, such as the gradual decrease of absolute population in non-metropolitan areas, the aging population in the whole country, the intensification of inter-regional competition, and the financial tension. In response, Japan's Ministry of Land, Infrastructure and Transport began to carry out land planning reform. The national comprehensive development plan based on the *Comprehensive Land Development Act* was abolished, and the land formation planning system was re-formed. In the new environment of medium and low-speed economic development, the natural and social environmental pressure brought by industrial agglomeration is no longer a major problem. So it is no longer necessary to restrict the development of agglomeration, and the policy areas designated by Capital Circle must also be adjusted accordingly. The original division of built-up area, urban development zone and suburban servicing area is gradually abolished. The former top-down planning process of the capital circle, central region and Kinki, prefecture and local planning are gradually transformed into wide-area local planning (wide-area planning for short) which attaches importance to local autonomy and emphasizes the independent cooperation of local governments at all levels (See Fig. 4.9).

Based on the new concept of wide area planning, Tokyo Metropolitan Area has carried out practice in industrial development, living environment, transportation

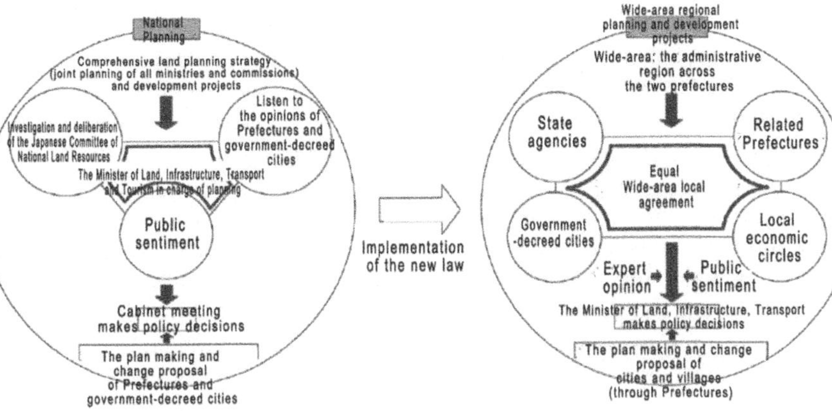

Fig. 4.9 Wide-area planning model of Tokyo Bay Area (*Source* You Ninglong et al. [2017])

system, environmental protection and other aspects. According to major issues such as public service, disaster prevention and mitigation, functional areas are divided and regional cooperation is carried out on this basis, instead of the original zoning control under the capital reconditioning area planning. The wide area planning of the capital area weakened the separation of administrative boundaries at all levels, and the units at any level of the state, prefectures, metropolitan circle, autonomous body and region can coordinate within the wide area circle. In order to strengthen the regional cooperation and enhance the administrative capacity under the wide-area planning system, the Japanese government has also implemented a matching "Wide-area Union" System. Specialized wide-area administrative service organs have been established to share the pressure of administrative affairs, and even to integrate the administrative affairs within the region, so that the wide-area planning presents more diversity and service functions. With strong practical operation, the wide-area union organization can put forward relevant requirements to administrative departments at all levels for tasks such as public service and disaster prevention and reduction, and each administrative department must respond to those requirements and reflect them in the wide area planning. The wide-area union organization can set up working organs in Prefecture and Municipality respectively. According to the actual needs of the region, it can draw up the regional planning within the wide area space, and realize the wide area administration through certain liaison and coordination mechanism. The work of the wide-area union organization is very flexible, which can not only focus on a specific public service, but also be responsible for a number of administrative affairs at the same time, so as to realize the regional governance of the wide area. For example, under the coordination of wide-area cooperation, the management of general waste in the charge of Municipality and the management of industrial waste in the charge of Prefecture can be effectively combined to jointly promote and improve the public service quality of garbage treatment in this district. Accordingly, the wide-area planning also provides the institutional basis for the involvement of the wide-area union organization in the specific public service work of its members. Under this kind of institutional arrangement, wide-area union organization has the right to advise its members on the relevant administrative affairs. In the case of garbage disposal mentioned above, the wide-area union makes specific provisions on the garbage disposal methods and garbage reduction countermeasures of the member units, and advises the members according to the requirements of the relevant planning. If the requirements are not met, the rectification suggestions can be put forward. Wide-area union organization can perform relevant functions and powers by accepting the entrustment of member units. The central government and the Prefecture can also entrust the wide-area union organization to perform the public service function by appointing the member units which are difficult to complete the relevant administrative tasks. Wide-area Union can be initiated through laws, decrees or regulations, and can directly handle the prescribed administrative affairs after the initiation. This innovative way of wide-area association and wide-area planning provides a new form and opportunity for the regional synergy development of the Tokyo Metropolitan Area.

4.3.3.2 Think Tanks

Think tanks play a vital role in the regional development and governance of Tokyo Metropolitan. To be specific, think tanks provide intellectual support for regional governance and act as a platform for social cooperation. The communication and coordination role of think tanks can be found in the planning of different levels and functional areas of the Tokyo Metropolitan. These think tanks have different backgrounds (some with deep official background, some typical private institutions), different sources of funds and different professional fields. Next, this section will make a brief introduction to the Capital Circle Port Joint Promotion Association and the Japan Development Conception Institute as typical examples.

The Capital Circle Bay Harbor Joint Promotion Association was established in 1976, and then the Tokyo Bay Harbor Joint Promotion Association was established in 1996. In 2002, it was renamed as the Capital Circle Port Joint Promotion Association. The association will be composed of the prefectural and municipal governments in charge of various harbors in Kanto, including Ibaraki-ken, Chiba-ken, Tokyo Metropolitan, Kanagawa-ken, Kawasaki, Yokohama, Yokosuka, and the Kanto Local Remediation Authority. The main functions of the Association include planning and coordinating the development, operation and maintenance of ports within Tokyo Metropolitan, developing and maintaining waterways, participating in important management matters of coastal areas near the waterways, studying the development of harbor areas within the metropolitan area, and participating in public relations activities related to the harbor area of Tokyo Metropolitan. Because of the close relationship between its operation and land use in Tokyo Metropolitan, the Association plays a very important coordinating role in the regional development and environmental governance of Tokyo Metropolitan.

Research Institute for Urban and Environmental Development (UED) in Japan is a research-oriented think tank under the Economic Planning Agency as the competent authority, and has close relations with the Cabinet Office and the Ministry of Land, Infrastructure and Transport. It is a consortium legal person. It focuses on the development of Tokyo Metropolitan and the investigation and consultation of regional higher education. It has participated in all aspects of work from land reconditioning to new city development in Tokyo Metropolitan, including redevelopment of old factories, development of new industries, distribution of recycling industries, logistics, passenger flow of freight lines, comprehensive environmental governance, disaster prevention and mitigation, etc.

UED has served Japan's central government and the local governments at all levels in Tokyo Metropolitan on land planning and industrial policy issues, and has won the trust of governments at all levels. As a result, it has gradually acquired a large amount of data from the central to the local level during its long-term service to them. These data not only reflect the national standards, but are also related to the development demands of Tokyo Metropolitan. It is involved in the vast majority of the relevant planning of Tokyo Metropolitan, and its vision is to guide the development of Tokyo Metropolitan with its own intellectual advantages, so that it can achieve its own interests, and at the same time consistent with the overall national deployment and related requirements, and mitigate and even eliminate the contradiction between local interest demands in the metropolitan area, and form a coherent set of Tokyo Metropolitan related planning scheme.

4.3.3.3 Public Transportation

Rail transit is the most important way to travel in Tokyo Metropolis. The Tokyo Metropolitan has the largest rail transit system with the highest utilization rate in the world, carrying a total passenger volume of 40 million passengers per day (in statistics, transfers in different rail transit operation systems are recorded as twice). The rail transit system in the Tokyo Metropolis has a total of 882 stations within the under its jurisdiction, 282 of which are metro stations, and hundreds more in the three outer prefectures. The whole rail transit network is operated by 32 operators, with a total of 121 passenger rail transit lines (102 of which serve Tokyo Metropolis, and more than 19 serve the metropolitan area outside of Tokyo).

Different from the mainstream practice in the metropolitan areas of developed countries in Europe and the United States, the Tokyo Metropolan has not carried out too much public ownership of rail transit in the region. Many rail transit lines in Tokyo Metropolitan are operated by private operators. Table 4.8 summarizes the basic situation of rail transit operators in Tokyo Metropolitan. Although the mixed operation mode of public, private and third-party companies has aggravated the fragmentation of rail transit lines, increased the difficulty of ticket management, and also raised some passenger traffic cost (the ticket price is usually calculated according to the one-way mileage, with the increase of total mileage, the fare per unit distance decreased gradually, but the mileage cannot be accumulated if the

Table 4.8 Basic information of rail transit operators in Tokyo Bay Area

Operators	Properties	Number of operating lines
East Japan Railway Company	Private	23
Keihin Kyukou Dentetsu	Private	5
Keio Corporation	Private	6
Keisei Skyliner	Private	7
Odakyu Electric	Private	3
SEIBU Railway	Private	13
TOBU Railway	Private	12
Tokyu Corporation	Private	8
Metropolitan Intercity Railway	Quasi-public	1
Tama Toshi Monorail sen	Quasi-public	1
TOKYO MONORAIL	Public	1
Tokyo Waterfront Area Rapid Transit, Inc	Quasi-public	2
yurikamome	Quasi-public	1
Tokyo Metro	Private	9
Tokyo Bay Area Government Bureau of Transportation	Public	4
Transportation Bureau, City of Yokohama	Public	2
Tōyō Rapid Railway	Quasi-public	1
Saitama Railway	Quasi-public	1
Chiba-monorail	Quasi-public	1
Maihama Resort Line Co., Ltd	Private	1
Enoshima Electric Railway	Private	1
hokuso-railway	Quasi-public	1
Sagami Railway	Private	3
NEW SHUTTLE	Quasi-public	1
Yokohama Shiisaido Rain	Public-to-be	1
Shibayama Railway	Public-to-be	1
Shin-Keisei Electric Railway	Private	1
shonan-monorail	Private	1
Nagareyama railway	Private	1
yamaman	Private	1
Yokohama Minatomirai Railway	Public-to-be	2

Source Sorted by the author

passenger changes to the line of different operators). However, it has improved the flexibility and profitability of rail transit operation, making the financial situation of rail transit operation in Tokyo Metropolis better than other major metropolitan areas in the world.

4.3.4 Summary and Referential Significance of the Governance of Tokyo Metropolitan

Different from the San Francisco Bay Area and New York Metropolitan Region in the United States, the special status of Tokyo Metropolitan Area makes its regional governance strongly supported by Japan's central government and parliament, and even guaranteed by the Japan's parliament in the form of special legislation. The central government of Japan and the local governments of Tokyo, Kanagawa-ken, Chiba-ken and Saitama-ken established the basic framework blueprint for the coordinated development of Tokyo Metropolis through the statutory wide-area planning system. Although the coordinating role of wide-area union organization in the regional governance of Tokyo Metropolis is guaranteed by legal system, the platform carriers for realizing regional cooperation are all kinds of non-governmental think-tanks. In addition, it is worth noting that for the construction and operation of regional transportation infrastructure, Japan has not followed the mainstream of regional governance in western metropolitan areas, but has carried out continuous privatization of major rail transit lines, and has maintained high efficiency after privatization. In general, contrary to the model of "consultative planning + special government grant/government-funded regional infrastructure operation and construction" in the two metropolitan areas of the United States, the Tokyo Bay Area has formed a model of "government-led planning + private capital investment and operation of infrastructure".

4.4 Research on Regional Synergy Development in China

Over the past 40 years of reform and opening up, China's economy has developed rapidly. Reform and opening up to a large extent liberated China's social productive forces, thus greatly changed China's urban and rural areas, and improved people's lives and livelihoods. In this sense, urban development is the embodiment of China's achievements in reform and opening up. The most direct reflection of urban development is the increase of urbanization rate. From 1978 to 2017, China's urbanization rate has increased from 17.9% to 58.5%,as shown in Fig. 4.10. Driven by urbanization, large cities and mega cities emerged in China, among which Beijing, Shanghai, Guangzhou and Shenzhen rank among the most developed cities. China's urbanization is both a trend and a positive policy. Rural residents migrate to big cities

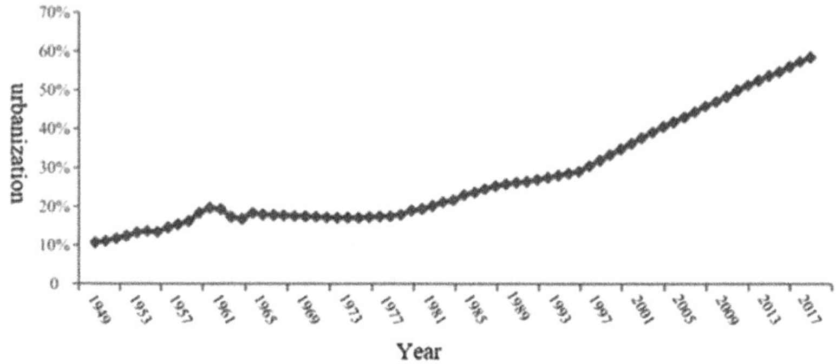

Fig. 4.10 China's urbanization development (*Source* State Statistical Bureau of China)

in search of higher-paying jobs. Urbanization has generated huge economic output through land mobilization, market opening, real estate development and infrastructure investment. However, the single urbanization model of urban–rural mobility not only increased the social gap between urban and rural areas, but also causes a heavy burden on the urban environment.

In 2006, the *11th Five-Year Plan for National Economic and Social Development* first proposed to "*take urban agglomeration as the main form for promoting urbanization*". Since then, based on the propulsion of urbanization, the trend of urban agglomeration expansion has become increasingly prominent in China. Currently, regional economy plays an increasingly important role in China's economic development, represented by the Yangtze River Delta Urban Agglomeration, Guangdong-Hong Kong-Macao Greater Bay Area and Beijing-Tianjin-Hebei Urban Agglomeration. The 2018*Urban Development Report of China*[2] points out that, besides Hong Kong, Macao and Taiwan, there are 34 central city metropolitan areas in China, accounting for 24% of the total area, 59% of the total population and 77.8% of the GDP. According to the different development degrees, the *Report* divides these metropolitan areas into three levels: mature, developing and nurturing. Among them, the seven metropolitan areas within the Yangtze River Delta and Pearl River Delta are the most developed areas, and have formed continuous and overlapping urban areas.

In China, as in many other economies, not only has the number, size and population of cities increased, but population and economic activity have also been concentrated in urban agglomerations. In addition to the three super large economic urban agglomerations of Pearl River Delta, Yangtze River Delta and Beijing-Tianjin-Hebei, China has completed the construction of 19 urban agglomerations. The economic development of the 19 urban agglomerations in China's *13thFive-Year Plan* (2016–2020) accounts for more than 90% of the national GDP.[3] As the most innovative

[2] *Urban Development Report of China in 2018*, Institute for China Sustainable Urbanization, Tsinghua University.

[3] Source: *Ranking of China's Urban Agglomeration Development Potential 2019.*

and internationally competitive clusters, the Pearl River Delta, Yangtze River Delta and Beijing-Tianjin-Hebei are expected to develop into world-class urban clusters in 2020, thus driving the national economic development.

The Chinese government plans to connect 19 urban agglomerations along "two horizontals and three verticals" corridors. "Two horizontals" refers to the Land-bridge Corridor and the Yangtze Corridor in the north of China, while "three verticals" refers to the Coastal Corridor, the Harbin-Beijing-Guangzhou Railway Corridor and the Baotou-Kunming Railway Corridor. To expand the international influence of China and its clusters, one of the horizontal corridors and one of the vertical corridors will be linked to BRI. The Yangtze Corridor will be partly connected to the land "economic belt", while the Coastal Corridor will be partly connected to the sea "road". China's main goal is to improve the distribution and layout of cities and population, as well as the management of natural and economic resources, by organizing the development of urban agglomerations in east–west and north–south corridors. The plan requires appropriate industrial division, coordination of planning and infrastructure, ecological protection and environmental improvement, to achieve integration and efficient development within urban agglomerations.

The strengthening of coordination across local administrative boundaries within the cluster region will bring a series of social, economic and sustainable benefits, including the increase of productivity and domestic consumption brought by the expansion of agglomeration economy. Since 2016, the central government has developed plans for each cluster in the 19 urban agglomerations in the *13th Five-Year Plan* to promote internal connectivity and governance coordination. The goal of this integration is to integrate economic clusters, labor markets and infrastructure, as well as to protect green open space, farmland and natural resources.

The development of urban agglomerations is the pillar of regional economic growth. When industrialization and urbanization develop to maturity, they will evolve into urban agglomerations. Through the inter-regional coordination mechanism of urban agglomeration, key cities in which can exert their own radiation effect, drive the development of surrounding cities, and thus drive the economic benefits of the whole urban agglomeration per unit area. The development imbalance between cities seriously affects the overall progress of regions. Regional coordination within urban agglomeration can effectively solve this dilemma. The rational allocation of regional elements and the rational flow of resources in urban agglomerations can realize the reasonable industrial layout of urban agglomerations, optimize the use of urban resource endowment from the perspective of comparative advantage, which is conducive to the overall promotion of regional competitiveness and the coordinated development of regional economy. It can be said that when we seize the city clusters, we have grasped the root of China's economy. At present, China's development has been transformed from high speed to high quality, which depends on the coordinated development of urban agglomeration. Moreover, with the increasing downward pressure on China's economy and the uncertainty of the external environment, urban agglomeration is also the key to stabilizing employment, foreign trade, investment, finance, foreign investment and expectations.

In order to achieve regional synergy development, it is usually necessary to make a lot of infrastructure investment in urban clusters and even at the national level, while coordinating the development of other policy areas. Interconnected infrastructure and transportation are crucial because the effective size of the labor market is defined by the average number of jobs available to each worker who commutes less than an hour. Cluster integration with more developed hubs and less developed peripheral cities can help China implement the policy of supply-side reform and high-quality growth. Through the coordinated development of urban clusters, resources will be redistributed from big cities to small cities. This will enable smaller cities in the early stage of industrialization to move up the value chain away from heavy polluting industries, while larger cities can further move up the value chain by focusing on innovation and *Made in China 2025* industries. Due to the size of clusters, each cluster will require effective coordination involving different levels of government.

Specifically, the synergy development of China's urban agglomerations mainly includes industrial labor division, transportation interconnection, scientific and technological innovation coordination and top-level governance coordination.

First, division of labor and cooperation of industries. Most of China's urban agglomerations are built around the largest hubs (such as Beijing, Shanghai, Guangzhou and Shenzhen), but the operation of urban agglomerations still depends on a large number of satellite cities. And those lower cities and towns will eventually become the core engine of the future development of urban agglomerations, with the greatest growth potential. Based on the industrial status and resource endowment of each city, different cities should have orderly division of labor and dislocation development, so as to build a reasonable industrial chain of urban agglomeration, realize the reasonable distribution of resources and the reasonable flow of elements, and help the coordinated development of the whole urban agglomeration.

Second, transportation interconnection. To some extent, the transportation infrastructure determines the urbanization process and the degree of interconnection between urban agglomerations. Therefore, different stages of traffic maturity and different traffic network design lead to a variety of urban morphology, spatial structure and intensity of urban agglomeration connection. Although there are various connectivity among cities, the connectivity should be based on their economic functions and their own characteristics. The flow of talents is the basis of the flow of various factors. The convenience of the flow of talents should be considered while ensuring the interconnection and convenience of urban economic functions, so as to do a good job in the basic work of transportation development.

Third, innovation and synergy as the driving force. Urban development in urban agglomerations varies from one city to another. In order to make full use of the advantages of more scientific research achievements and faster innovation and development in some cities, scientific innovation collaboration should be carried out among urban agglomerations, and resources should be reasonably allocated and introduced. The establishment of technology park, the establishment of strategic emerging industry development platform and other ways can achieve innovation, so as to achieve the optimization of resource utilization among cities.

Finally, governance collaboration. The governance coordination of urban agglomerations is to effectively solve the fragmentation problem faced by the each city. Within the urban agglomeration area, there are many administrative entities, each of which has independent authority in various policy areas, including tax and budget system, land-use planning, transportation infrastructure and traffic management, industrial park development, open space planning and environmental protection, and even the labor market. Cross-jurisdictional coordination has begun, but institutionalized coordination is still in its early stages.

The synergy development of Beijing-Tianjin-Hebei and Yangtze River Delta urban agglomerations are studied in this section in order to understand the current situation and future trends of the coordinated development of the two mega city agglomerations in China and provide enlightening advice for the development of GBA.

4.4.1 Synergy Development of Beijing-Tianjin-Hebei Urban Agglomeration

4.4.1.1 An Overview

Beijing-Tianjin-Hebei Urban Agglomeration is the largest urbanization cluster in northern China, including Beijing, Tianjin and 11 cities in Hebei Province. The entire area covers more than 200,000 km^2, more than twice the area of South Korea. Beijing-Tianjin-Hebei Urban Agglomeration has its own advantages in specific fields. Beijing is the center of politics, education, culture and R&D. Tianjin is known as the logistics center of north China due to its port and other advantages, owning one of the busiest ports in the world. Hebei Province is famous for its heavy industry and plays an important role in steel production. However, if each city is static and only focuses on its current advantages, the development of the Beijing-Tianjin-Hebei Urban Agglomeration will not make a qualitative leap. The coordinated development of Beijing Tianjin Hebei Urban Agglomeration will require the regional resources (including industries with excess capacity) to be rebalanced more optimally, while the whole Beijing-Tianjin-Hebei region needs to become more active by using and adjusting its existing advantages, which is more important for the next stage of China's economic development, the upstream development of the value chain.

President Xi Jinping called for a coordinated development of Beijing and the two neighboring regions at a forum on February 26, 2014. On April 30, 2015, the *Integrated Development Plan of Beijing, Tianjin and Hebei* was approved, making it clear that the region will build a world-class city cluster with the capital as the core. The three local governments have been cooperating in environmental protection, including afforestation and air pollution abatement. The Strategy in Coordinated Development of the Beijing-Tianjin-Hebei Region, an important part of China's national strategy, has yielded tangible results since its implementation and helped the government redistribute the resources and industries of Beijing to nearby areas, so as to achieve better growth. At present, the total GDP of Beijing-Tianjin-Hebei accounts for about 10% of China's GDP, with a population of more than 100 million, accounting for 8% of China's population, which is three times the population of the Tokyo Bay Area.

The Beijing-Tianjin-Hebei region is also facing a series of challenges. Conceptually, an urban agglomeration is an urban combination that brings together many small and medium-sized satellite cities and is led by the core city. However, a supercity cluster requires not only the core city to have strong economic strength, but also the satellite city to have economic strength, in order to effectively share and support the economic activities of the whole cluster. Among the Beijing-Tianjin-Hebei Urban Agglomeration, except that Beijing is far ahead and Tianjin is well developed, the urban development of Hebei province is relatively backward, showing a large development gap within the region. For the development of Beijing-Tianjin-Hebei Urban Agglomeration, the focal point is Beijing, the key point is Hebei, and the difficult point is the coordination of the three regions. In the Beijing-Tianjin-Hebei Urban Agglomeration, Beijing and Tianjin are by far the most important cities, while other cities are not as well-known or economically important in China. Beijing's per capita GDP reached 106,000 yuan in 2015, while the per capita income of Shijiazhuang, capital of Hebei province, was only 50,800 yuan.[4] Such a huge gap means that before the whole Beijing-Tianjin-Hebei region can develop harmoniously, local governments must spend time and money to bridge the gap between the surrounding cities. In addition, Beijing must coordinate with Hebei and Tianjin to better share knowledge and information and to take advantage of each other's comparative advantages (such as banking system, ports and relatively cheap labor costs) so that target industries can be more effectively distributed.

4.4.1.2 Spatial Synergy

Since the implementation of the *Strategy in Coordinated Development of the Beijing-Tianjin-Hebei Region*, transportation integration, as the key area of the first breakthrough, has achieved remarkable results. Infrastructure plays a key role in the physical connectivity of each urban agglomeration, with shipping ports and international airports being the most important. The "one-hour traffic circle" of Beijing-Tianjin-Hebei has changed the integration of the three places from space integration to time integration. It also makes the people of the three places feel that this development strategy is been realized from blueprint. The improvement of the transportation network is not only a manifestation of the diversification of transportation modes, but also an important link in the process of urban planning and construction and regional synergy development, with the continuous improvement of the integration degree of transportation among the three places.

In November 2016, the National Development and Reform Commission released a plan to build an intercity rail network in the Beijing-Tianjin-Hebei region, aiming

---

[4] Source: *China Statistical Yearbook* (2016).

to cut train travel time between nearby small towns and satellite cities and the capital to less than one hour. The extension of Tianjin-Baoding railway and Beijing-Tianjin railway has been completed. It takes only 1 h from Tianjin to Baoding and from Beijing to Tianjin Binhai New Area, instead of the previous 3 h. On December 28, 2017, Shijiazhuang Jinan high-speed railway was put into operation. Echoing the Tianjin-Baoding railway from north to south, and with the Beijing-Shanghai and Beijing-Guangzhou high-speed railway lines as the skeleton, the high-speed railway network will be connected in the Beijing-Tianjin-Hebei region in the shape of Chinese character "井" and arranged in stages, and The Beijing-Tianjin-Hebei rectangular high-speed railway ring network will be formed with Beijing, Tianjin, Shijiazhuang and Dezhou as the base points. More convenient transportation has brought Beijing, Tianjin and Hebei closer, laying the foundation for the development of regional integration.

After initiation of the Beijing-Tianjin-Hebei coordinated development strategy, more than 800 roads and expressways within the urban agglomeration have been upgraded. Major railway projects, such as the expansion of the intercity railway between Beijing and Tianjin, the extension of the railway between Tianjin and Baoding, and the connection between Zhangjiakou and Tangshan in Hebei Province, have been completed. By 2018, more than 40 trans provincial bus lines with a total length of 2800 km[5] have been operated between Beijing and 17 neighboring regions or cities in Hebei Province. The high-speed railway connecting Beijing and Zhangjiakou in Hebei Province has been put into operation, and the expressway between Yanqing District of Beijing and Chongli of Zhangjiakou will also be in operation, which are the two main venues for the 2022 Winter Olympic Games. The Tianjin municipal government also announced that the construction of high-speed rail connecting Tianjin and Beijing Daxing District new airport will also be accelerated.

To reduce train travel times, nine new intercity lines (with a total length of 1100 km) will be built by 2020, which the National Development and Reform Commission says will require a total investment of 247 billion yuan.[6] By 2020, there will be 9500 km of railways and 9000 km of expressways in the Beijing-Tianjin-Hebei Urban Agglomeration, which means that the train travel time between any major cities in the region will be less than 1 h and the driving time will be less than 3 h. In addition, 16 intercity railway lines will be added by 2050.[7]

Important progress has also been made in aviation links in the Beijing-Tianjin-Hebei region. Beijing Daxing International Airport, located at the junction of Daxing District of Beijing and Langfang in Hebei province, has begun operation. It will become an aviation tourism hub in northern China and help improve airport resource utilization efficiency in Tianjin and Shijiazhuang, capital of Hebei province. The completion of the new airport will help promote the development of four strategic

---

[5] Source: *Beijing-Tianjin-Hebei Blue Paper: Report on the Development of Beijing-Tianjin-Hebei (2019).*

[6] Source: National Development and Reform Commission of the PRC http://www.ndrc.gov.cn/.

[7] Source: National Development and Reform Commission of the PRC http://www.ndrc.gov.cn/.

areas, namely Beijing New Airport Economic Zone, Hebei Caofeidian Comprehensive Development Zone, Tianjin Binhai New District Airport Industrial Zone and Hebei Zhangjiakou-Chengde Ecological Zone. Tangshan Airport in Hebei province has been expanded and Cangzhou airport in Hebei province has been put into use. Beijing-Tianjin-Hebei Urban Agglomeration will establish a strong and coordinated air transportation system.

In addition, the governments of Beijing, Tianjin and Hebei have launched the *Beijing-Tianjin-Hebei Connectivity Card* to facilitate internal travel in the urban agglomeration. By the end of 2017, a total of 720,000 Beijing-Tianjin-Hebei traffic "One-Card" were issued in Hebei Province. More than 800 urban bus lines have been set in 11 districts and cities of Hebei province, and about 13,500 city buses and Shijiazhuang subway have been upgraded, basically realizing the "One-Card" Connectivity with Beijing, Tianjin and Hebei.

4.4.1.3 Industrial Synergy

Relying on the coordinated development of Beijing-Tianjin-Hebei Region, Tianjin undertakes high-end industries transferred from Beijing and distributes homogeneous industries to Hebei. The Beijing-Tianjin-Hebei region has traditionally been engaged in heavy industry and manufacturing. Tianjin's strength has been in aviation, logistics and shipping. Beijing complements this economic activity with strong petrochemical, education and R&D industries. Rich in agricultural and mineral resources and with a strong traditional industrial base, Hebei is the province with the largest output of steel and cement. However, overcapacity in heavy industry in Hebei has caused severe environmental pollution, and the manufacturing industry has become homogeneous as that in Tianjin.

Orderly industrial transfer has been carried out in Beijing-Tianjin-Hebei Urban Agglomeration. According to the *Outline of the Coordinated Development Plan for The Beijing-Tianjin-Hebei Region* released in April 2015, the core of the coordinated development of the Beijing-Tianjin-Hebei region is the orderly relocation of Beijing's non-capital functions, and Beijing will give priority to key functions of politics, culture, international exchanges and technological innovation, while other departments will be moved out of Beijing. An important task of the Beijing-Tianjin-Hebei strategy is to remove non-essential functions from Beijing to ease urban problems such as traffic congestion and pollution in the capital. At the same time, the orderly industrial decentralization can also drive the economy of Tianjin and Hebei to embark on a new stage of development.

Due to the gap of industrial layout, innovation ability and natural resources among the three regions, the income gap between Beijing and Hebei has been very large, and the orderly decentralization of industries can inject new endogenous power into Hebei Province, and promote its industrial upgrading and development. High-value-added and energy-efficient manufacturing of Beijing moving to Hebei could help Hebei optimize its industrial structure. Beijing's manufacturing industries, such as mobile phones and cars, are relatively light and advanced. Therefore, the vitality of

Beijing's manufacturing industry can radiate to Hebei and transfer more employment opportunities to the province. Beijing will become "the center of national political, cultural and international exchange activities" and the center of technological innovation. Tianjin will become a national R&D base for advanced manufacturing, a shipping hub in north China, a demonstration area for financial innovation and a pilot area for further reform and opening up. And Hebei province will become an important national trade and logistics base, a pilot zone for industrial transformation and upgrading, a demonstration zone for modern urbanization, a coordinated development zone for urban and rural areas, and an ecological buffer zone. In terms of industrial coordination, Beijing-Tianjin-Hebei Urban Agglomeration will move unnecessary functions out of Beijing, which will help to adjust the regional economic structure, cultivate new growth sectors, and solve the problems of large cities such as overpopulation, pollution and resource scarcity.

Speeding up industrial transfer is the key area to promote the coordinated development of Beijing, Tianjin and Hebei. On December 21, 2017, the Beijing-Tianjin-Hebei Cooperation Office issued the Suggestions on Strengthening the Construction of Key Platforms for Industrial Transfer and Undertaking in Beijing-Tianjin-Hebei Region, which made a major decision on the industrial coordinated deployment of Beijing-Tianjin-Hebei, and initially defined the distribution of important platforms of Beijing-Tianjin-Hebei industry (see Fig. 4.11). The release of Suggestions on the Construction of Key Platforms provides support for the realization of integrated and coordinated urban agglomeration development, defines the roles of different regions and encourages them to follow their own development models.

4.4.1.4 Synergy of Technology and Innovation

The depth of coordinated development of Beijing-Tianjin-Hebei Urban Agglomeration depends on the depth of various industries in science and technology. From the perspective of the development of Beijing-Tianjin-Hebei Urban Agglomeration, the high-tech industry in the region presents regional agglomeration development. However, due to the lack of collaborative innovation mechanism among cities, there is an obvious regional gap in the development level of scientific and technological innovation. Beijing has the largest number of science and technology innovation resources, and innovation elements are gathered, so the development of science and technology innovation industry is ahead of Tianjin and Hebei. In terms of technological innovation, there were 56,900 invention patents granted in the Beijing-Tianjin-Hebei region in 2017, of which 46,100 were granted in Beijing alone, accounting for 14.10% of the country, higher than other developed provinces and cities, with outstanding technological innovation output advantages. Since 2012, Tianjin's high-tech industry has achieved rapid development. However, Hebei's high-tech industry has been developing slowly, and the growth rate of its total output value lags behind that of Beijing and Tianjin. For a long time, the lack of national strategic landmark innovation platform in Hebei has been considered as an important factor that makes it difficult for Hebei to connect national resources, undertake innovation spillovers

15 Coordinated Development Platforms	3 Modern Agricultural Cooperation Platforms	20 Modern Manufacturing Platforms
Beijing and Tianjin Scientific Town	Zhuozhou National Agricultural high-tech Industrial Development Zone	Langfang Economic and Technological Development Zone
Future Science City in Beijing-tianjin Cooperation Demonstration Zone	Jingzhang Bashang Vegetable Production Base	Beijing Yizhuang Yongqing High-tech Industrial Development Zone
Wuqing National University Innovation Park	Jingcheng Agricultural Cooperative production base	Tianjin Economic-Technological Development Area
Jinan New Area		Tianjin Binhai New District Airport Industrial Zone
Xingdong New Area		Tianjin Huaming Donglihu District
Zhengding New District	**8 Service Industry Platforms**	Tianjin Beichen High-end Equipment Manufacturing Park
Baoding-Zhongguancun Innovation Center		Tianjin Haihe Education Park
Baiyangdian Science and Technology City	Baigou New Town of Baoding City	Bohai New Area
Beijing and Tianjin Zhongguancun Science and Technology City in Baodi	Langfang Yongqing Lingang Economic bonded trade park	Cangzhou Economic Development Zone
Caofeidian Circular Economy Demonstration Zone	Shijiazhuang Lesheng international Trade City	Tianjin Xiqing South Station Science and Technology Business District
Zhongguancun Haidian Garden Qinhuangdao Sub-park	Cangzhou Pearl Trade City	Baoding High-tech Industrial Development Zone
Beidaihe Life Health Industrial Innovation Area	Xianghe Wantong trade logistics City	Shijiazhuang High and New Technology Development Zone
Bazhou Economic Development Zone	Xingdong Production City Integration Demonstration Area	Shijiazhuang Economic and Technological Development Zone
Hengshui Binhu New District	Jinghai Tuanbo Health Industrial Park	Handan Economic and Technological Development Zone
Qinghe Economic Development Zone	Yanda International Health City	Xingtai Economic and Technological Development Zone
		Tangshan High-tech Industrial Development Zone
		Qinhuangdao Economic and Technological Development Zone
		Jing jin Zhou he Sci-Tech Industrial Park
		Gu'an Economic Development Zone
		Hengshui New Industrial Zone

Fig. 4.11 Key platforms for industrial transfer and undertaking in Beijing-Tianjin-Hebei Region (*Source*: *Suggestions on Strengthening the Construction of Key Platforms for Industrial Transfer and Undertaking in Beijing-Tianjin-Hebei Region* [December 21, 2017])

from Beijing and Tianjin, and promote regional flow of innovation elements. The main reason for this unbalanced development is that a well-functioning innovative and coordinated mechanism of Beijing-Tianjin-Hebei has not yet been established.

An inter-regional innovative and coordinated mechanism should be established to support Beijing-Tianjin-Hebei coordinated development of science and technology innovation due to the different resource endowments and industrial development stages among different cities. The coordinated development of Beijing-Tianjin-Hebei has become a national strategy, which gradually clarifies the regional functional positioning and industrial positioning, and promotes the coordinated development of high-tech industries in Beijing-Tianjin-Hebei region. In June 2016, the State Council approved the *Pilot Program for Promoting Comprehensive Innovation and Reform in Beijing, Tianjin and Hebei*, which stressed that the deep integration of industrial chain, policy chain, capital chain and innovation chain should be strengthened to enhance the level of coordinated innovation, and then create an innovation community. Since the implementation of the *Strategy for Coordinated Development of the Beijing-Tianjin-Hebei Region*, Beijing has continuously exported cutting-edge technologies to nearby cities. In 2016, Beijing's technology export value to Tianjin and Hebei was 15.4 billion yuan, up 38.7% year-on-year; the paid in investment of Beijing enterprises in Tianjin and Hebei increased by 26% and 100% respectively.[8] Hebei has introduced 4100 projects from Beijing and Tianjin, with a total investment of 382.5 billion yuan, according to the Beijing Municipal Commission of Development and Reform.

The Beijing-Tianjin-Hebei region will build a coordinated innovation community and a leading innovation highland in China. As one of the regions with the most intensive innovation resources and the most abundant scientific and technological innovation achievements in China, Beijing-Tianjin-Hebei are actively exploring a new mode of co- building science and technology parks, giving full play to Beijing's technical resources and professional resources of productive services, and forming Tianjin Binhai-Zhongguancun Science and Technology Park and Baoding-Zhongguancun Innovation Center. The two innovation centers, which combine Beijing's innovation achievements and resources with local manufacturing capabilities, bring the greatest benefits to both sides. Tianjin Binhai-Zhongguancun Science and Technology Park mainly undertakes the science and technology innovation and R&D transformation industries in Beijing, and jointly promotes the construction of a key demonstration area of new innovation and entrepreneurship ecosystem with Zhongguancun science and technology park. Baoding-Zhongguancun Innovation Center, with the help of Zhongguancun's advanced scientific and technological resources, creates a new engine for the development of emerging industries in Baoding.

4.4.1.5 Governance Synergy

The *Strategy for Coordinated Development of the Beijing-Tianjin-Hebei Region* will be implemented with top-level design as the guidance. In order to meet the challenge of governance fragmentation, it is crucial for the top-level design of urban agglomeration. This coordinated governance includes not only planning authority over connectivity infrastructure, but also financial management authority over revenue and budget to effectively implement and manage plans and manage infrastructure. As a national strategy, the coordinated development of the Beijing-Tianjin-Hebei requires corresponding cross regional governance structure and mechanism as an important guarantee for the implementation of the strategy. Since the coordinated development of the Beijing-Tianjin-Hebei region has risen to the national strategy in February 2014, the central government has successively issued the Outline of the Coordinated Development Plan for The Beijing-Tianjin-Hebei Region and the Plan for the national economic and social development of Beijing-Tianjin-Hebei during the *13th Five-Year Plan* period, giving the region a clear top-level design.

The internal structure of Beijing-Tianjin-Hebei Urban Agglomeration is complex. Beijing has a special political status as the capital, Tianjin has the status of a municipality directly under the central government, and the cities in Hebei have relatively weak discourse power–there is a wide gap in administrative status among the three.

---

[8] Source: Beijing Development and Reform Commission.

Although the function center is different from the administrative center that undertakes the responsibility of building a specific function center, the construction of the function center needs the participation of enterprises, finance, education, medical and other multiple institutions, social organizations and even individuals, forming a multi-center and multi-level governance mode based on the positioning of the function center under the national strategic planning. In the future, with the further promotion of Beijing-Tianjin-Hebei cooperation and the gradual implementation of the functional orientation of each region, the interdependence and coordinated development among the functional centers will gradually deepen into a symbiotic relationship, forming a virtuous cycle system in which each functional center supports and helps each other. The internal operation of the system will be smoother, and the upgrading from multi-center governance mode to symbiotic governance mode will be gradually realized.

China has a very strong national and municipal governance system, a strong infrastructure capacity and the ability to provide effective public services. The future development challenge of Beijing-Tianjin-Hebei Urban Agglomeration will be to create strong institutions to achieve similar good governance on the scale of urban clusters. From the perspective of governance, the coordinated development of The Beijing-Tianjin-Hebei region is a national strategy, and the strategic coordination at the national level is indispensable. This level is composed of the central government, relevant ministries and commissions, and the three local governments. Its core function is to formulate a national strategy for the coordinated development of the region. Therefore, based on the Chinese context, the government level is still the key subject of coordinated governance, and it is necessary to play the role of bridge and link between the above and the below, implement the national strategy upward, and coordinate social resources downward. The coordination at this level directly affects the level and level of the coordinated development of the whole region (see Fig. 4.12).

From the perspective of coordinated intensity, the priorities of coordinated governance of The Beijing-Tianjin-Hebei Urban Agglomeration include economic development, public services and environmental protection. Different dimensions of coordinated governance adopt different strategies and methods. From the perspective of the government as the key coordination subject, the economic field mainly relies on the regulation of the market mechanism, supplemented by the regulation of the administrative mechanism. Meanwhile, the coordination between the two mechanisms has a good foundation and conditions, so the required coordination intensity is relatively weak. At present, the environmental protection field mainly relies on administrative mechanism to promote coordinated governance, and the market mechanism is actively promoted as a supplementary. Moreover, how to effectively connect the two mechanisms needs to be further explored, so the coordinated intensity is relatively strong. And the scope of public services is relatively broad, and the coordinated intensity is between the former two. Therefore, effectively identifying different governance types and providing differentiated coordination according to governance categories can effectively facilitate the future development of The Beijing-Tianjin-Hebei urban agglomeration.

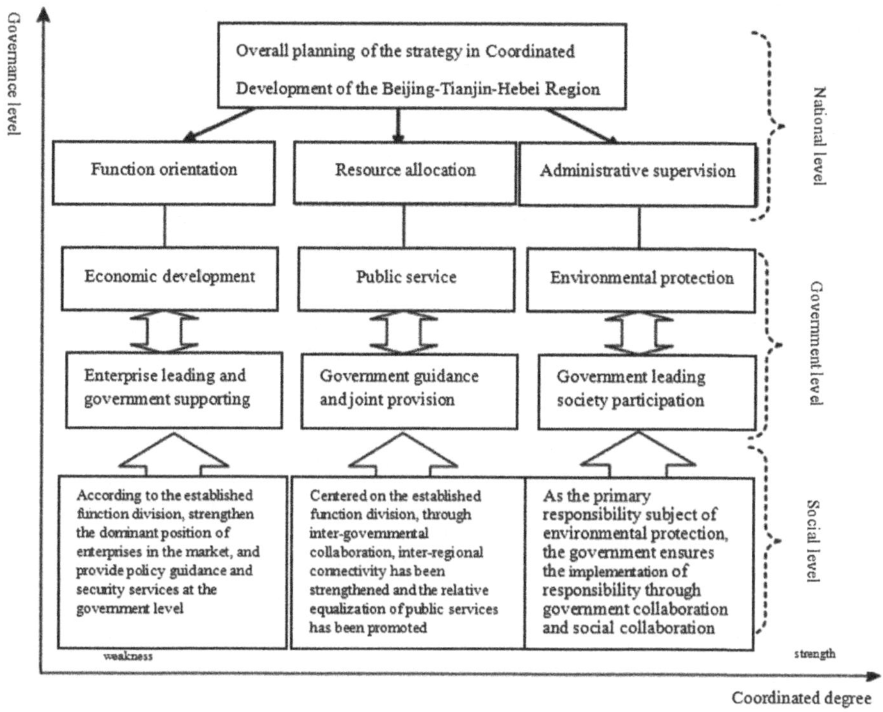

Fig. 4.12 Coordinated governance structure of Beijing-Tianjin-Hebei Region (*Source*: *On coordinated governance of the Beijing-Tianjin-Hebei Region: model selection, governance structure and social participation* (Wang Xin 2017)

4.4.2 Synergy Development of the Yangtze River Delta Urban Agglomeration

4.4.2.1 An Overview

The Yangtze River Delta Urban Agglomeration, with Shanghai as the center and Nanjing, Hangzhou and Hefei as the sub-centers, includes three provinces and one city, namely, the provinces of Jiangsu, Anhui and Zhejiang and the city of Shanghai. Hangzhou Bay Area and Wanjiang City Belt, as well as some parts of Wenzhou-Taizhou City Cluster and Zhejiang City Cluster are also in this region. It is one of the most dynamic regions in China, with the highest degree of opening up and the strongest innovation capacity. It is a powerful driving force of China's economy and an important window of China's national competitiveness. In May 2016, with the approval of the State Council of *Development Plan for the Yangtze River Delta Urban Agglomerations*, the Yangtze River Delta Urban Agglomeration was officially expanded, and Anhui Province joined the Yangtze River Delta Urban Agglomeration development plan. From the perspective of urban composition, Yangtze River

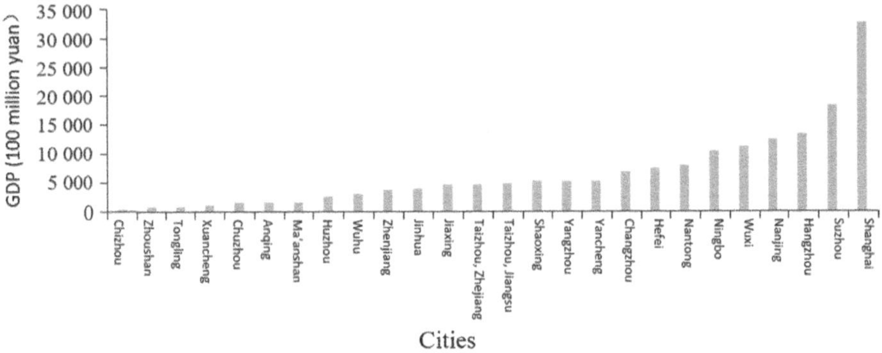

Fig. 4.13 GDP of cities in Yangtze River Delta Urban Agglomeration in 2018 (*Source* State Statistical Bureau of China)

Delta Urban Agglomeration contains Shanghai, the municipality directly under the Central Government, and 26 cities in the three provinces of Jiangsu, Zhejiang, Anhui, including 3 sub-provincial cities of Hangzhou, Nanjing and Ningbo, and 22 prefecture-level cities. In his speech at the opening ceremony of The 2nd China International Import Expo on November 5, 2018, President Xi said China would "*support the integrated development of the Yangtze River Delta region and turn it into a national strategy*".

The cities of the Yangtze River Delta are already highly industrialized, with advanced transportation infrastructure such as highways, high-speed railways, airports and ports. Shanghai dominates in finance, banking, real estate, automobiles and logistics. Suzhou is a strong manufacturing base for foreign companies. Nanjing is the hub of automobile industry, electronics, education, energy and steel industry. And Ningbo is a developing economic port that provides import and export routes to neighboring provincial capitals. At present, the Yangtze River Delta Urban Agglomeration is the largest urban agglomeration with the largest economic aggregate in China. In 2018, the GDP of the Yangtze River Delta urban agglomeration exceeded 21 trillion yuan, accounting for about 20% of the national GDP and more than twice that of the Beijing-Tianjin-Hebei Urban Agglomeration (the GDP of which in 2018 was about 8.5 trillion yuan). The Yangtze River Delta Urban Agglomeration accounts for 1/3 of China's total import and export, with a population of about 150 million, accounting for 11% of China's total population.[9] Although the comprehensive economic development of the Yangtze River Delta Urban Agglomeration is outstanding, there is a huge gap in the total urban economic volume. Shanghai ranks first with GDP of more than 3 trillion yuan, while Chizhou of Anhui Province has only 65.4 billion yuan, a difference of about 50 times (see Fig. 4.13). From the provincial perspective, Jiangsu has the best performance, with a relatively fast overall development and a small gap among cities, while Anhui

[9] Source: Official website of China's State Statistical Bureau.

has the weakest overall strength. Except for Hefei and Wuhu, other cities are in the backward position in the urban agglomeration.

4.4.2.2 Spatial Synergy

The transportation infrastructure of Yangtze River Delta Urban Agglomeration supports interconnection. The Yangtze River Delta Region enjoys good infrastructure conditions. Before China's reform and opening up, the railways of Shanghai-Nanjing, Shanghai-Hangzhou and Nanjing-Hangzhou were already the busiest. With the advent of reform and opening up, the Yangtze River Delta took the lead in the construction of interregional railways and expressways since the 1980s.Since then, the regional transportation network has developed by leaps and bounds. At present, the four administrative regions in Yangtze River Delta Urban Agglomeration have realized the traffic interconnection.

The Yangtze River Delta region takes the lead in realizing county-to-county high-speed access. It is estimated that by 2020, the mileage of expressways will reach 300,000 km, realizing a clear and convenient road network structure, which is conducive to promoting the industrial integration development of the Yangtze River Delta. The main structure of a new railway bridge over the Yangtze River in Wuhu city, Anhui province, has been completed, paving the way for the operation of high-speed trains to Shangqiu, Hefei and Hangzhou by 2020. The railway is designed to have a top speed of 350 km/h, which will further reduce travel time between Hefei and Hangzhou.

In addition to railways and expressways, the construction of bridges across the river and sea in the Yangtze River Delta has further enhanced the regional compactness. Among them, the construction of Su-Tong Yangtze River Highway Bridge and Hangzhou Bay Bridge has a great impact on the economic reconstruction of the Yangtze River Delta. Su-Tong Yangtze River Highway Bridge has broken the separation of the two sides of the Yangtze River, effectively connecting the high-speed railways along the Yangtze River and Yancheng-Nantong High-speed Railway on the north and south sides of the Yangtze River, opening up the passage for Shanghai to go northward, and playing the leading role of Shanghai in Northern Jiangsu. Hangzhou Bay Bridge shortens the distance between Shanghai and Ningbo, and improves the ability of southeast and Southwest Zhejiang to accept the radiation from Shanghai. The two bridges make the transportation between north and south of the Yangtze River Delta more convenient.

The transportation network integrating land, sea and air is improving day by day. Shanghai has built four major shipping service clusters, namely Lujiazui, Waigaoqiao, Yangshan port and airport area. The integrated development of Zhoushan Port in Ningbo, Zhejiang province promotes the construction of a new pattern of port development in the Yangtze River Delta region. At present, there are five airports in the region, including Shanghai Pudong International Airport, Shanghai Hongqiao International Airport, Hangzhou International Airport, Nanjing Lukou International Airport and Nantong Xingdong International Airport. The high-speed railway and urban rail transit between the airports rapidly connect several airports, forming a closely connected Yangtze River Delta airport cluster.

Although the construction density of major transportation infrastructure units in the Yangtze River Delta Urban Agglomeration is higher than the national average,[10] there is a significant gap in the construction density of transportation infrastructure units in provinces and cities of Yangtze River Delta. Most indicators of Shanghai are far ahead, while Anhui Province is relatively backward, and the imbalance of regional infrastructure construction is more obvious, which is also an important consideration in the process of regional integration in the future.

4.4.2.3 Industrial Synergy

Industrial dislocation between cities in the Yangtze River Delta region is providing impetus for regional synergy development. Three provinces and one city in Yangtze River Delta have different resource advantages in industry. Since the beginning of the twenty-first century, the Yangtze River Delta region has gradually broken the barrier of market segmentation on factor flow, and gradually established an industrial system with Shanghai as the leader, orderly and gradient internal structure, and effective complementary cooperation within the region. As a financial center, Shanghai has many financial institutions, such as banks, securities and insurance companies, together with active investors. Jiangsu has a solid foundation of manufacturing industry. Zhejiang Province has an active private economy. Anhui Province has rich land and human resources. Similar to the Tokyo Bay area, the Yangtze River Delta region presents a pattern of prominent core and multi center development.

As the leader of the Yangtze River Delta region, Shanghai has been playing a leading role in economic development and radiating the surrounding areas. The opening up of Pudong in the 1990s improved the opening-up level of the entire Yangtze River Delta region. Other cities in the region took the initiative to connect with Shanghai, actively positioned urban functions, relied on the power of the market, and actively participated in the industrial cooperation of the Yangtze River Delta, gradually forming several regional central cities such as Hangzhou, Nanjing, Suzhou and Ningbo, etc. With the establishment of the Shanghai Pilot Free Trade Zone in 2013, Shanghai has continued to deepen reform and opening-up, standing at the forefront of further opening-up, and providing guidance for other regions in the Yangtze River Delta to deepen reform and opening-up. Since the reform and opening up, Jiangsu has actively docked with Shanghai, making full use of Shanghai's radiation capacity and realizing the effective allocation of resources. In the 1980s, Suzhou and Shanghai established a talent sharing mechanism, and *the Sunday Engineer Program* has successfully enabled technical talents to be shared between Shanghai and Suzhou. Since 2000, Suzhou has taken the initiative to connect with Shanghai's capital and

[10] Source: *Urban agglomeration leading the second half of infrastructure construction, Yangtze River Delta integration enjoying more advantages*. Report from Guotai Junan Securities.

market, give full play to the advantages of industry and technology intensive, undertake the transfer of Shanghai's technology, industry, talent and mode, and form a high-level coordinated development with Shanghai. Hangzhou is a famous city of the Internet and culture and innovation. Hangzhou has seized the opportunity of the Internet and "Made in China 2025", based on the frontier of science and technology and market, and formed an economic system driven by the Internet. By the end of 2018, Hangzhou's per capita GDP has exceeded 20,000 US dollars. Hangzhou has taken the initiative to connect with Shanghais capital and market, and promoted the rapid development of the Internet industry.

4.4.2.4 Synergy of Technology and Innovation

Cities in the Yangtze River Delta Urban Agglomeration promote the sharing of scientific and technological resources and jointly build a scientific and technological innovation platform. The region is coordinating the industrial layout to establish world-class industrial clusters in the fields of integrated circuits, artificial intelligence, biomedicine, high-end equipment, new materials and new energy vehicles, and seeks to use innovation communities to achieve breakthrough technologies in several key areas. Shanghai, Jiangsu, Zhejiang and Anhui, which have never been so closely linked as they are today, are working together to develop the region into a strong and powerful pole of growth and a world-class urban agglomeration with global competitiveness. From small chips to large aircraft, from cloud computing to the Internet of things, these four places are jointly promoting the further integration of the industrial chain.

G60 Science and Innovation Corridor promotes the coordinated development of human resources, technology, capital, equipment, facilities, projects and policies in the core cities of the Yangtze River Delta. As one of the most active economic zones in China, G60 Science and Innovation Corridor includes nine cities—Shanghai, Jiaxing, Hangzhou, Jinhua, Suzhou, Huzhou, Xuancheng, Wuhu and Hefei, covering an area of 76,200 km^2. On May 24, 2016, Songjiang District of Shanghai took the lead in proposing to build a science and innovation corridor combining industry and city along the G60 High-speed Railway, to drive the development of the whole region towards "Songjiang Creation".

The G60 Science and Innovation Corridor has entered its 1.0 era. On July 12, 2017, Songjiang, Shanghai, Hangzhou and Jiaxing, Zhejiang signed the *Strategic Cooperation Agreement on the Construction of Shanghai-Jiaxing-Hangzhou G60 Science and Innovation Corridor*, marking the beginning of the 2.0 era of the Corridor. The three regions will conduct in-depth cooperation in scientific innovation and industrial upgrading. Currently, the G60 Science and Innovation Corridor is an alliance of nine major cities in the Yangtze River Delta, which is committed to promoting infrastructure construction and creating a better business environment. After taking the first step to connect the Yangtze River Delta, the Corridor signed agreements with Jinhua, Suzhou, Huzhou, Xuancheng, Wuhu and Hefei in June 2018, once again expanding its reaches. Named after the G60 High-speed Railway running through Shanghai and its three neighboring provinces, the G60 Science and Innovation Corridor aims to break down regional barriers between provinces and promote strong entrepreneurship in scientific innovation. Together, these cities will provide faster approval procedures and more friendly services for enterprises in the Corridor, aiming to break the market access barriers that have plagued scientific innovation in the Yangtze River Delta for a long time. So far, the corridor has achieved remarkable results. In the future, the corridor will continue to serve as a hub for leading and connecting scientific innovation in the Yangtze River Delta, with a focus on supply-chain structural reform.

In order to promote the free flow of innovation resources within the region, the Yangtze River Delta has established an innovation platform for the Yangtze River Delta Science and Technology Innovation Circle to promote cross-regional scientific and technological cooperation. Scientific and technological resources represented by scientific research equipment and scientific information are indispensable conditions for the development of scientific and technological innovation. The scientific research institutions in the Yangtze River Delta are rich in resources. The annual budget of the universities and research institutes in this region is more than 10 billion yuan, most of which is used to purchase experimental equipment. The coordinated development of science and innovation has given new impetus to the regional integration of the Yangtze River Delta. A major achievement is to give full play to the function of "the Yangtze River Delta large instrument network" and promote the resource integration of large scientific instruments. By the end of 2018, more than 450,000 large instruments have been integrated to achieve efficient utilization of large instruments in the Yangtze River Delta. In early July 2019, representatives from three provinces and one city jointly launched A Proposal to Build an Innovation Platform for Yangtze River Delta Science and Technology Innovation Circle, which will further promote the free flow of scientific and technological resources. The national strategy of Yangtze River Delta integration has entered a new starting point of practice.

Based on the advantages of the gathering of high-tech enterprises, scientific research institutions and talents, and based on the positioning of Shanghai and Hefei as two comprehensive national science centers, the three provinces and one city of the Yangtze River Delta will jointly promote the construction of the center, give full play to their respective advantages, build the Yangtze River Delta science and technology innovation circle, jointly make breakthroughs of a series of "strangle hold" technologies, promote data sharing, and build the Yangtze River Delta big data trading platform. On the basis of large instrument cooperation, a perfect science and technology resource sharing platform will be formed to provide innovation and entrepreneurship services such as technology transformation and trading, and promote the implementation of industry university research in the region.

4.4.2.5 Governance Synergy

The multi-directional cooperation mechanism among cities in the Yangtze River Delta ensures regional synergy. Today, Shanghai, Jiangsu, Zhejiang and Anhui are working together on a common blueprint, rather than one foe each. The Yangtze River Delta has entered a new era of active docking and deep interaction among provinces and cities in the region. Shanghai is the core city of Yangtze River Delta, seeking to "actively go out". The surrounding regional key cities such as Jiaxing and Nantong actively dock with Shanghai for innovation practice of regional synergy to generate compound innovation power. A new model of regional synergy in the Yangtze River Delta is formed by the planning leading power of national major development strategy, the consensus and collaborative power of multi-level, multi-field and multi-theme in the Yangtze River Delta, and the initiative of Shanghai, the core city of the Yangtze River Delta, as the interactive power for the active docking with the peripheral cities.

Since the late 1990s, cooperation mechanisms at multiple levels have been gradually established in the Yangtze River Delta, including the Joint Meeting System of Provinces and Mayors, the System of Symposium on Economic Cooperation and Development of Jiangsu-Zhejiang-Shanghai, and the Joint Meeting of Co-organizations (Committee) of Yangtze River Delta. With the further development of the Yangtze River Delta cooperation, Anhui Province has gradually joined the development of the Yangtze River Delta region, which has changed from two provinces and one city to three provinces and one city. On December 3, 2015, officials of the three provinces and one city held a forum and reached an agreement on further promoting the integration of the Yangtze River Delta.

The central planning and positioning of the Yangtze River Delta is the main driving force for the integrated development of the Yangtze River Delta. In 2010, the National Development and Reform Commission issued the *Development Plan for the Yangtze River Delta Urban Agglomerations*, aiming to break the pattern of homogenized development and vicious competition among urban agglomerates. In 2015, the *Development Plan of the Yangtze River Delta Urban Agglomerations* adopted by the State Council put Anhui Province into the scope of Yangtze River Delta integration development, and promoted the establishment of cross regional linkage cooperation mechanism. In November 2018, the comprehensive development of the Yangtze River Delta was upgraded to be a national strategy. In January 2019, the Shanghai, Jiangsu, Zhejiang and Anhui signed the *Memorandum of Cooperation on the Integration of Yangtze River Delta Marketing System and the Market Rules, Credit Governance and Market Supervision*. In March 2019, Shanghai, Jiangsu and Zhejiang announced that three regions will set up Yangtze River Delta Integration Demonstration Area along their borders. At present, planning and institutional design are being carried out.

4.5 A Comparison of Synergy Development of Global Bay Areas and Prediction of Synergy Development of Urban Agglomerations in China

4.5.1 A Comparison of Synergy Development in Global Bay Areas

Through the study of the three bay areas in San Francisco, New York and Tokyo, we can find that these three metropolitan areas have formed their own distinctive regional governance models due to their different conditions (see Table 4.9). They are the most successful bay areas in the world, and only a successful bay area economy can breed the successful free trade port, which plays a huge supporting and promoting role in the bay area economy.

Table 4.9 Comparison of regional governance among the three metropolitan areas

Area	Core city	Leading government institutions	Governance platforms	Major participants
San Francisco Bay Area	Multiple	The State of California	San Francisco Bay Area Government Association, San Francisco Bay Area Metropolitan Transportation Association	State government, city government, state statutory bodies, non-profit consulting agencies
New York Metropolitan Area	Single	New York City Government	Regional Planning Association (RPA)	City government, state government, state statutory bodies, city statutory bodies, non-profit consulting agencies
Tokyo Bay Area	Single	Wide-area union organization	Think-tanks	Central government, non-profit consulting agencies, prefectural governments, wide-area union organization, and enterprise legal persons

Source Sorted by the authors

Under the explicit decentralization system of the three-level government of "federal-state-local government" in the United States, coupled with the broad consensus of emphasizing local autonomy in the American society, it is difficult for San Francisco Bay Area and New York Metropolitan Region to form a strong regional government or quasi-government agency to promote regional governance from the top down. There is no absolute central city in the Bay Area, so the regional comprehensive planning and governance is mainly coordinated by the San Francisco Bay Area Government Association, a platform organization for consultation and cooperation among district and county local governments. For transportation, housing, and environmental issues of widespread local concern, the solution is driven by single functional government management agencies supported by special funds from the federal government and state governments, such as the San Francisco Bay Area Metropolitan Transportation Association and other statutory agencies.

In the New York Bay Area, although the hot issues of regional governance, such as transportation, are also promoted by the single-function statutory bodies established by the federal government and the state government, the establishment and operation of these statutory bodies often require the consultation and cooperation between the two states due to the problem of cross-district joint governance. New York City is the absolute core of New York Metropolis, so the New York City government plays a leading role in the regional collaborative governance of the metropolitan area, and also has a lot of capital investment. And as the most influential non-profit planning consulting institution in this area, the Regional Planning Association also promoted the regional planning of New York Metropolitan Region to incline to the regional central city, and further consolidated the single core and multi circle structure of regional development.

The regional synergy of Tokyo Bay Area has been strongly supported by Japan's central government, and even targeted arrangements at the legislative level. Japan has established a wide-area planning system covering the whole country, regions, prefectures and Municipality, thus forming an institutional guarantee for regional coordinated governance. However, at the specific implementation level, non-governmental organizations play a more important role. Thinktanks serve as a platform for local government cooperation and provide sustained intellectual support for regional governance; while private and third-party legal entities have played a huge role in the construction and operation of important infrastructure such as rail transit.

Although there are many differences in the regional governance model of the three metropolitan areas, we can still find some rules from the practice of regional governance in these three metropolitan areas, which can be regarded as the necessary factors for the success of free trade port. First, regional synergy development is often jointly promoted by different organizations, including government agencies (central or federal governments and local governments at all levels), non-governmental statutory bodies, public and private enterprises, non-profit consulting agencies, etc. Secondly, transportation infrastructure is the most important factor in the implementation of regional cooperation, because the deployment of transportation infrastructure will directly affect the spatial structure of regional development and the mode of land development and utilization, and it is also the most intensive element of regional cooperation. Thirdly, regional synergy needs the guidance of special institutions and the support of special funds, which is the necessary and insufficient condition for effective regional synergy.

4.5.2 Prediction of Synergy Development in China

4.5.2.1 Direction and Future for the Synergy Development in Beijing-Tianjin-Hebei Urban Agglomeration

Beijing-Tianjin-Hebei Urban Agglomeration needs to establish an industrial integration system with different strengths and coordinated division of labor within industries. The development gap between Beijing, Tianjin and Hebei is obvious, and the level of industrial coordinated development is low. As the coordinated development of the Beijing-Tianjin-Hebei Region has become a national strategy, the pattern of one-way population flow, uneven public services and traffic separation will be broken in the future. Beijing-Tianjin-Hebei will fully utilize the unique geographical and population advantages, based on the comparative advantages of the three regions, to reshape the regional industrial division pattern and to construct a gradient and interconnected industrial system.

With the construction of Xiong'an New Area as the supporting point, we will promote the equalization of economic development and financial expenditure among Beijing, Tianjin and Hebei. Taking Xiong'an as the support does not mean that the problem can be solved simply by diverting the non-core resources of Beijing and Tianjin to Xiong'an, but that the construction of Xiong'an should be taken as an opportunity to promote the balanced development of other cities in Hebei.

With Beijing Tianjin Hebei Urban Agglomeration as the engine power, it will coordinate the development of Bohai Economic Circle.

As the only mature urban agglomeration in North China, Beijing-Tianjin-Hebei Urban Agglomeration should establish a large pattern in its development. In the current economic transformation of China, how to achieve the great development of Bohai Economic Circle through the development of Beijing-Tianjin-Hebei Urban Agglomeration and the neighboring Shandong Peninsula Urban Agglomerations and Liaozhongnan City Groups is the focus of overall consideration for the next top-level design.

4.5.2.2 Direction and Future for the Synergy Development in Yangtze River Delta Urban Agglomeration

The regional integration of the Yangtze River Delta has made positive progress and laid a solid foundation. However, compared with other urban agglomerations (especially that of the Pearl River Delta), there is much room for improvement. More efforts are needed in the following aspects.

First, identify the development goals for each city and determine the development pattern of urban agglomeration. Shanghai is the only Chinese city among the top 10 financial centers in the world. It has obvious advantages in economy, finance, science and technology, education, talent, culture, location and urban governance. As a promoter of reform and opening up and a pioneer of innovative development, Shanghai is destined to lead and drive the future development of the Yangtze River Delta. In order to promote the healthy development of the Yangtze River Delta Urban Agglomeration, provinces and cities in the urban agglomeration will need to cooperate with each other and focus on their own comparative advantages, so as to avoid duplication, achieve regional complementarity and maximize the cooperative effect. Measures should be taken to cope with certain disordered competition in petrochemical and metallurgical fields in the region, and there is a gap between its economic efficiency and that of world-class urban agglomerations. In addition to focusing on the current advantages, the Yangtze River Delta must also make use of its innovation ability to develop new comparative advantages in modern service industry and advanced manufacturing industry. Therefore, by developing the priority industries in the "Made in China 2025" industrial strategy, the Yangtze River Delta Urban Agglomeration will play a leading role in the next stage of China's economic development.

Second, pay attention to the unbalanced development of urban agglomerations and realize synergy development from multiple perspectives. The Yangtze River Delta has a good market foundation and the core area composed of Shanghai, Southern Jiangsu and Hangzhou-Jiaxing-Huzhou is highly developed and balanced, whereas, the weaker areas in Anhui and Northern Jiangsu are underdeveloped. In the future, the spatial distribution of industries should give priority to mend this gap, give full play to the resource endowment advantages of these regions, and accelerate the optimized allocation of factors under the marketization based on infrastructure connectivity. In addition, it is necessary to strengthen the connection and integration of regional planning (especially urban planning). The necessity of synergy development and the depth of cooperation among provinces and cities in the region need to be deepened constantly. At present, the central government's focus on infrastructure construction is to "make up for the weaknesses". The linkage of provinces and cities in the Yangtze River Delta region needs to update and upgrade the infrastructure according to local conditions, industry conditions and policies. In terms of policy coordination, we should give priority to sharing financial resources in the process of industrial transfer, to improve regional financial equalization, and promote equalization and institutional cohesion of regional public services on this basis.

Third, create investment infrastructure asset categories to reduce government burden. The Yangtze River Delta Urban Agglomeration is currently the largest urban agglomeration in China, covering 26 cities. The main goal of its development is to better integrate Anhui, Northern Jiangsu and Southern Zhejiang and other developing regions into its overall development plan. This will be achieved mainly through the expansion of infrastructure scheme in four key areas: transportation, telecommunications, energy and water conservation. The scale of these initiatives is large and will pose a huge challenge to funding. Therefore, the local governments of Yangtze River Delta Urban Agglomeration need to utilize private investments as an alternative source of funding for large-scale infrastructure projects. Advantage fund for Yangtze River Delta Cooperation of 100 billion yuan (US $14 billion) has been set up by the government and measures to establish public–private partnerships have been taken. However, opportunities for private participation in the scheme remain limited as financing is dominated by local state-owned enterprises. To facilitate this process and establish benchmark transactions, best practice pilot transactions can be established with stakeholders such as the Asian Infrastructure Investment Bank (AIIB).

References

Wang X (2017) Research on Beijing-Tianjin-Hebei collaborative governance: mode selection, governance structure, governance mechanism and social participation. City and Environmental Research 2:16–33

You NL, Shen ZJ, Ma Y et al (2017) The change and impact of development and planning system for redevelopment and planning in the capital area of Japan: a case study of wide area planning. Urban and Rural Planning 2(15–24):59

Chapter 5
Research on the Development Foundation of GBA Combined Ports

In Chapter 4, meticulous study is conducted on the developmental process and advanced experience of the San Francisco Bay Area, the New York Bay Area and the Tokyo Bay Area, as well as on regional synergy development and innovation measures of Beijing-Tianjin-Hebei Urban Agglomeration and Yangtze River Delta Urban Agglomeration. Chapter 5 aims to discover and study the current situation of and development basis for the Combined Ports of GBA in order to further clarify the general condition, economic development and social operation of the "9 + 2" GBA City Cluster. Horizontal comparisons are made between GBA and the three famous international bay areas to identify advantages and disadvantages of GBA Combined Ports.

5.1 An Overview of the GBA

The GBA City Cluster consists of nine cities from Guangdong Province that include Guangzhou, Foshan, Zhaoqing, Shenzhen, Huizhou, Zhuhai, Zhongshan and Jiangmen, and two Special Administrative Regions, i.e., Hong Kong Special Administrative Region (HKSAR) and Macao Special Administrative Region (MSAR). It forms the "9 + 2" Mode, one of the regions with the highest degree of openness and the strongest economic vitality in China, and the important spatial carrier for China to participate in global competition. According to statistics in the end of 2018,[1] GBA is about 56,000 square kilometers, covering 0.6% of China's total area. Its resident population is 71,160,000, covering 5.1% of China's total population. South of GBA is near Southeast Asia and South Asia. It is connected with the west coast of the Straits Economic Zone and Taiwan on the east. On the north, it is immediately adjacent to the Yangtze River Economic Belt. On the west it is connected with the Beibu Gulf

[1] Source: Wind, *Statistical Yearbook of Nine Cities of Guangdong* (2018), National Bureau of Statistics of China, 2018.

© Xiamen University Press 2022

S. Ba et al., *Collaborative Innovation Mechanism of GBA in China*,
https://doi.org/10.1007/978-981-19-2251-0_5

Economic Zone. The location advantage is obvious. It will serve as a key gateway for the Belt and Road once the whole GBA is mobilized and developed.

5.1.1 Developmental Process of the GBA

The concept of GBA was initiated in 2015 and intensive study was carried out in 2017. Finally, it was officially pronounced on February, 18, 2019. Fig. 5.1 provides a summary of development stages of the initiation of GBA.

In March, 2015, China's National Development and Reform Commission, Ministry of Foreign Affairs and Ministry of Commence issued *Vision and Proposed Actions Outlined on Jointly Building Silk Road Economic Belt and 21st Century Maritime Silk Road* (To be abbreviated as *the Vision*). The three departments jointly proposed to deepen cooperation with Hong Kong and Macao and to construct the Greater Bay Area.

In March, 2016, GBA was formally proposed in China's *13th Five-Year Plan*. The central government pledged to "*support Hong Kong and Macao to play important roles in the cooperation with the Pan-Pearl River Delta Region, and promote the building of major cooperation platforms between GBA and cross-provincial regions*."

In March, 2017, GBA was written into the *Government Work Report* with the tasks to "*promote deeper cooperation between the mainland and Hong Kong and Macao, study and formulate the development plan of GBA City Cluster, give full play to the unique advantages of Hong Kong and Macao, as well as raise their role and function in national economic development and opening to the outside world*."

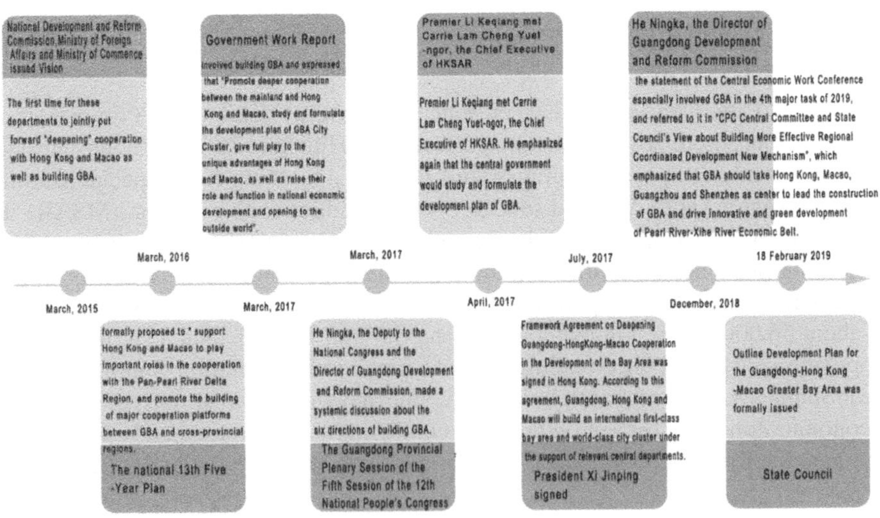

Fig. 5.1 The development stages of the GBA (*Source* Sorted by the authors)

In March, 2017, in the Guangdong Provincial Plenary Session of the Fifth Session of the 12th National People's Congress, He Ningka, an NPC Deputy and Director of Guangdong Development and Reform Commission, made a systemic clarification of the six tasks in the construction of the GBA. Firstly, strengthen infrastructure interconnectivity, form an infrastructure system that matches the regional economic and social development, focus on jointly building *One Center and Three Nets* and form an overall transport system that radiates home and abroad. Secondly, create a global innovation highland, make joint efforts to build a global sci-tech and innovation platform, construct an open innovation system, perfect the system and mechanism of innovation cooperation, build an innovation community of GBA and gradually turn GBA into a major innovation center of sci-tech industry worldwide. Thirdly, construct an open new structure of the BRI, deepen the infrastructure interconnectivity and economic and trade cooperation with countries along the belt and road, further advance the liberalization of service trade in Guangdong, Hong Kong and Macao, and create the upgrading version of *Closer Economic Partnership Arrangement* (CEPA).Fourthly, foster the benefit-shared industry value chain, speed up the pace of stepping into the high end of global value chain and build a modern industry pilot area with international competitiveness, accelerate the transformation and upgrading of manufacturing industry, and put emphasis on fostering and developing strategic emerging industrial clusters including the new-generation information and technology, biological technology, high-end equipment, new materials, energy conservation and environmental protection, and new-energy vehicles. Fifthly, jointly build the financial core circle, promote competition and cooperation in order as well as coordinated development of Guangdong, Hong Kong and Macao in finance, foster new platform of financial cooperation, expand two-way openness and connectivity of financial market elements between the mainland and Hong Kong and Macao, create the financial hub that leads the Pan-Pearl River Delta Region, radiates Southeast Asia and serves BRI, and form the GBA financial core that takes Hong Kong as dragon head, relies on Guangzhou, Shenzhen, Macao and Zhuhai, and takes Nansha, Qianhai and Hengqin as node. Finally, jointly build the good-quality life circle of GBA, focus on improving social well-being, create an international education highland, perfect the service system of employment and entrepreneurship, promote cultural prosperity and development, together build healthy bay area and advance social coordinated management so as to develop GBA into a world-class city cluster that is green, suitable to live, work and travel.

In April, 2017, when Premier Li Keqiang met Carrie Lam Cheng Yuet-ngor, the Chief Executive of HKSAR, he emphasized the central government's plan to study and formulate a development outline for the GBA.

On July, 1, 2017, while celebrating the 20th anniversary of Hong Kong returning to China, President Xi Jinping, signed the *Framework Agreement on Deepening Guangdong-HongKong-Macao Cooperation in the Development of the Greater Bay Area*, which further clarified that Guangdong, Hong Kong and Macao will build an international first-class bay area and world-class city cluster under the support of relevant departments under the central government.

On the statement issued by the 2018 Central Economic Work Conference (Held from December 19 to 21), the construction of GBA was listed as the fourth priority task of 2019. In the State Council's document *On the Establishment of a more Effective New Mechanism for Regional Coordinated Development*, it is stated that GBA should put Hong Kong, Macao, Guangzhou and Shenzhen at the center to lead the construction of GBA and drive innovative and green development of the Pearl River-Xijiang River Economic Belt.

On February, 18, 2019, the *Outline Development Plan for the Guangdong-Hong Kong-Macao Greater Bay Area* was formally issued. The target is to build a world-class city cluster, an international center of sci-tech innovation, an important support of BRI, and a demonstration zone of deep cooperation between the mainland and Hong Kong and Macao in GBA. At the same time, GBA should develop a quality living circle for living, working and travelling which serves as a model in China. The specific goals include the formation of an international first-class bay area and a world-class city cluster in GBA by 2022 and turning GBA into an international first-class bay area that is suitable for living, working and travelling by 2035.

5.1.2 An Overview of Economic Development in the GBA

5.1.2.1 Large Economy Volume vs. Uneven Economy Distribution

The GBA is an advanced urban agglomeration leading China's opening up with Hong Kong and Macao as international windows, Guangzhou and Shenzhen as regional centers, and multi-city linkages between the Circle of Guangzhou, Foshan and Zhaoqing, the Circle of Shenzhen, Dongguan and Huizhou, and the Circle of Zhuhai, Zhongshan and Jiangmen. In 2018, the total GDP of GBA (9 + 2) is about RMB 10.86 trillion yuan (see Fig. 5.2), accounting for around 12% of China's GDP, second to the Yangtze River Delta Urban Agglomeration (at RMB 17.79 trillion yuan), and higher than that of the Beijing-Tianjin-Hebei Urban Agglomeration (at RMB 8.5 trillion yuan).[2] Compared with the three bay areas in the world, GBA's GDP is 82.2% of that of the Tokyo Bay Area, 83.7% of the New York Bay Area and 163.5% of the San Francisco Bay Area.

However, the GDP of individual cities in GBA is imbalanced. On the one hand, the distribution of GDP is uneven among the cities (see Fig. 5.2). According to statistics in 2018,[3] in terms of GDP, Hong Kong, Shenzhen and Guangzhou took the first, second and third place respectively among GBA "9 + 2" cities, creating 65.4%

---

[2] Source: Wind, *Statistical Yearbook of Guangdong Nine Cities* (2018), Yangtze River Delta city cluster includes Shanghai, Nanjing, Wuxi, Changzhou, Suzhou, Nantong, Yancheng, Yangzhou, Zhenjiang, and Taizhou of Jiangsu Province, Hangzhou, Ningbo, Jiaxing, Huzhou, Shaoxing, Jinhua, Zhoushan, and Taizhou of Zhejiang Province, and Hefei, Wuhu, Maanshan, Tongling, Anqing, Chuzhou, Chizhou and Xuancheng of Anhui Province; GDP of Beijing-Tianjin-Hebei city cluster comes from *Beijing Daily* (April, 4, 2019).

[3] Source: Wind, *Statistical Yearbook of Nine Cities of Guangdong*.

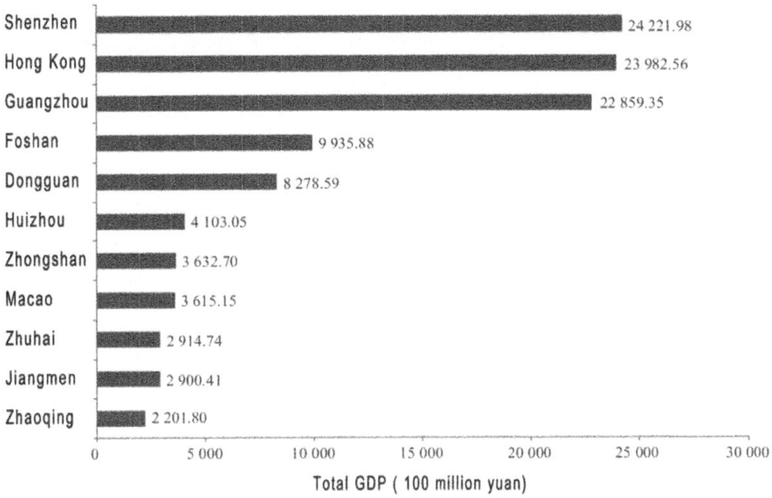

Fig. 5.2 The total GDP of GBA city clusters (*Source* Wind)

of the total GDP in GBA, while the total GDP of Huizhou, Zhongshan, Zhaoqing, Jiangmen, Zhuhai and Macao SAR combined falls below that of Guangzhou. On the other hand, there is huge differences in production capacity of each city (see Fig. 5.3). Hong Kong and Macao are in the first tier. GDP per capita surpassed RMB 300,000 yuan in Hong Kong, and RMB 500,000 yuan in Macao (ranking No. 2 in the world). The second tier cities include Shenzhen, Zhuhai and Guangzhou with GDP per capita above RMB 150,000 yuan. The third tier cities include Foshan, Zhongshan and Dongguan with GDP per capita above RMB 90,000 yuan. The third tier cities are located close to the second tier cities, benefiting from economic spillover effect. Huizhou, Jiangmen and Zhaoqing are in the fourth tier whose economy volume is smaller and GDP per capita is between RMB 50,000 and 90,000 yuan.

According to data from *Fortune* in 2019 (Table 5.1), 20 GBA enterprises are among the Fortune 500. Their businesses cover science and technology, finance, real estate, retail and others. 7 are from Hong Kong, 7 from Shenzhen, 3 from Guangzhou, 2 from Foshan, and 1 from Zhuhai. The data testify the strength of the first tier GBA cities, especially that of Hong Kong, Shenzhen and Guangzhou.

5.1.2.2 High Economic Growth vs. Low Economic Density

According to Wind database and 2018 statistical yearbook of nine cities in Guangdong, from 2012 to 2018, the total economy volume of the GBA rose from RMB 6723.8 billion yuan to 10864.6 billion yuan (see Fig. 5.4), with 62% growth rate

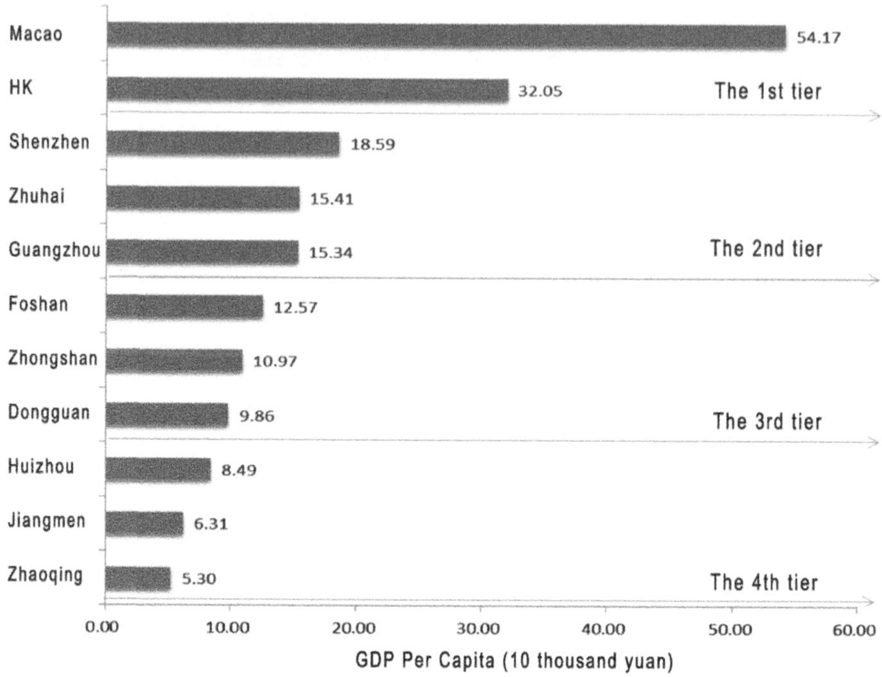

Fig. 5.3 The GDP Per Capita of GBA city clusters (*Source* Wind)

within 6 years and nominal annual growth rate of 8.33%which is far higher than that of 2.26% over the same period in the world.[4]

The production per unit area in the GBA is 24.78 million dollars per square kilometer, accounting for about 20% of the Tokyo Bay Area and 31% of the New York Bay Area.[5] This reflects that GBA's economy density is relatively low and its unit economic production capacity is still far from that of the world-class bay areas. On the other hand, it also reflects that Guangdong, Hong Kong and Macao have not been over-squeezed in their economic space as they have adequate land resource supply backed by the mainland, and the space for low-end industrial transfer and industrial space reconstruction is ample.

[4] Source: Wind.

[5] Source: Sorted by the author. PS: San Francisco Bay Area (San Jose-San Francisco-Oakland Metropolitan Statistical Region); New York Metropolitan Area (New York-Newark-Jersey City Metropolitan Statistical Region);Greater Tokyo Bay Area (One Capital Three County), Statistical Year: 2016.

Table 5.1 A List of Fortune 500 in GBA (2019)

Enterprise	Location	Ranking	Industry
Ping An Insurance (Group) COMPANY OF CHINA, LTD	Shenzhen	29	Insurance
Huawei Technologies Co., LTD	Shenzhen	61	Communication equipment
China Resources	Hong Kong	80	Retailing
China Southern Power Grid Company Limited	Guangzhou	111	Electricity
Amer	Shenzhen	119	Non-ferrous medal
Evergrande Group	Shenzhen	138	Real estate
Country Garden	Foshan	177	Real estate
China Merchants Bank	Shenzhen	188	Banking
Guangzhou Automobile Group Co., Ltd	Guangzhou	189	Automobile manufacturing
Lenovo	Hong Kong	212	High tech
Tencent	Shenzhen	237	High tech
China Vanke Co., Ltd	Shenzhen	254	Real estate
China Merchants Group	Hong Kong	280	Diversity
Jardine Matheson	Hong Kong	280	Diversity
Cedar Holdings	Guangzhou	301	Diversity
Media Group	Foshan	312	Household appliance
CK Hutchison Holdings Limited	Hong Kong	352	Retailing
AIA	Hong Kong	388	Financing
Zhuhai Gree Group Co., Ltd	Zhuhai	414	Household appliance
China Taiping Life Insurance Co., Ltd. (TAIPING LIFE)	Hong Kong	451	Financing

Source Fortune (2019)

5.1.2.3 Regional Differentiated Industrial Distribution Coexisting with Certain Repetitive Industrial Competition

According to Wind database and 2018 city statistical yearbook of nine cities in Guangdong, the ratio of the primary industry, secondary industry and tertiary industry of nine cities in Guangdong is 1.55:41.20:57.25; whereas the ratio of the tertiary industry is 88.9%[6] in Hong Kong and 93.3%.[7] The disparity is obvious between the nine cities and the two SARs.

From the perspective of the industry structure (Table 5.2 and Fig. 5.5), the supply chain of up and down stream industries within GBA is adequate, and there is gradient

[6] Wind database: Census and Statistics Department of Hong Kong SAR.

[7] Wind database: Census and Statistics Department of Macao SAR.

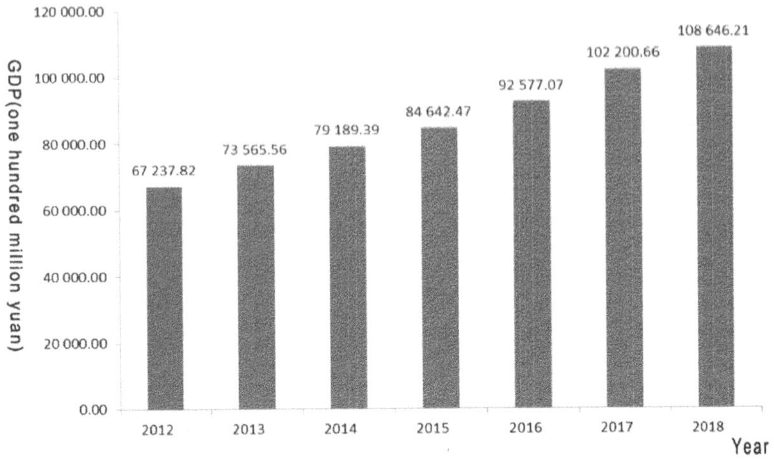

Fig. 5.4 GDP of GBA between 2012–2018 (*Source* Wind)

among industries, so they can complement one another to realize differentiated development. In terms of industry distribution, nine cities in Guangdong can make up for "industry hollowing" of Hong Kong and Macao, while Hong Kong and Macao can feed back to the mainland, supporting export of manufacturing industry of the nine cities. Besides, core cities and two-wing cities of nine cities in Guangdong can achieve coordinated development where high-end manufacturing industry of Zhuhai and special market base of Zhongshan can complement one another, and advanced manufacturing industry and high-end service industry of Guangzhou can complement with industrial base of Foshan. Overall, the secondary industry of the GBA focuses on advanced manufacturing industries such as electronics processing industry and medical equipment as well as traditional equipment manufacturing industry; the tertiary industry focuses on financial service, internet, tourism industry and modern service industry. Known from Table 5.2, Hong Kong plays solid roles as a financial center, trade center, logistics center and education center; Macao stands out for gambling, tourism, finance and other service industries with special functions. Nine cities of Guangdong formed seven industry clusters including textile industry, building materials industry, household electric appliance industry, electronics and information industry, pharmaceutical industry, machine industry, and automobile industry. Seen from the distribution of specifically classified industries in each city, the industries of Guangdong, Hong Kong and Macao exist staggered division of labor for long time, but part of industries exist overlapping and mutual competition. According to research conducted by Tan Chenglin and Pan Dandan (2018), in the inner layer of manufacturing industry, there is high degree of similarity in structure of manufacturing industry between Shenzhen and Dongguan, Shenzhen and Huizhou, Dongguan and Huizhou; there is serious convergence in industrial structure among Zhuhai, Foshan and Zhongshan and exists overlapping competition in part of industries.

Table 5.2 Strategies and industrial positioning of GBA cities

Industrial Cluster	Feature	City distribution
Textile Industrial cluster	The industrial chain is complete, mainly exported through Hong Kong and Macau markets, keeping up with international trends	Zhongshan, Shenzhen, Dongguan
Construction material Industrial cluster	Large cluster, complete product categories, occupying most of the domestic market	Foshan, Jiangmen
Household appliance Industrial cluster	Household appliances have a complete range of products, occupy most of the domestic market, and form a certain brand effect	Foshan, Zhongshan, Zhuhai
Electronic information Industrial cluster	The industrial chain is complete, and the cluster is large. It mainly produces electronic computers and communication equipment. It has basically formed a manufacturing base in Shenzhen Suihui, Dongguan	Guangzhou, Shenzhen, Dongguan, Foshan, Huizhou
Medicine Industrial cluster	A good international environment, accepting large-scale investment from multinational companies, focusing on bio-services, bio-technology and bio-medical equipment industries	Guangzhou, Shenzhen, Zhongshan, Zhuhai, Hong Kong
Mechanical Industrial cluster	Focus on the development of technology-intensive, capital-intensive, talent-intensive machinery industry and high-input, high-value-added export machinery industry	Guangzhou, Shenzhen, Foshan, Zhongshan
Automobile Industrial cluster	The automobile industry cluster led by the three major foreign automobile companies has basically taken shape. Focusing on supporting enterprises, starting with the introduction of foreign capital and advanced technology	Guangzhou, Zhaoqing, Foshan, Jiangmen

Source Sorted by the authors

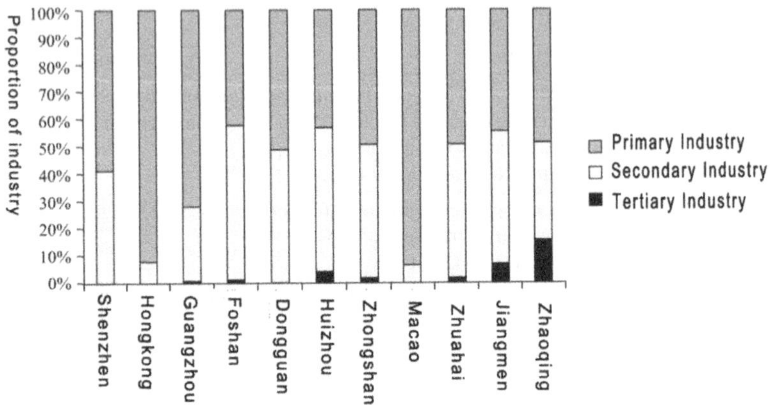

Fig. 5.5 Proportion of three industries in GBA in GDP (2018) (*Source* Wind
PS: The statistic scale of the tertiary industry of HK and Macao is not completely in align with that of the nine cities in Guangdong)

5.1.3 An Overview of Social Development in the GBA

5.1.3.1 Obvious Population Concentration and Reasonable Population Structure

GBA's population concentration effect is significant in Guangdong and in China driven by favorable economic and employment opportunities. According to Wind database, its resident population exceeded 70 million by 2018, reaching 71.1598 million, an increase of 1.5882 million over the previous year. In 2018, the resident population of the nine cities in Guangdong Province was 63,009,900, with an increase of 1,504,500 over the previous year, a slight decrease of 0.09% year-on-year, but an increase of 0.86% over the same period in Guangdong Province, which shows that population absorption capability of GBA is strong and population concentration effect is significant.

In 2018, resident population of the nine cities made up 88.55% of the total population of GBA, and Hong Kong and Macao took up 10.52 and 0.94% respectively. In 2018, the growth rate of Guangdong resident population reached 2.45%, surpassing the 2.28% growth rate of the GBA over the same period, 1.51% higher than Hong Kong and 0.26% higher than Macao. Seen from population density (Table 5.3 and 5.4), in 2018, the density of resident population in GBA was 1,273 per square kilometer. Due to the level of urbanization and the large area of administrative areas, the population density of Macao and Hong Kong is very high, reaching 21,954 and 7,126 per square kilometer respectively. Shenzhen ranks 3rd with the population density of Shenzhen reaching 6,523 per square kilometer, close to the figure in Hong Kong. The low population density of the other cities indicates that GBA has great potential for population absorption.

Table 5.3 Basic demographic statistics of GBA

Index	2015	2016	2017	2018
Total population of Guangdong Province at the end of the year (10,000 people)	10849	10999	11169	11346
The total population of the GBA at the end of the year (10,000 people)	6669.92	6800.96	6957.16	7115.98
Total population of nine cities in Guangdong Province (10,000 people)	5874.27	5998.49	6150.54	6300.99
total population of Hong Kong (10,000 people)	730.97	737.71	741.31	748.25
total population of Macao (10,000 people)	64.68	64.49	65.31	66.74
Population density of GBA (person/km 2)*	1193	1217	1244	1269

Source Wind, *Guangdong Statistical Yearbook* (2015–2018)
PS: Population density of GBA is based on the areas and population of the 9 + 2 cities

Table 5.4 Social and economic index of GBA

City	Area (km^2)	Population in 2018 (ten thousand)	Population in 2017 (ten thousand)	GDP in 2018 (one hundred million yuan)	GDP per capita in 2018 (ten thousand yuan)	Population density (per person/km^2)
Shenzhen	1997	1302.66	1252.83	24221.98	18.59	6523
HK	1050	748.25	741.31	23982.56	32.05	7126
Guangzhou	7434	1490.44	1449.84	22859.35	15.34	2005
Foshan	3798	790.57	765.67	9935.88	12.57	2082
Dongguan	2460	839.22	834.25	8278.59	9.86	3411
Huizhou	11347	483.00	477.70	4103.05	8.49	426
Zhongshan	1784	331.00	326.00	3632.70	10.97	1855
Macao	30.4	66.74	65.31	3615.15	54.17	21954
Zhuhai	1736	189.11	176.54	2914.74	15.41	1089
Jiangmen	9509	459.82	456.17	2900.41	6.31	484
Zhaoqing	14891	415.17	411.54	2201.80	5.30	279

Source Wind

In terms of the economic effects of the population, the total population size of GBA is about 5% of China's total, but it has created more than 12% of the China's GDP. The economic benefits of population agglomeration are remarkable.[8] Figure 5.6 shows that GBA is rich in human resources, with reasonable age structure as nearly 60% of the population are between the ages of 25 and 34. In Shenzhen nearly 70% of the population are between the ages of 25 and 34.It indicates that GBA is full of vitality and has a very strong talent team and development momentum. Seen from

[8] Source: Wind.

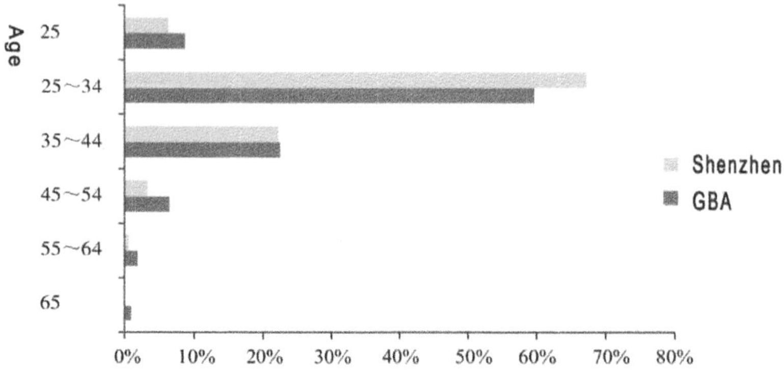

Fig. 5.6 Age distribution of talents of GBA (*Source The Research Report on Digital Economy and Talent Development of Guangdong-Hong Kong-Macao Greater Bay Area*, Tsinghua School of Economy and Management)

Fig. 5.7, among educational background owned by middle-and-high-end talent in GBA, bachelor degree accounts for the most, the second is college degree or below and master degree, and the number of doctor and post doctor degree is relatively small. This talent structure is similar to that of the Yangtze River Delta region. But in comparison, the proportion of masters and doctors in Beijing, Tianjin and Hebei is evidently higher than that in GBA, which shows that there is space for improvement in talent strength of GBA.

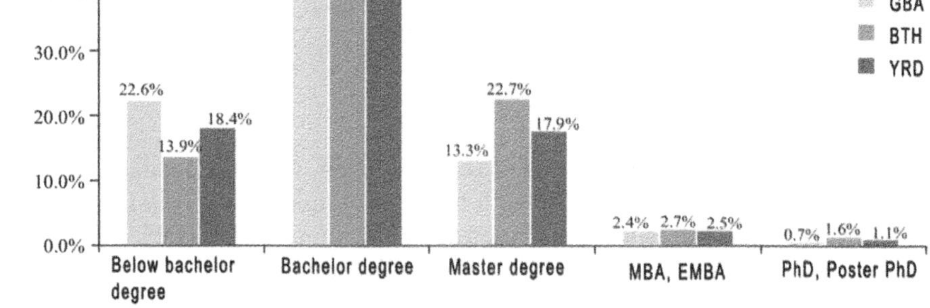

Fig. 5.7 Educational structure of high-end talents in GBA, BTH and YRD (*Notes* BTH refers to Beijing-Tianjin-Hebei region. TRD refers to Yangtze River Delta region. *Source The Report on Middle-and-high-end Talent Development of GBA*, Hunter [2019])

5.1.3.2 Spillover of GBA Population and Further Optimization of Its Population Concentration and Outflow

There is gradient distribution of population in the GBA. Population agglomeration is obvious in Guangdong, while population spillover is also common in the GBA, leading to an optimized population distribution. According to Wind database, the resident population in the GBA has grown by 1,588,200 in 2018. The number of the nine cities is 1,504,500, accounting for 94.73% of the total. Figure 5.8 reveals that differences in different parts. The population of the two core cities, i.e., Guangzhou and Shenzhen, increased 406,000 and 498,300 respectively. The growth rate of the resident population of the two cities accounted for 51.09% of the growth rate in Guangdong Province during the same period. Foshan and Dongguan continue to keep high population growth momentum, with an increase of 249,000 and 125,700 respectively in 2018. The growth rate is lower in Huizhou, Zhuhai, Zhongshan, Jiangmen, Zhaoqing, Hong Kong and Macao, with an increase under 100,000. GBA has sustained and strengthened its advantage of talent attraction. Meanwhile, its population distribution is becoming more and more optimized as population agglomeration is no longer over concentrated in core cities such as Guangzhou, Shenzhen and Dongguan and areas with intensive manufacturing industries. Instead, population flow changes with the change of industrial structuring. Compared with Guangzhou, Shenzhen and Donguan, the trend of talent spillover in Hong Kong and Macao is not significant due to *the One Country Two Systems* policy. Talent concentration is still significant and there is a trend of sustained growth.

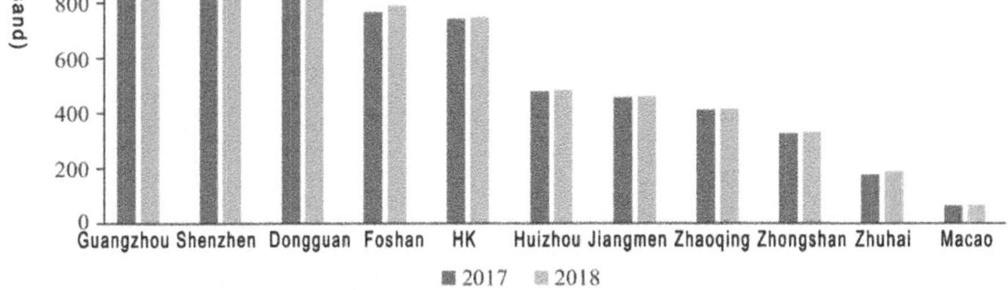

Fig. 5.8 Trend of spatial changes of resident population in GBA (*Source* Wind)

5.1.3.3 Significant Spatial Difference of Internal Social Resources Setting Obstacles for Regional Synergy

The distribution of education resource in the GBA is uneven. Hong Kong possesses high-quality and diverse higher education resource, where The University of Hong Kong, The Chinese University of Hong Kong, The Hong Kong University of Science and Technology, The Hong Kong Polytechnic University and City University of Hong Kong rank among the top 100 in the world. There are has 10 degree-granting institutions of higher learning in Macao, which are University of Macau, Macao Polytechnic Institute, Macao Institute For Tourism Studies, Macau Security Force College, City University of Macau, The University of Saint Joseph, Kiang Wu Nursing College of Macau, Macau University of Science and Technology, Macau Institute of Management and Macau Millennium College. The number of colleges and universities in Guangdong is 147, second only to 166 in Jiangsu. Of these, 5 universities are directly under the central government, 62 are undergraduate institutions and 85 are higher vocational (specialty) institutions (Xian Xuelin and An Dongping, 2017).

Universities on the QS top 100 list are all in Hong Kong. There is significant uneven distribution of education resources in nine cities. Guangzhou hosts more than 60% of colleges and universities in GBA, and almost all of the top universities in GBA. Statistically, Guangzhou is far ahead of the other eight cities. The second is Zhuhai and Shenzhen is the last (See Fig. 5.9). In terms of the number of universities in the hundreds of billions of GDP, Guangzhou is as high as 3.72, 12 times that of Shenzhen, 4 times that of Dongguan and 1.4 times that of Zhuha (See Fig. 5.10).

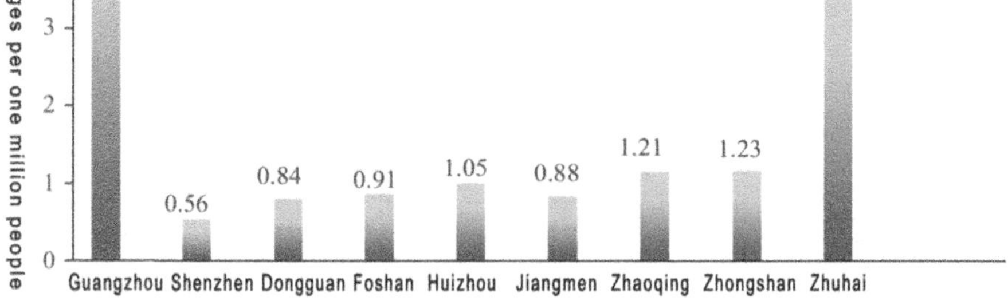

Fig. 5.9 Spatial distribution of institutes of higher learning in GBA per million people (*Source* Xian Xuelin and An Dongping [2017])

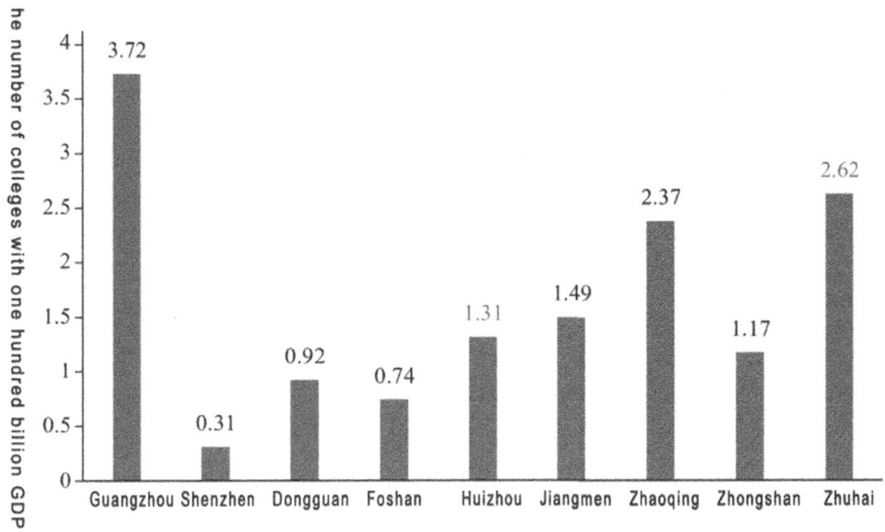

Fig. 5.10 Spatial distribution of universities over 100 billion GDP in GBA (*Source* Xian Xuelin and An Dongping [2017])

Talents are unevenly distributed in different parts of the GBA. According to relevant researches,[9] based on the social media LinkedIn, personnel with higher degrees are referred to as high-level talents. Figure 5.11 shows that the concentration degree of high-level talents in the GBA varies from city to city. Guangzhou does not have the largest number of talents, but its talent distribution in different industries is the most balanced. In software and IT services, consumer goods, tourism and vacation, retail, transportation logistics, education and other industries, Guangzhou retains a slight advantage compared to the overall level of GBA. Besides Guangzhou, the talent distribution in other seven municipalities is featured in different ways. Shenzhen has a very high level of talent concentration in the ICT (software and IT services, computer networks and hardware) industry, enjoying a leading advantage in ITC and certain advantage in manufacturing, transportation and logistics. Zhuhai has obvious talent advantages in the manufacturing and tourism and vacation industries, thanks to its unique geographical location. Dongguan, Foshan and Huizhou have talent advantages in the manufacturing and consumer goods industries. On the whole, there is a greater homogeneity of talents in the cities in Guangdong, but there is also an obvious talent disadvantage in the financial and educational industries. Compared with overall level of GBA, Hong Kong has high concentration of talents in finance, education and enterprise service industries, while the talents of Macao gather in

[9] Source: *The Research Report on Digital Economy and Talent Development of Guangdong-Hong Kong-Macao Greater Bay Area*, Tsinghua School of Economy and Management.

PS: only eight cities are compared as statistics on Zhaoqing, Jiangmen and Zhongshan is not available on LinkedIn.

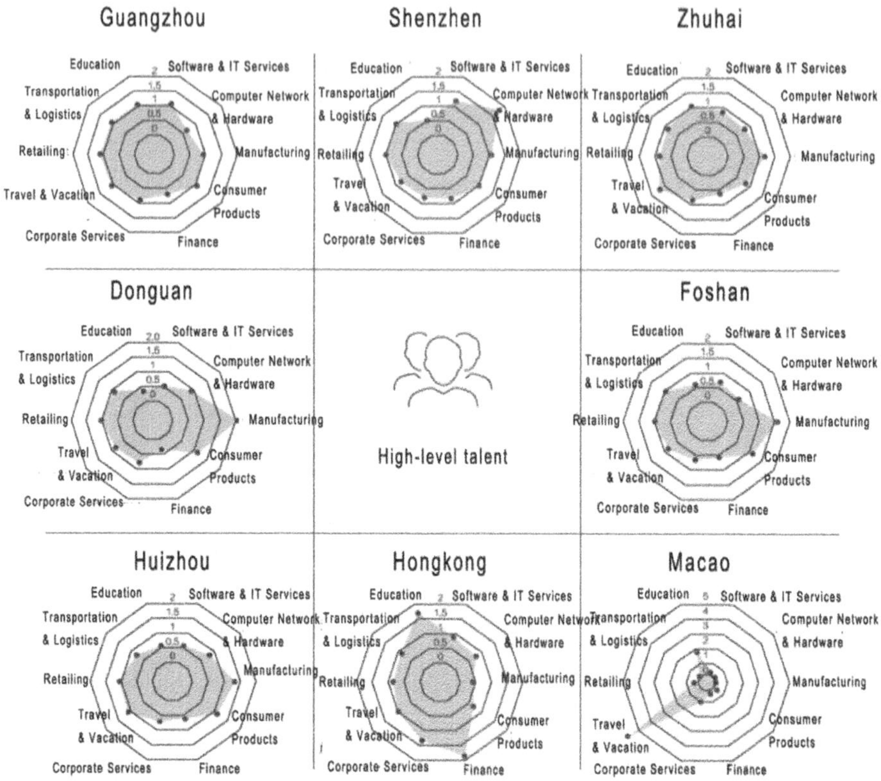

Fig. 5.11 Distribution of talents in GBA (*Source Report on Digital Economy and Talent Development of Guangdong-Hong Kong-Macao Greater Bay Area*, Tsinghua School of Economy and Management)

education and tourism and vocation industries, the latter of which is the most characteristic industry in Macao. The two SARs and the nine cities can be complementary in utilizing talent advantages.

Medical resources in the GBA are distributed unevenly as significant disparities exist in spatial distribution. Hong Kong is second only to the United States in the world in terms of medical standards. It even surpasses Europe and the United States in a number of medical fields such as the treatment for stomach and lung cancer. Hong Kong has been at the forefront of the world in terms of doctors and technology, medical equipment and drug application. Based on 2018 statistic data of Wind database, seen from the number of medical institution, Table 5.5 demonstrates that Shenzhen and Guangzhou among Guangdong nine cities take absolute advantage with more than 4,000 medical institutions. The second is the circle of Zhaoqing, Huizhou and Dongguan with more than 2,400 institutions. The total number of institutions in Foshan and Jiangmen is more than 1,600. Zhongshan and Zhuhai have a relatively smaller number of institutions, which is less than 1,000.Seen from

Table 5.5 Basic statistics of medical resources in GBA

City	No. of medical institution	No. of hospital beds (ten thousand)	No. of doctors (ten thousand)
Hong Kong	140*	3.97	1.43
Macao	692*	0.16	0.18
Guangzhou	4058	9.00	5.00
Shenzhen	4049	4.00	3.30
Zhuhai	742	0.90	0.60
Foshan	1715	3.50	1.80
Dongguan	2446	3.00	1.80
Zhongshan	806	1.50	0.80
Huizhou	2725	2.30	1.30
Jiangmen	1608	2.30	1.00
Zhaoqing	3079	1.70	0.80

Source Wind

PS: Medical institutions of Hong Kong include public hospitals and institutions under the administration of Hospital Authority, private hospitals, caring institutions and hospitals under the administration of disciplinary institutions. Medical institutions of Macao include hospitals and primary health treatment sites

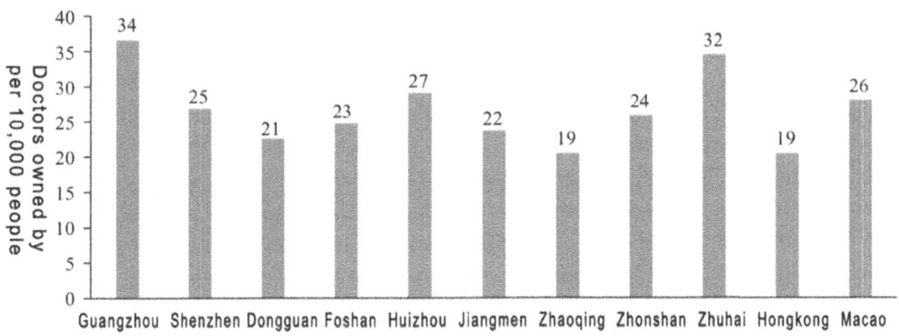

Fig. 5.12 Spatial distribution of no. of doctors per 10,000 people in GBA (*Source* Wind)

the number of doctors owned by per ten thousand people, Fig. 5.12 shows that per ten thousand people have about 30 doctors in Guangzhou and Zhuhai. The number is 25 in Huizhou and Shenzhen and 20 in Zhongshan, Foshan, Jiangmen, Dongguan and Zhaoqing. As for the number of hospital beds owned by per ten thousand people, Fig. 5.13 shows that per ten thousand people have about 60 hospital beds in Guangzhou. The number is 50 in Jiangmen, Huizhou and Zhuhai, 45 in Foshan and Zhongshan, 35 in Zhaoqing and Dongguan, and 30 in Shenzhen, which is the lowest. In addition, according to China hospital ranking in 2017,[10] 10 hospitals of

[10] http://rank.cn-healthcare.com/

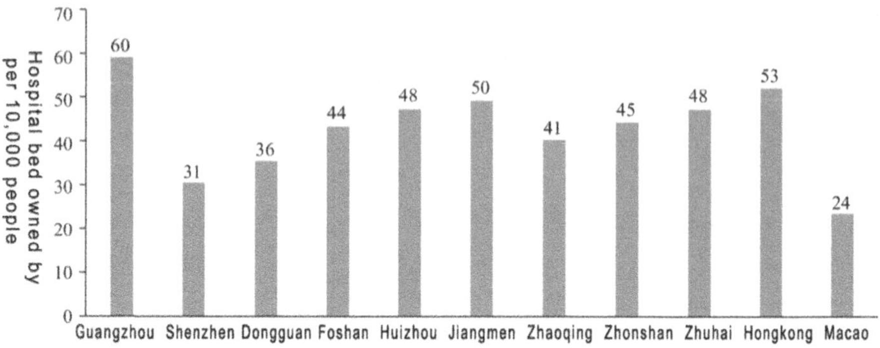

Fig. 5.13 Spatial distribution of no. of hospital beds per 10,000 people in GBA (*Source* Wind)

Guangzhou entered the top 100, among which First Affiliated Hospital of Sun Yat-sen University is No.7 in China. Hospital from the other eight cities fail to enter the top 100. The uneven distribution of medical resources in GBA is reflected both in quantity and in quality.

The scale of rail transit network in the GBA is not adequate, and the space layout of rail transit system is not reasonable. According to *13th Five-Year Plan of Transportation in Guangdong*, the data shows that by 2020, Guangdong expects to invest RMB 1.8337 trillion in the field of rail transit and double its operation mileage to 9,900 km, which is an increase of 5,428 km. The scale of urban rail will be further expanded to be 1,430 km, about 26.3% of the total added mileage. However, as of the end of 2018, only Hong Kong, Guangzhou, Shenzhen, Foshan and Dongguan have urban rail transit in GBA (9 + 2) with the total of 972.8 km. The line density is as low as 0.01 km per square kilometer. Guangzhou-Foshan subway is the only cross-city subway.[11] Taking Hong Kong, Macao, Guangzhou and Shenzhen as traffic hub core, the rail transit system of GBA includes inter-city railway, general speed railway, high speed railway, commuter rail and urban subway, making up about 11.5, 24.8, 31.9, 1.1 and 30.6%. By comparison, the development of commuter rail and inter-city railway is lagged, and the ratio of rail transit construction is unreasonable. The problem is prominent in terms of inner-city rail construction, which generally has many problems such as low technique standard, unreasonable station layout and long construction time consumption, as well as inadequate connectivity to national key trunk. Many problems cause that the length of Guangzhou- Foshan- Zhaoqing railway is only 110 km, but time consumption of journey tends to pass 60 min (the longest is 90 min), having no competitiveness compared to other transit tools. In addition, part of inter-city trains exist many problems such as stopping in the outer-city stations and over long time consumption of shuttle, which is hard to satisfy the demand of inter-city passenger flow.

[11] *Reform the Approval System of Rail Transit Planning and Build One Net for Cross City Rail Transit in GBA* [EB/OL]. http://www.sohu.com/a/300145848_99970599

Table 5.6 A general comparison of the four bay areas

Bay area	Population (ten thousand)	Area (km^2)	GDP (trillion dollar)	Proportion in national GDP (%)
San Francisco Bay Area	937	35280	0.85	4.54
New York Bay Area	2003	20787	1.66	8.87
Greater Tokyo Bay Area	3629	13376	1.69	34.30
GBA	6801	56095	1.39	12.45

Source Sorted by the authors
PS: San Francisco Bay Area of San Jose-San Francisco-Oakland Metropolitan Statistical Region; New York Bay Area of New York-Newark-Jersey City Metropolitan Statistical Region; and Greater Tokyo Bay Area of One Capital Three Counties. Statistical Year of 2016

5.1.4 Comparison of GBA with the World's Three Bay Areas

5.1.4.1 Differences in Geo-Spatial Structure

Compared with the world's three bay areas (See Table 5.6), the GBA has the largest area and population base with an outstanding optimization potential in land development and utilization, demographic dividends and population structure. The population density of GBA is slightly higher than that of the New York Bay Area, but lower than that of the Tokyo Bay Area. The Tokyo Bay area has the highest population density, with 2,713 people per square kilometer. The geographical distribution of land and population shows that GBA has the capacity to absorb more people and optimize intensive land use. By contrast, the San Francisco Bay Area is located in a narrow strip, similar to the Tokyo Bay Area, with limited ability of urban extension. Although the New York Bay Area is backed up by hinterland like GBA, its hinterland area is far less, restricting its regional synergy development.

5.1.4.2 Differences in Economic Development

Compared with the world's three bay areas, the overall economic strength of GBA is still weak, but it has obvious growth potentials. Table 5.6 shows that Tokyo Area has the biggest GDP, reaching 1.69 trillion dollars, whereas San Francisco Bay Area has the smallest GDP at 0.85 trillion dollars. However, its GDP per capita is the largest and contributes the largest per capita output value to the per capita land area, which is about 2 times that of the Tokyo Bay Area and more than 4 times that of the GBA. From the perspective of the local economic contribution rate, the Tokyo Bay Area contributes about 34% of Japan's GDP, ranking first among the four bay areas. The second place is taken by the GBA at about 12%, with huge growth potential.[12] The

[12] Source: Wind, National Bureau of Statistics of China.

third and fourth places are taken by New York and San Francisco respectively. The contribution rate of local economy in these bay areas depends on their economic environment. The land is narrow and natural resources are limited in Japan, offering limited expansion space for the economy of the Tokyo Bay Area. By contrast, the US economy is developed and mature. While Japan's economic development is overly dependent on the Tokyo Bay Area, the contribution of the economy of New York and San Francisco to the US is much less significant. China is an emerging economy in the period of economy transformation. Compared with the mature economies of the three international bay areas, China's domestic inland market is broad and unbalanced, signifying huge market opportunities. Relying on the domestic market volume and a good economic development environment, the GBA has a greater potential for development when compared with the three international bay areas.

5.1.4.3 Differences in Industrial Structure

In terms of industrial structure (Table 5.7 and Fig. 5.14), service industry of the three international bay areas occupies the most important position, while in GBA traditional manufacturing industry still takes up considerable proportion. Among them, the tertiary industry takes up the highest proportion of GDP in the New York Bay Area, with almost all of the primary industry moved outside the Bay Area. Figure 5.14 shows that the proportions of GDP taken up by service industry in the San Francisco Bay Area, New York Bay Area and Tokyo Bay Area are 82.8, 89.4 and 82.3% respectively. The industrial structure of San Francisco Bay Area is similar to that of Tokyo as innovation and entrepreneurship of Silicon Valley require considerable high-end manufacturing industry to start up business and practice technological achievements, while based on its industry, the two industrial belts in Greater Tokyo Area shows overlapping development with financial service industry. In comparison, the proportion of the tertiary industry in the GBA is the lowest, only 62.2%. Its

Table 5.7 Major industries in the four bay areas

Bay Area	Major industries
New York Bay Area	Finance and insurance industry, professional and technological service industry, real estate industry, medical and health industry, wholesale and retail industry
San Francisco Bay Area	Finance and insurance industry, professional and technological service industry, real estate industry, medical and health industry, wholesale and retail industry, information industry, manufacturing industry
Greater Tokyo Bay Area	Real estate industry, wholesale and retail industry, manufacturing industry, finance and insurance industry, communication and media industry
GBA	Manufacturing, import and export trade, finance, wholesale and retail, real estate, warehousing and logistics, computer services and software

Source Sorted by the authors

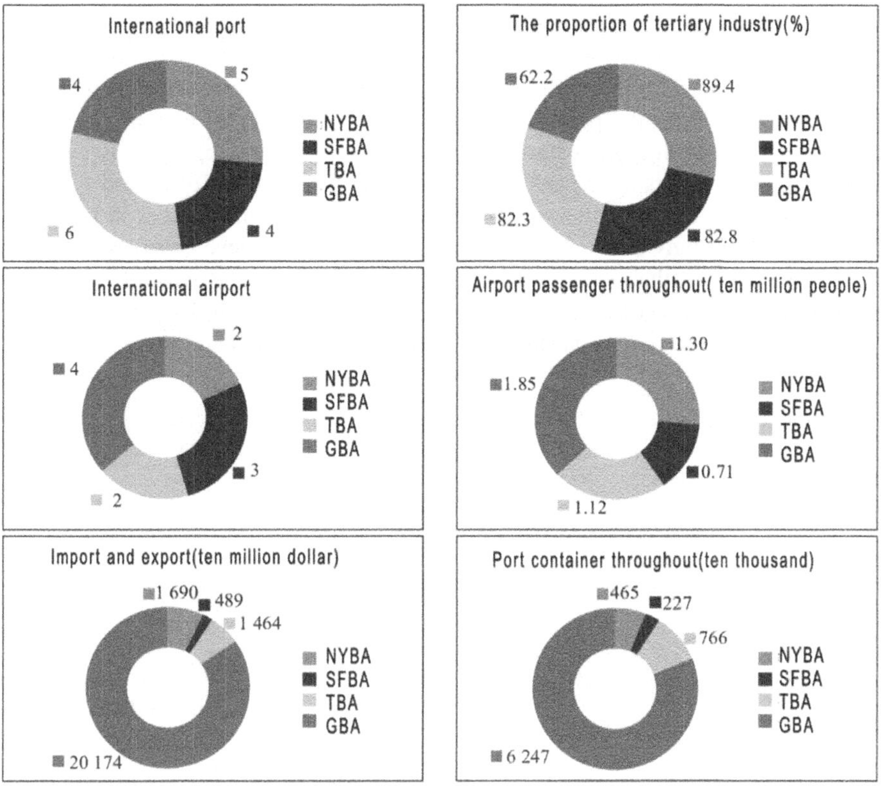

Fig. 5.14 Comparison of certain development indexes of the four bay areas (*Source* R&D Department of CSC Financial Co., Ltd)

primary industry still takes up certain proportion. Although it possesses considerable basis of manufacturing industry, optimizing industrial structure is required to occupy higher position in the global value chain.

5.1.4.4 Differences in development foundation

In terms of development foundation (See Fig. 5.14), the number of international ports, international airports and passenger throughout in GBA is comparable to that of the three international bay areas. Its export and import as well as container throughout have surpassed the other three bay areas, having absolute advantage. It is safe to say that GBA has laid a sound development foundation. In recent years, the economy growth rate of Tokyo is slowing down. The GBA is also affected by the slowing down of the world economy. If its current growth momentum can be sustained, GBA is expected to surpass the Tokyo Bay Area to be the largest bay area economy in the world.

5.1.4.5 Differences in Innovation Capabilities

An important index to measure bay area development is comparing their innovation capabilities from the perspective of innovation features of bay area economy. Figure 5.15 shows that GBA has greatest number of patent applications, which is 176,000. The numbers are 35,000 in San Francisco, 22,000 in Tokyo and 12,000 in New York respectively. However, taking into account the differences in the patent licensing system between countries, in order to further achieve comparability, it is more feasible to use the total number of global top 200 scientific research institutions in each bay areas to compare their innovation capabilities. Figure 5.15 shows that San Francisco Bay Area has the strongest innovation capability, and the second is New

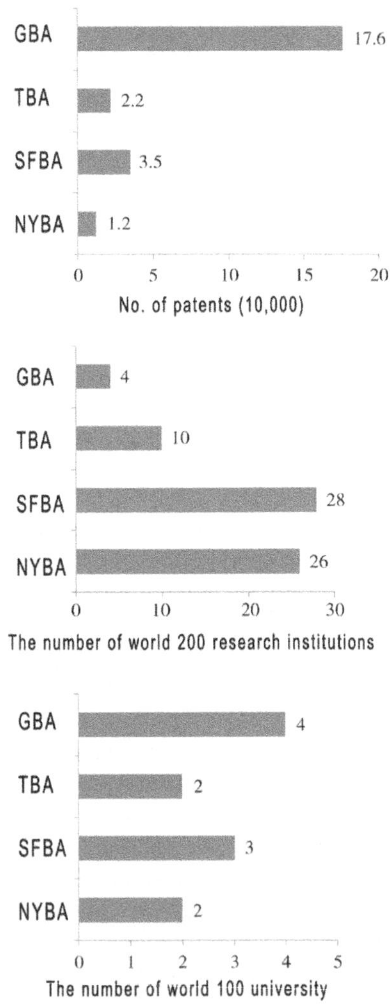

Fig. 5.15 Comparison of scientific innovation index of the four bay areas (*Source* Sorted by the authors)

York Metropolitan Area. The Tokyo Bay Area and GBA have relatively weak innovation capabilities. GBA falls far behind San Francisco and New York. The difference can also be observed in the number of universities in these bay areas. Although there are four Top 100 universitiesin GBA, all of them are in Hong Kong. San Francisco has produced many Nobel Prize, Fields Medal and Turing Award winners, attracting even more internationally renowned scholars. GBA is not a match for the time being or the near future. In addition, research and innovation capability can be indirectly reflected by research level. Of the top 50 leading scientific research institutions in the international rankings, Hong Kong University of Science and Technology is the only one from GBA (Fig. 5.16). According to *2thinknow* (a famous think tank from Australia) ranking of *World Innovation Cities*, Tokyo, San Francisco and New York are among the world's leading innovation hubs. Hong Kong stands at 27, being the first among Chinese cities. The second is Shanghai(35) and the third is Beijing(37). Shenzhen ranks 55 and Guangzhou ranks 113, which shows that the influence of sci-tech and innovation of GBA falls far behind that of the three bay areas (See Table

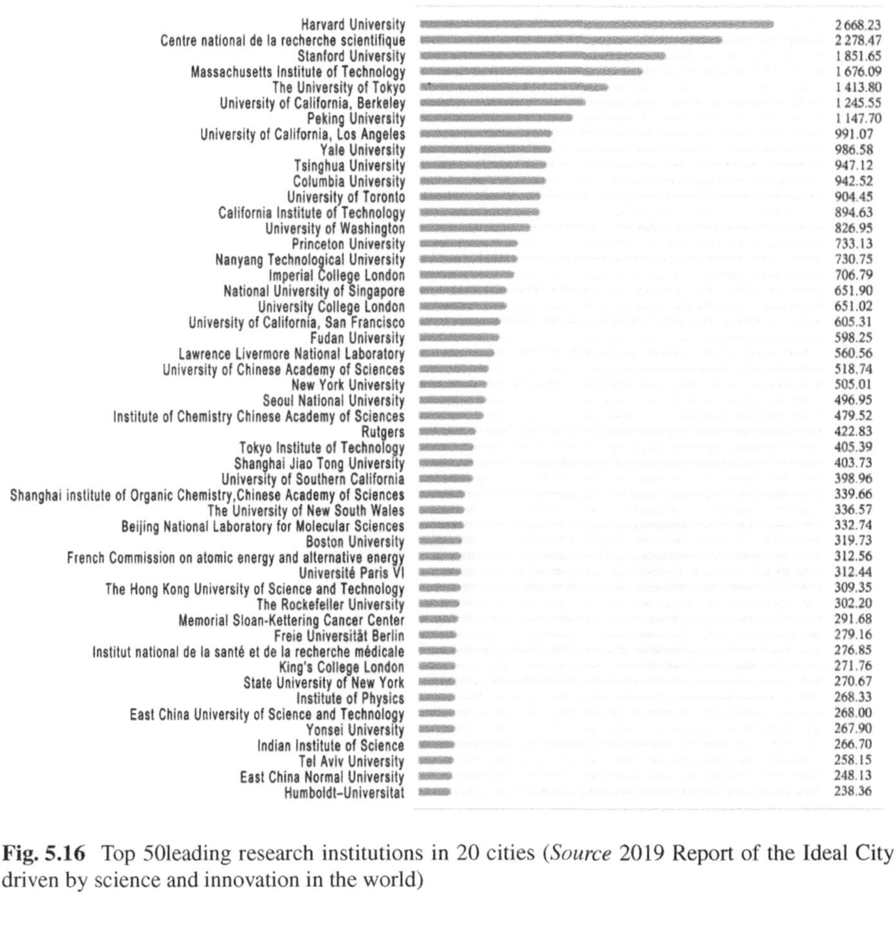

Fig. 5.16 Top 50leading research institutions in 20 cities (*Source* 2019 Report of the Ideal City driven by science and innovation in the world)

Table 5.8 Ranking of Innovation Cities

Ranking	City	Country
1	Tokyo	Japan
2	London	UK
3	San Francisco-San Jose	USA
4	New York	USA
5	Los Angeles	USA
6	Singapore	Singapore
7	Boston	USA
8	Toronto	Canada
9	Paris	France
10	Sydney	Australia
27	Hong Kong	China
35	Shanghai	China
37	Beijing	China
55	Shenzhen	China
113	Guangzhou	China

Source 2thinknow city ranking

5.8). In addition, Fig. 5.17 shows that most of R&D personnel in GBA are enterprise employees with a low proportion of scientists, which is another shortcoming of GBA. Enterprise R&D focuses on incubating and amplifying results of known researches, seeking faster returns with fewer investment. In-depth thinking is rare and it is difficult to achieve deep integration of research and innovation. The rational structure of enterprise R&D and scientific research should complement each other and be able to combine production, research and development. The deficiency will directly affect the innovation ability of GBA.

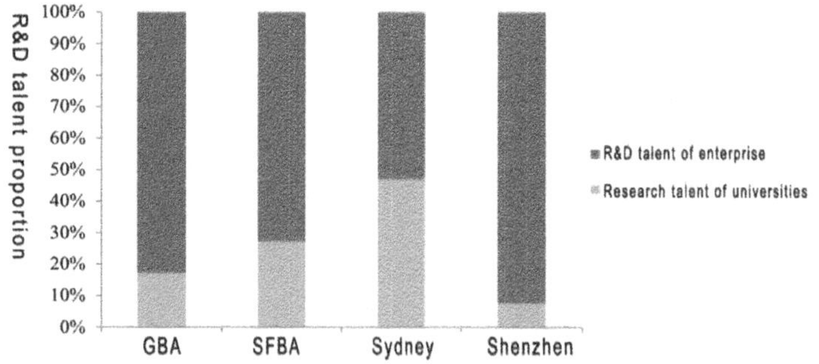

Fig. 5.17 Type of research talents in SFBA and GBA (*Source* Sorted by the authors)

5.1.5 Developmental Advantages and Disadvantages of the GBA

5.1.5.1 Developmental Advantages

The GBA has inborn advantages such as strong economic vitality, homogeneous city cluster culture and frequent communication. GBA ports stretch well into the hinterland. Its systems of economy, industry, sci-tech and transport are endowed with favorable conditions for world-level economic growth. Four comprehensive advantages can be created in GBA through the construction of a platform economy on top of the *One Country Two Systems and Three Tariff Zones.*

First, GBA's strength in institution and mechanism innovation, which is the basis for making a breakthrough in upgrading the status of the GBA. Its institutional advantage is manifested in *One country, Two systems and Three Tariff Zones.* Under the background of "one country", Hong Kong retains its original institutional advantages within a highly liberal and open policy environment. By adopting a common law system and both Chinese and English as the legal language, HK can be fully integrated with the international community while enjoying the convenience of the Two Systems. With the 1, 2 and 3 model in place, a flexible institutional arrangement is created for GBA to connect internationally.

Second, GBA's economy is large, which is the basis for further bay area economic development. Three rivers flow through GBA. It faces the Pacific Ocean and impacts the Pan-Pearl River Delta, having the largest hinterland among the four bay areas. It is larger than the total bay areas of New York, San Francisco and Tokyo. Its waterfront is close to the world's first golden route, covering the important passages of the Maritime Silk Road and enjoying obvious location advantage as the "crossroad" between Asia and Oceania, and Pacific Ocean and Indian Ocean. The total population of GBA ranks first among all four bay areas, but its proportion to the national population is much less significant than that of New York or Tokyo, which indicates that there is much space for talent absorption in GBA.

Third, GBA's potential for industrial development is great, which is the basis for industrial upgrading. Its upstream and downstream supply chains are complete, and its industrial ecosystem is perfect. Advanced manufacturing industry and modern service industry dominate its industrial structure. More than 300 industrial clusters with their own features strongly complement each other, granting special overall competition advantage in the GBA. The headquarter effect is outstanding. GBA also possesses the advantage of population structure. The age structure of its population is relatively young with high-proportion labor force and strong sustainable population driving force. Though the proportion of tertiary industry in GBA is less than that of other bay areas, difference in development gradient is beneficial for the concentration and radiation of industry and economy. Therefore, seen from industrial chain ecosystem, population structure and industrial population, GBA's development potential is greater than the other three bay areas.

Fourth, GBA's advantages of scientific and technological innovation provide impetus for further development. The GBA has outstanding performance in sci-tech research, development, and transfer. High-level universities, research institutions, high-tech enterprises and national science projects can be found in Hong Kong, Guangzhou and Shenzhen. GBA's strong innovative elements, research basis and development potential can provide continuous drive for the development of the GBA.

5.1.5.2 Developmental Disadvantages

There are also limitations in system connectivity of *One Country Two Systems and Three Tariff Zones*, which serves as the foundation of providing innovative institutional mechanism for the development of the GBA, but also generates obstacles that GBA must overcome to achieve regional synergy development. There are gaps in the legal system, administrative system, economic system and social governance model, as well as in the dimensions of market openness and social welfare in Hong Kong, Macao and Guangdong Province. This is an obstacle of institutional mechanism.

Economic differences are obvious and regional economic integration is low in the GBA. Cities like Hong Kong and Shenzhen have first-mover advantages whose industrial layout is basically complete and the development is basically stable. The later-comers' development space is thus squeezed as space is limited. Cities other than Hong Kong and Macao lag behind in marketization, internationalization and institutional inclusiveness and adaptability.

Differentiation in social factors is obvious and regional social unfairness is a reality. Social factors such as health care, education, the annual increase in the resident population, etc., are inherently and innately unequally distributed. Quality resources are obviously concentrated in Hong Kong, Macao and Guangzhou. As a city with high level of economic development in the GBA, Shenzhen has less and inferior social resources when compared with Guangzhou. The social resources of the remaining cities are basically in line with the level of economic development, that is, in areas with poor economic development, there are also problems of weak medical and educational resources, low annual added value of the resident population and limited level of sustainable development.

Differentiation in soft power is obvious which is hard for regional synergy. There are still obstacles to cultural exchange and integration in GBA. The strength of the cultural and creative industries is not strong and the inclusive and open social atmosphere is still weak. People in Hong Kong and Macao still have some doubts about the opening up and integration of the GBA and worry about losing their status and space. Guangzhou and Shenzhen face many non-market disturbing factors such as local protection, administrative obstacles and disorderly competition in economic development. Their degree of social inclusion and market openness needs to be further improved.

Cross-border infrastructure is not yet perfect, and regional spatial integration still faces problems. Distribution of social and economic resources is uneven in the GBA, which is related to the imperfection of transportation, especially fast rail transit facilities. There are a few channels across the Pearl River estuary and the inter-connection is loose. The effect of economic westward radiation is insignificant. Airport and port functions are overlapped with weak coordination and homogeneous competition is fierce. Scientific planning in land resources and environmental protection is lacking. Problems in land use and environmental pollution are becoming increasingly serious when each city acts on its own will without coordination. Disparities exist in cities' ability to attract first-class enterprises and talents.

5.2 Opportunities for Combined Free Trade Ports of GBA

The current situation of development of the GBA shows that there is room for improvement in the development of "9 + 2" city cluster economy integration. There is still a gap between the realization of regional synergy development, the integration of urban and rural development, and the construction of a scientifically structured, intensive and efficient development pattern of GBA.

It is for this reason that the Chinese central government has included the construction of combined free trade ports in the GBA as a national priority strategy. Innovating and breaking current building pilot free trade zone is a major exploration made by China to deepen reform and opening up, optimize resource allocation and integrate port resource from the global prospective. Building combined free trade ports is expected to advance the building of GBA and beneficial to deepening exchange and cooperation between mainland and Hong Kong and Macao. It is of great significance for Hong Kong and Macao to participate in national development strategy, raise their competitiveness, and maintain long-term prosperity and stability. Therefore, it is necessary to identify the opportunities for building combined free trade ports of GBA and to explore the construction direction and path in order to promote high-quality integration development in the GBA.

5.2.1 Uniquely Favorable Geographical Conditions for the Construction of GBA Combined Ports

GBA is endowed with superior land and maritime factors for developing international trade. Located in China's coastal areas with a vast sea area and the coastline accounting for about a quarter of the China's coastline, GBA enjoys natural geographical advantages and unique port development conditions. It is one of the regional port groups with the largest capacity and the best water depth conditions in the world, and its ports' throughput is the highest in the world. The GBA is located in the subtropical monsoon climate zone of Eurasia, with high temperatures and plenty rainfalls. It is neither troubled by sea water freezing in winter in high-latitude coastal areas which poses restrictions on shipping, nor is it troubled by harsh coastal environment caused by proximity of desert in the same latitude under the control of subtropical high pressure. It is one of the most advantageous areas in the world for land and sea factors. Excellent ports are created in GBA thanks to its coastline and climate advantages. Historically, the GBA ports have been favored by overseas trade.

GBA features high density in spatial distance, which is conducive to the formation of close and integrated port groups. The geography of GBA is characterized with closeness to sea and harbor and easiness of group forming. Such high density of spatial distance provides great convenience and possibility for combined development, which is beneficial to promoting close integration of city, port and industry, and forming highly modernized port groups.

With Hong Kong and Macao included, GBA has the advantage of deep integration development. The nine municipalities are all adjacent to either Hong Kong or Macao, the two islands on the two sides of the Pearl River estuary. As an international trade center, financial center, shipping center and tourism center, Hong Kong is one of the freest economies in the world. Shenzhen and Hong Kong are adjacent and have convenient transportation, which is conducive to close cooperation between the two sides, promoting rapid contacts between enterprises and forming networks, and contributing to the deep integration and development of both sides. Hong Kong has established close economic ties with Southeast Asia and countries along the Maritime Silk Road to serve as a wealth management center in the region. The concerted development of the GBA can better serve the China's BRI and promote common regional development.

5.2.2 *Innovative Genes of* One Country Two Systems and Three Tariff Zones *Providing Impetus to Building GBA Combined Ports*

At present, there is an urgent need for Hong Kong and Macao to jointly build combined ports to cultivate new momentum as a means to cope with the constraints of current systems and mechanisms. GBA has always been the major pilot area for national system and mechanism innovation. Hong Kong is not only an internationally famous financial, shipping, trade and aviation hub, but a financial, shipping and trade center in GBA. However, in the current stage, Hong Kong is confronted with predicaments such as weak growth, lagging development of sic-tech cultural industry. Macao is tourism leisure center, and an important service platform of commerce and trade cooperation between China and Lusophones. At present, gambling industry dominates the economy of Macao. The industrial ecological chain environment is too simple and the port development is limited. The concept of "one country, two systems" is an innovation of the China's reform and opening-up in order to give full play to the comprehensive advantages of Hong Kong and Macao, promote the interconnection between Hong Kong and Macao and the Mainland, promote the complementary advantages of Hong Kong and Macao and the Mainland, and realize the common development of the region. The innovation of GBA is to integrate Hong Kong and Macao into the overall development of the country, further expand their development space, cultivate new dynamics for development and promote coordinated regional development.

The three free trade zones of Guangdong carry innovative genes to inject impetus for the construction of GBA Combined Ports. The nine municipalities include one pilot demonstration zone of Socialism with Chinese Characteristics in Shenzhen and two National Innovation Demonstration Zones in Shenzhen and Pearl River Delta. The three pilot free trade zones are Qianhai-Shekou of Shenzhen, Nansha of Guangzhou and Hengqin of Zhuhai, It shows that GBA has the innovative gene and innate advantage of developing free trade ports. The three pilot zones are set up to experiment innovation to inject new impetus into the combined ports initiative. The innovative gene of Nansha New Area is embodied in the expansion and opening up to the whole world, providing advanced integrated hub services, taking the lead in developing high-end manufacturing, productive services, shipping logistics and specialty metals, and creating an international high-end productive service industry factor gathering highland. The innovation gene of The Qianhai-Shekou Area is embodied in deepening the cooperation between Shenzhen and Hong Kong, characterized by financial opening and innovation, using science and technology as leverage to further the opening up of high-end service industry, and building a pilot demonstration window for the opening up of China's financial industry, an important base for global trade in services and an international hub port. The innovative gene Hengqin New Area is reflected in the deep cooperation with Macao, focusing on the development of the health industry, leisure tourism, culture, science and education as the focus, high-tech support, to create the most open international business services leisure area and an open pilot area for culture and education. It can be seen that the three zones focus on differentiated development positioning, aiming at synergy development backed up by Hong Kong and Macao, which helps to create innate advantages for the construction of GBA Combined Ports. At the same time, it also injects innovative impetus into the construction of the Combined Ports, and catalyzes the early completion of the Combined Ports.

The innovation of the existing institutional mechanism in GBA helps to pave the way for the construction of the GBA Combined Ports. Firstly, the perfection and innovation of the legal system help to pave the way for the maritime commercial cooperation in GBA. Taking Qianhai-Shekou Zone as an example, firstly, a system of legal rules in line with internationally accepted commercial rules has been established here. Three basic legislations are in place, including *Regulations on the Modern Services Cooperation Zone in Qianhai Shenzhen-Hong Kong, Shenzhen Special Economic Zone, Interim Measures of the Administration of Modern Services Cooperation Zone in Qianhai, Shenzhen*, and *Interim Measures for the Administration of the Bonded Port Area of Qianhai Bay of Shenzhen.* At the same time, legal construction entities are encouraged to settle in Qianhai to jointly create an environment of international first-class rule of law, accelerate the reform of the judicial system mechanism in Qianhai, and build an international and diversified dispute resolution mechanism.

Secondly, an international legal service platform has been set up in Qianhai to safeguard Chinese enterprises to go international. Finally, Qianhai has exerted great efforts in law cooperation between Shenzhen and Hong Kong, learning from and mirroring Hong Kong's experience in regional legal system.

Secondly, the perfection of the social credit system helps to pave the way for GBA Combined Ports to regulate the market business environment. Firstly, Shenzhen municipal government, as an example of the other cities in Guangdong, issued regulations to severely punish the breach of trust of individuals and enterprises, including *Measures for the Administration of Personal Credit and Credit Rating* and *Management Measures for Enterprise Credit and Evaluation.* Personal and enterprise credit information system platform is made to facilitate internet search. Relying on the joint application of credit information data, the relevant departments in Shenzhen have carried out credit classification supervision system to varying degrees in various key areas, and actively promoted the construction of trustworthy incentive and breach of trust disciplinary mechanism. Secondly, the enterprise credit information system of Shenzhen and some other cities in Guangdong is directly connected to the national enterprise credit information disclosure system of China's State Administration for Industry and Commerce. In so doing, the geographical restrictions are broken. Personal credit system is connected with those of the Ministry of Public Security, the Ministry of Education and the General Administration of Industry and Commerce to establish long-term cooperative relations. In so doing, real-time sharing of the individual household registration, education and enterprise organization code and other information is available to ensure that the social credit system is continuously transparent and convenient. As a pioneer, Shenzhen has served as an exploration zone to improve social credit and business environment for servicing free trade ports.

Thirdly, simplification of approval system paves the way for investment facilitation of GBA Combined Ports. In order to promote investment facilitation, administrative approval reform is carried out in Guangdong to raise administrative service level for reducing formalities required in business operation in order to reduce enterprise cost. Taking administrative approval reform of Qianhai as an example, it has adopted an innovative service model of *One Hall and One Net* to provide enterprises with complete services from business establishment to operation relying on one administrative hall and one online administrative hall, and taking the enterprise web page as the carrier. Great efforts are made to advance online business and service to create time saving business environment for enterprises.

Fourthly, financial innovation paves the way for combined ports to realize cross-border finance. For forming competitiveness of financial service and concentration, Guangdong distinguished Pilot Free Trade Zone of Guangdong Qianhai-Shekou, Nansha and Hengqin from their differentiation, achieved interconnectivity with international financial market and built unique mechanism of cross-border capital market linkage relying on the advantage of Hong Kong as an international financial center. Guangdong effectively controls the risk of cross-border capital flow as the opening level of China's financial market is raised. Active explorations are conducted in Pilot FTZs of Guangdong such as developing diverse cross-border finance tools and innovating cross-border financial business. Innovations such as cross-border use of

RMB, relaxation of access to financial institutions, opening up of financial markets and improvement of financial regulatory methods within the FTZs are implemented to provide more convenience in cross-border settlement in GBA Combined Ports, to provide institutional basis for cross-border financial development, and to further promote the integration of GBA Combined Ports into the international market.

5.2.3 Existing and Planned Industrial Conditions for Laying a Solid Foundation for the Construction of GBA Combined Ports

5.2.3.1 GBA's Strong Industrial Base Serving as the Basis for GBA Combined Ports

Firstly, GBA's shipping industry has obvious foundational advantages. China is a major exporter and importer in the world. For many years, Guangdong's export and import ranks first in China with huge primary cargo throughout, having comparative advantage in port space expansion, infrastructure and operation cost. Hong Kong is the only region in China that provides internationally recognized overall shipping service (such as maritime arbitration, hull insurance and financing). In Hong Kong, the legal environment is stable; enterprise registration is convenient and quick; tax rate is low; and capital in–out is free. It is more suitable to develop high-end shipping service industries represented by hull management, shipping broker, shipping financing, shipping insurance and law. Therefore, from the perspective of shipping industry development, synergy development of the GBA is a better solution to avoid regional vicious competition. Secondly, continuous expansion in trade scale between Hong Kong, Macao and mainland spontaneously promotes the building of combined free trade ports. Since 2012, trade volume between Hong Kong and China's mainland has taken up more than half of Hong Kong's total trade volume. According to statistics from Hong Kong General Administration of Customs, in 2018, trade export volume from Hong Kong to mainland reached 314.33 billion dollars, covering 55.2% of total export volume; import volume reached 274.36 billion dollars, covering 43.7% of total import volume.[13] Hong Kong's trade surplus mainly comes from mainland. There is strong complementary in service industry between Guangdong and Hong Kong, which naturally promotes the building of combined free trade ports. Thirdly, the basis of interconnectivity in financial field is good, which is helpful to advance the building of combined free trade ports. Hong Kong conveniently and effectively realizes interconnectivity in international capital market by innovation models such as Shanghai-Hong Kong Stock Connect, Shenzhen-Hong Kong Stock Connect and Bond Stock Connect. Interconnectivity in financial infrastructure and market is an important basis for building combined free trade ports. Meanwhile, financial interconnectivity can not only effectively consolidate Hong Kong's role as international financial center,

[13] Source: http://m.askci.com/news/maoyi/20190214/1018081141537.shtml.

but provide security for mainland enterprise financing with the help of Hong Kong capital market, which is helpful for promoting effective building of combined free trade ports. Fourthly, complementary and cooperation in sci-tech and innovation fields among Guangdong, Hong Kong and Macao provide driving force for building combined free trade ports. Sci-tech cooperation and exchange among Guangdong, Hong Kong and Macao become gradually frequent, presenting good cooperation momentum. Hong Kong will cooperate with Shenzhen to build "Hong Kong- Shenzhen Innovation & Sci-tech Park" in Luomazhou and Hetao, Qianhai "Shenzhen-Hong Kong Youth Dream Factory", together building "Shenzhen-Hong Kong Innovation Circle" with international competitiveness, which provide vast development space for future sci-tech and innovation industries of GBA combined free trade ports, feasible cooperation model for driving sci-tech innovation and industrial upgrading of whole GBA and cultivating new economic driver, and mechanism security of sustainable development for making the GBA the first sci-tech and innovation bay area in the world.

5.2.3.2 GBA's Sound Industrial Ecosystem Enhancing the Feasibility of GBA Combined Ports Initiative

GBA has adequate up-and-down-stream supply chain, and perfect industrial ecosystem, which provide basis for in-depth combined development. Guangzhou and Shenzhen have good basis of manufacturing industry, possess perfect industrial clusters in medicine, electronic information industry and mechanical industry, and gradually transform and upgrade to finance, sci-tech service and IT. Taking Pearl River as boundary, other cities are separated into two zones of manufacturing industry. The east bank of Pearl River bears advanced electronic manufacturing industry formed by Shenzhen, Dongguan and Huizhou being a group. Shenzhen occupies the two ends of the "Smile Curve", who is responsible for high value-added activities including R&D design and brand marketing. Based on finance service and business service offered by Shenzhen, many major mobile phone factories such as Huawei, OPPO and VIVO locate in Dongguan and Huizhou as the two cities accept technology spillover of electronic information industry in Shenzhen. The west bank of Pearl River bears advanced equipment manufacturing industry and light industry made up by Guangzhou, Zhuhai, Foshan, Zhaoqing and Zhongshan. Guangzhou also occupies the two ends of the "Smile Curve", who is responsible for R&D and high value-added activities. Zhuhai, Foshan, Zhaoqing and Zhongshan respectively undertake hull and ocean engineering, smart equipment manufacturing, energy reduction and environmental protection, and new-energy equipment.

GBA possesses industrial opportunity to build combined free trade ports, boasting over 300 modern-service-oriented industrial clusters with their own features and perfect regional industrial division. In addition, GBA boasts many high-tech industries and high-end manufacturing industries such as artificial intelligence, cloud computing, new materials and smart manufacturing, which lay industrial foundation and provide sci-tech support for building GBA combined free trade ports. GBA also possesses developed manufacturing industry and sound industrial system, which provide industrial basis for combined free trade ports coordinating development of production service industries including R&D, logistics, finance, IT, business, energy reduction and environmental protection.

5.2.3.3 GBA's Misalignment of Industrial Structure Providing Space for the Construction of GBA Combined Ports

Seen from industrial structure (Fig. 5.18), GBA has adequate up-and-down-stream supply chain. Up-stream industries and down-stream industries can complement each other and achieve differentiated development as gradients exist in industries. In terms of industrial output, China's mainland can compensate the "industry hollowing" of Hong Kong and Macao, while Hong Kong and Macao can feedback mainland, supporting export of manufacturing industry in the nine municipalities. At the same time, core cities and two-wing cities can implement differentiated development. For example, advanced manufacturing industry and high-end service industry in Guangzhou can complement with industrial base in Foshan. Modern service industry in Shenzhen can complement with high-end manufacturing industry in Dongguan. High-end manufacturing industry can complement with special market base in Zhongshan. If GBA is promoted to be coordinated as the whole, achieves factor interconnectivity and provides one-stop service, the competitiveness of enterprises in international market will be greatly raised. Then, a super combination of

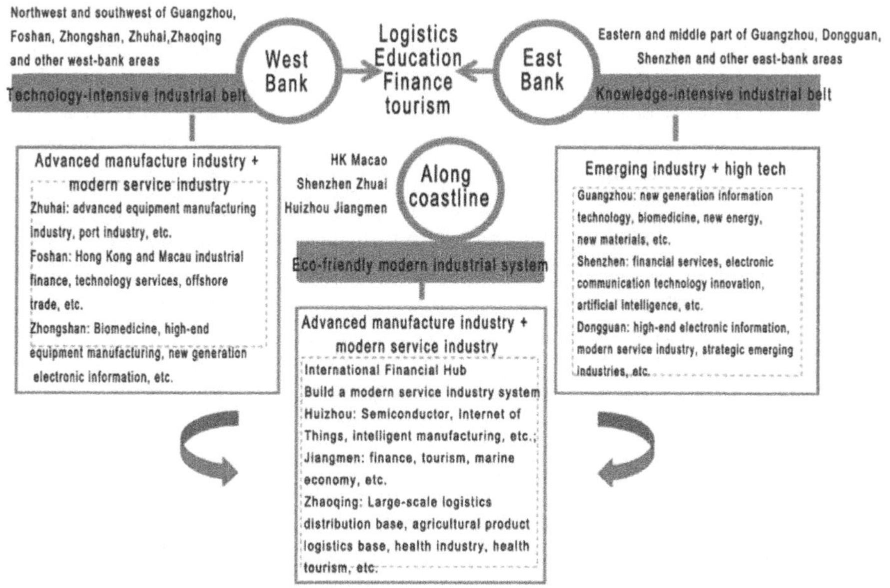

Fig. 5.18 An ecological map of industries in GBA (*Source* Sorted by the authors)

Hong Kong, Shenzhen and Dongguan", that is "$1 + 1 + 1 > 3''$, will be expected to be the world's new Silicon Valley. From now on, it may be a new normal that creativity is generated in Hong Kong, developed in Shenzhen, and finally finished in Dongguan.[14] This differentiated and complementary industrial ecologic map helps to lay the foundation for the combination of ports, being one of major advantages for GBA to develop combined ports.

5.2.4 Continuously Perfected Land-Sea-Air Connectivity Infrastructure for the Smooth Construction of GBA Combined Ports

As a large-scale infrastructure and national strategic material, the improvement of the competitiveness port clusters depends on the coordinated development after the overall planning. Port clusters can reduce logistics cost and avoid cross-border transit. In addition, port cluster is beneficial to strengthening network effect of urban road and bridge resource. GBA planning shows that in the future several years, land- sea- air connectivity infrastructure in the GBA will be continuously improved, which provides infrastructure support for coordinating development of each port and building combined free trade ports.

5.2.4.1 GBA Owning the world's Largest Airport Complex

At present, there are four major international airports in GBA, located in Hong Kong, Macao, Guangzhou and Shenzhen respectively, reaching all corners of the world. GBA also owns Zhuhai Jinwan Airport, Huizhou Pingtan Airport, as well as the planned construction of Guangzhou Second Airport, Pearl River Delta Hub (Guangzhou New) Airport. It takes no more than 5 h to fly from Hong Kong International Airport to cities lived by half of the world population. There is seamless connection between GBA airports and urban transits. Both Guangzhou-Dongguan-Shenzhen urban rail and Guangzhou-Foshan urban rail can reach Guangzhou Baiyun International Airport terminal.

5.2.4.2 GBA's World-Class Transit Network Supporting *One-Hour Living Circle*

Transit facilities of land interconnectivity in GBA are continuously improved (Fig. 5.19). In September, 2018, GBA opened its high-speed rail which passes by Guangzhou South, Shenzhen North, Futian and Hong Kong West Kowloon, a less than one-hour trip between the two terminals. Guangzhou South Railway Station is

[14] Huang Wentao. *Industrial Opportunities Contained by GBA* [EB/OL]. http://finance.eastm.

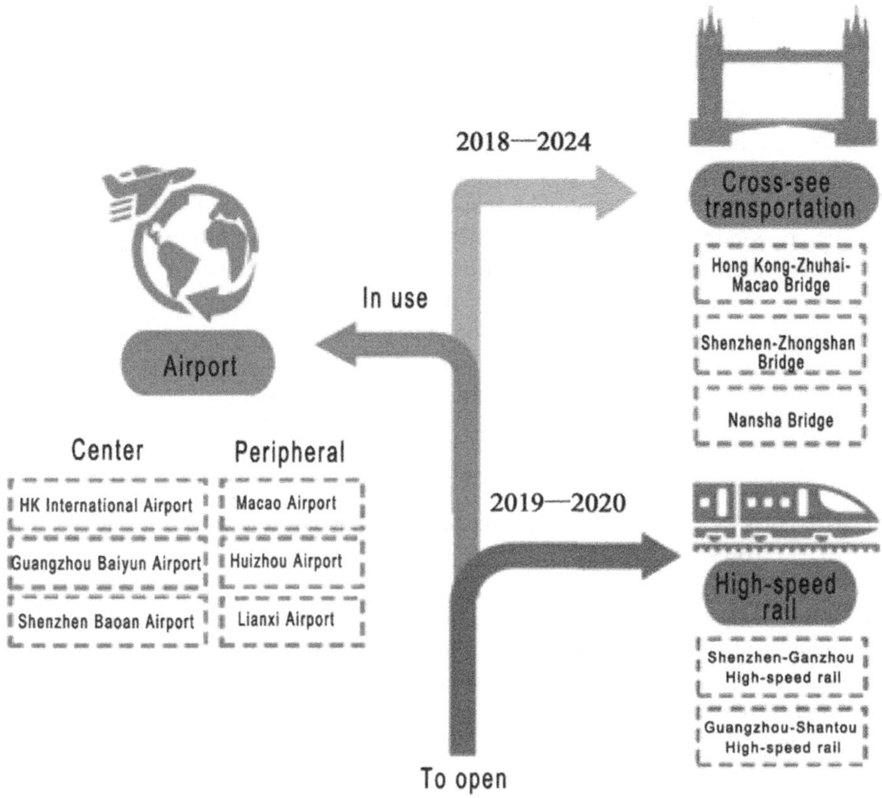

Fig. 5.19 Diagram of major infrastructure construction in GBA (*Source A Special Report on Guangdong-Hong Kong-Macao Greater Bay Area*, iiMedia Report)

connected to national high-speed rail network in the mainland, being able to transfer and access to 44 cities in the mainland. With the opening of Hong Kong-Zhuhai-Macao Bridge and connectivity of east and west ports in Pearl River, residents along the west coast of Pearl River Delta have entered a three-hour transit circle to reach Hong Kong. The travel time from Zhuhai to Hong Kong airport is reduced to 45 min. In addition, GBA plans to build Shenzhen-Zhongshan thoroughfare and Shenzhen-Zhuhai cross-sea urban rail. In addition to easing traffic pressure on the Humen Bridge, it connects the east and west sides of the Pearl River, allowing the relatively slow-growing west coast of Zhuhai to catch the fast train of Shenzhen's economic growth.

The spatial feature of current main transportation infrastructure in the GBA displays transit an intensive traffic network centered around Guangzhou, Shenzhen, Hong Kong and Macao. The transportation infrastructure under construction or planning presents the direction of the construction of Guangzhou as the central axis to extend to the wings. The uneven spatial distribution of infrastructure is often limited by the level of urban development. The relative independence of the GBA cities and the restriction of inter-city connectivity, especially the inadequate infrastructure services in the less developed areas, often further aggravate the imbalance of economic development in the GBA. Compared with the existing infrastructure projects, the planned projects can solve the problem of low density of peripheral transportation infrastructure to a certain extent, and solve the problem of uneven spatial distribution of the original transportation infrastructure in GBA.

The cross-border communication infrastructure has been initially established in the GBA. International Communication Accesses are established in Guangzhou, Shenzhen, Zhuhai and other cities by the Ministry of Industry and Information. The three major Chinese communication operators have completed the Hong Kong-Zhuhai-Macao Bridge cross-border fiber optic cable system and provided wireless coverage on the East and West manmade islands, enabling connectivity with operating communications enterprises in Hong Kong and Macao.

5.2.4.3 GBA's Foundation Supporting the Construction of the world's Largest Port Cluster

There are many sea ports in the GBA, including internationally renowned ports of Guangzhou, Shenzhen and Hong Kong and ports of Dongguan, Huizhou, Zhongshan, Macau, Jiangmen and Foshan which possess unique advantages. In addition, river-sea combined transport is convenient in the GBA, which is helpful for inland river ports to build combined ports. GBA is endowed with resources and advantageous conditions for constructing combined free trade ports.

A triangular balance is established among the ports of Guangzhou, Shenzhen and Hong Kong and progressive division of labor is shared among the other ports along the Pearl River banks. Among all the ports, the ports of Guangzhou, Shenzhen and Hong Kong have always occupied the core position. 25 Chinese ports are listed in the 2019 Lloyd's Top 100 Global Ports, six of which are in the top 10. Guangzhou Port moved up to the 5th place, up 2 places from 2018, surpassing Hong Kong Port and Busan Port. Shenzhen Port ranked 4th and Hong Kong Port ranked 7th. Over the years, the strength of the three core ports has been changing, and all have achieved common progress in the competition. Relying on developed foreign trade, Shenzhen is mainly positioned as cargo container international transport of the Pearl River Delta region, becoming the cargo import and export seaport of the east bank of the Pearl River estuary and the southern hinterland of Jiangxi. Guangzhou has the vast hinterland of the west bank of Pearl River estuary, northern Guangdong, Hunan, north-central Guangxi and Guizhou and can serve as the coastal seaport for import and export of the inland containers from these places. Relying on the advantages of low taxation and tax exemption, Hong Kong can continue to develop its re-export business and become an international transit port serving the whole Greater Bay Area. Such a balanced triangular port eco system is most beneficial for the construction of combined ports in the GBA.

Although the surrounding ports on both sides of the Pearl River estuary are not as weighty as the three leading ports in terms of port size, economic hinterland and routes, they have made full use of their advantages, embraced group development, and achieved great results. As the fourth largest port in the GBA, Dongguan Port ranks 46th in Lloyd's 2019 Global Port 100. As the "factory of the world", Dongguan has a huge demand for shipping, whose strength cannot be underestimated. Huizhou Port is a national first-class port and is a rare natural port in southern China. It will gradually develop into a multi-functional and integrated port for the shipping of petrochemical products, containers-based cargo, as well as general and bulk cargo. Relying on the local developed manufacturing industry and convenient transportation, Zhongshan Port will strive to build a world-class manufacturing base in the GBA, and build a regional integrated transportation hub. Zhuhai Port is one of the 25 major coastal ports in China. With the transfer of energy-intensive enterprises in the Pearl River Delta to the west of Guangdong, and the spillover of bulk cargo from Guangzhou and Shenzhen to the surrounding ports, Zhuhai Port is expected to achieve further rapid development. The ports in the GBA are making common progress with increasingly clear division of labor, providing guidance for the positioning and direction of GBA Combined Ports.

The GBA has a wealth of inland waterway resources, and is strategically located in the land and connected with the sea. Its convenience in connected river and sea transport is favorable for the construction of combined inland river ports. Zhaoqing Port is located in the Xijiang Corridor and the key area of the Pan-Pearl River Delta, enjoying superior location advantages and shipping conditions. Driven by the growth effect of Guangzhou-Fushan-Zhaoqin economic belt, Zhaoqing Port is expected to continue to maintain rapid growth and become a transit port connecting the Pearl River Delta and Guangxi. With 76 navigable rivers and a navigable range of more than 1,350 km, Foshan Port is the largest inland port in the Pearl River basin. Nansha Port Hub is jointly constructed by Foshan, Guangzhou and Zhongshan, which will become a booster for port cooperation on the west bank of the Pearl River estuary, contributing to the foundation construction of GBA Combined Ports.

5.3 Challenges for GBA Combined Free Trade Ports

With the establishment of Guangdong-Hong Kong-Macao coordinated mechanism in shipping, trade, finance and sci-innovation and the construction of GBA Combined Ports, a pattern of complementary advantages and differentiated competition will be made possible in the GBA, avoiding vicious homogeneous competitions and enhancing the international competitiveness of the Greater Bay Area. GBA has become a world-class bay area in terms of total economic volume, port group density, urban group size, hinterland space potential, and industrial system integrity. However, compared with the high degree of interconnection within the world's three bay areas, the large-scale synergy effect has not yet been formed in the GBA. The construction of GBA Combined Ports is facing many challenges.

5.3.1 *Coordination Barriers Brought by the Differences of* Two Systems

The existing four institutions under the *Two Systems* are restricting the flow of elements in the GBA and are difficult to coordinate. They are the institutions of customs, currency, tax and law. The system by which customs exercise the functions of supervision and administration of imports and exports in accordance with the laws and administrative regulations of the country (or region) is a specific system for regulating the movement of goods and persons in the free trade area. The currency system refers to the structure and organization of currency circulation determined by the government of a country (or region) in legal form. In FTZ, it involves the settlement of cross-border currency, the centralized operation of foreign exchange funds at the headquarters of multinational corporations, and the two-way fund pool of foreign currency. The tax system includes not only the tariff system, but also the relevant taxes and fees paid by enterprises that invest directly in the free trade area, the personal income in the free trade area, and so on. The construction of the legal institution includes laws and regulations up to a country's constitution, to laws and regulations common within a country's sovereignty, and to regulations within FTZ, regulating and guiding all economic activities in FTZ.

The implementation of the *Two Systems* in the GBA represents its uniqueness and outstanding advantages, However, if not handled well, the elements cannot flow efficiently and conveniently. It will become a barrier and obstacle to further deepening cooperation between Guangdong, Hong Kong and Macao. It may become the biggest obstacle to the construction of the GBA. Under *One country Two systems*, different social systems, legal systems and tariff areas exist in the GBA. The level of market connectivity needs to be improved step by step and efficient and convenient flow of factors of production has not yet been formed. The cooperation between the three regions has entered the deep water area. Many deep problems in the development of Hong Kong and Macao need to be solved through deep regional cooperation. Due to the lack of smooth regional coordination, the three regions choose to make their own plans and seek independent development, becoming the leading cause of the stagnation of the flow of factors in GBA and creating an institutional barrier characterized by the phenomenon of "open gates with closed doors". One of the major challenges for GBA Combined Ports is to remove this barrier and allow the elements to flow freely in the GBA (Table 5.9).

5.3.2 *Homogeneous Competition Brought About by the Rapid Development of the GBA Port Clusters*

The dense water network and its many ports and docks are the advantages of GBA Combined Ports. But if homogeneous competition exists among the ports, its current

Table 5.9 Regional differences and complementary advantages in GBA

System	Guangdong	Hong Kong	Macao	Complementation and coordination
Investment	Concentrate on big things	International Business Rules	World Tourism and Leisure Center	Promote the further upgrading of modern service industries and advanced manufacturing high-tech industries
Trade	Strong decision-making execution	International Business Network	Business service platform between China and Portugal	Maintain trade multilateralism and promote globalization
Finance	Separate operation, foreign exchange settlement and sale system	Mixed operation, open exchange control	Mixed operation, open exchange control	Enhance the lubricant effect of finance on the real economy of the Guangdong-Hong Kong-Macao Greater Bay Area
Law	Socialist Law System (Department of Statutory Law)	Common law system	Civil Law System (Statutory Law System)	Inter regional judicial assistance
Political system	socialism	Capitalism and a high degree of autonomy	Capitalism and a high degree of autonomy	Improve the quality of opening up
Economic system	Government-led	Active non-intervention	Between the two	Make full use of both domestic and foreign markets, rationally allocate resources, accelerate the formation of new development methods, and promote the strategic adjustment of economic structure
Talent	Frontier science and technology, basic science talents	Finance and shipping talents	Portuguese-speaking countries, tourism and hotel management talents	Industry-University-Research Cooperation Highland

(continued)

Table 5.9 (continued)

System	Guangdong	Hong Kong	Macao	Complementation and coordination
Industry	Advanced manufacturing and high-tech	Fintech and Shipping Technology	Tourism and Gaming	Industry diversification, integration of new economic growth points

Source Sorted by the authors

advantages and competitive strength will be greatly weakened. The vicious competition of existing ports, including deliberately lowering market prices or blindly investing in order to expand market share, forces the convergence of the structure of cargo transport between ports, and can lead to regional oversupply. Some port cities have stepped up financial subsidies and administrative intervention in order to make temporary gains. These competitive means may fail to improve the efficiency of the ports and affect the overall competitive strength of the whole region.

Surveying the current functions of GBA ports, we find that with the rapid rise of Shenzhen Port and Guangzhou Port, Hong Kong's shipping business is bound to be affected by the diversion of both. Hong Kong was once the most important trade transit port in the GBA, and were chosen by the vast majority of enterprises in the hinterland of Chinese mainland. In recent years, on the one hand, the cost of loading and unloading in Hong Kong, including labor costs and land costs, has been higher than that of Mainland ports; on the other hand, the ports of Shenzhen and Guangzhou have developed rapidly with lower costs and smoother connections with China's economic hinterland. It is inevitable that Hong Kong Port will be significantly weakened and its basic shipping operations will be diverted. According to statistics from Hong Kong Maritime Department, in recent 5 years from 2012 to 2016, 4 years have witnessed negative growth in total number of Hong Kong ocean shipment cargo. In terms of container throughput, Hong Kong's global ranking has fallen from No. 3 in 2012 to No. 5 in 2016. As similar free trade ports are constructed in Guangdong, the number and gross tonnage of mainland vessels docked in Hong Kong for a short period of time will likely continue to be diverted by ports of Guangdong. Hong Kong's basic shipping services sector will inevitably be affected. In the medium to long term, the three major GBA ports have their own advantages. Guangzhou Port is close to Shanghai Port in terms of cargo throughput. Shenzhen Port has an advantage in passenger throughput. Hong Kong has an advantage in a highly liberal and open system. The Combined Ports Initiative is conducive to the formation of differentiated positioning and development, and enhance the overall efficiency of the regional port clusters in the GBA. The construction of free trade ports and the establishment of a coordination mechanism for the shipping industry in the GBA will help promote the differentiated competition of shipping services in Hong Kong, Guangzhou and Shenzhen, enhance the overall competitiveness of regional shipping and avoid ineffective price competition. It will also expand new varieties and markets in the shipping business, enhance the influence of the global shipping index, enhance the advantages of the international shipping market over competitors such as Singapore, and enhance the global competitiveness of the shipping industry in Guangdong, Hong Kong and Macao (Table 5.10).

However, ports of GBA inevitably exist such problems as transport category overlapping and homogeneous competition. It is one of huge challenges to build combined free trade ports and an important path to gain advantage in global value chain competition that how to differentiate port cluster function, avoid homogeneous competition, help leverage coordinated effect among ports in middle-and-long term, realize resource sharing and raise production efficiency.

Table 5.10 A comparison of shipment index of five ports in 2018

Port	Container throughput (10,000 TEU)	Cargo throughput (10,000 ton)	Cargo foreign trade throughput (10,000 ton)	Passenger throughput (10,000 persons)
Guangzhou Port	2187	59396	13782	101
Shenzhen Port	2574	25127	18728	698
Shanghai Port	4201	68392	40206	315
Singapore Port	3660	63000	N/A	N/A
Hong Kong Port	1960	25850	N/A	N/A

Source Ministry of Transport of China, Transport Department of HKSAR, Transport Department of Singapore

5.3.3 Industrial Restructuring and Imbalanced Industrial Development

GBA also faces great challenges in industrial restructuring and imbalanced industrial development. Against the background of Sino-US trade friction, as international industrial output is reconstructed and economy of the GBA is typically outward-oriented economy. Potential economic growth in the U.S. and Europe has declined since 2008, which directly weakened demand of developed country market for China's products and influenced export processing trade of the GBA. The slowdown of export trade will form chain reaction, which not only slows down market demand, but leads to reduction in profits of domestic shipment market, finally directly affecting port investment.

Currently, the degree of industrial development in each city in the GBA is still not coordinated, which is mainly reflected in that there is a huge difference in industrial development level among cities on the two banks of Pearl River and the leading industry is not prominent. In contrast, the world's three great bay areas all have precise positioning and distinctive leading industries. For example, the New York Bay Area is the financial innovation hub; the Tokyo Bay Area is the industrial hub, and the San Francisco Bay Area is the scientific innovation hub. While the GBA covers high-end manufacturing, high-tech industries, and financial industries, it has not been able to form a dominating industry.

In addition, Hong Kong's economic growth lacks sustained and solid support, and Macao's economic structure is relatively single and its development resources are limited. The market economy system of the nine municipalities needs to be perfected. Although the *Outline Development Plan* emphasizes on differentiated development, which will promote further development in the GBA, the gap between urban development within the GBA is still large, and synergy needs to be improved. There is still homogeneous competition and resource mismatch in certain areas in the GBA, and it is very necessary to carry out synergy development through the construction of GBA Combined Ports. How to link manufacturing and service industries through the Combined Ports, achieve good balance and beneficial interaction between high-tech and traditional industries, and promote co-development of the core urban hinterland through radiation effect remains a challenge for GBA Combined Ports.

5.3.4 *Fierce Competition from Domestic and Foreign Port Groups*

It is inevitable that GBA ports will face competition from domestic and foreign port groups in the process of development. From a global perspective, Asia is one of the most port-intensive regions in the world. Competition among Asian port clusters has always been fierce as ports choose to maximize performance for the pursuit of individual interests. This gives GBA even greater pressure in its way to the top. On the domestic front, the GBA is facing the challenges of the Yangtze River Delta Port Cluster. Table 5.11 shows that from 2008–2018, Yangtze River Delta represented by Shanghai Port and Ningbo Zhoushan Port has the largest port density in China, whose container throughput covers half of the whole throughput in China. In recent years, though Shenzhen Port and Guangzhou Port have quickly risen, Yangtze River Delta port cluster is still a strong competitor for GBA. The rapid development of the mainland ports has also made the hinterland of ports further extend to interior of the mainland. The port clusters of Yangtze River Delta, Fujian, and Southwest China are constantly taking away businesses used to belong to Pearl River Delta. Container throughput at Hong Kong Port was 1.493 million TEUs in June 2019, down 11.3% year-on-year, which is the 17th consecutive month of decline. It is a second double-digit decline after February 2019, which was 17.9%. As a beneficiary of the Sino-US trade war, Vietnam's port container throughput exceeded that of Hong Kong by 1.5 million TEUs in June, 2019. Since competition from home and abroad is inevitable, the success of GBA Combined Ports lies in regional synergy development and precise development positioning.

Table 5.11 A comparison of container throughput of Chinese and foreign ports from 2008 to 2018

Port	2018	2017	2016	2015	2014	2013	2012	2011	2010	2009	2008
Shanghai Port	4201	4023	3653	3654	3529	3362	3253	3174	2907	2500	2798
Singapore Port	3660	3367	3092	3092	3390	3260	3160	2994	2843	2587	2992
Hong Kong Port	1959	2077	2011	2011	2228	2235	2310	2422	2370	2098	2425
Shenzhen Port	2574	2521	2420	2421	2403	2328	2294	2250	2251	1825	2141
Zhoushan Port	2635	2461	2062	2063	1945	1733	1617	1464	1316	1050	1123
Guangzhou Port	2192	2037	1762	1740	1616	1531	1452	1431	1255	1119	1100

Source Ministry of Transport of China, Transport Department of HKSAR, Transport Department of Singapore

5.3.5 Mismatch Between Scientific Discovery and Technological Application

There is mismatch between basic scientific research and technological transfer and application in the GBA. Science discovery and application of industrial technology are two important stages of innovation. Scientific discovery represents the ability of breaking through basic science and front-edge science problems, and often is measured by the number of published high-level papers. Application of industrial technology represents the ability of using scientific discovery results to produce social economy value and increase business value creation capacity for total factor productivity with new production capacity. It is often measured by the number of patent applications. In comparison, science discovery requires a long production cycle, but once breakthrough progress is achieved, productive force will be greatly raised. It is the cornerstone of technological progress. The application of industrial technology is the embodiment of the commercial value of scientific discovery, which can make scientific discovery constantly tested and get feedback in the market.

The number of SCI journals measures the impact of a city's scientific discovery, and the number of SCI journals owned by a city represents the concentration of high-level science in the city. As can be seen from Table 5.12, the gap between China's cities and other international cities in the publication of high-level papers is still large. Beijing has 14 SCI journals, but is ranked 35th compared to other international cities

Table 5.12 Geographical location of SCI journals (in cities)

City	No	City	No	City	No	City	No
New York	545	Palo Alto	42	Heidelberg	17	Auckland	9
Malden	507	Bethesda	35	Munich	17	Kyoto	9
Oxford	297	Paris	34	Abington	16	Leiden	8
Amsterdam	250	Claire	34	Alexander	15	Taipei	8
London	245	Stuttgart	32	Beijing	14	Warsaw	7
Philadelphia	218	Ottawa	28	Los Angeles	14	Madison	7
Dordrecht	117	Oxon	27	Cary	12	Providence	6
San Diego	113	Chicago	27	Edinburgh	12	Bangalore	6
Washington	97	Lausanne	26	Boston	12	Boulder	6
New Jersey	78	Lawrence	22	Sao Paulo	12	Texas	6
Basel	61	Vienna	21	New Rochelle	12	Dutak	6
Saint louis	55	Berlin	19	Victoria	11	Helsinki	6
Bristol	47	Reston	19	Singapore	12	Cleveland	6
Tokyo	47	Jena	19	Leeds	11	Cambridge (USA)	5
Cambridge (UK)	43	Hertford	18	Abingdon	11	Shanghai	3

Source Li Jian. *The Origin of Knowledge Output in Global Innovation Network* [A]. Tu Qiyu. *Report on Development of International Cities* (2017) [M]. Beijing: Social Sciences Academic Press, 2017

Table 5.13 No. of scientific publications and patents owned by major city clusters in China

City cluster	Major cities	No. of publications	No. of patents
GBA city cluster	Shenzhen-Hong Kong	45393	55433
	Guangzhou	59762	4029
Total	—	105155	59462
Beijing-Tianjin-Hebei city cluster	Beijing	222668	23014
	Tianjin	37,572	807
Total	—	260240	23821
Yangtze River Delta city cluster	Shanghai	114395	8736
	Nanjing	75749	1440
	Hangzhou	44950	3773
	Hefei	26560	350
	Suzhou	13692	2119
Total	—	275346	16418

Source The Global Innovation Index 2019, Cornell University, INSEAD, and World Intellectual Property Organization

in the table. Shanghai ranked 60th. No GBA city is on the list. In contrast, of the other three bay areas (Table 5.12), the New York Bay Area is the strongest, with two cities in the top 10. New York City topped the list with 545 SCI journals and New Jersey ranked 78th, demonstrating the scientific strength of the New York Bay Area. The second is Tokyo Bay Area, where Tokyo ranked 14th thanks 47 SCI journals. In addition, Kyoto in Japan also entered the top 60. Oakland in San Francisco Bay Area also entered the top 60. GBA has an obvious disadvantage in terms of comprehensive scientific influence.

When compared with other Chinese cities, GBA is also weak in scientific influence. As of March, 2019 (Table 5.13), the number of scientific publications published by Beijing is 222,668, and the number by Shanghai is 114,395. The number of publications in Beijing and Tianjin is used to represent the number of publications of the Beijing-Tianjin-Hebei Urban. The number of publications in Shanghai, Nanjing, Hangzhou, Hefei and Suzhou is used to represent that of Yangtze River Delta Urban Agglomeration. The number of publications in Guangzhou, Shenzhen and Hong Kong is used to represent that of GBA. As can be seen from Table 5.13, the number is 260,000 in Beijing-Tianjin-Hebei Urban Agglomeration, nearly 280,000 in the Yangtze River Delta Urban Agglomeration, but less than 110,000 in GBA, which is only 42% of Beijing-Tianjin-Hebei and 39% of the Yangtze River Delta. There is still a big gap between GBA and high-level cities and urban agglomerations in scientific research. To build a highland of scientific and technological innovation, it is necessary for GBA to increase cooperation with universities and research institutes in basic technology.

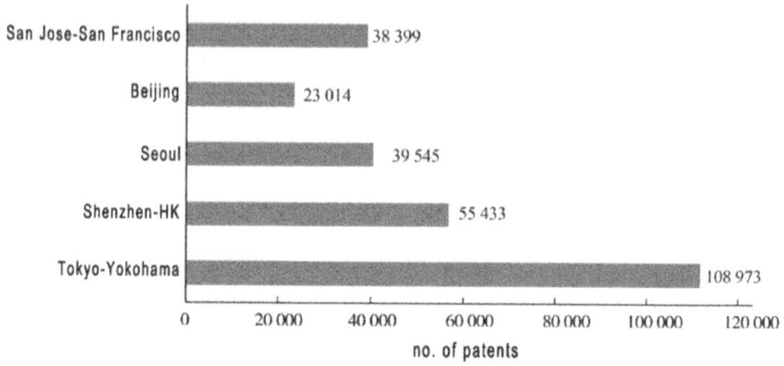

Fig. 5.20 Top 5 city clusters based on the no. of patents (*Source The Global Innovation Index 2019*, Cornell University, INSEAD, and World Intellectual Property Organization)

Technological application is measured by the number of patent applications. *2019 Global Innovation Index*[15] indicates the number of PCT patent application. The number of patents in the GBA, represented by Shenzhen-Hong Kong and Guangzhou, is 59,462. The number of patents for Beijing-Tianjin-Hebei Urban Agglomeration, represented by Beijing and Tianjin, is 23,821. The number of patents for the Yangtze River Delta Urban Agglomeration, represented by Shanghai, Nanjing, Hangzhou, Hefei and Suzhou, is 16,418. Figure 5.20 shows that the Shenzhen-Hong Kong cluster has the second largest number of patents in the world, at 55,433, but is only 51% of the first cluster of Tokyo-Yokohama. The third, fourth and fifth places are taken by Seoul, Beijing and San Jose-San Francisco, and there is little difference in the number of patent applications. In conclusion, GBA has advantages in patent applications, but it's a far cry from the first place.

Taking the two stages of innovation, namely scientific discovery and technological application, into consideration, it is not difficult to see that Tokyo-Yokohama is the dual center of scientific discovery and technology application among the four bay areas of the world. New York is relatively focused on scientific discoveries, which are an important stepping stone to the application of technology. The San Francisco Bay Area is also advanced on both dimensions. In contrast, the GBA is at a disadvantage in scientific discovery and is more focused on being a manufacturing hub. There is mismatch between scientific discovery and technological application. The GBA is in urgent need to build a solid foundation for scientific discovery, to gather momentum for innovation, and to avoid being frequently cornered by dilemmas in scientific and technological innovation. These are the major challenges to the development of the GBA.

[15] Source: *The Global Innovation Index 2019*, Cornell University, INSEAD, and World Intellectual Property Organization.

References

Tan CL, Pan DD (2018) An analysis of the convergence and agreeableness of the industrial structure of the Guangdong-Hong Kong-Macao Greater Bay Area. Rev Econ Manag 34(3):15–25

Xian XL, An DP (2017) Discussion on the current situation of higher education in Guangdong, Hong Kong, Macao and the Greater Bay Area and the mode of cooperation. Shenzhen Inform Vocat Technol J Shenzhen Inform Vocat Technol Coll 15(4):7–11

Hunter (Liepin), at https://wow.liepin.com/

Chapter 6
Preliminary Conception of Combined Free Trade Ports of the GBA

The GBA aims at building a world-class bay area and city cluster. The key to achieving this goal is to design, plan and construct the "9+2" cities[1] as an overall system. The coordinated development of the entire GBA will be realized through the interconnection and deep integration among these cities. Based on the previous experience of free trade ports and regional coordinated development and the basic analysis of the development of the GBA, this chapter discusses in detail the conception of "9+2" urban coordinated development in the GBA from seven dimensions, including space, industry, finance, science and innovation, system, governance and talent.

6.1 Conception of Spatial Synergy in the GBA

6.1.1 The Integrated Spatial Layout Framework of the GBA and the Choice of Strategic Key Areas

6.1.1.1 Overall Layout: A Beaded Pattern with an Axial Belt Support and "One Pole, Three Main Projects and Multiple Regions"

The GBA generally presents a "9+2" spatial system with features of multi-cores, multi-nodes, bay area-hinterland linkage, and development around the bay. It is a prerequisite for the spatial coordinated layout to clarify the core nodes, strategic key areas and hinterland expansion directions. From the night light data, the overall degree of integration in the core area of the GBA has been relatively high. From either the global or the national perspective, Hong Kong is the most mature and well-developed important international free trade port in the GBA while Shenzhen, as a

[1] The "9+2" cities in the GBA is a city cluster consisting of nine mainland cities—Guangzhou, Foshan, Zhaoqing, Shenzhen, Dongguan, Huizhou, Zhuhai, Zhongshan and Jiangmen, as well as Hong Kong and Macao.

© Xiamen University Press 2022

S. Ba et al., *Collaborative Innovation Mechanism of GBA in China*,
https://doi.org/10.1007/978-981-19-2251-0_6

pilot demonstration zone of socialism with Chinese characteristics, is the innovation engine of the GBA. In combination with its own advantages and national positioning, Shenzhen-Hong Kong combined free trade ports are taken as the leading core (one pole) of the Bay Area, whose focus is placed on the promotion of the collaborative construction of three free trade twin ports–Shenzhen and Hong Kong, Zhuhai and Macao, Guangzhou and Foshan around the Pearl River Bay (three main projects). Meanwhile, relying on both the coastal and the riverside strategic supporting axes, the Bay Area will accelerate the coordination in the pan regional layout and synergy construction capacity (multiple regions), and comprehensively promote the multi-level network interaction and integrated development among different port groups at all levels in order to form a Bay Area free trade ports group system featuring foreign trade and complementary functions. It is aimed at building a beaded pattern of "one pole, three main projects and multiple regions", namely, having Shenzhen-Hong Kong as the pole, Hong Kong-Shenzhen, Guangzhou-Foshan and Macao-Zhuhai as the three main projects, relying on the regions along the sea or the Pearl river and promoting the interactive development.

With regard to the spatial transmission, efforts are made to promote the integrated spatial layout of the GBA through the three-level gradient radiation of the strategic core area–strategic key area–strategic expansion area. The strategic core area gives priority to leading functions such as the pilot testing, demonstration and promotion of major reform and innovation policies. The strategic key area mainly undertakes specific functions such as the implementation of major policies of the free trade ports. The strategic expansion area is an important potential strategic area because it undertakes functional expansion and will achieve a regional integrated layout.

6.1.1.2 The Strategic Core Area: Strengthening the Core Hub Status of the Shenzhen-Hong Kong Free Trade Port, and Sparing no Effort to Construct Combined Free Trade Ports in the Socialist Pilot Demonstration Zone with Chinese Characteristics (Shenzhen)

The Hong Kong-Shenzhen dualcity cores under the "one country, two systems" principle have been fostered by their geographical advantages, the landscape pattern of the adjacent to the sea and the special institutional relationship. The Hong Kong-Shenzhen built-up area presents a dual-city-center structure of Hong Kong Central-Kowloon and Shenzhen Luohu-Futian-Qianhai. The dual city centers are connected by ring roads and crossing passages, with continuous mountains as isolated green space, which forms a "palm" shape with the green land. The roads diverge radially outwards, and the built-up areas extend like fingers, forming a typical semi-radial spatial structure of coastal cities. The strong industrial linkages between Hong Kong and Shenzhen have initially formed a cooperation model of "Hong Kong providing international access and high-tech elements while Shenzhen applying research and development, and transforming the achievement highly effectively". Meanwhile, the financial industry in both places has reached a relatively high level. All these contribute to the potential of combined free trade ports (Li Xun et al. 2018).

The Shenzhen-Hong Kong combined free trade ports will serve as a polar core leader and be built into the forefront and general engine of the development of the export-oriented market economy in the GBA, giving full play to the core hub function of the spatial system of the combined free trade ports. The Shenzhen-Hong Kong strategic core area has extremely high talent density, capital density, science and technology industry density, and financial density. It can provide necessary and sufficient elements for the construction of combined free trade ports of the GBA, and promote high-quality transformation and development in the adjacent and hinterland areas through spatial spillover of elements. From the perspective of the key points of the cooperation between Shenzhen and Hong Kong, the focus will be put on the following three points. First, grasping the opportunities in the construction of the Shenzhen-Hong Kong Modern Service Industry Cooperation Zone in Qianhai of Shenzhen and the Shenzhen-Hong Kong Science and Technology Innovation Cooperation Zone in the bend of the Pearl River, and promoting the integration of the financial reform and innovation, innovation in the scientific and technological innovation system and mechanism, customs clearance and logistics services. Second, encouraging a high degree of openness and cooperation between Shenzhen and Hong Kong in all aspects, such as in taxation, public services, talent services, and informatization; 3. giving high preferential treatment in terms of investment and talent introduction.

Shenzhen should seize the great historical opportunity of building a pioneering demonstration zone of socialism with Chinese characteristics and provide experience and reference for GBA in the coordinated construction of free trade ports. It is highly suggested to win the central government's support to build combined free trade ports in the socialist pioneering demonstration zone (Shenzhen) with Chinese characteristics at the national level, in accordance with the valuable experience of major free trade ports in the world and the national conditions of socialism with Chinese characteristics and the development needs of the GBA, which aims to realize the integration of internationalization and localization of the construction of free trade ports, and provide for the reform and innovation of free trade ports in the country and the world with "Chinese solutions" and "Shenzhen wisdom". In general, Shenzhen should take the reform of the socialist market economy system as the overall focus, fully implement the new requirements for building a pioneering demonstration zone of socialism with Chinese characteristics and a global benchmark city, and provide reform and innovation experience and typical model demonstrations for the comprehensive promotion of the construction of a free trade port of the GBA. In the specific implementation process, a "single window" one-stop service of multimodal transportation from other parts of the GBA to Shenzhen will be promoted in advance with Shenzhen as the strategic core hub, to realize the integration of customs clearance. The purpose is to build highly integrated GBA combined free trade ports system around Shenzhen.

6.1.1.3 Strategic Key Area: Building Three Major Free Trade Twin-Ports with the Focus on the Pearl River Bay

The free trade twin-ports are the fundamental level of the spatial coordinated layout and are also a major innovative attempt to build combined free trade ports, which aims to promote the full opening and development of the GBA through strong alliances. After 40 years of opening up and development, the GBA's endogenous and integrated growth development system has continued to mature, and the process of cooperation between cities has been significantly accelerated. The three twin ports of Shenzhen-Hong Kong, Zhuhai-Macao and Guangzhou-Foshan have become the top priorities of the collaborative construction. Unlike other integrated regions in China, the GBA not only has the characteristics of cross-administrative regions, but also has its biggest feature of the spatial agglomeration of different systems, different tax systems, different legal systems, and different currencies. The promotion of the economic integration of Shenzhen-Hong Kong and Zhuhai-Macao will not only blur the geographical boundaries of the GBA, but will also push forward the efficient integration of the two different systems. The greater potential for the free and open development of the GBA will be unleashed by the spatial reorganization of the diverse and complementary elements of talents, technologies, funds and institution. The GBA will become a model for the integration of free trade under the special background of "one country, two systems" and "three tax zones, three laws and three currencies". The promotion of the three free trade twin ports of Shenzhen-Hong Kong, Zhuhai-Macao and Guangzhou-Foshan with the focus around the Pearl River Bay will initially realize the joint construction of combined free trade ports at the local level. Then the optimization and reorganization of functions will be realized, as well as the energy level integration and amplification, via the consultation, contribution and shared benefits of the collaborative construction model of the three twin ports, so as to establish a closely related, collaborative and shared free trade community of the GBA.

Firstly, the construction of Shenzhen-Hong Kong free trade twin ports. The important opportunities will be seized in the pilot construction of Qianhai Shenzhen-Hong Kong Modern Service Industry Cooperation Zone, China (Guangdong) Pilot Free Trade Zone in Shekou Area of Qianhai, Shenzhen, Shenzhen-Hong Kong Science and Technology Innovation Cooperation Zone. Being fostered as the centre of global science and innovation, and the forefront of reform and opening up, Shenzhen is encouraged to join forces and cooperate with Hong Kong, the important global financial centre and a free trade port, in the fields of finance, trade, and technological innovation etc., to build a core demonstration area and main engine for the construction of combined free trade ports of the GBA. All the above will raise the regional energy level of Qianhai-Shenzhen-Hong Kong cooperation engine area and give full play to the pivotal role of the reform and innovation of the combined free trade ports.

Secondly, the construction of the Zhuhai-Macao free trade twinports. The major opportunities of the China (Guangdong) Pilot Free Trade Zone in Hengqin New Area ofZhuhai, the Guangdong-Macao Cross-border Financial Cooperation (Zhuhai)

Demonstration Zone will be seized, while the advantages of the two places will be combined together to promote the cooperation in key fields such as characteristic finance, technological innovation and leisure tourism etc., all of which serve for the purpose of building the West Coast Free Trade Centre of the GBA. A major Hengqin-Zhuhai-Macao cooperation platform will be built. And the cross-border financial cooperation, economic and trade investment, and cross-regional joint construction of universities and new research and development institutions will take the lead on the platform.

Thirdly, the construction of Guangzhou-Foshan free trade twinports. The major opportunities of China (Guangdong) Pilot Free Trade Zone in Nansha New District, Guangzhou, Guangdong-Hong Kong-Macao Comprehensive Cooperation Demonstration Zone in Nansha of Guangzhou will be seized, and the comprehensive cooperation among Guangdong, Hong Kong and Macao will be supported on the major platform of Guangzhou-Foshan, especially in finance, technological innovation and global shipping, so as to establish a Guangzhou-Foshan Free Trade Port Financial Island. A major cooperation platform in the Nansha-GBA will be deployed, and the integration of transportation infrastructure construction, public service layout and the integration of spatial planning will be advanced first.

6.1.1.4 Strategic Development Area: Expanding the Bearing Function of Hinterland and Accelerating the Promotion of Pan-Regional Layout

The hinterland of the GBA will be taken as the main strategic core area and the function expansion area of the strategic key area, providing an important reserved land for the development of a new main free trade port area in the future. The resources that used to be accumulated in the center will be gradually distributed to different places, which relies on the supporting axes and accelerates the pan-regional layout of free trade ports and the integrated development of multiple areas, and finally will realize the integrated development pattern of free trade ports and the GBA. From the perspective of expansion directions, the focus will be put on the hinterland of the GBA and the Pan-Pearl River Delta (hereinafter shortened as PRD) region. The expansion will rely on the construction of the Pearl River-Xijiang Economic Belt and the Guangdong Coastal Economic Belt, and will continue to extend the functions of the combined free trade ports to the inland and outer coastal zones, and finally form the integrated, global and full opening general layout of the combined free trade ports of the GBA.

From the perspective of development model, the target will be realized in the following three ways. Firstly, establishing combined free trade ports zone in the hinterland through function takeover and strengthening the joint development of the free trade economy of the headquarters and the free trade economy of the enclave, in order to realize the layout of one port and multiple regions. Secondly, establishing a free trade port cooperation zone in the hinterland through complementary functions when it has developed to a certain level, so as to achieve a "1 + 1> 2"win–win cooperation. Thirdly, building a free trade port in the hinterland to cultivate important new growth poles. Focus of the construction will be put on the future industrial direction while the priority will be given to the cultivation of a number of free trade port construction potential areas, such as the case of the China-Korea (Huizhou) Industrial Park which will be upgraded to the Guangdong-Hong Kong-Macao Free Trade Port (Huizhou) Synergy Zone.

6.1.1.5 Strategic Support Shaft: Relying on the "Dual Axis" Co-Support to Enhance the Closeness of Spatial Connection

The spatial coordination of the GBA is in urgent need of a strategic support shaft. As being divided by the two key geographical boundaries of the Pearl River Bay and the Pearl River, the GBA actually consists of three major regional economic plates, namely the east coast, the west coast and the hinterland. The key to the increasing closeness of spatial ties in the GBA is to remove the barriers to interconnection among the three major regional economic sectors and to rely on the construction of a strategic support shaft to form a seamless and integrated development pattern, with an aim of strengthening the spatial connection, the economic connection, the market connection, the social connection, and the information connection altogether.

Firstly, coastal strategic support shaft. Both the two sub-axes of the GBA, the East Coast and the West Coast will be taken as the focus of the medium and long-term port system space expansion. We will regard Dongguan, Huizhou, Zhongshan, and Jiangmen as the functional expansion regions of the current main port cluster and important reserved areas for future development of new ports. And we will gradually transfer the pattern of accumulating the resources in the center to one that distributes resources to different places and promote multi-sector integrated development. The three-dimensional planning and construction of sea, land and air infrastructure along the coast outside the Gulf will be accelerated. The airport facilities, expressways and secondary road networks, and port infrastructure will be optimized. For example, the construction of the Shenzhen-Zhongshan Passage and the Shenzhen-Maoming Railway will be promoted. The support function of the axle belt will be enhanced. The focus will be put on the Hong Kong-Zhuhai-Macao cross-sea corridor to realize the interconnection and intercommunication of the transportation infrastructure of the east–west coastal axle belt, and to break the traffic barrier between the east and the west.

Secondly, strategic support axis along the river. The layout along the Pearl River will be emphasized to realize the spatial coordination pattern of sea-land interaction and river-sea combined transportation, the two-way joint development of both the pan-GBA and the Guangdong-Hong Kong-Macao and the hinterland in order to give full play to the driving effect of the GBA Free Trade Port on the hinterland. The construction of the three-dimensional Pearl River-Xijiang River channel will be promoted. Zhaoqing will be taken as an important fulcrum, while the construction of Zhaoqing Airport will be accelerated, which serve for the goal of a modern, environment-friendly and intelligent Pearl River waterway port system, and a new international land-sea trade channel with the Pearl River Estuary as the frontier outlet.

6.1.2 Strategic Conception of the Construction of a Networked Spatial System of and the Interconnection in the GBA

6.1.2.1 Building a "Three-Level" Network Pattern and Comprehensive Transportation Support System in an All-Round Way

We will comprehensively promote the three gradient networked interaction among neighboring areas, different cities, countries and regions at different levels as well as the integrated development of ports and cities. We will implement the strategy of spatial cooperation in different places and the construction of "enclave economy". We will stimulate the overall cooperation ability and comprehensive competitiveness of free trade port groups through orderly flow of factors and optimization and integration of resources. The construction of three gradient networked spatial system is mainly based on the coordination and linkage of space, information and relationship in different regions. Firstly, the high integration of free trade port and city will be realized through local linkage strategy, and a "global" free trade port will finally be built. Secondly, the construction of networked spatial system in neighboring areas will be promoted through short-range linkage strategy, which will enhance the dependence and complementarity of mutual development. Thirdly, the networked connection pattern among Guangdong, Hong Kong, Macao and the mainland and the global market will be promoted through the long-distance linkage strategy. The networked pattern will be established on the base of the thoughts of "*Outline Development Plan for Guangdong-Hong Kong-Macao GBA*", and the rapid transportation network as well as the port group and airport group which mainly consist of high-speed railway, intercity railway and high-grade highway.

In regard to supporting measures, we should focus on transportation infrastructure and information interconnection to promote the free and reasonable flow of various production factors in Guangdong, Hong Kong and Macao. In particular, we should build a comprehensive transportation support system that is efficient, perfect and connected to the world, promote the formation of a free trade network among Guangdong, Hong Kong and Macao Bay area and the Mainland and global markets, and enhance the fast access ability of green wisdom of free trade combination Hong Kong. With regard to function cultivation, the GBA will be strengthened as a global hub and gateway, whose free passage at all times and all weather with major international trade markets will be established. The top-level hub supported by the intersection of major international traffic corridors will be constructed, and the global air and port passenger and cargo transportation system will be built and improved.

6.1.2.2 Internal Communication Strategy: Improving Intercity Rail Transit Network and Expressway Network in Order to Form a "One Hour Free Trade Circle"

The realization of internal interconnection is the leading strategy to ensure the internal integration of the GBA. Combined with the urban network pattern of Guangdong, Hong Kong and Macao and the relevant planning, the intercity transportation support system of pan-Bay Area and the internal traffic support system of main cities are taken as the core, and the intercity rail transit network and expressway network are mainly improved. Finally, a green, modern and efficient comprehensive transportation system of Guangdong, Hong Kong and Macao Bay area will be built, and so will a "one hour freedom" be formed in the "Bay Area Trade Circle".

With regard to the construction of intercity rail transit network, the core of two comprehensive intercity transportation hubs in Guangzhou and Shenzhen, as well as important regional intercity transportation hub nodes such as Zhuhai, Huizhou, Zhaoqing and Jiangmen, will be formed on the base of the planning and construction foundation of "ring + radiation" network of intercity railway during the 13th Five Year Plan period. We will strengthen the intercity traffic connection with Hong Kong and Macao, explore and implement a more convenient and efficient passenger clearance system in order to realize the integration of public transport in the GBA. We will focus on the construction, optimization and upgrading of intercity rail transit in the GBA, and enhance the line construction in areas where the transportation infrastructure is comparatively weak, such as the east–west outer coast of the Pearl River Estuary and Zhaoqing. In terms of major projects, Guangzhou-Zhongshan-Macao high-speed railway will be upgraded on the basis of Guangzhou Zhuhai urban rail transit to promote major projects of a number of major intercity railway networks, such as GuangfoRing Line, Guangzhou-Dongguan-Shenzhen and Guangzhou-Foshan-Zhaoqingintercity railway will be promoted to complete a radial high-speed railway network around the Pearl River Estuary. As for the highway network construction, based on the general goal of "6 expressways linked with Hong Kong and Macao" included in the 13th Five Year Plan, we should strengthen the expressway connection project in the GBA, and formulate a rapid customs clearance mechanism for social vehicles. We will continue with the construction of cross sea and river crossing channels in the Pearl River Estuary and strive to increase the number of existing channels to 12 in accordance with *The Overall Planning of River Crossing Channels at the Pearl River Estuary*. We will focus on major infrastructure projects such as the Shenzhen branch line of the Hong Kong-Zhuhai-Macao Bridge, Shenzhen-Zhongshan Channel, Lianhuashan River Crossing Channel and Nansha-Dongguan River Crossing Channel. At the same time, we should strengthen the traffic linkage between the port and the city, and optimize the high-speed transportation system of the port.

6.1.2.3 Internal And External Connectivity Strategy: Building a World-Class Airport Cluster and Port Cluster, Building a Global Maritime and Air Transport Hub, and an Important Support Area for the Construction of the "Belt and Road" and "Air Silk Road"

The construction of the world-class airport group and port group system in the GBA will be implemented with an aim to exert the multi-port linkage effect of the airport group and the harbor group, enhance the comprehensive competitiveness of the three international hubs of Guangzhou, Shenzhen and Hong Kong, and build the global maritime and shipping hub as soon as possible. In regard to the airport construction, guided by the principles of dislocation and coordinated development and avoiding homogeneous competition, the existing airport bearing capacity shall be increased in advance according to the international market demand. In accordance with the *Outline of Development Plan for Guangdong-Hong Kong-Macao Greater Bay Area* and the *Three year Action Plan* (2018–2020) *of Guangdong Province to Promote the Construction of Guangdong-Hong Kong-Macao Greater Bay Area,* we will focus on both the reconstruction and expansion of Guangzhou, Shenzhen and Hong Kong airports, and the construction of a new Guangzhou airport and a Zhaoqing airport. We will reasonably allocate the basic business types of airports according to the requirements of the international market, and enhance the density and collaborative development capacity of regional airports and general airports. As for the port construction, we should concentrate on the optimization of the port cooperation network of the GBA, and the enhancement of the construction capacity of the eastern and western outer coastal port of the Pearl River Estuary. Meanwhile, the comprehensive function of the port area is enhanced through the collaborative construction of the port international cooperation industrial park, international logistics base and bonded zones. The port group cooperation construction is promoted substantially by establishing the Port Alliance in the GBA. Finally, through the comprehensive construction of international three-dimensional passageway of sea, land, air and large-scale traffic infrastructure, a comprehensive transportation support system of the GBA with complementary functions and coordinated development will be constructed to establish its status as the global transportation hub.

The comprehensive transportation support system of the GBA should be closely integrated with the national BRI to build an important support area for the BRI and "Air Silk Road" construction. Based on the geographical advantages of the GBA, it will open up trade channels with major global markets, focusing on three aspects: the Maritime Silk Road, trade links between Guangdong, Hong Kong and Macao and ASEAN, South Asia, Europe and the United States, and the air trade in the "Air Silk Road". The first is to build a new fulcrum for the 21st Century Maritime Silk Road and form a global internal and external linkage pattern facing the international market. The second is to focus on supporting the trade liaison among markets like Guangdong-Hong Kong-Macao and ASEAN, South Asia, Europe and the United States, etc. The Guangdong-Hong Kong-Macao-ASEAN land-sea linkage pattern will be started, and the feasibility of integrating Guangdong-Hong Kong-Macao into the China-ASEAN high-speed rail construction plan will be studied. Hengqin-Macao China-Latin America economic and trade cooperation platform is taken as the frontier to build a long-term and stable international trade channels among China-Portuguese-speaking countries. The Guangdong-Hong Kong-Macao Logistics Cooperation Park will serve as a node to build Sichuan-Guizhou-Guangzhou-Hong Kong and Macao-South Asia international logistics channel. The China–Europe train will be taken as an opportunity to carry out the "road-rail combined transport" plan for Guangdong-Hong Kong-Macao-Europe bonded goods. The third is to seize the opportunity of building a world-class airport cluster, integrate the GBA into the national "Air Silk Road" construction, enhance the function of Guangzhou Baiyun International Airport as an international aviation hub, and increase international routes and flights from Guangzhou and Shenzhen to ASEAN countries.

6.1.2.4 Information Connectivity Strategy: Building the Information Highway Network and Big Data Center in the GBA to Create the Master Node of the Global Information Network

Based on the global flattening trend in the information age, we will make every effort to shape the spatial pattern of flows in the GBA, and attach importance to the positive impact of informatization and connectivity on spatial coordination. We will focus on strengthening the interconnection of information infrastructure in order to build GBA information highway network on the base of advantages of local information technology innovation, to promote the integration and sharing of information resources in the region, and to create a global information network master node. In accordance with the requirements of the "*Outline of the GBA Development Plan*", the work will be specifically implemented from the three aspects of information infrastructure construction, smart bay area construction and network security. Firstly, we will promote the upgrade and transformation of the Internet in the GBA and fully realize the large-scale deployment of Internet Protocol Version 6 (IPv6), and promote the construction of Enhanced Ultra High Throughput (EUHT) wireless coverage in the new era. Secondly, we will promote the construction of national smart pilot cities and the PRD National Big Data Comprehensive Pilot Zone, and to promote the construction of a world-class smart city cluster in the GBA. Thirdly, we will promote the construction of a network security system in the GBA and create a national-level network security innovation demonstration zone. In terms of information node construction, we will concentrate on the construction of the GBA big data center and the international big data trading center with an aim of the "Guangzhou-Shenzhen-Hong Kong-Macao" science and technology innovation corridor, and a global big data research and development center.

6.1.3 Conception of Major Support Measures for the Spatial Synergy Layout in the GBA

6.1.3.1 A Set of Comprehensive Land Spatial Planning Scheme Will Be Formed with Planning Synergy as the Guide

The intensive land development and utilization in the GBA necessitates a comprehensive spatial planning scheme to integrate the main function zoning, the overall land use planning and the overall urban and rural planning so as to scientifically solve the prominent contradictions of population growth, urbanization, economic development and resource environment. We should design a sustainable medium and long-term development blueprint of the GBA and stick to it to the end. Meanwhile, it is important for us to clarify the reasonable boundary between dos and don'ts. We should increase investment in scientific and technological innovation, accelerate the marketization process of modern service industry, and at the same time, strictly limit the direction of space development and utilization in terms of the top- level design.

To promote the integration of the land and space planning system of the GBA, we shall make efforts in the following four aspects. First, we cannot overpass 3 red lines during the high-quality transformation and development of the GBA: 1. the ecological protection, 2. the bottom line of environmental quality, 3. the upper limit of the use of resources. Second, we shall set up a collaborative management mechanism that helps to strengthen the cooperation between Guangdong provincial Party Committee and Government, the Provincial Department of Natural Resources and relevant functional departments at all levels, and the relevant functional departments in Hong Kong and Macao. It will enable the exploration and the construction of a new cross regional collaborative planning system under the special background of "one country, two systems", as well as the optimization of the land space development pattern of the GBA, and the building of a beautiful bay area. Third, we shall reinforce the comprehensive planning of land protection, development and management, which will coordinate the important planning achievements of ecology, urbanization and agriculture. It will help promote the "three-in-one" collaborative planning of the strategic pattern of ecological security, urbanization and agricultural development in combination with the national strategic positioning, so as to promote the formation of both a new pattern of urban–rural coordination and green modern development of the GBA, and a model of coordinated development of human and land in the new era. Fourth, we shall enhance the technical level of grid management that will help realize the accurate planning, scientific and efficient utilization of "every inch of land" in the GBA, and strictly follow the conception of refined spatial planning during the specific construction.

Furthermore, on the basis of the existing Guangdong Provincial Urban–Rural Planning Committee, a metropolitan planning cooperation task force and an intercity planning cooperation coordination meeting will be established to form a multilevel inter-city planning cooperation organization. The functions of the Urban and Rural Planning Committee of Guangdong Province will be reinforced. It will also

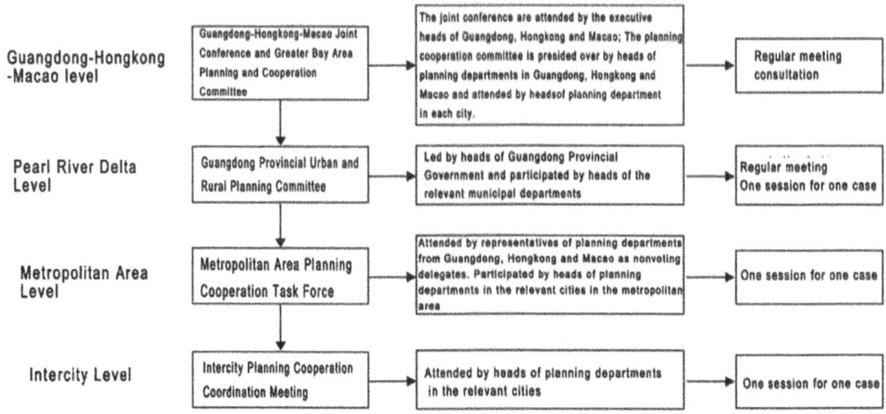

Fig. 6.1 Multi-level framework for urban planning collaboration in the GBA (*Source* Yao Jiangchun et al. [2018])

be granted the authority to review and coordinate important issues involving the entire PRD, the location of major regional projects, regional green space, and the construction of major infrastructure channels. The metropolitan areas planning cooperation task force for Guangzhou-Foshan-Zhaoqing, Zhuhai-Zhongshan-Jiangmen and Macao, Shenzhen-Dongguan-Huizhou and Hong Kong will be improved and functioning with the participation of the heads of the planning departments of the three metropolitan areas, and attended by representatives from the planning departments of the Guangdong provincial government as nonvoting delegates. In addition, an inter-city planning cooperation coordination meeting mechanism will be set up drawing on the experience of existing Shenzhen-Hong Kong, Zhuhai-Macao and Guangzhou-Foshan intercity cooperation mechanism, which will be participated by planning department heads from relevant cities, and extended to cities in the GBA (Fig. 6.1) (Yao Jiangchun et al. 2018).

6.1.3.2 Having the Infrastructure Connectivity as the Guarantee While Giving Priority to the Major Planning of Transportation Infrastructure Interconnection

The cross-border traffic construction has promoted the interconnection of infrastructure in the GBA. From 2000 to 2008, the average annual growth rate of high-speed railway mileage in Guangdong reached 16%, while the average annual growth rate of railway mileage in the same period was comparatively slow. However, from 2008 to 2015, the average annual growth rate of Expressway slowed down to 10%, and the average annual growth rate of railway reached 18%. In addition, the construction of large-scale infrastructure has also promoted the connectivity between the east and the west of the GBA. For example, the completion and opening of the Hong Kong-Zhuhai-Macao Bridge, a world-class sea crossing channel project, connects

Hong Kong's Lantau Island, Macao Peninsula and Zhuhai City. It takes only half an hour from Hong Kong to the mainland, significantly improving the accessibility level among the three places. With the opening of Guangzhou-Shenzhen-Hong Kong high-speed railway, the train speed reaches 350 km/h. It takes only 14 min from West Kowloon Terminus in Hong Kong to Futian, Shenzhen. The total length of Guangzhou-Dongguan-Shenzhen intercity railway is 116.62 km. Its opening has formed an hour economic circle on the east bank of the Pearl River, which has greatly promoted the development integration level there. The 24-km-long Shenzhen-Zhongshan channel, which is still under construction, connects Shenzhen and Zhongshan City, crosses the Pearl River Estuary and connects the eastern and western banks of the Pearl River. On the basis of relieving the pressure of Humen Bridge, it promotes the exchange between the east and the west banks of the Pearl River, connects the three major free trade zones in Guangdong, and connects the "Shenzhen-Dongguan-Huizhou" and "Zhuhai-Zhongshan-Jiangmen" clusters, which is of great significance to the integration of the GBA (Table 6.1).

We attach great importance to the construction of infrastructure interconnection, which will be enacted by special groups such as the leading group for construction and special group for infrastructure interconnection in the GBA. They will take the lead in the plan and construction of various transport infrastructure. Regarding the specific responsibilities, on the one hand, it is necessary to regularly track the construction progress of major transportation infrastructure to ensure the construction schedule and construction period. On the other hand, it is necessary to strictly implement the responsibility supervision system, and the leaders of Party and government departments at all levels shall directly take the lead in supervising the progress and safety of construction projects. In addition, attention should be paid to the coordination and implementation of inter-regional transportation infrastructure interconnection. With regard to the supporting policy, the transport infrastructure planning of the GBA will be incorporated into the overall layout of the nation, and the core projects will be included in the major special plans in the 14th "Five-Year-Plan" such as the modern comprehensive transportation system planning and civil aviation development planning. Priority should be given to the implementation of core projects. Concerning the fund guarantee, the trillion capital demand will be met by various ways such as government bond and PPP financing, etc. Under the the "Belt and Road" Initiative, we actively rally support from Asia Investment Bank and China Development Bank, and establish a financial cooperation mechanism for Guangdong, Hong Kong and Macao to jointly ensure steady progress in infrastructure construction.

In terms of ports and shipping, relying on the advantages of Hong Kong as the center of economy, trade, finance, information and international shipping, the port groups of Guangdong, Hong Kong and Macao have given full play to the role of ports such as Guangzhou, Shenzhen and Shantou. While consolidating the status of Hong Kong as an international shipping center, they have formed a situation of complementary advantages, clear division of labor, fair competition and common development with Hong Kong port. In addition to the water transportation, the linkage among ports still needs to serve South China and part of Southwest China through a comprehensive transportation system composed of railways, highways, Xijiang

Table 6.1 Newly-built large-scale infrastructure projects in the GBA

City	Project	Description
Guangzhou	Baiyun International Airport	Construction of a new terminal and two additional runways for a business aviation service base
	Zhengguo International Airport	Construction of the second civil airport to be started in 2020
	Nansha Port	Phase III and Phase IV construction stage; Phase I construction for Nansha Cruise Terminal
	Intercity Rail Transit	Large scale expansion, access to Foshan, Jiangmen and Huizhou
	Railway	Jiangmen-Shenzhen section of Shenzhen-Maoming railway and Guangzhou-Shantou high-speed railway
Shenzhen	Rail transit	Construction of Line 3 in Longgang
	Expressway	Construction of Shenzhen-Huizhou Expressway
	Shenzhen-Zhongshan Bridge	Shenzhen-Zhongshan Bridge is scheduled to open in 2024
Foshan	PRD High-speed Railway Airport	As part of Guangdong's plan to build 9 major airports (i.e. 5 airports in the PRD and 4 airports in the east, west and north of Guangdong Province), a new airport has been prepared
	Jiangmen	Expressway
	Intercity Rail Transit	Jiangmen section of Shenzhen-Jiangmen-Maoming Expressway
	Huizhou	Pingtan Airport
	Expressway	Huizhou section of Hunan-Huizhou Expressway
Zhongshan	Expressway	Zhongshan section of Shenzhen-Zhongshan expressway, Zhongshan-Kaiping expressway, Zhongshan-Jiangmen expressway, etc
Zhuhai	Intercity Rail Transit	Guangzhou-Foshan-Jiangmen-Zhuhai Intercity Railway
Zhaoqing	Expressway	Construction of Shenzhen-Zhaoqing Expressway
	Intercity Rail Transit	Construction of Zhaoqing-Nanhai Intercity Railway
Dongguan	Humen Bridge	The second Humen Bridge was opened in 2019

(continued)

Table 6.1 (continued)

City	Project	Description
	Intercity Rail Transit	Guangzhou-Dongguan-Shenzhen intercity rail, Dongguan-Huizhou intercity rail, Foshan-Dongguan intercity Rail, Zhongshan- Humen-Longgang intercity rail and Dongguan-Shenzhen high speed transportation
Macao	Clearance channel	A new crossing point will be built near the present inspection station in Gongbei to increase the passenger transport volume
	Hong Kong-Zhuhai-Macao Bridge	Opened in the summer of 2018
Hong Kong	Hong Kong International Airport	Construction of a third runway
	Guangzhou Shenzhen-Hong Kong high speed railway	Opened in the third quarter of 2018

Source An Yong. *GBA–A Booming Project*

shipping trunk lines, the shipping network and oil pipelines in PRD, aviation, etc., so as to strengthen the exchanges among Guangdong Province, inland areas and Hong Kong SAR and Macao SAR.[2]

It is to meet the competitions from ports in the worldwide and the need to enhance its international competitiveness that the ports in the GBA coordinate their development with each other. They promote the transformation and upgrading of port groups and high-quality development, and reduce the internal homogenized competition. First of all, the development of Shenzhen and Hong Kong should be highly integrated in order to form the world's leading port and shipping center in the GBA. This requires the reinforced strategic division of labor in, dislocation development of and complementary and win–win direction among the ports in the GBA. The strategic complementary advantages of Shenzhen and Hong Kong will be given full play under the current system, in order for a further integration and development and a regional level growth pole on the basis of the existing ports. Along with the development of Shenzhen-Hong Kong combined free trade ports, Guangzhou port should give play to its advantages of closer geographical distance with the economic hinterland and multi-functions. Diversified and professional developmental strategies will be adopted to build a comprehensive port hub and a regional shipping center, which forms a strategic differentiation division of labor with Hong Kong and Shenzhen, and becomes the important supplement and support for the construction of Hong Kong-Shenzhen free trade integrated port. Guangzhou port should concentrate its advantages to build a comprehensive hub port in the near future and become a regional shipping center. Macao port should take its advantage of language towards the Portuguese speaking countries so as to build a world tourism and leisure center.

[2] *National coastal port layout planning.*

As the core hub port on the west bank of the Pearl River, Zhuhai port should cooperate with Hengqin free trade zone to focus on the bulk cargo transportation and the port industry. As a regional auxiliary port, Humen Port is an important supplement to the Guangzhou port and Shenzhen port. Huizhou, as the main loading and unloading port of crude oil of the GBA, which should focus on serving the chemical industry base of the PRD; Zhongshan port should provide services for the local economy, mainly feeding transportation (Zhang Guoqiang 2019).

6.1.3.3 Cross Regional Coordination Organization and Information Maintenance Management Platform to Be Established on the Basis of Unified Service Management

Each city in the GBA has relatively independent government departments and industrial structure. It is encouraged for the governments in different cities in the GBA to innovate the mode of coordination. And a cooperation mechanism and an appropriate mode will be established among the three governments under the background of regional integration. It is recommended to establish a governments' alliance among Guangdong, Hong Kong and Macao to facilitate the coordination so as to promote the integrated management of the three places. It is also suggested to establish a direct dialogue mechanism among important cities such as Guangzhou, Shenzhen, Hong Kong and Macao, for the convenience of direct communication and consultation on major development issues. In the specific implementation, in accordance with the requirements of deepening social governance cooperation in the *Outline Development Plan for the Guangdong-Hong Kong-Macao Greater Bay Area*, we should focus on strengthening the coordination of clean government mechanism in the GBA, further promoting the administration by law, creating a high-quality, efficient and clean government, with an aim to improve the service efficiency of the government and the people's sense of gain. In order to promote the further implementation of relevant affairs in Guangdong Province, the system of leaders taking the responsibility shall be strictly enacted in each city, and the leading group offices at national, provincial and municipal levels for the construction of the GBA shall be promoted. In addition, integrated management will be strengthened with the help of information service platform and the process of intelligent and efficient management of the GBA will be promoted through the construction of digital government and online smart government.

6.2 Conception of Industrial Synergy in the GBA

6.2.1 Building a "Comprehensive Industrial Bay Area" Focusing on Science and Technology Innovation Industry, High-End Manufacturing Industry and Modern Service Industry

On the basis of the comprehensive analysis of the industrial advantages of the GBA, the industrial types and cooperation channels are accurately positioned, and a "comprehensive industrial Bay Area" will be built, which will be mainly composed of science and technology innovation industry, high-end manufacturing industry and modern service industry. With regard to industrial system planning, focus will be put on the overall goal of "a modern industrial system with international competitiveness". The transformation and upgrading of traditional manufacturing industry and the cultivation of modern service industry will be promoted, so as to form three leading pillar industries of strategic emerging industry, high-end manufacturing industry and modern service industry, and finally build the world's base of emerging industry, advanced manufacturing industry and modern service industry.

6.2.1.1 Agglomerating World-Class Scientific and Technological Innovation Resources and Cultivating and Strengthening Strategic Emerging Industries

As per the Outline Development Plan for *the Guangdong-Hong Kong-Macao Greater Bay Area*, each city cluster in the GBA should, according to its own characteristics, build and improve the high-tech industrial chain, with reliance on the scientific research resources and industrial foundation advantages of financial and innovative core cities such as Hong Kong, Macao, Guangzhou and Shenzhen. They will leverage the innovative platform advantages of the PRD National Independent Innovation Demonstration Zone, National High-tech Zone, national innovative city and Nansha National New Area in Guangzhou, to form strategic emerging industrial clusters with international competitiveness, so as to enhance the new momentum of economic development. Under the guidance of this plan, according to their own characteristics and industrial chain foundation, the PRD cities have defined the development direction of strategic emerging industries in the future. According to the strategic development plan of emerging industries formulated by each city at present (see Table 6.2), the key industries to be developed in the future are high-tech manufacturing industry and advanced manufacturing industry, which will jointly build a science and technology-led innovative industrial cluster chain.

In terms of the cultivation of key industries, in accordance with the requirements of the *Outline Development Plan for the Guangdong-Hong Kong-Macao Greater Bay*

Table 6.2 Strategic planning and layout of emerging industries in key cities of PRD

City	Strategic planning and layout of emerging industries
Guangzhou	Biomedicine, new materials, new energy vehicles, information technology
Shenzhen	Biomedicine, Internet, environmental protection, information technology, life and health, intelligent equipment, marine industry
Zhuhai	Intelligent manufacturing, ship and ocean engineering, aerospace, rail transit, new energy vehicles
Foshan	New energy vehicles, biomedicine, electronic information, digital economy
Dongguan	Information technology, high-end equipment manufacturing, new materials, new energy, life science, biotechnology

Source Sorted by the authors

Area, the GBA will focus on the promotion of the development of four types of industries as the new pillar industry, including new generation information technology industry, biotechnology industry, high-end equipment manufacturing industry and new materials industry. In terms of the cultivation of key institutions, it is necessary to promote the construction of enterprise R & D forces and new R & D institutions, and promote the upgrading of emerging industrial chain by relying on the combination of the industry, university and research institution. In addition, it is suggested to establish a collaborative innovation community of the GBA to accelerate the formation of a new mode of "R&D-transformation" innovation and cooperation among departments and regions.

Shenzhen and Dongguan are the leaders of the high-tech manufacturing industry in the nine municipalities of the PRD (PRD). According to the data issued by the Statistics Bureau, by the end of 2018, the number of high-tech enterprises and the industrial value added in the two cities were both in the forefront of the country. Shenzhen ranked first among the 9 cities in PRD, and second in China, having over 14,000 high-tech enterprises and the value added of high-tech industries at the amount of RMB¥ 829.663 billion. Dongguan ranked the fifth in China, with a total of 5,798 high-tech enterprises and the value added of high-tech industry of RMB¥ 152.062 billion. Compared with Shenzhen and Dongguan, the rest of the nine municipalities in PRD still have much room for improvement. In the future, an industrial strategic planning and layout of emerging industries is expected to be issued in the GBA, with the aim to continuously optimize and adjust the industrial structure layout, and to increase the proportion of high-tech manufacturing industry and advanced manufacturing industry in the value added of industrial manufacturing industry.

6.2.1.2 Accelerating the Development of High-End Manufacturing Industry with Technological Upgrading as a New Driving Force

As the forefront of national reform and opening up, after over 40 years of rapid development, the city cluster in the GBA has witnessed the great adjustment and changes in the industrial structure in this area. Generally speaking, the proportion of the secondary industry in the GBA has decreased year by year in recent years while the industrial structure has been continuously optimized and improved. In view of the fact that the service industry accounts for more than 90% in both Hong Kong and Macao, the value added of the industrial manufacturing in the GBA mainly comes from the nine municipalities in the PRD. In 2018, the high-tech manufacturing industry accounted for 31.5% of the industrial value added of the industrial enterprises above designated size in Guangdong Province, and the percentage reached 56.4% in the advanced manufacturing industry, while the high-tech manufacturing industry and the advanced manufacturing industry accounted for 35.8% and 59.4% respectively of the industrial value added of the industrial enterprises above designated size in the nine municipalities of the PRD, which were 0.7% and 0.8% higher than those in 2017, and about 4.3% and 3.0% higher than the average level of Guangdong Province.

Statistics show that in 2018, the high-tech manufacturing industry of the nine municipalities in the PRD increased by 8.2% year-on-year, the proportion of high-tech manufacturing industry output value continued to rise, and the industrial structure continued to be optimized. In terms of absolute scale, Shenzhen is far ahead of other cities. In 2018, the value added of high-tech manufacturing industry was close to RMB 580 billion, accounting for 58.7% of the total value added of the PRD. Dongguan ranked second with value added of RMB 143.4 billion, accounting for 14.5% of the total value of nine cities in the PRD. In terms of growth rate, Jiangmen, Guangzhou, Zhuhai and Dongguan saw strong growth in high-tech manufacturing industry in 2018.

In terms of industrial manufacturing industry, the industrial structure adjustment of nine cities in the PRD have shown great differences in recent years. Among the nine municipalities, it is in Dongguan and Zhongshan that the degree of concentration in manufacturing industry increased significantly. Having the electronic equipment manufacturing industry as the largest pillar industry, the degree of concentration in the manufacturing industry in Dongguan has significantly increased. The proportion of industrial value added in the manufacturing output value increased from 22.64% in 2007 to 36.73% in 2017. In terms of industrial restructuring, Shenzhen, Dongguan and Huizhou turned to electronic equipment manufacturing, while Zhuhai, Zhongshan and Foshan focused on developing electrical machinery and equipment manufacturing. With the continuous upgrading of science and technology industry, electronic equipment manufacturing industry and electrical machinery manufacturing industry can gradually transform into high-tech manufacturing industry, so as to further adjust and optimize the industrial structure of each city.

Under the background of gradual adjustment of industrial structure, the cities in the GBA can actively establish national intelligent manufacturing demonstration area, national manufacturing innovation center and national green transformation development demonstration area by virtue of the platform innovation advantages of national new industrialization industry demonstration base, so as to promote the transformation and upgrading of manufacturing industry to intelligent and green direction. On this basis, Shenzhen, Guangzhou, Hong Kong and Macao should give full play to their advantages of innovation level to promote the gradient transformation and upgrading of the traditional manufacturing industry in the hinterland of the pan GBA, and jointly form an ecological system for the innovation and development of manufacturing industry with the core cities.

6.2.1.3 Taking the Opportunity of Financial Cooperation Between Guangdong, Hong Kong and Macao to Vigorously Promote the Development of Modern Service Industry

In light of the *Outline Development Plan for the Guangdong-Hong Kong-Macao Greater Bay Area*, the GBA should speed up the development of modern service industry and build a modern service industry system. In 2018, the economic volume of the "9+2" city cluster in Guangdong, Hong Kong and Macao Bay area accounted for about 10.8% of the national GDP, while the tertiary industry dominated by service industry accounted for 66.1% of the GDP of Guangdong, Hong Kong and Macao Bay area, and the proportion was still increasing year by year. As economically developed regions, Hong Kong and Macao both accounted for more than 90% of their industrial structure in 2018. Among them, Hong Kong's tertiary industry accounted for 93% and Macao's tertiary industry accounted for about 92%. Therefore, the driving force for the development of modern service industry in the GBA City Cluster mainly comes from the nine municipalities in the PRD (see Table 6.3).

Compared with the traditional service industry, modern service industry is one with higher technology and cultural content, which appeared and develops on the basis of the demand of modern city and human development. Modern service industry generally includes basic services such as communication and information, production and market services such as finance, logistics and e-commerce, personal consumption

Table 6.3 Changes in the asset scale of the tertiary industry in the nine municipalities of the PRD in 2018

City	Asset scale in 2017 (billion RMB yuan)	Asset scale in 2018 (billion RMB yuan)	Year-on-year growth (billion RMB yuan) (%)
Guangzhou	1525.437	1640.184	7.52
Shenzhen	1315.302	1423.794	8.25
Zhuhai	133.917	143.083	6.84
Dongguan	389.601	422.634	8.48
Foshan	384.022	417.743	8.78
Zhongshan	164.971	179.088	8.56
Huizhou	164.681	176.550	7.21
Jiangmen	117.794	129.057	9.56
Zhaoqing	101.186	107.929	6.66

Source Sorted by the authors

services such as education, medical treatment, culture and entertainment, and public services such as public management and health care. The nine municipalities in the PRD have made some achievements in the development of modern service industry according to their practical situation. Shenzhen and Guangzhou have always been in the forefront of the nine municipalities in the PRD in terms of the development of modern service industry. Guangzhou regards the building of a modern service industry as an important support for its high-quality development, which has encouraged various new service industries and emerging service models. As an epitome of the rapid progress of modern service industry in Guangzhou, Pazhou boasts of a number of well-known Internet enterprises such as Tencent, Alibaba, Fosun International, Gome, Xiaomi, YY and VIPSHOP that have settled there. It is becoming a high-quality economic growth pole for the integrated development of modern service industries such as internet innovation industry, convention and exhibition industry, headquarters economy etc., and agglomeration development of export oriented and innovative economy. It is also an important symbol of Guangzhou's future economic form. Meanwhile, Guangzhou also proposed to vigorously develop modern business, culture, tourism, health and other service industries, arranged special funds to support 64 high-end productive service industry projects, and introduced a number of brand exhibitions such as ReMaTec Asia and Global Mobile Internet Conference. According to the data of Tianhe District in 2018, the GDP of Tianhe District reached 460.88 billion yuan, an increase of 9.2% compared with that in 2017. Both the total amount and growth rate of GDP ranked first in the city. According to a study of the contribution of various industries to GDP, it is found that the service industry accounts for the highest proportion, which has reached 93% of GDP. What's more, the modern service industry represented by finance, modern commerce and new generation information technology accounts for 61.8% of GDP, and its value added increased by 11.4% compared with that in 2016, among which the value added of financial industry exceeded 100 billion yuan. In the first half of 2019, Guangzhou's modern service industry continued to maintain a good momentum of development. The value added of information transmission, software and information technology service industry increased by 19.1%, the financial industry increased by 8.6%, and the modern logistics industry increased by 8.2%. There were 5 new listed companies and 7 enterprises listed on the new OTC market. In the context of the continuous development of the high-tech industries such as mobile Internet, cloud computing and big data, the industrial cooperation between modern service industry and traditional manufacturing industry is further deepened. Due to the solid development foundation of Guangzhou's manufacturing industry, there have been many enterprises transforming from production-oriented manufacturing to service-oriented manufacturing, and the emerging service industries are developing rapidly.

As one of the central cities in the GBA, in terms of the modern service industry, Shenzhen's functional form has been transforming from special economic zone to international city, while its development has also turned from agglomeration-oriented development to radiation-oriented development. The development level of modern service industry is an important indicator to measure the degree of modern social and economic development. Shenzhen is gradually speeding up the pace of moving towards the high end of the value chain at the same time of its functional transformation. Its economic form has also changed from industrial economy to service economy. At present, Shenzhen has a number of brand service enterprises, such as Ping An and China Merchants Bank in the financial field, Vanke and Jindi in the real estate field, Tencent in the information service field, etc. The development of Shenzhen's service industry has always been market-oriented. It attaches great importance to science and technology and information technology. It is highly sensitive to development efficiency and production efficiency. Its labor productivity is far higher than that of manufacturing industry and life service industry. It has strong innovation and development ability and high industry agglomeration effect. In recent years, domestic service enterprises have been distributed intensively in Shenzhen. However, compared with metropolitans like Hong Kong, Beijing, Shanghai, the industrial structure of modern service industry in Shenzhen still needs to be improved, the service scope of modern service industry needs to be expanded, and the industry environment needs to be improved. For example, the proportion of professional services such as accounting and lawyers is not high, and the relatively lagging of professional services will affect the development of other services such as finance and scientific and technological services to some extent. In addition, the service industry has higher demand for the construction of the rule of law, orderly market, fair competition, etc. than asset operation. Therefore, it also has higher requirements for the formulation of supporting industrial policies. In this context, Shenzhen can adjust relevant industrial policies to promote the construction of an impartial, fair, transparent and predictable business environment, maintain orderly market competition, build a credit system and standard system of the service market, ensure orderly competition of market operators, and promote the further development of modern service industry in Shenzhen.

To promote the further development of the service industry in the nine municipalities of the PRD is the key to accelerate the construction of the service industry system in the GBA. Considering the proportion of service industry in nine cities of the PRD is increasing year by year, we can further rely on the advantages of Hong Kong International Financial Center to vigorously develop characteristic financial industry. The Qianhai Shenzhen-Hong Kong modern service industry cooperation zone is the support platform to strengthen the construction of Qianhai Shenzhen-Hong Kong Financial Cooperation Demonstration Area. It supports the priority development of science and technology finance, green finance and cross-border finance, and promote the construction of offshore financial center for RMB in Hong Kong. In light of the *Outline Development Plan for the Guangdong-Hong Kong-Macao Greater Bay Area*, Macao will give full play to its advantages of Chinese and Portuguese financial cooperation nodes, jointly build with Zhuhai a financial cooperation demonstration zone for Portuguese speaking countries to provide financial services. Supports will be give to build a regional private equity market and green financial reform and innovation pilot area in Guangzhou, and to improve the green financial market system, green credit product innovation mode and financing channels, green insurance product business model and green financial standards. All serve for the final target of the construction of modern financial industry system in the GBA with resort to the major platforms of Shenzhen-Hong Kong, Zhuhai-Macao Financial Cooperation Demonstration Zone and Guangzhou green financial reform and innovation pilot area.

6.2.2 *Supporting the Regional Cooperation of Industries and Technology Diffusion, and Building the Industrial Cluster Network and Industrial Collaborative Innovation Ecosystem*

The industrial system of the GBA is stratified and relatively balanced. There are not only high-end industries close to those in the developed countries, but also relatively low-end industries. The industrial levels are diversified. Each city constructs its own industrial system according to its own role positioning, such as information technology industry in Shenzhen and Guangzhou, financial service industry in Hong Kong and high-end manufacturing industry in Dongguan, etc. In accordance with the *Outline Development Plan for the Guangdong-Hong Kong-Macao Greater Bay Area*, it is necessary to "leverage the radiating and leading function of the GBA, coordinate the productivity layout of the nine PRD municipalities and eastern, western and northern Guangdong, and foster development in nearby areas at a faster pace; to facilitate the flow of factors of production and relocation of industries in the Pan-PRD region, and establish a stratified and complementary industrial cooperation system with a reasonable division of labor". This requires the industries of each city in the GBA to give full play to their competitive advantages, further improve the industrial division cooperation mode and mechanism of the GBA, promote the transfer of superior technology and surplus technology of innovative cities and enterprises through the market-oriented way, and construct the modern industrial system with international competitiveness which is jointly developed by industrial cluster network and industrial collaborative innovation ecosystem.

6.2.2.1 Information-Technology Industry

In today's world, the rapid development of artificial intelligence (AI), big data and virtual reality technology have brought about changes in people's production and life style, so as in the economic society. The new generation of information technology is one of the seven strategic emerging industries identified by the State Council (see Fig. 6.2), mainly including integrated circuits, artificial intelligence, cloud computing, big data and the internet of things, etc. Among the nine PRD municipalities in the GBA, Shenzhen and Guangzhou have taken the lead in seizing the historical opportunities of technological and industrial changes, and vigorously

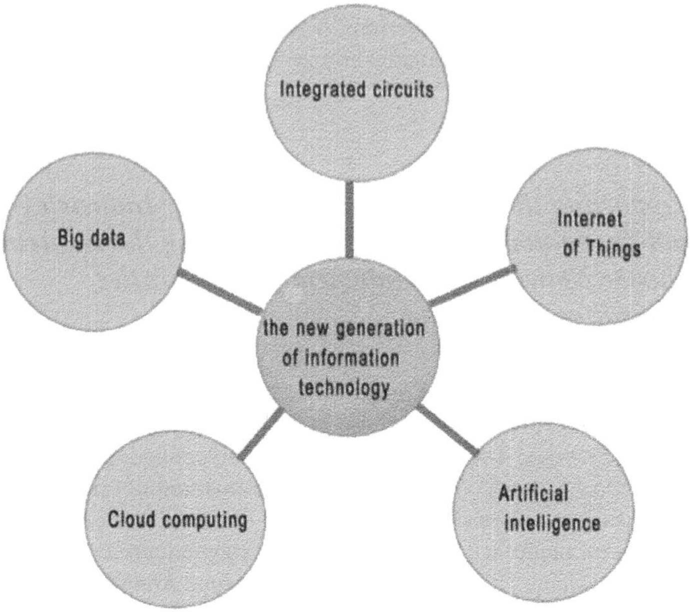

Fig. 6.2 Composition of the new generation of information technology (*Source* Sorted by the authors)

developing a new generation of information technology industry to support sustainable development in the future, which has effectively promoted the development of information technology industry in the GBA.

Development of IT Industry in Shenzhen

In terms of the development of information technology industry, Shenzhen focuses on cross-border industrial integration and intelligent development, aiming to build a global leading electronic information industry base. Specifically, Shenzhen has taken the lead in implementing the leapfrog development project of integrated circuit industry, improving the whole industrial chain covering design, packaging and testing, wafer manufacturing, and industrial supporting, creating a highland for integrated circuit cluster development; seizing the opportunity of artificial intelligence development, accelerating the industrialization of applied technologies such as computer audio-visual perception and new human–computer interaction, and building a global leading artificial intelligence industry demonstration area. We should seize the window period of the development of the fifth generation mobile communication (5G), promote the development of core technologies, standards and key products, stepping up efforts to promote the technology, and establish a leading area for 5G industrial development. At the same time, we should comply with the

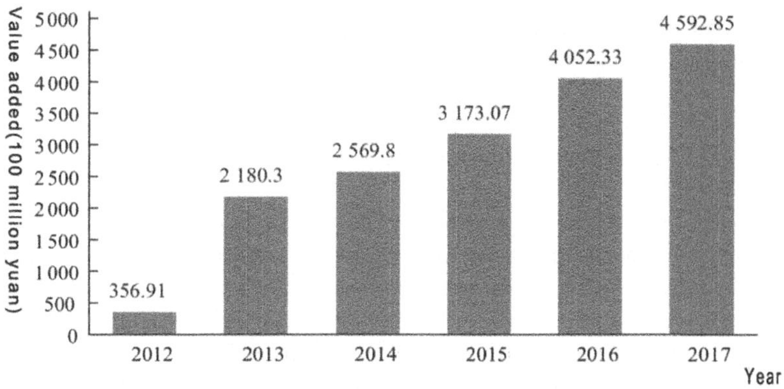

Fig. 6.3 Value added of new generation IT in Shenzhen from 2012 to 2017 (*Source* Sorted by the authors)

new trends and requirements of the internet of things (IOT), accelerate the construction of its commercial network, and vigorously promote the typical demonstration application of it.

At present, Shenzhen has become an important manufacturing base, R & D base, export base and logistics center of China's IT industry. Headquarters and regional headquarters of the top 10 electronic information industry enterprises are all located in Shenzhen. In 2017, the value added of Shenzhen's new generation information technology industry reached RMB 459.285 billion yuan, an increase of 13.3% over 2016, which was higher than the GDP growth rate in the same period (see Fig. 6.3). The existing IT industrial parks mainly include Shenzhen Software Industry Base, Shenzhen Bay Technology Ecological Park, Banxuegang Science and Technology City, and representative local enterprises such as Huawei, ZTE and Hainengda etc.

Founded in 1987, Huawei, as a representative of Shenzhen's IT industry, is a global leading provider of ICT (information and communication) infrastructure and intelligent terminals, and its business covers more than 170 countries and regions around the world, providing products in the fields of communication network, IT, intelligent terminal and cloud services for customers, solutions and services including operator business, enterprise business, consumer business and cloud business for more than 3 billion customers. According to its annual report of 2018, Huawei's global revenue reached 721.2 billion yuan, a year-on-year increase of 19.5%; its net profit was 59.3 billion yuan, a year-on-year increase of 25.1%. In terms of consumer business, by the end of the second quarter of 2019, Huawei has surpassed Apple in terms of pixel and AI technology, as well as the excellent quality of its flagship products and P-Series products, maintaining the second largest global share for two consecutive quarters. Regarding R & D investment, Huawei's R & D expenditure in 2018 was as high as 101.5 billion yuan, more than 14% of its sales revenue. In the past 10 years, the total R & D expenditure of Huawei exceeded RMB 480 billion yuan. According to the data released by the World Intellectual Property Organization

(WIPO) of the United Nations, Huawei submitted 5,405 patent applications to the organization in 2018, ranking first among all enterprises in the world.

Development of IT Industry in Guangzhou

In recent years, Guangzhou has seized the development opportunities of industries such as new generation information technology, mobile Internet, artificial intelligence, big data etc., to promote the innovation and development of electronic information and software service industry. As of April 2017, the output value of Guangzhou's electronic information manufacturing industry reached 73 billion yuan, a year-on-year increase of 9%; the main business income of software and information service industry hit RMB 114.2 billion yuan, a year-on-year growth of 26.8%.

At the same time, Guangzhou continues to promote the development of a new generation of information technology industry. In the field of new display, by the end of 2017, there were 10 new display manufacturing enterprises among the top 20 electronic information manufacturing enterprises in the city, with an output value of 139.3 billion yuan. With Foxconn's 10.5-generation display project that brings an investment volume of 61 billion yuan settled in Zengcheng District, Guangzhou's new display industrial cluster has entered the era of "dual core" driven by Guangzhou Development Zone and Zengcheng District.

Guangzhou and Shenzhen are the two poles and core of Guangzhou-Shenzhen Science and technology corridor in the development of information technology industry. In terms of industrial base, there are 14,400 high-tech industries in Shenzhen at present, ranking second in China; there are 11,000 high-tech enterprises in Guangzhou, ranking third in China, a little behind Shenzhen. In terms of information technology innovation foundation, Guangzhou has 83 universities and colleges including Sun Yat-Sen University and South China University of Technology, ranking first in terms of quality and quantity. In terms of innovation environment, there is a big gap between Guangzhou and Shenzhen: first, the R & D investment by information technology enterprises in Guangzhou is lower than that in Shenzhen in 2018; second, the number of listed enterprises is less in Guangzhou than that in Shenzhen. As of November 2019, there are 106 A-share listed companies in Guangzhou while 312 A-share listed companies in Shenzhen. There are 53 Hong Kong stock listed companies in Guangzhou and 99 Hong Kong listed companies in Shenzhen. There is a certain gap between Guangzhou and Shenzhen (as shown in Fig. 6.4). In general, although Guangzhou has advantages in industrial innovation foundation, Guangzhou still lags behind Shenzhen in terms of technical level and output value scale.

6.2.2.2 Financial Services

In the GBA, Hong Kong, Macao and the nine municipalities in the PRD belong to three different development systems. Their industrial characteristics and economic

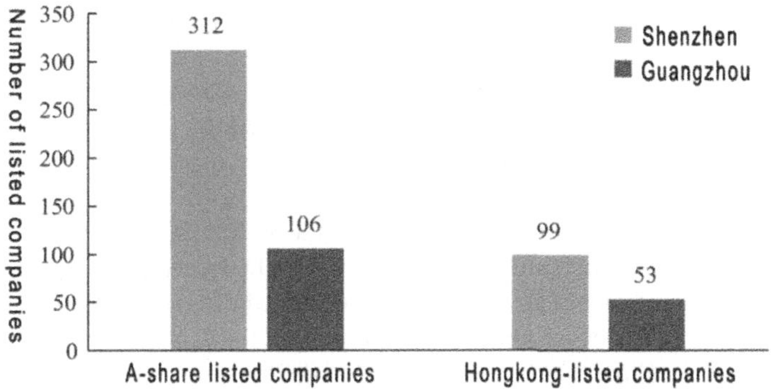

Fig. 6.4 Comparison of the number of listed companies in Guangzhou and Shenzhen (as of November 2019) (*Source* Wind)

strength are significantly different. Thus the development states of financial industry in different cities in the GBA are also different.

Generally speaking, Hong Kong, Shenzhen and Guangzhou have obvious advantages in the breadth and depth of financial development. Financial institutions in the GBA, such as commercial banks, securities companies and insurance companies, are mainly concentrated in these three cities whereas their comparative advantages are different. Hong Kong's overall financial industry is at the highest level with absolute advantages in terms of development volume. It is the international asset and risk management center of the GBA.

In terms of financial infrastructure, due to the concentration of science and technology enterprises, there are a large number of active financial infrastructures in the GBA, such as Shenzhen Stock Exchange and Hong Kong stock exchange. With the continuous promotion of payment and settlement interconnection among Guangdong, Hong Kong and Macao, the composition of payment service subjects is also more diversified. Guangzhou Branch of the People's Bank of China first built and successfully operated the leading Guangdong-Hong Kong joint bill settlement system, which can realize the real-time payment of foreign currency between Guangdong and Hong Kong. In terms of regional payment, the settlement system has launched a cross-border payment system between Guangdong and Hong Kong, making the market infrastructure more perfect. On this basis, Hong Kong and Macao actively promote the cross-border payment system of RMB, further accelerate the construction of all-weather and multi-currency modern payment and settlement channels among Guangdong, Hong Kong and Macao, so as to make cross-border fund payment more convenient. As of June 2019, through the introduction of large amount payment system in Guangdong Province, there are 8,946 banking institutions that can carry out cross-border payment and settlement. Among them, 492 banking institutions can handle regional payment and introduce market infrastructure to carry out joint settlement business between Guangdong and Hong Kong. From January to May of 2019, Guangdong Province, Hong Kong and Macao alone conducted more than 2.1 billion payment and settlement businesses in the payment and clearing systems of qualified financial institutions, with a total amount of 476 trillion yuan, an increase of more than 15%.

In terms of financial market development, the financial market integration development of the GBA is mainly reflected in three aspects: equity financing, debt financing and green financial market. With regard to the equity market, its financing performance is active in the GBA. Statistics show that in 2018, 40% of China's IPO companies came from the GBA. From 2018 to the first half of 2019, the total amount of initial capital raised by nine municipalities in the PRD exceeded 80 billion yuan, and the enterprises mainly concentrated in new economic fields such as information technology. In terms of the development of debt market, the cross-border bond issued in the GBA is mainly China Corporate USD Bond. Enterprises in the GBA are the main participants of China Corporate USD Bond, whose issuance scale accounts for 40% of the total amount of China Corporate USD Bond issued in Hong Kong. Statistics show that in the first half of 2019, the scale of China Corporate USD Bond issued in Hong Kong exceeded US $60 billion, an increase about 20% year-on-year. In terms of the development of green bond market, the financial institutions in the GBA have an outstanding performance and are in the forefront of the country. As a national green financial reform pilot zone, Guangzhou has issued more than 30 billion yuan of green bonds since 2016, which is the leader of green credit development in the GBA.

In terms of the development of financial institutions, the banking industry in the GBA has been developing steadily. The total assets, deposit balance and loan balance of the banking institutions have all reported a continuous increase. There are 51 more outlets of large commercial banks in Guangdong Province. By the end of 2018, the balance of domestic and foreign currency deposits in Guangdong Province's banking industry hit 20.8 trillion yuan, a year-on-year increase of 6.9%, and the loan balance reached 14.5 trillion yuan, a year-on-year increase of 15.2%;there were 152 licensed banks in Hong Kong and 29 in Macao. In the securities industry, there were 28 securities companies, 32 fund firms and 22 futures companies, a total of 588 listed companies and 2,905 licensed institutions of the Hong Kong Securities Regulatory Commission, who were all headquartered in Guangzhou by the end of 2018. In regard to the insurance industry, in 2018, there were 34 insurance institutions headquartered in Guangdong Province, with a total premium income of over RMB 460 billion yuan; there were 24 insurance financial institutions in Macao with a total premium income of MOP $21.1 billion; and the total premium income of Hong Kong insurance industry in 2018 reached HKD 432.9 billion. The top three premium income companies are AIA, Prudential Insurance and HSBC Life, accounting for more than half of the total market share. In terms of financial products, statistics show that by the end of 2018, the banking deposits in the GBA exceeded 30 trillion yuan. Due to the high density of technology enterprises in the GBA, in order to meet the financing needs of technology enterprises, commercial banks in the GBA have set up science and technology branches. At present, there are dozens of science and technology branches in the GBA; in the securities industry, as of the end of 2018, 289 and 1,277 listed companies were registered in Shenzhen and Hong Kong respectively; in the fund industry, by the end of 2018, the number of private funds registered in Guangdong Province was about 18,000, and the total scale of funds under management exceeded 2.4 trillion yuan.

In the process of promoting the establishment of large-scale financial institutions and the construction of important financial infrastructure in the future, we can give full play to the strengths of central cities and promote the formation of agglomeration effect of financial industry development, so as to better play the radiation role and provide financial services for the real economic development of the GBA and even Southeast Asia. At present, a number of financial work in the bay area has initially shown a financial agglomeration effect, such as the establishment of Guangdong equity trading center, the promotion of the establishment of the silk road insurance company in Guangzhou, and the preparation for the establishment of the International Commercial Bank in the GBA. According to the *Outline Development Plan for the Guangdong-Hong Kong-Macao Greater Bay Area*, in terms of financial innovation and development, the GBA can open up direct financing channels through regional equity trading market. In order to give full play to Hong Kong's "leading role" in the financial field and constantly consolidate and strengthen Hong Kong's position as an international financial center, we should vigorously promote the participation of Hong Kong's private equity funds in the financing activities of high-tech enterprises in the GBA, actively guide qualified high-quality high-tech enterprises to join the financing platforms for listed companies in Hong Kong, and build Hong Kong into an innovative technology industry financing base for GBA. In terms of financial markets connectivity, we should encourage Hong Kong to build green bond certification institutions, develop more financial risk management tools like offshore RMB, commodity futures and options etc.; we should also support the establishment of green finance pilot zone in Guangzhou, promote the establishment of carbon futures exchange, set up regional private equity trading market and regional trading center for property rights and bulk commodities, and focus on the development of special financial services such as shipping finance, science and technology finance, financial leasing etc., so as to enhance the level of internationalization. We will support Shenzhen to establish an insurance innovation and development pilot zone, promote the bulk commodity trading and financing platform with the Hong Kong Stock Exchange Qianhai joint trading center as the core, and accelerate the financial opening up. In terms of industrial layout, Macao will be supported to build a RMB based securities market, a green financial platform and a Sino-Portuguese financial service platform, establish an export credit insurance system, and explore the construction of Macao-Zhuhai cross-border financial cooperation demonstration zone.

In addition, the government can also plan and develop its own financial functions according to the regional function orientation, endowment characteristics and service demand of each city. It is expected that through the development and accumulation of experience after a certain period of time, the characteristic finance coordinated with the real economy of the city will gradually form a cluster and form a new financial pattern. Take the *Three-year Initiative (2018–2020) of Guangdong Province to Promote the Construction of the Guangdong-Hong Kong-Macao Greater Bay Area* that was issued on July 5, 2019 as an example. According to the real economic foundation and industrial development characteristics of each city in the GBA, the development priorities of financial industry in each city are deployed. It is proposed to promote the construction of Shenzhen insurance innovation and development pilot zone, support reinsurance product and system innovation in Qianhai District, research and launch businesses such as catastrophe bonds, and innovate and develop shipping insurance, financial leasing insurance, cross-border e-commerce insurance.

6.2.2.3 Advanced Manufacturing

In the era of economic globalization, advanced manufacturing industry is the core force of global competition and the "ballast" and "stabilizer" to maintain stable economic growth. In 2018, among the high-tech manufacturing industries in the nine municipalities of the PRD, the output value of both Shenzhen and Dongguan exceeded 100 billion yuan respectively, far ahead of other cities in the GBA.

Survey of Advanced Manufacturing Industry in Shenzhen

Shenzhen has always been an intelligent manufacturing base for China's strategic emerging industries and a high-end base for advanced manufacturing industries. In 2018, the value added of Shenzhen's advanced manufacturing industry reached RMB 656.5 billion, accounting for 72% of the value added of industries whose annual revenue are of 20 million yuan or more from their main business operations. In the first quarter of 2019, the value added of industries whose annual revenue are of 20 million yuan or more in Shenzhen increased by 8.6% year-on-year, 4.6% higher than that from January to February, 2.1% higher than that of the whole country (6.5%), ranking first among the four first tier cities of Beijing, Shanghai, Guangzhou and Shenzhen, and the growth rate is higher than other cities in the nine municipalities of the PRD.

The development of advanced manufacturing industry is the "hard core" of Shenzhen's industrial development. As emphasized in the *Outline Development Plan for the Guangdong-Hong Kong-Macao Greater Bay Area*, "focus shall be put on the cultivation and development of new industries, new formats and new models, support shall be given to the transformation and upgrading of traditional industries in order to accelerate the development of advanced manufacturing industry." To achieve this goal, Shenzhen will build the core of world-class advanced manufacturing industry clusters, such as electronic information industry, which will have global influence and competitiveness. According to statistics, the industrial value added of Shenzhen exceeded 900 billion yuan, with a year-on-year growth of 9%, ranking first in large and medium-sized cities in China for two consecutive years. Shenzhen became the first and only city with industrial value added exceeding 900 billion yuan in China. In addition, the contribution rate of Shenzhen's industry to GDP growth exceeded 40%, and the growth rate exceeded the GDP growth rate and tertiary industry growth rate in the same period for two consecutive years.

Shenzhen is one of the first batch of key cities to develop 5G industry. Huawei, ZTE, CSOT, DJI and Han's Laser are all headquartered in Shenzhen, which provides a good foundation for Shenzhen to strengthen and optimize the emerging manufacturing industry. Among them, Huawei is a global leader in the communication industry with its continuous efforts in intelligent terminals; CSOT has successfully broken the monopoly of foreign-funded panels by laying out large-scale LCD board production lines; Hytera has accelerated the layout of high-level frequency digit machines and gradually increased its market share in the international market.

On the basis of maintaining the advantages of Internet, 5G and new generation of display and communication technology, Shenzhen can continue to vigorously develop intelligent manufacturing and equipment integration technology, including high-speed and high-precision processing equipment and intelligent complete sets of equipment. In the future, Shenzhen manufacturing will also radiate to other key fields such as medical diagnosis and 3D printing, and the development space will continue to expand.

Survey of Advanced Manufacturing Industry in Dongguan

Technological innovation has become the core competitiveness of enterprises in Dongguan. According to the statistics, by the end of 2018, the number of high-tech enterprises in Dongguan has reached 5,798, ranking the first among the prefecture-level cities in Guangdong Province. The proportion of advanced manufacturing industry in GDP of the whole city is also rising, with an average growth rate of 19.9% in the past five years. And various emerging industries develop rapidly, including new materials, robots, lithium batteries, etc. At present, Dongguan is actively promoting the construction of a national innovative city. In this process, we need to accelerate the cultivation and development of emerging industries, strengthen the "transformation of scientific and technological innovation achievements", and build Dongguan into an advanced manufacturing center in the GBA.

In order to achieve this goal, on the basis of promoting the core competitiveness of enterprises driven by scientific and technological innovation, Dongguan also gathers high-end industrial chain through precise investment promotion, so as to realize the transformation of Dongguan from "follower" to "leader". Dongguan's industrial cluster is gradually taking shape. In 2018, more than 100 major industrial projects involving new materials, new energy, high-end electronic information and other fields were discussed, with the amount of intended investment reaching a trillion yuan. With the continuous improvement and aggregation of high-end industrial chain in Dongguan, Dongguan manufacturing industry is further moving towards intelligent, networked and digital development, which provides a solid guarantee for Dongguan to build an advanced manufacturing center in the GBA.

As mentioned in the *Outline Development Plan for the Guangdong-Hong Kong-Macao Greater Bay Area*, "the cities in the GBA should focus on in-depth cooperation in the fields of entrepreneurship incubation, science and technology finance, achievement transformation, international technology transfer, and science and technology service industry, and jointly build achievement transformation platforms such as national scientific and technological achievements incubation base and youth entrepreneurship and employment base of Guangdong, Hong Kong and Macao." At the level of technology transfer, we should establish a public service platform for technology transfer and a list of technology transfer projects in Guangdong-Hong Kong and Macao GBA, scientifically guide hinterland regions to carry more advantageous technology transfer through the construction of enclave parks, and promote the rational flow of industrial innovation elements. In addition, efforts should be made to cultivate some world-class industrial clusters with an aim at international advanced standards and the improvement of the level of industrial development, and promote complementary, close cooperation and linkage development of industries. For example, we will comprehensively strengthen the R & D of information technology and the construction of financial service headquarters economic clusters in Shenzhen, Guangzhou and Hong Kong; we will vigorously build world-class advanced manufacturing industrial clusters with Shenzhen and Dongguan as the core; we will vigorously promote the construction of Guangzhou as the capital of design to form a global landmark of design industrial cluster; we will vigorously build the world-class petrochemical industrial cluster in Daya Bay to promote the transformation and upgrading of ecological development.

On this basis, many industrial clusters form an industrial cluster network through division of labor and cooperation and innovation resonance, in which various innovation elements realize free allocation and reorganization based on market-oriented power, and jointly form the industrial collaborative innovation ecosystem of Guangdong, Hong Kong and Macao; through the establishment of various industry alliances, the industrial innovation forces of Guangdong, Hong Kong and Macao are gathered to realize subversive collaborative innovation in key fields.

6.2.3 Sprinting for the Top of the Global Value Chain of Scientific and Technological Innovation and the Source of Emerging Industries

We should seize the great opportunity of the construction of the international science and technology innovation center in the GBA, taking the top of the global science and technology innovation value chain as the general anchor point, strive to build GBA into a global industrial innovation highland, strive to promote the collaborative sharing of the value chains of scientific and technological innovation, promote the upgrading of industry led innovation, and form an important source of global emerging industries.

Table 6.4 Comparison of R & D centers and laboratories in the GBA, Jiangsu Province, Beijing and Shanghai

R & D centers and laboratories	GBA	Jiangsu Province	Beijing	Shanghai
Provincial new R & D institutions (number)	191	346	—	—
National Independent Innovation Demonstration Zone (number)	1	1	1	1
state key laboratory (number)	43	20	79	32

Source Sorted by the authors

6.2.3.1 Rapid Gathering of Top Innovative Resources and Talents so as to Promote the Combination of Industries, Universities and Research Institutions and the Transformation of Scientific Research Achievements

At present, there are 43 state key laboratories and 150 universities in the GBA, with 16 state key laboratories and 6 national engineering technology research sub centers in Hong Kong, 1 state key laboratory and 1 state laboratory in Macao. In addition, there are 1 national independent innovation demonstration zone, 3 national innovative cities, 25 national engineering research centers and 191 provincial new R & D institutions in the GBA (see Table 6.4). There are many famous universities in the GBA, including nine in the top 500 universities of Times Higher Education World University Rankings. However, as for the gathering of top innovative talents and resources, as of the end of 2017, there were only 43 academicians of Chinese Academy of Sciences and Chinese Academy of Engineering in Guangdong Province, less than those in Jiangsu Province, Shanghai and Beijing. The GBA should speed up the layout of national R & D centers and laboratories, gather top innovative talents and resources, and further promote the combination of industries, universities and research institutions and the transformation of scientific research achievements.

6.2.3.2 Giving Full Play to the Role of the Technological Innovation of Enterprises and Taking the Lead in the Global Industrial Transformation in Fields Like Information Technology Industry and Other Fields

In 2017, the number of R & D institutions in Guangdong Province reached 23,300, with a year-on-year increase of 62.7%. Among them, there were more than 20,000 R & D institutions in industrial enterprises with annual revenue of 20 million yuan or more from their main business operations, with a year-on-year growth rate of 69.3% and a coverage rate of 37.1%, an increase of 14.4% over the previous year (see Fig. 6.5). In 2017, the number of R & D projects in Guangdong province increased from 135,700 in 2016 to 170,200, an increase of more than 25%.

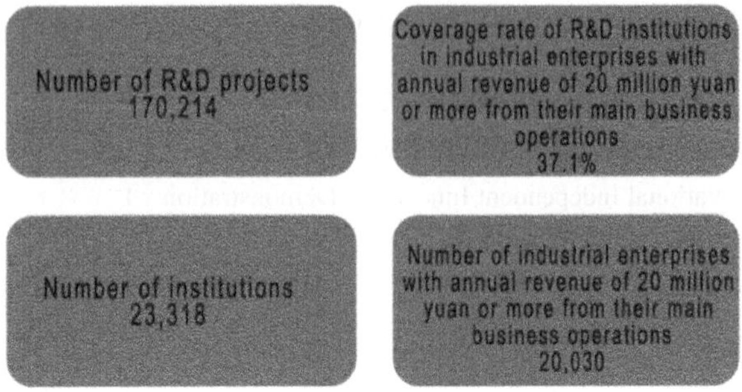

Fig. 6.5 A survey of the R&D institutions in Guangdong Province (*Source* Sorted by the authors)

By the end of 2017, there were about 33,000 high-tech enterprises in Guangdong Province, ranking first in China (see Fig. 6.6). Among them, there were 30,000 cities in the PRD, accounting for 90% of the province. The top two cities were Shenzhen and Guangzhou. As the main force of innovation, Shenzhen boasted of its 10,988 high-tech enterprises while Guangzhou had nearly 9000, far higher than the numbers in other cities. The representative enterprises include Tencent, Huawei, BYD, ZTE, DJI and BGI, etc.

As the representative of excellent enterprises with a certain scale, listed companies play a great role in the study of the development level of local advantageous industries. Statistics show that, since 2013, R & D expenditure of listed companies in the GBA has been increasing year by year. From 2013 to 2017, the compound growth rate of R & D investment of listed companies in the GBA in A-share market and Hong Kong stock market exceeded 30% (see Table 6.5).

On this basis, the GBA should give full play to the role of the technological innovation of enterprises, relying on important enterprises to achieve pinpoint innovation, especially in fields such as the IT industry, etc. to take the lead in the global industrial change.

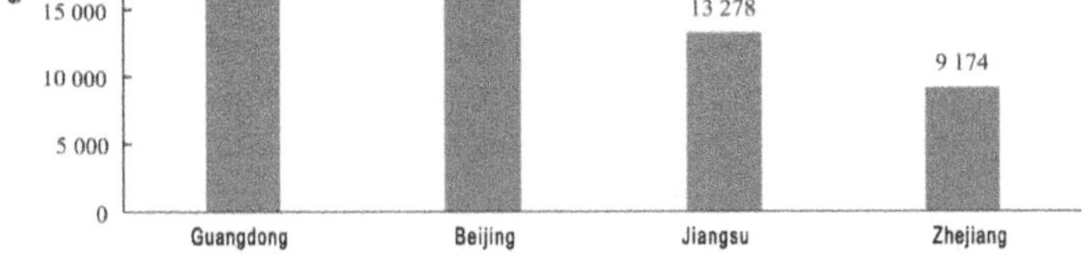

Fig. 6.6 No. of high-tech enterprises in different regions by the end of 2017 (*Source* Sorted by the authors)

Table 6.5 A survey of scientific research expenditure of listed high-tech enterprises

Name of enterprises	Industries	Scientific research expenditure in 2017 (RMB billion)	Proportion of total income (%)
Google	Internet	108.6	15.00
Microsoft	Internet	88.3	14.49
Intel	IT	85.5	20.85
Apple	IT	76.8	5.05
Huawei	IT	89.7	14.95
Tencent	Internet	17.4	7.31
ZTE	IT	12.9	11.85
Midea	Consumer goods	8.5	3.51
Foxconn	IT	7.9	2.23
BYD	Consumer goods	6.2	5.85
GREE	Consumer goods	5.7	3.80
China Merchants Bank	Finance	4.7	2.13
TCL	Consumer goods	4.7	4.21
GAC Group	Consumer goods	3.0	4.19
OFILM	IT	1.7	5.03

Source Wind, SINO-INNO RESEARCH

6.2.3.3 Scientific Promotion of the Transformation and Upgrading of Industrial Structure, and Realization of Upgrading Traditional Manufacturing Industry to the High-End

With a sound manufacturing industry system, the GBA has always been a world-class manufacturing base, which is also an important driving force for the economic development of the GBA. The *Outline Development Plan for the Guangdong-Hong Kong-Macao Greater Bay Area* calls for accelerating the development of advanced manufacturing, building an internationally competitive base of advanced manufacturing, cultivating and strengthening strategic emerging industries, and improving the ecological system for innovative development of manufacturing in the PRD.

At present, the GBA has formed two camps of traditional manufacturing industry and high-end manufacturing industry in the layout of manufacturing industry. The traditional manufacturing industry represented by the equipment manufacturing industry is mainly concentrated in the west bank of the Pearl River, while the high-end manufacturing industry represented by the electronic information manufacturing industry is mainly concentrated in Shenzhen, Huizhou, Dongguan and other cities on the east bank of the Pearl River. The east bank of the Pearl River is also the region in the lead for the development of information industry in China. In accordance with the *Outline Development Plan for the Guangdong-Hong Kong-Macao Greater Bay Area*, it is very important to realize the industrial transformation and upgrading to

Table 6.6 Industrial transfer trend in Guangdong Province from 2011 to 2018

Cities	Industries of absolute transfer
Guangzhou	Agricultural and sideline food processing industry, wine and beverage and refined tea manufacturing industry, textile industry, textile clothing industry, leather, fur and feather products and footwear industry, wood processing and rattan palm grass products industry, culture, education, industry, sports and entertainment products manufacturing industry, petroleum processing and coking and nuclear fuel processing industry, chemical raw materials and chemical products manufacturing industry, ferrous metal smelting and processing industry, metal products industry, railway, ship, aerospace and other transportation equipment manufacturing industry, and industry of comprehensive utilization of waste resources
Shenzhen	Leather, fur, feather and its products, footwear industry, culture, education, industry, sports and entertainment products manufacturing, ferrous metal smelting and processing industry
Zhuhai	Liquor and beverage and refined tea manufacturing industry, textile industry, textile clothing industry, leather, fur and feather products and footwear industry, printing and recording media reproduction industry, culture, education, industry, sports and entertainment products manufacturing industry, nonferrous metal smelting and processing industry, general equipment manufacturing industry, electrical machinery and equipment manufacturing industry, and other manufacturing industries
Foshan	Petroleum processing and coking, nuclear fuel processing and other manufacturing industries
Huizhou	Petroleum processing and coking, nuclear fuel processing industry, ferrous metal smelting and processing industry, comprehensive utilization of waste resources
Dongguan	Liquor and beverage and refined tea manufacturing industry, textile industry, petroleum processing and coking and nuclear fuel processing industry, other manufacturing industry, comprehensive utilization of waste resources
Zhongshan	Food manufacturing industry, textile industry, textile and clothing industry, leather, fur and feather products and footwear industry, wood processing and wood, bamboo, rattan, palm and grass products industry, paper and paper products industry, printing and recording media reproduction industry, culture, education, industry, sports and entertainment products manufacturing industry, petroleum processing and coking and nuclear fuel processing industry, chemical raw materials and chemical products manufacturing industry, rubber and plastic products industry, non-metallic mineral products industry, ferrous metal smelting and processing industry, non-ferrous metal smelting and processing industry, metal products industry, special equipment manufacturing industry, electrical machinery and equipment manufacturing industry, comprehensive utilization of waste resources, gas production and supply industry
Jiangmen	Textile industry, textile and clothing industry, leather, fur, feather and its products and footwear industry, wood processing and wood, bamboo, rattan, palm and grass products industry, furniture manufacturing industry, printing and recording media reproduction industry, culture, education, industry, sports and entertainment products manufacturing industry, petroleum processing, coking and nuclear fuel processing, chemical raw materials and chemical products manufacturing, rubber and plastic products industry, ferrous metal smelting and processing industry, non-ferrous metal smelting and processing industry, metal products industry, railway, ship, aerospace and other transportation equipment manufacturing, electrical machinery and equipment manufacturing, instrumentation manufacturing, other manufacturing, comprehensive utilization of waste resources industry

(continued)

Table 6.6 (continued)

Cities	Industries of absolute transfer
Zhaoqing	Textile industry, textile and clothing industry, leather, fur and feather products and footwear industry, pharmaceutical manufacturing industry, ferrous metal smelting and processing industry, nonferrous metal smelting and processing industry, railway, ship, aerospace and other transportation equipment manufacturing industry, electrical machinery and equipment manufacturing industry, computer communication and other electronic equipment manufacturing industry, and other manufacturing industries

Sources Official websites of related municipal governments

the high-end. At present, the economic transformation and upgrading and structural adjustment in the PRD is in the lead in China, and the continuous development of intelligent technology will undoubtedly provide new momentum for this adjustment and transformation process.

With the acceleration of scientific and technological innovation, the continuous integration of artificial intelligence, big data and other emerging technologies with the real economy has provided a foundation for the transformation, upgrading and optimization development of the manufacturing industry. In this context, as a world-class manufacturing base, the GBA should constantly improve the level of division of labor and cooperation among industries, encourage win–win cooperation between the upstream and downstream of the industrial chain, and accelerate the construction of a world-class competitive high-end manufacturing base with high technology as the link.

While actively promoting the development of advanced manufacturing industry, it is also necessary to continuously develop strategic emerging industries in theGBA. We should make full use of the advantages of the central cities in the GBA in terms of high-tech industrial foundation and scientific research resources, and further play the role of gathering high-quality elements of the GBA as a national new area, a national independent innovation demonstration zone and a national high-tech zone, so as to jointly build a strategic emerging industrial cluster with a complete industrial chain, and provide continuous momentum for the economic development.

The industries transferred out of Guangdong Province are mainly concentrated in food processing and manufacturing industry and heavy industry, including nonferrous metal smelting and processing industry, general equipment manufacturing industry, special equipment manufacturing industry, automobile manufacturing industry, electrical machinery and equipment manufacturing industry, etc., which are meanwhile also industries that have been planned to be transferred out or are being sped up in the transfer according to the *Outline Development Plan for the Guangdong-Hong Kong-Macao Greater Bay Area.*

Industry hollowing-out will appear in the process of industrial transfer, which has been highly concerned by the central cities. The GBA should form a reasonable regional development plan through continuous improvement, and cities in the GBA should avoid the phenomenon of "industrial hollowing-out" in the process of industrial transfer through reasonable division of labor.

6.2.3.4 Speeding up the Construction of Science and Technology Incubator, and Providing Start-Up Enterprises with Integrated Services of Funds and Policies

Science and technology start-up enterprises participate in the whole process of science and technology innovation in China. These enterprises can use relatively few resources to realize technology creation and product innovation. At present, there are a large number of science and technology-based start-ups in China, with remarkable achievements in technological innovation, which is an important driving force for the progress of science and technology in China. The development mode and industry focus of technology-based start-ups in different countries are different, but throughout the world, technology-based start-ups are facing similar financing difficulties. Generally speaking, the financing channels of technology-based start-ups can be divided into internal financing and external financing. Internal financing mainly includes internal financing within the enterprise, retained earnings and founder's investment; external financing can be divided into policy financing, direct financing and indirect financing. Generally speaking, enterprises prefer internal financing for the promotion of its development for the reasons that on the one hand, the financing cost of internal financing is far lower than that of external financing; on the other hand, internal financing is also a financing mode more suitable for the practical development needs of enterprises. However, the ability of internal financing is often closely related to the ability of both the enterprise and the founder. Nonetheless, at the initial stage of development, technology-based start-ups are generally characterized by poor profitability and large financing demand, which often can not meet the capital needs of enterprises through internal financing. Hence the development of technology-based start-up enterprises often depends on external financing.

Commercial Banks are generally less motivated to lend to technology start-ups because they are generally small without much fixed assets for mortgage and are not capable enough to take risks. In view of this situation, some domestic commercial banks set up special branches to serve science and technology enterprises, such as Beijing Zhongguancun Park Branch of Bank of Communications, Zhongguancun Haidianyuan Branch of Bank of Beijing, etc. However, due to the lack of clear risk control and isolation mechanism in the development process of these characteristic branches, their business development is confronted with many problems. In the GBA, the support of financial institutions for science and technology enterprises also relies on the characteristic technology branches of commercial banks. There are still not enough venture capital and venture capital institutions related to science and technology.

In 2016, the financial office of Guangdong Provincial People's government issued the *Opinions on Further Promoting the Standardized Development of Micro-credit Companies*, which clearly pointed out that the entry threshold of Guangdong micro-credit companies should be further lowered, their investment and financing channels should be expanded, and the threshold to establishing small-credit companies with capital from Hong Kong and Macao should also be lowered, and the corresponding restrictions on shareholding ratio of shareholders should be removed. In practice, although high-quality micro-credit companies can pilot launching the joint investment and loan business for science and technology enterprises, the proportion of equity investment still can not break through the limit of 20%. In 2018, the GBA established a joint industrial fund with a scale of RMB 10 billion yuan. Generally speaking, though there are about 608 science and technology enterprise incubators in the GBA, there is still a lack of cooperation and sharing platform for the interconnection of science and technology credit and investment and financing. Therefore, there is huge potential of the investment and financing business of scientific and technological enterprises.

In this context, the GBA should accelerate the establishment of the investment and financing interconnection platform for science and technology enterprises, speed up the construction of science and technology intermediary and incubator, provide more helpful policy and financial support for the scientific and technological enterprises, and promote the development of the technology-based start-ups in the GBA.

6.2.4 Actively Embedding into Global Production Network and Establishing Global Promotion Center of Domestic Manufacturing

Relying on the strong manufacturing production capacity of the PRD, and taking industrial internationalization as an important strategy, we should strive to build a global advanced manufacturing innovation center. Seizing the opportunity of a new round of global science and technology revolution and the new trend of international labor division, we should actively adjust the role of the global industrial division of the GBA, get rid of the geographical limitations of the traditional supply chain network layout, and actively integrate into the global high-tech industry transformation tide with the help of the "Internet +" industrial upgrading opportunity, and strive to become a new leading node of the global production network.

6.2.4.1 Enhancing the Competitiveness of Both Ends of the Industrial Value Chain, and Fully Promoting the Construction of the Industrial R & D, Brand Building and Marketing Capacity of the GBA

As Michael Porter of Harvard Business School puts forward in his book *Competitive Advantage*, "*every enterprise is a collection of various activities to assist its products in the design, production, sales and the sending of, all of these activities can show that value chain*". Industrial chain, originated from the field of industrial economics, refers to the chain type relationship among various industrial sectors based on the technical and economic relations, and objectively formed according to a certain space–time layout and logical relationship. According to Michael Porter, any enterprise is in a certain link of an industrial chain. If an enterprise wants to maintain its competitive advantage, it requires not only the perfection of its internal value chain, but also the effective connection between its value chain and its customers, sellers and suppliers in the industrial value chain. Throughout the world, all well-known enterprises are based on successful brand building. The promotion and construction of enterprise brand is related to the survival and development of enterprises. At present, the competition among enterprises is not only the competition of product quality and service, but also the competition among brands. Brand is not only a unique symbol of product quality and service, but also a pass for enterprises to enter the market and a bridge between the enterprise and consumers, which can bring huge market share and economic benefits for the enterprise.

At present, the majority of private enterprises in China are still small and medium-sized. They generally are lacking in understanding of the concept of brand. They do not pay attention to the construction and promotion of the brand. Most of the enterprises focus on product design and R & D, ignoring brand construction and marketing strategies. Good brand building can bring high popularity, high credibility, large market share and huge economic benefits for enterprises.

The GBA, which is positioned as the world city cluster and the center of international science and technology innovation, shoulders the responsibility of internationalizing China's industrial development. Enterprises in the GBA should pay attention to product R & D and design, and at the same time, focus on improving their brand construction and marketing ability, pay attention to the self promotion ability of manufacturing brands in the GBA, and establish global promotion centers for domestic manufacturing in key cities like Shenzhen, Guangzhou, Hong Kong, Macao, etc..

6.2.4.2 Promoting the Integration of the Local and Global Production Networks in the GBA, and Playing a Leading Role in Scientific and Technological Innovation

The GBA enjoys good economic development. Manufacturing industry is an important part of the economy of the GBA, and it is also an important driving force to promote the sustainable development of the economy. The total economic volume of the GBA reached 10.87 trillion yuan in 2018 and is expected to continue to grow steadily in the following five years and become the largest in the world. The second industry accounted for more than 30% of the GBA, and the upstream and downstream industrial chains of the cities in the bay area are relatively complete and complementary. The development of manufacturing industry will benefit from the coordinated development and will become an important driving force for the sustainable development of the GBA economy. The GBA has a strong manufacturing foundation. At present, it has initially formed the advanced equipment manufacturing industrial belt on the west bank of the Pearl River and the electronic information industry cluster on the east bank of the Pearl River.

Under the promotion of factors like policy, technology and market etc., intelligent manufacturing is becoming the core field of manufacturing upgrading in the GBA, which has initially shown the characteristics of development of industrial cluster. With the information and communication industry as the core, data-driven system level intelligence based on comprehensive interconnection and the continuous improvement of digitization, automation and single point intelligence based on industry itself, the intelligent revolution of manufacturing industry has come, and the cities in the GBA have issued various policies to support the development of intelligent manufacturing industry. With the support of factors such as technology and policy, the intelligent manufacturing industry in the GBA shows the characteristics of cluster development. According to the statistics issued by the Ministry of industry and information technology, the number of Intelligent Manufacturing Industrial Parks in the PRD accounted for 28.16% of the whole country as of the end of the third quarter of 2019. And the data from the *Development Trend Report (2019) of the World Intelligent Manufacturing Center* shows that, in 2018, the number of intelligent manufacturing industrial parks in the PRD accounted for 11% of the whole country.

The transformation and upgrading of manufacturing industry can not be realized without the promotion of technological innovation. The GBA has industrial and technological foundation in several fields such as artificial intelligence, integrated circuit technology, new materials and biomedical technology, which will effectively promote the reform of manufacturing industry in the GBA. In the field of artificial intelligence, the GBA boasts of its advantages in R & D innovation, application scenarios, integration development and other aspects, which has laid a sound foundation for the future development of robot manufacturing industry. In the field of integrated circuit technology, the GBA will rely on top leading enterprises such as Huawei and Hisilicon, which are far ahead in the core technology of integrated circuit design. In the field of new materials, the GBA has the advantages of superior industrial clusters in polymer materials, metal materials and electronic information materials, etc. The industrial integration of the GBA will further promote the development of advanced equipment industrial cluster. In the field of biomedical technology, the advantages of leading enterprises of medical instruments clustering in the GBA will enhance the core technical ability of biomedicine in the GBA, and promote the formation of the industrial chain of the high-end medical equipment. Under the background of the internationalization of global production system, the GBA should further promote the integration of local production network and global production network by virtue of its advantages in the field of production and manufacturing; in terms of scientific and technological innovation and manufacturing upgrading, it should support the embedding of advanced links in global production network and encourage multinational enterprises to set up international headquarters and global R & D center in the GBA.

6.2.5 Vigorous Fostering of New Service Economy Such as Cross-Border e-commerce Finance, Port Economy, High-End Old-Age Care, and Medical Tourism

Through the cultivation of new economy and new business forms, the diversity of industrial ecosystem in the GBA will be enhanced, focusing on the industrial advantages and cooperation potential of Guangdong, Hong Kong and Macao, and vigorously cultivating new service-oriented economy such as cross-border e-commerce finance, port economy, high-end old-age care and medical tourism. First, we will vigorously promote the cluster of cross-border e-commerce, financial insurance and other related industries, focusing on the construction of four comprehensive pilot zones of cross-border e-commerce in Guangzhou, Shenzhen, Zhuhai and Dongguan, support the pilot operation of trade finance blockchain platform in the GBA with an aim to promote the construction of e-commerce globalization capacity in the GBA. Second, relying on the ports of Shenzhen-Hong Kong and Zhuhai-Macao, we will vigorously build the port economic belt of the GBA and explore the operation mechanism, system and mode of an innovative port, enhance the port's passenger and cargo clearance capacity, and promote the free flow of people, goods, capital and information in the GBA. Third, we will build an ecological and livable bay area, giving priority to the convergence of endowment insurance and medical insurance among Guangdong, Hong Kong and Macao, speeding up the diversified construction capacity of pension service institutions. We will also introduce a series of measures to support Hong Kong and Macao residents to go to the mainland to enjoy the old-age care service, build a national cross-border pilot zone for the elderly in the GBA, and promote the development of high-end pension industry in the GBA. Fourth, we will support the development of international medical and health care tourism services in the GBA, vigorously improve the construction of local medical service system and its international competitiveness, welcome the high-quality medical resources from Hong Kong and Macao to the mainland, and establish branch medical institutions and medical centers, and build up important international medical tourism destinations.

6.2.5.1 Cross-Border e-commerce

Since the pilot project of cross-border e-commerce was carried out in Zhengzhou, Hangzhou, Chongqing, Shanghai and Ningbo in 2012, China's cross-border e-commerce has maintained a rapid growth. As of December 2018, the number of cross-border e-commerce service pilot cities increased from 15 to 37, basically covering large and medium-sized cities in China (see Table 6.7).

Table 6.7 37 pilot cities of cross border e-commerce import services

Approval time	Approval document	City
August 2012	Division for Innovation and High Technology Development, National Development and Reform Commission [2012] No. 2218	Zhengzhou, Hangzhou, Chongqing, Shanghai, Ningbo
September 2013		Guangzhou
July 2014		Shenzhen
October 2015		Tianjin
December 2015		Fuzhou, Pingtan
January 2018	Speech of spokesperson of the Ministry of Commerce	Hefei, Chengdu, Dalian, Qingdao, Suzhou
December 2018	Finance Division, Ministry of Commerce [2018] No. 486	Beijing, Hohhot, Shenyang, Changchun, Harbin, Nanjing, Nanchang Wuhan, Changsha, Nanning, Haikou, Guiyang, Kunming, Xi'an, Lanzhou Xiamen, Tangshan, Wuxi, Weihai, Zhuhai, Dongguan, Yiwu

Source Sorted by the authors

At the same time, the volume of cross-border e-commerce transactions is also growing at a high speed, accounting for about 30% of foreign trade imports and exports in 2018, up from 6.8% in 2011. The absolute value of transactions is expected to exceed 10 trillion yuan in 2019 (see Fig. 6.7). According to the current rate of growth, it is expected to double in the coming years.

Although the cross-border e-commerce market is huge, there are few financial institutions involved in the hidden financial business. At present, the cross-border e-commerce financial business mainly includes warehouse financing, accounts receivable financing, and financing by using big data risk control model, etc., whose overall

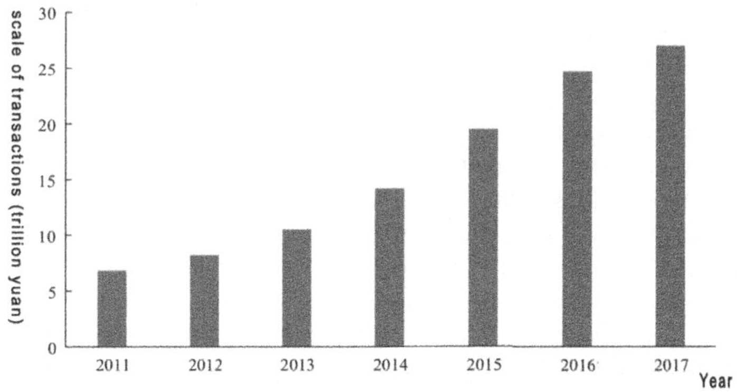

Fig. 6.7 The scale of cross-border e-commerce transactions in China (*Sources* General Administration of Customs, iiMedia Research, Enfodesk, Ali Research)

penetration rate is less than 10%, and the penetration rate of export cross-border financial business is even lower. This is in sharp contrast to the fact that there are so many participants in the consumer finance market that they are almost everywhere and the competition is extremely fierce. With the progress of science and technology and the improvement of consumption concept, China's cross-border consumption volume has ushered in a blowout growth trend. According to relevant data, from 2015 to 2017, the total amount of cross-border imports in the GBA exceeded 40% of the domestic total, while the total value of cross-border goods also exceeded 40% of the domestic total. In accordance with the information released by customs, the total value of the retail import and export commodities on the customs cross-border e-commerce management platform in 2018 was 1.5 times of that in 2017, reaching RMB 134.7 billion yuan, of which the export volume accounted for 41.6%, an increase of 67% compared with the previous year, and the import volume accounted for 58.4%, which exceeded 78.5 billion yuan, an increase of 39.8% compared with 2017. The issuance of *Outline Development Plan for the Guangdong-Hong Kong-Macao Greater Bay Area* will help the cross-border e-commerce industry to a new level.

According to the data in *China E-commerce Development Index Report*, the e-commerce development index of Guangdong Province in 2018 was 65.6, ranking first in China. As a pilot city of cross-border e-commerce, Guangzhou takes the lead in import and export volume of cross-border e-commerce in China, accounting for nearly 30% of the total import and export of cross-border e-commerce in China, with its products being sold to more than 180 countries and regions around the world.

As the birthplace of cross-border e-commerce industry, Shenzhen is home to more than 70% of cross-border sellers, with high-quality upstream and downstream service providers and suppliers with the highest cost performance ratio. It is also the most active and influential cross-border e-commerce industrial zone in China. At the same time, the GBA with its unique geographical location, will become the core hub of "Belt and Road" development in the future. Along with the market opportunities and competition, Internet e-commerce has entered a golden period of development, and a large number of high-quality pioneer enterprises have emerged. At the same time, sourcing factories specializing in cross-border e-commerce have sprung up. The unique geographical location and overall industrial positioning of the GBA have incubated a large number of high-quality cross-border e-commerce suppliers of goods.

The upgrading of national consumption and the improvement of consumers' raised demand for product quality and product types have promoted the development of cross-border e-commerce market. At the same time, the promulgation of the "*E-commerce Law*" provides a standardized development environment for the industry. Consumption upgrading promotes the improvement of customer demand and the continuous standardization of the whole industry, as well as the improvement of market structure. On such a basis, the scale of cross-border e-commerce transactions will continue to expand in 2019, and will be expected to reach more than 10 trillion yuan. In such an industrial background, the GBA should rely on its unique location and advantages of goods supply, and vigorously cultivate cross-border e-commerce finance and promote the development of cross-border e-commerce industry.

6.2.5.2 Port Economy

According to the definition of Port economy, ports are usually taken as carriers, import and export trade as the basis, while other liquidity factors such as manpower, capital, materials and information, etc. as two-way economic feedback, so as to promote the development of related industries and infrastructure construction, reflecting the overall function of the economic system.

The port economy can take the port as the foundation, radiates continuously from the port to the peripheral area, thus forming the diffusion effect. According to the correlation between ports and economic activities, the port economy can be divided into three levels: the first level is the most basic and important part of port economy, that is, the economic activities of related ports, including the fees to be charged by the port management department and the taxes and fees collected by the inspection departments, as well as the related activities of the transportation system and port characteristic services; the second level is "port-centered industry", which has a direct relationship with the port, including material processing and bonded factories, as well as production and business activities such as bonded zones and free trade zones developed by relying on the advantages of the port; the third level is the export-oriented economy indirectly related to the port of import and export enterprises developed by relying on the import and export advantages of the port.

Take Shenzhen as an example, the land ports that have been opened for communication between Shenzhen and Hong Kong include Futian, Shatoujiao, Luohu, Wenjindu, Shenzhen Bay and Huanggang ports. In 2019, at the seventh session of the Sixth National People's Congress of Shenzhen, the work report of Shenzhen government clearly pointed out that it was necessary to improve the development and construction level of Shenzhen-Hong Kong Science and technology innovation cooperation zone in the bend area of Shenzhen River, so as to promote the construction of a more open and creative collaborative mode which can fully integrate and embody the advantageous system of "one country, two systems". It also pointed out that Shenzhen should strive to lead the way in the full flow of personnel and materials, improve the access mechanism of vocational qualifications, constantly innovate relevant rules and preferential systems, and regulate the development of new drugs and medical devices, so as to promote the more effective cross-border use of Shenzhen-Hong Kong research funds through measures like "implementation first, pilot first" etc. At the same time, Shenzhen plans to promote the construction of a new platform for trade, tourism and consumption with Hong Kong in 2019. The main measures are to actively promote the construction of port economic belt, re-build the Shatoujiao and Huanggang ports, and continue the opening and construction of the New Liantang port. As for Luohu and other ports, their quality needs to be improved, and Shenzhen needs to constantly improve its functions in leisure and culture, so as to promote the formation of cross-border consumer business circles and promote cross-border cultural exchanges. The in-depth cooperation between Shenzhen and Hong Kong is accelerating. From the west to the east, the "Qianhai Cooperation Demonstration Zone of GBA", "Shenzhen-Hong Kong Science and Technology Innovation Cooperation Zone" and "Shatoujiao-Luohu-Shenzhen-Hong Kong International Tourism and

Consumption Cooperation Zone" will be formed, which will enable Shenzhen and Hong Kong to form a closer strategic layout. Other cities in the GBA can learn from Shenzhen's advanced experience in port economic development and jointly build the port economic belt into a strategic support point and an important development pole of the GBA.

6.2.5.3 High-End Pension and Medical Tourism

In October 2016, the CPC Central Committee and the State Council issued the *Healthy China 2030 Planning Outline*, which proposed to take improving people's health as the core, integrate health into all policies, and ensure people's health in an all-round and full cycle way. It is estimated that by 2020, the scale of China's health industry will reach 8 trillion yuan, close to 10% of China's GDP at that time, and become the pillar of the national economy. As one of the regions with the strongest economic vitality and the highest degree of openness in China, the GBA has actively responded to and implemented the *Healthy China 2030 Planning Outline*, and continued to increase investment in the health industry. Statistics show that by the end of 2018, the total GDP of the GBA exceeded 10 trillion yuan, ranking second in the world after Tokyo Bay Area. The GDP of health industry accounted for about 7% of the total GDP in the GBA. However, in the developed countries such as the United States and Germany, the ratio of health industry to GDP is more than 15%. Therefore, compared with developed countries or regions in Europe and America, the GBA still has great potential in the development of health industry.

According to the *Outline Development Plan for the Guangdong-Hong Kong-Macao Greater Bay Area*, it is proposed to continuously support the cooperation in pension services between mainland cities and Hong Kong and Macao. The government should enhance its support in all aspects of the pension industry, continuously deepen the pension reform, put forward innovative policies for the elderly, actively support the private-owned pension enterprises, and accelerate the implementation of effective measures to alleviate the endowment pressure. At the same time, the government should also make the pension industry develop in an orderly and healthy way. The pension service is of great significance to the whole society. It is a field worthy of in-depth discussion and research no matter at present or in the future. In addition, the development of the pension industry is also inseparable from the improvement of the social service system for the elderly, which can more effectively promote the comprehensive construction of the pension industry. This requires the active promotion of exchanges between the pension industries in the mainland and Hong Kong, who work together to cultivate professionals in the elderly service, etc., so as to make up for the existing talent gap in this field in China. Only in this way can the complementary social function of the pension industry and the elderly service be enhanced.

In terms of the medical industry, the launch of the *Outline Development Plan for the Guangdong-Hong Kong-Macao Greater Bay Area* has brought new opportunities to the development of the medical industry in the GBA. The GBA has a large economic aggregate, active economy and great demand for medical services. The development of the medical industry also plays an important supporting role in the economic development of the GBA.

On November 6, 2019, the Construction Leading Group Meeting of the GBA approved 16 policies in three categories to benefit the people and facilitate the development of Hong Kong's professional sectors in the GBA (hereinafter referred to as "16 Policies"), of which Article 7 clearly states that "Hong Kong registered drugs and commonly used medical instruments are allowed to be used in designated Hong Kong funded medical institutions in mainland cities of the GBA". In order to facilitate Hong Kong people working and living in the GBA to seek medical treatment locally, the central government has accepted the proposal of the SAR government to allow designated Hong Kong funded medical institutions in mainland cities of the GBA to use drugs and medical equipment registered in Hong Kong. The Hong Kong Food and Health Bureau will discuss specific arrangements with the authorities concerned in the mainland, including the Shenzhen Hospital of the University of Hong Kong as a pilot. This policy provides an important support for the opening and coordinated development of the medical industry within the GBA. Take HPV vaccine as an example. Since 2013, young women from the PRD and even many mainland provinces have chosen to go to Hong Kong for HPV vaccination. As the vaccination needs to be taken three times, the cost of the round trips is high. If the policy is implemented in the future, the designated Hong Kong funded medical institutions in the mainland cities of the GBA can also use the drugs registered in Hong Kong and the commonly used medical equipment, then similar vaccination is expected to be carried out in Hong Kong funded clinics in the PRD, and it will be more convenient for mainland residents to receive similar vaccination. As of November 2019, more than 27 Hong Kong funded medical institutions have been opened in the PRD, and eight Hong Kong funded medical institutions have been established in Shenzhen. These Hong Kong funded clinics are mainly specialized in Ophthalmology, Stomatology and Pediatrics.

From the perspective of the GBA, Hong Kong has an obvious advantage in the medical market and is more advanced in terms of medical system and medical service management, which is convenient to be in line with the international standards. This provides valuable learning experience for the development of the medical industry in the GBA. Cities in Guangdong province can actively learn from the advanced management model of Hong Kong's medical industry and set up a mutual recognition mechanism for the professional qualifications of Hong Kong doctors and mainland doctors, so as to further promote the sharing of medical resources between the two places and promote the development of the medical industry in the GBA. Local governments in the GBA will increase investment, introduce endowment enterprises to cover the pension and medical market in the GBA to alleviate the pressure of insufficient supply of endowment resources in the mainland and Hong Kong, and build a modern pension system with full coverage in the GBA.

Tourism plays a very important role in the economic development of Guangdong, Hong Kong and Macao. Statistics from the National Tourism Administration show that tourism contributes a lot to industries such as accommodation, civil aviation and railways, as well as catering and cultural entertainment. In recent years, the tourism market of Guangdong province has been developing new forms of business and opening up new markets, and the tourism competitiveness of all cities in the province has been significantly improved. Since 2017, Guangdong Province has continuously strengthened the tourism market cooperation with major tourist source regions and countries such as Europe, the United States and ASEAN, and accelerated the development of tourism cooperation with central Europe and South America, seizing the opportunities of relevant industries in emerging tourism areas to attract more tourists, so as to make Guangdong Province more competitive in the international tourism market.

Tourism departments at all levels in Guangdong Province have set up 27 tourism cooperation and promotion centers abroad, which have conducted promotion of tourism related activities in more than 30 countries or regions. The establishment of the Center for International Cooperation Promotion and the training of Chinese-speaking tour guides have greatly promoted the development of tourism and related industries in Guangdong province. In addition, in terms of cruise tourism, Guangdong Province also gives full play to its geographical advantages and keeps up with the new tourism trend and continuously expands relevant business of cruise tourism through Nansha and Shekou, two high-quality cruise home ports. In 2017 alone, the Nansha and Shekou ports operated 180 inbound and outbound cruise ships, receiving 580,000 passengers from various countries. In particular, Guangzhou operated over 120 cruise ships, accounting for 69% of the total, an increase of more than 20% over the previous year and ranking among the top three in China.

In the GBA, cities like Guangzhou, Shenzhen, Zhuhai, Jiangmen, etc. have strong tourism city competitiveness; meanwhile, in the radiation area of the GBA, the attraction of Shaoguan, Maoming and Zhanjiang has also been recognized nationwide (see Table 6.8).

The completion and operation of such basic transportation construction projects as the Hong Kong-Zhuhai-Macao Bridge and the Guangzhou-Shenzhen-Hong Kong high-speed railway have made the travel of tourists more convenient and efficient, shortened the time spent in transportation, which not only improves the tourism quality of tourists, but also provides a growth point for the tourism industry in the project radiation area. Guangdong, Hong Kong and Macao are also carrying out frequent cooperation on tourism business. The establishment of "GBA Urban Tourism Association" in 2017 has greatly promoted the tripartite cooperation in tourism. All parties have been actively deepening the research on the investment in relevant industries. Not long ago, Hong Kong Disneyland launched the "Special Discount Package for Residents of the GBA", and the Hong Kong Travel Industry Council is preparing to make an electronic tourism information platform for Hong Kong and the GBA. The tourism industry in the GBA is upgrading its tourist attractions and developing rapidly to make things easier for the people. On this basis, each city in GBA should start from their own characteristics to further promote the coordinated development of the tourism industry in the GBA.

Table 6.8 Evaluation of tourism competitiveness of cities in the GBA (2017)

City	Evaluation/Ranking
Guangzhou	Among the world's ten fastest growing tourist cities, Guangzhou ranks second Guangzhou's tourism comprehensive competitiveness ranks the third in China and the first among the sub provincial cities In the list of top 100 tourism destination cities in the world in 2017, Guangzhou ranked 18th in the world
Shenzhen	In the list of top 100 tourism destination cities in the world in 2017, Shenzhen ranked 11th in the world
Zhuhai	Among the top 100 tourist destination cities in the world in 2017, Zhuhai ranked the 63rd in the world and has been awarded as one of the first "Model Cities for Tourism and Leisure in China" by the National Tourism Administration
Jiangmen	It was approved by the United Nations World Tourism Organization as the ninth in China and the first in Guangdong, World Tourism Organization observation point of sustainable development in tourism
Shaoguan	"Ecological and Natural Tourism City" on the 2017 Most Beautiful China List
Maoming	"Most Popular Charming City in 2017" and "Top 10 Charming Cities"
Zhanjiang	"Excellent and charming city, Charming Chinese City in 2017"

Source Sorted by the authors

6.3 The Conception of Financial Synergy in the GBA

In the construction of the GBA, financial coordination is one of the keys to build a complete financial service system. In terms of the financial sector, the *Outline Development Plan for the Guangdong-Hong Kong-Macao Greater Bay Area* clearly puts forward the requirements of "*accelerating the development of modern service industries and promoting the connectivity of financial markets in an orderly manner*". This puts forward higher requirements for cross-border financial coordination in the GBA. At present, the GBA has taken the lead in cross-border financial cooperation and achieved good results.

In terms of cross-border financing policies, support will be given to financial leasing companies or leasing project subsidiaries registered in Guangdong province to introduce cross-border RMB funds from financial institutions operating RMB business in Hong Kong to broaden financing channels. In terms of cross-border financial innovation, policies concerning cross-border lending, QFLP (Qualified Foreign Limited Partner), QDLP (Qualified Domestic Limited Partner), and participation of foreign investors in carbon emission trading have been introduced. In terms of cross-border RMB business, we will deepen financial cooperation between Guangdong, Hong Kong and Macao, expand cross-border RMB use, and accelerate the establishment of a pilot innovation zone for cross-border RMB business. In terms of cross-border payment service innovation, we will support commercial banks in Hong Kong and Macao in engaging in payment service business in the public service sector within the free trade zone in accordance with the law. In terms of cross-border two-way equity investment, foreign-funded enterprises and individuals may, in accordance with the law, set up equity investment enterprises in Guangdong Province, raise funds from domestic and foreign investors in a non-public way and invest in non-public equity of enterprises.

In consideration of the shortcomings in the current pattern of financial coordination in the GBA in the aspects of institutional diversification and financial supervision, focus should be put on the aspects of financial infrastructure, financial markets coordination, financial institutions coordination and financial products coordination in the process of promoting the financial coordination in the GBA, to strive to build a financial coordinated development ecosystem in the GBA.

6.3.1 Synergy of Financial Infrastructure in the GBA

As clearly stated in the *Outline Development Plan for the Guangdong-Hong Kong-Macao Greater Bay Area*, the financial infrastructure needs to be further consolidated and improved in cities like Hong Kong, Macao, Guangzhou, Shenzhen, Macao, Zhuhai etc., in order to realize the connectivity among the three places. The 'Outline' also puts forward that "*we will give full play to Hong Kong's leading role in the financial sector, consolidate and enhance its status as an international financial center, and build an investment and financing platform for the construction of 'Belt and Road'. We will support Guangzhou in improving its modern financial service system, building a regional private equity trading market, building a regional trading center for property rights and bulk commodities, and raising its level of internationalization. We will support Shenzhen in developing a capital market with the Shenzhen Stock Exchange as the core in accordance with regulations and accelerate financial opening and innovation. We will support Macao in building a financial service platform between China and Portuguese speaking countries, establish an export credit insurance system, and become a RMB clearing center of Portuguese speaking countries. The advantages of the Sino-Portuguese Fund headquarter will be leveraged in Macao to undertake the financial cooperation services between China and Portuguese speaking countries. Work will be done on the research and exploration of the construction of Macao-Zhuhai cross-border financial cooperation demonstration zone*". On this basis, the following three synergy conceptions are proposed for the financial infrastructure in the GBA.

6.3.1.1 Promoting Payment and Settlement Interconnection Among Guangdong, Hong Kong and Macao

In accordance with the global experience, the major international Bay areas will be supported by a strong financial center, and the interconnection of payment and market infrastructure constitutes the foundation for the core of financial circle in the

GBA city cluster. The most important thing is to create an environment for faster and more efficient circulation of elements for the enterprises in Guangdong, Hong Kong and Macao.

Currently, the cross-border settlement account system of Guangdong FTZ is mainly OSA (offshore account) and NRA (overseas non-resident account). In 2009, the State Administration of Foreign Exchange encouraged and supported the opening of domestic foreign exchange accounts by overseas institutions, and the volume of transactions conducted through NRA accounts increased year by year. In early 2017, the People's Bank of China promulgated a notice entitled "*PBOC Circular Regarding the Prudent Macro Management of Full-range Cross-border Financing*". It clarifies that domestic and foreign currency deposits deposited by overseas entities in financial institutions shall not be included in the calculation of the weighted balance of cross-border financing risks, which has further encouraged more and more banks to carry out foreign NRA account related finance business. Meanwhile, the People's government of Guangdong Province launched *Circular Regarding Further Promoting the Use of NRA Accounts*, in which it proposes to "further promote the use of domestic bank settlement accounts (NRA accounts) of overseas institutions" and required "relevant authorities in Guangzhou, Shenzhen, Zhuhai and other provinces" to actively guide and promote enterprises and financial institutions to open NRA accounts and use NRA accounts to carry out cross-border financial business. In 2018, the detailed rules for the implementation of Guangdong FTZ clearly stated that "*Banks with registration and business sites in the zone are allowed to handle foreign exchange settlement business for overseas institutions in domestic foreign exchange account (Foreign exchange NRA account)*", and NRA account has become the focus of cross-border settlement financial innovation in Guangdong FTZ.

In terms of NRA account practice, domestic banks not only handle fund collection and payment for overseas institutions holding foreign currency NRA accounts, but also add foreign currency NRA accounts into the settlement flow to design and launch different product portfolios. The main functions of NRA account include pledge loan, liquidity loan, fund collection and payment, L/C opening, import bill negotiation and so on. As of the end of June 2018, there were 324 NRA accounts opened in the banks of Guangdong FTZ, and the account balance reached 927 million US dollars.

OSA accounts are also known as offshore accounts. Each foreign entity may open an offshore account at the offshore business department of a domestic bank that has legally obtained the offshore banking qualification. In the *Outline Development Plan for the Guangdong-Hong Kong-Macao Greater Bay Area*, it is proposed that the GBA should "promote financial openness and innovation, expand OSA functions, learn from the Free Trade Account system (FTA) of the Shanghai Pilot Free Trade Zone, and actively explore the effective path of capital item convertibility". OSA accounts are subject to fewer foreign exchange controls than NRA accounts; OSA accounts are more secure from a security standpoint than NRA accounts and are therefore less subject to regulatory restrictions from State Administration of Foreign Exchange.

6.3.1.2 Accelerating the Opening of the Credit Rating Market

In recent years, the degree of China's financial market opening to the outside world has increased significantly, and then the opening of bond market to the outside world has also been accelerated. As the "gatekeeper" of credit risk in the bond market, credit rating has also ushered in the situation of opening up. In July 2019, Office of the Financial Stability and Development Commission of The State Council announced a series of policies and measures to further open the financial industry to the outside world, which explicitly allows foreign institutions to grade all kinds of bonds in the inter-bank bond market and the exchange bond market when conducting credit rating business in China. Credit rating is one of the important infrastructure for the development of bond market. In recent years, with the marketization and legalization of credit risk and default disposal in bond market, whether credit rating agencies can effectively play the role of credit risk disclosure has been increasingly concerned by the market. The opening of the rating industry to the outside world will attract more overseas issuers and investors to enter the Chinese market, meet the demands of international investors in allocating diversified RMB assets, and enhance the internationalization level of the bond market. At the same time, it will also provide more decision-making reference for domestic investors and provide more abundant services for credit risk pricing and credit risk management of bond market participants.

On this basis, new measures can be taken to further open up the credit rating market, such as opening up the credit rating market in the loan business and the credit rating market of small loan companies and financing guarantee companies. At the same time, domestic credit rating agencies will focus on giving full play to the advantages of localization, to strengthen the effectiveness of the ratings and the degree of differentiation, enhance market credibility, and consolidate customer base, with more excellent service to meet competitive challenges, build rating services for foreign investors, and promote the internationalization of business operation level, promote the development of the internationalization of China's financial markets.

6.3.1.3 Establishing a Market Platform for Intellectual Property Transactions in the GBA

The *Outline Development Plan for the Guangdong-Hong Kong-Macao Greater Bay Area* proposes to strengthen the protection and application of intellectual property rights, make use of the regional intellectual property cooperation mechanism in the Guangdong-Hong Kong, Guangdong-Macao region and Pan PRD, in order to comprehensively strengthen the cooperation in intellectual property protection and professional personnel training in the GBA, carry out intellectual property transactions and promote the rational and effective circulation of intellectual property rights relying on existing trading places. With more and more China-manufactured goods replaced by China-created ones in the market, the importance of intellectual property transactions is becoming increasingly prominent. The realization of the market-oriented trading of intellectual property rights is of great significance to the construction of the GBA, the collection of excellent resources at home and abroad, and the promotion of the transformation and application of innovative elements.

In the field of intellectual property rights, Hong Kong and Macao have advanced innovation culture, developed market economy and better protection of intellectual property rights. On the other hand, cities in the PRD such as Shenzhen and Guangzhou have high-quality high-tech manufacturing foundation and rich intellectual property reserves. Therefore, Guangdong, Hong Kong and Macao can work together to create an environment of respecting intellectual property rights, unify the intellectual property evaluation system of the GBA, establish commonly recognized evaluation indicators and evaluation processes, promote mutual recognition of intellectual property evaluation results in the GBA. The three places can also join hands together to establish a trading platform of intellectual property in, promote the interconnection of intellectual property pledge financing in the GBA, to escort innovation, attract innovative talents from all over the world to settle in the GBA, build a top talent pool and stimulate innovation dividends.

6.3.2 Synergy of the Financial Market in the GBA

The *Outline Development Plan for the Guangdong-Hong Kong-Macao Greater Bay Area* also raises certain requirements on the communication mechanism and market security of the financial market: "*We should establish the coordination and communication mechanism of financial supervision in the GBA, and strengthen the supervision of cross-border financial institutions as well as the cooperation on the monitoring and analysis of capital flow. We will improve cooperation and information exchange mechanisms among Guangdong, Hong Kong and Macao in combating money laundering, terrorist financing, and tax evasion. We will establish and improve a system for early warning, prevention and resolution of systemic risks, and jointly safeguard the security of the financial system.*" Under this condition, the following two conceptions are proposed.

6.3.2.1 Learning from the EU's "Single Pass" System to Promote the Integration of the Financial Market in the GBA

Market coordination means to promote the connectivity of the financial markets of Guangdong, Hong Kong and Macao, promote the orderly flow of financial elements in the GBA, and provide efficient financial services for the optimal allocation of resources in the GBA. Most of the financial connectivity measures in the GBA used to be based on the product level, which was a pipelined or "external" transfusion model for the economy. As a result, when the product reaches a certain stage of development, it will face a lot of bottlenecks, such as product fragmentation, unbalanced pace of policy introduction, and even regulatory arbitrage and policy game, etc., which will lead to the downslide of the efficiency of the whole connectivity. The "Single Pass" system may be the key to moving from "external" transfusion to substantive integration. The minimum standards established under the "Single Pass" system will enable the enterprises to practice within the uniform rules, while enterprises in some regions could also set higher standards to boost the investors' confidence and strengthen global recognition of the region. The GBA can learn from the EU's "Single Pass" system and its corresponding mutual recognition mechanism, promote the conformance of financial business rules in the region, gradual transition from differences to convergence, and promote the integration of financial markets in the GBA.

Promoting the integration of financial services in the GBA of Guangdong, Hong Kong and Macao and promoting the efficient allocation of financial resources in the region will be an important driving force for the economic transformation and upgrading in the region and the further development of the financial industry in the three regions. With the mainland's accelerating financial opening up, the institutional arrangements for financial institutions from Hong Kong and Macao to enter the mainland's cross-border trade have partly broken through the CEPA framework. However, the current barriers to entry and restrictions on capital flows, as well as the differences between regulatory systems and tariff systems, are still the main reasons why the cross-border financial demands of the three cities cannot be met for a long time. We propose in this section to learn from the experience of the EU's "Single Pass" system. We suggest to broaden the range of freedom that used to be limited to the banks and insurance agencies, to different qualified financial institutions in Guangdong, Hong Kong and Macao where they will enjoy the service freedom. We will first open access to areas with strong cross-border demand, such as cross-border car insurance and payment, or business areas that do not involve the central authority, such as small loans, commercial factoring, financing guarantee and financial leasing. At the same time, the financial supervision cooperation and coordination mechanism of Guangdong, Hong Kong, Macao. A sustainable supervision mode for cross-border development of financial institutions of the three places with "passes", so as to establish a "common market" of Guangdong, Hong Kong, Macao. On the one hand, the legal coordination of financial regulation in the Bay Area should be gradually promoted. In the initial stage, "minimum coordination" can be carried out for financial institutions, financial business access and prudential supervision rules applicable to the "Single Pass" system. When conditions are ripe, the scope of coordination can be gradually expanded and the degree of coordination can be improved. On the other hand, we should improve the procedural institutional arrangements for the regulatory coordination and cooperation among the three places, including establishing the regulatory dialogue mechanism, clarifying the framework of information exchange and regulatory cooperation among the three places, coping with the changes in the economic, financial and regulatory environment, and ensuring the implementation of the regulatory coordination and cooperation arrangements as well as the fulfillment of the rights and obligations of all parties.

6.3.2.2 Broadening the Market Communication Mechanism of Various Financial Products

Article 5 of the "16 Policies" proposes "*to explore the establishment of a two-way financing mechanism to open up a broader market and business space for the financial industry of the two places on the premise of controllable risk and appropriate protection of investors*". At present, Shenzhen-Hong Kong cross-border interconnection financial products mainly include Shanghai-Hong Kong Stock Connect Program, Shenzhen-Hong Kong Stock Connect Program, QFII (qualified foreign institutional investors) and RQFII (RMB qualified foreign institutional investors), Bond Connect and mutual recognition funds issued by the two places. It's reasonable to induct that China's cross-border financial products opening measures are constantly advancing from the following events: the establishment of the Shanghai-Hong Kong Stock Connect Program in 2014, the establishment of Shenzhen Hong Kong Stock Connect Program in 2016, the cancellation of the total two-way investment quota of Shenzhen-Hong Kong Stock Connect Program, the establishment of Bond Connect in 2017, the control relaxation of one-day limit of two-way investment of Shanghai-Shenzhen Hong-Kong Stock Connect Program in 2018, the launch of Shanghai-London Stock Connect in June 2019, and measures like the cancellation of investment limit on QFII/RQFII in September of the same year by State Administration of Foreign Exchange. When Shenzhen-Hong Kong Stock Connect was launched in December 2016, the CSRC of the two places issued a Joint Announcement saying that they would jointly study other financial products such as ETF interconnection. As of September 2019, Shanghai-Shenzhen-Hong Kong Stock Connect, QFII and RQFII have become the main means for foreign financial institutions to invest in A-shares. The market value of stocks held through these two channels exceeds 1.3 trillion yuan, of which the Shanghai-Shenzhen-Hong Kong Stock Connect accounted for 62%, while the QFII and RQFII channels accounted for 38%. The cumulative net capital inflow of Shanghai Stock Connect and Shenzhen Stock Connect reached as high as RMB 461.6 billion and RMB 367 billion respectively. Since the opening of the Bond Connect, the stock of RMB bonds held by foreign investors has exceeded 1.9 trillion yuan.

As of September 2019, there were 26 mutually recognized funds in the mainland, with the latest total size of 38.924 billion yuan. There were 43 mutually recognized funds in Hong Kong, with the latest total size of 74.896 billion yuan. According to the data of cross-border issuance of securities investment funds between the mainland and Hong Kong released by the SAFE, in the same year, the accumulated net inward remittance of the sales funds of the mainland funds in Hong Kong was RMB 302 million, and that of the Hong Kong funds was RMB 15.392 billion. With the flow of personnel elements in the two places and the extensive and in-depth cross-border use of RMB, the residents' demand for investment in cross-border financial management and asset management products has gradually increased. It is urgent to develop two-way cross-border financial products that can meet the diversification and liquidity needs of customers.

In order to meet the cross-border wealth management needs of residents in the two places, financial institutions in the GBA should explore cross-border business cooperation mode, design diversified cross-border financial products, and broaden cross-border use and circulation channels of RMB. At the same time, we can learn from the EU's "Single Pass" model to promote mutual recognition of joint venture financial institutions and cross-border financial products in the GBA, promote cross-border fund management platform through the exchange mode of fund, asset management and bank financial products, and realize the registration of products in one place and issuance in difference places (within the GBA). Financial institutions in Guangdong Province can try to create innovative and anchored value blockchain cross-border financial products in order to attract Hong Kong and Macao residents to open financial accounts in the mainland and convert foreign currencies into RMB to invest in diversified wealth management products in the mainland. Following the mechanism of Shanghai-Shenzhen-Hong Kong stock connect, the financial regulatory authorities in the mainland can design the annual cross-border quota management system and closed-loop capital supervision mode to realize cross-border financial connection, and effectively break through the approval problem of cross-border capital flow in the current capital account on the premise of risk control.

6.3.3 Synergy of Financial Institutions in the GBA

The Outline Development Plan for the Guangdong-Hong Kong-Macao Greater Bay Area points out the direction of the coordinated development for many financial institutions, including "supporting Hong Kong institutional investors to raise RMB funds in the GBA to invest in the Hong Kong capital market in accordance with regulations, and to participate in the investment of domestic private equity funds and venture capital funds; supporting the development of more offshore renminbi, commodities and other risk management tools in Hong Kong; supporting insurance institutions in the mainland, Hong Kong and Macao to carrying out cross-border RMB reinsurance business; continuous improving of the Shanghai-Hong Kong Stock Connect, the Shenzhen-Hong Kong Stock Connect and the Bond Connect; supporting qualified Banks and insurance institutions from Hong Kong and Macao to set up business offices in Qianhai of Shenzhen, Nansha of Guangzhou and Hengqin of Zhuhai". Under this outline, the following four collaborative modes are proposed for financial institutions in the GBA.

6.3.3.1 Exploring the Co-Operation Mode of Financial Institutions in Guangdong, Hong Kong and Macao

In order to realize the coordinated development of financial institutions in the bay area, we need to accelerate the exchange and cooperation among various financial institutions in the bay area, provide support for the all-round and multi-level high-quality construction of the financial system in the GBA, so as to realize the innovation of cooperation mode among Hong Kong, Macao and the mainland, gather professionals from relevant industries in the Bay Area, and constantly improve the coordinated development system of regional financial market in the GBA.

First of all, we should combine China's opening-up policy with the development of the financial market in the GBA, and make full use of various preferential policies. We should not only support the "going abroad" of mainland enterprises, but also provide more independent operation rights for overseas investment institutions in China, so that they can compete with the mainland enterprises in the GBA on an equal footing, and jointly build Guangdong-Hong Kong- Macao GBA. We should take advantages of the coordinated development of financial institutions in the GBA to provide new opportunities for all entities in the GBA. At the 2018 Boao Forum For Asia, President Xi Jinping proposed that China would further open its financial markets and implement more open policies in related industries like banking, securities and insurance, etc. to help Hong Kong and Macao financial institutions develop their businesses in the mainland. In order to further improve the opening level of China's financial market, while seizing the opportunity to enjoy the preferential policies in the GBA, Hong Kong and Macao financial institutions should play a leading role and strive to show the achievements of China's opening up to the international market, and attract more international financial institutions to settle in the GBA.

Secondly, the GBA also provides development opportunities for cross-border financial products of financial institutions in the three places, which is conducive to the innovation of relevant products and systems in the Bay Area. When residents and enterprises in the GBA conduct cross-border business and consumption activities, they will have a series of demands for products related to cross-border financial industry. However, under the existing conditions, the supply of cross-border financial products in the market can not meet the huge demand, which provides opportunities for banks, insurance and other financial institutions in the GBA.

Thirdly, the leading science and technology and a large number of science and technology innovation enterprises in the GBA can provide financial institutions with opportunities in product and technological innovation. Under the preferential policies of the municipal governments in the GBA, the start-up technology enterprises in the GBA are facing more rapid development. Under this background, financial institutions such as VC / PE and banks will get more investment opportunities. At the same time, compared with start-ups, the Hong Kong Stock Exchange, Shanghai Stock Exchange and Shenzhen Stock Exchange have issued corresponding preferential policies for the stock listing for the mature emerging and innovative industries. The Hong Kong Stock Exchange has been accelerating the reform of the listing system, allowing biotech companies with the same share but different rights, no profits and barely any earnings to be listed in Hong Kong; the Shanghai Stock Exchange has set up the science and technology innovation board and pilot registration system to improve its ability to serve technological innovation enterprises; Shenzhen stock exchange actively promotes the reform of the registration system of the GEM, improves the listing, refinancing and merger and reorganization system of the GEM, and increases its support for the listing of science and technology innovation enterprises. Mature science and technology innovation enterprises in the GBA can make full use of the preferential policies of the three major exchanges–Hong Kong Stock Exchange, Shenzhen Stock Exchange and Shanghai Stock Exchange in terms of the stock listing of scientific and technological innovation enterprises, so as to speed up their listing and financing process, which will bring new growth points for the investment and financing business of major financial institutions at home and abroad.

6.3.3.2 Relaxing the Access Threshold for Hong Kong and Macao Financial Institutions to Conduct Business in the Mainland

At present, securities companies from Hong Kong and Macao carry out securities business in the mainland with resort to Supplementary Agreement X of CEPA. In order to further open up the financial market, the CSRC published the new *Administrative Measures For Foreign-invested Securities Companies* in 2018, which made major adjustments to the shareholding ratio, business scope, shareholder restrictions and the change and recognition of the nature of domestic-invested securities companies. Most of the adjustments involved in the new *Administrative Measures For Foreign-invested Securities Companies* are consistent with CEPA's preferential access to Hong Kong and Macao securities companies, which reflects the pilot role of the GBA in the policy of opening up to the outside world. The *Administrative Measures For Foreign-invested Securities Companies* represents the positive attitude of China's financial opening up, and is of great significance for speeding up the entry of Hong Kong and Macao securities companies into the mainland to carry out business.

The process of further opening up China's securities market continues. In July 2019, the website of the People's Bank of China released relevant measures to further expand the opening up of the financial industry, including the advancement of the time point of abolishing the restrictions on foreign shares of securities companies, fund management companies and futures companies from 2020 to 2021; permission to foreign institutions to obtain Class A principal underwriter's license for the interbank bond market. With the further promulgation of the opening policy of the securities industry, the business scope of joint venture securities companies and the proportion of their foreign shares will be further relaxed. There is no doubt that this will attract more and more Hong Kong and Macao securities companies to set up joint venture securities companies to carry out business in the mainland, thus promoting the coordinated development of the securities industry in the GBA.

The asset management industry involves many cross-border businesses. The investment channels of the asset management industry in the GBA can be divided into cross-border investment, stock and bond market interconnection, mutual recognition of funds, public fund business, private fund management, etc. Under various channels, the main latest laws and regulations on which the GBA asset management institutions operate are listed in Table 6.9.

Cross-border investment is mainly carried out by qualified foreign investor (QFII), RMB qualified Foreign institutional investors (RQFII), qualified foreign limited partners (QFLP), R-QFLP, foreign-invested venture capital enterprises, other domestic investment platforms of foreign-invested companies, qualified domestic institutional Investors (QDII), qualified domestic investor overseas enterprises (QDIE), qualified domestic limited partners (QDLP) and foreign direct investment. Stock and bond market connectivity mainly realized on the Shanghai-Hong Kong Stock Connect,

Table 6.9 Asset management policies related to cross-border business

Cross-border business in the asset management industry	Relevant policy
Mutual recognition of funds	Interim Provisions on the Administration of Mutually Recognized Fund in Hong Kong
Public funds	Special Administrative Measures for Foreign Investment Access (Negative List) (2018 edition)
Private equity investment funds	Answers to Questions related to Private Fund Registration and Filing (10)
The interconnection of stock and bond markets	Shanghai-Hong Kong Stock Connect Pilot Program of Shanghai Stock Exchange
	Measures for the Implementation of Shenzhen-Hong Kong Stock Connect Business of Shenzhen Stock Exchange
	Interim Measures on The Administration of The Mainland and Hong Kong Bond Market Connectivity Cooperation
Cross-border investment	Measures for The Administration of Domestic Securities Investment by Qualified Foreign Institutional Investors
	Measures for The Pilot Investment in Domestic Securities of RMB Qualified Foreign Institutional Investors
	Provisions on the Administration of Foreign-Invested Venture Capital Enterprises
	Provisions on The Establishment of Investment Companies by Foreign Investors
	Catalogue of Industries for Foreign Investment
	Trial Measures for The Administration of Overseas Securities Investment by Qualified Domestic Institutional Investors

Sources The website of the People's Bank of China and the website of China Securities Regulatory Commission. Sorted by the authors

Shenzhen-Hong Kong Stock Connect and Bond Connect. Mutual recognition of funds is mainly conducted through mutual recognition of funds in the Mainland and Hong Kong. Public fund business is carried out through the establishment of joint venture fund management companies in China, while private fund management (PFM) business is mainly conducted through the establishment of wholly foreign-owned enterprises (WFOE) in China.

In the banking and insurance industry, in order to attract more financial institutions from Hong Kong and Macao to enter the mainland, the GBA needs to relax the entry threshold for foreign banks and insurance companies in Hong Kong and Macao. The limit on the proportion of foreign shares is 51% (*Administrative Measures for Foreign Invested Securities Companies*), which can be gradually relaxed to 100% in the GBA. This will help attract more qualified foreign banks to settle down and serve the real economy. The threshold for foreign-invested securities companies to enter the mainland will be lowered. According to the current legislation, the appraisal indicators include "the business scale in the recent 3 years" and "revenue and profit ranking in the forefront of the world". However, the definition of "the forefront of the world" is not clear enough, and the evaluations in different countries are inconsistent. This requirement also limits the entry of some innovative and fast-growing small and medium-sized financial institutions. It is suggested that the threshold of the mainland be lowered in terms of the scale and profit of enterprises, in order to enhance the development momentum of small and medium-sized enterprises.

6.3.3.3 Realizing the Interconnection Between the Domestic and Overseas Markets, Promoting the Coordinated Development of Banking Institutions in Guangdong, Hong Kong and Macao

For banks in Hong Kong and Macao, the main policy basis for their business in the mainland is the CEPA Supplementary Agreement IV and Supplementary Agreement VI and the *Overall Plan of China (Guangdong) Pilot Free Trade Zone*. To further open up the financial market, in 2018, the CBRC issued the *Decision of the CBRC on the Amendment of the Measures for the Implementation of the Administrative Licensing of Foreign Funded Banks by the CBRC*, which has a significant impact on foreign banks' banking business in China and provides an important legal basis for foreign banks to carry out equity investment in the banking industry, such as improving the convenience of foreign banking institutions to develop their business, adding new wholly foreign-owned banks, and the conditions for Sino-foreign joint venture banks to apply for investment and establishment, and to take shares in domestic banking financial institutions, changing the examination and approval system to the reporting system for businesses such as the foreign bank's overseas financial management for clients, the trusteeship of overseas financial management for clients, the trusteeship of securities investment funds, and the withdrawal of interest bearing assets from the liquidated foreign financial institutions.

In an interview on May 1, 2019, Guo Shuqing, chairman of the China Banking Regulatory Commission (CIRC), mentioned 12 new measures to be released for the financial opening up. Those involved with banking industry include the following: the restriction on the shareholding ratio of a Chinese commercial bank will be exempted for a single Chinese bank and a single foreign bank in accordance with the principle of consistency between domestic and foreign investment; the total assets requirement of US $10 billion for foreign banks to set up foreign-funded legal person banks in China and US $20 billion for foreign banks to set up branches in China will be abolished; the restrictions on Chinese shareholders of Chinese and foreign joint ventures will be relaxed; the requirement will be removed that the sole or major Chinese shareholder of joint ventures must be a financial institution; the approval will be canceled for foreign banks to conduct RMB business, and permission will be granted to foreign banks to conduct RMB business when they open their business; and permission will also be granted to foreign banks to operate the business of "agency collection and payment service".

On July 20, 2019, the People's Bank of China issued relevant measures to further expand the opening up of the financial industry, including encouraging overseas financial institutions to participate in the establishment and investment of financial management subsidiaries of commercial banks, and allowing foreign institutions to obtain class A underwriter license for the inter-bank bond market, and further facilitating foreign institutional investors to invest in the inter-bank bond market. The accelerating process of China's banking industry's opening to the outside world has provided greater space for the coordinated development of the banking industry in the GBA. In terms of cross-border banking services, banks in Hong Kong and Macao have rich experience while banks in Guangdong Province have rich resources in terms of clients and banking outlets. Hong Kong funded banks should leverage their advantages of cross-border business and promote the coordinated development of banking institutions in Guangdong, Hong Kong and Macao; at the same time, with the help of Macao's advantage of connecting with Portuguese speaking countries, Guangdong's financial institutions' efforts will be promoted to expand their international business. Commercial banks can also give full play to their professional advantages in international operation, open up domestic and overseas markets, flexibly use markets and resources to meet the needs of enterprises and individual clients, helping them to save capital costs, and providing support for the interconnection of talent flow, logistics, capital flow and information flow in the GBA.

6.3.3.4 Taking Insurance Institutions as a Breakthrough to Build the Interconnection of Insurance Industry in Guangdong, Hong Kong and Macao

Statistics show that the insurance premium income of Guangdong, Hong Kong and Macao reached about US $116 billion in 2018, equivalent to one fourth of the total amount of the whole country. It reveals the strong demand for insurance sales and service in the GBA. On April 27, 2018, the CIRC issued the *Circular Regarding*

Liberalizing the Business Scope of Foreign Insurance Brokerage Companies, which proposed to further expand the business scope of foreign insurance brokers. Prior to the promulgation of the circular, foreign insurance brokerage companies were not allowed to engage in small and medium-sized commercial insurance brokerage or personal insurance brokerage business. They were only allowed to engage in large-scale commercial insurance brokerage businesses such as international marine, aviation and transportation insurance brokerage and reinsurance brokerage business. The promulgation of the circular will be conducive to Hong Kong and Macao insurance institutions to engage in small and medium-sized commercial insurance and personal insurance business with a wider clients and greater prospects in China.

In May 2019, the China Securities Regulatory Commission (CSRC) and the People's Bank of China (PBOC) respectively issued liberalization measures related to the insurance industry, including abolishing the requirement that foreign insurance brokers must meet the 30-year operation period and total assets of no less than 200 million US dollars to operate insurance brokerage business in China; allowing foreign-funded insurance groups to establish insurance institutions; allowing domestic foreign-funded insurance groups to establish insurance institutions with reference to the qualification requirements of Chinese insurance groups; advancing the transition period from the original 2021 to 2020 during which the limit on the proportion of foreign capital shares in life insurance will be raised from 51 to 100%; abolishing the rule that domestic insurance companies hold no less than 75% of the total shares of an insurance asset management company, and allowing foreign investors to hold more than 25% of the total shares.

Hong Kong's insurance products have always been attractive to mainland residents, and mainland tourists have become the main force in Hong Kong's insurance market. Statistics show that the proportion of mainland residents' cross-border insurance purchase accounted for 25% of the scale of Hong Kong's insurance market. In 2018, the new cross-border insurance premium of mainland residents reached as high as HK $47.6 billion. Under the background of further opening up of the insurance industry, insurance companies in Hong Kong and Macao will have the opportunity to directly serve residents in the mainland, and they can cooperate with domestic institutions in terms of channels and products, so as to form a coordinated development. The mature development of insurance institutions in Hong Kong can bring more new elements and development experience to the insurance industry in the mainland. We support Hong Kong insurance institutions in setting up the "GBA Insurance Service Center" in the Mainland to provide after-sales services of life insurance and medical insurance for Hong Kong policies holders who live or work in the mainland.

6.3.4 Synergy of Financial Products in the GBA

The *Outline Development Plan for the Guangdong-Hong Kong-Macao Greater Bay Area* clearly points out that "we should expand the space for cross-border investment between Hong Kong and mainland residents and institutions, and steadily expand the channels for Hong Kong and mainland residents to invest in each other's financial products. Under the premise of legal compliance, we will orderly promote cross-border transactions of funds, insurance and other financial products in the GBA, continuously enrich the categories of investment products and investment channels, and establish an exchange mechanism between funds and products". Financial institutions in the GBA need to make good use of the preferential policies of CEPA and free trade zone, etc. focusing on the collaborative innovation of various cross-border financial products, so that enterprises and individuals can enjoy all-round and high-quality financing and risk protection services in the GBA.

6.3.4.1 Promoting the Development of a Mechanism for Mutual Recognition of Financial Products in the GBA

We will optimize the trading structure of cross-border real estate investment trust (REITs), promote the innovation of dual currency, swap and credit risk mitigation, and establish commercial syndicated loan, bond underwriting and investment banking integrated financial services for listed REITs; realize the data interconnection of insurance asset management products; promote the construction of cross-border insurance policy services in the mode of blockchain; orderly expand cross-border stock index futures and option derivatives, and promote international investors to participate in the mainland futures market. As put forward in *Outline Development Plan for the Guangdong-Hong Kong-Macao Greater Bay Area*, we will "orderly promote the interconnection of financial markets and gradually expand the scale and scope of cross-border use of RMB in the GBA". The cross-border financial activities in the GBA are more frequent, which is the endogenous driving force for the financial development of the GBA. There is a large demand for cross-border products in cross-border financial activities, but there is a shortage in the supply of cross-border financial products. The interconnection of financial markets in Guangdong, Hong Kong and Macao provides a basis for the innovation of cross-border products of financial institutions.

Frequent cross-border financial activities of enterprises or residents will bring a large number of demands for cross-border payment and settlement, followed by the need to reduce business risks and transaction costs. This provides a rare development opportunity for commercial banks in the GBA, who can develop cooperatively in product design and management mode, expand business scope, design and launch financial products to meet the cross-border payment and settlement needs of enterprises or residents, such as RMB spot and forward foreign exchange trading business, cross-border RMB lending business, etc.. At present, some banks in the GBA have piloted in cross-border financial product innovation. For example, in 2019, Bank of China firstly launched "Easy Account in the GBA" in Hong Kong, which enables Hong Kong customers to conveniently handle personal class II and III accounts of Bank of China in the mainland without going to the mainland in person; the Industrial and Commercial Bank of China has also launched a similar "Cross-border Business Link" to streamline the business registration process to a large extent, providing remote cross-border business registration services for Hong Kong enterprises, and has established a "cross-border business platform" in the Nansha Free Trade Zone on a pilot basis. The platform, jointly created by the Industrial and Commercial Bank of China and a number of banking institutions, focuses on providing comprehensive financial services such as comprehensive capital settlement for domestic and foreign enterprises, and cross-border asset management package services such as remittance and exchange.

In addition, we should also promote the interconnection and cooperation among scientific and technological financial institutions in the GBA. According to statistics from the Hong Kong Monetary Authority, 40% of mainland consumers choose fintech related methods when they pay, and 35% of them use fintech based insurance products. Fintech related products are highly accepted in the Mainland. At present, the development of fintech in the mainland is ahead of that in Hong Kong and Macao. This will enhance the openness of fintech in Hong Kong, promote cooperation between mainland technology enterprises and traditional financial institutions in Hong Kong, and form financial and technological connectivity between Hong Kong and Macao and the mainland.

6.3.4.2 Promoting the Interconnection Between Cross-Border Insurance Services and Products

Generally speaking, the insurance market of the GBA is an important part of China's insurance market, and it develops rapidly. In 2018, the growth rate of premium income in the GBA was as high as 6.8%, far higher than the national growth rate of 3.3%. Statistics show that, from 2014 to 2018, the premium income of insurance market in the GBA had always been accounting for more than 20% of the total national premium income (see Fig. 6.8).

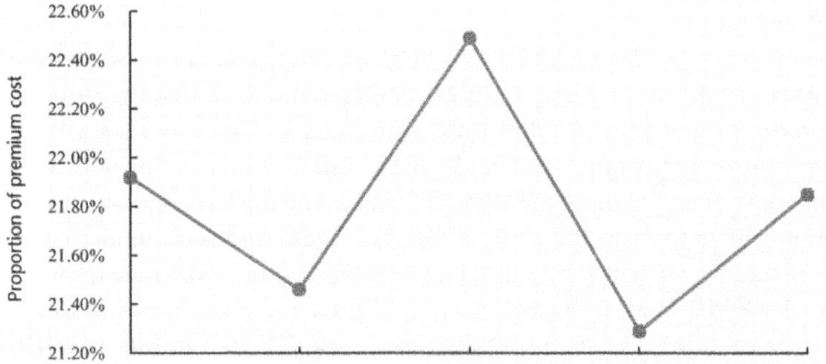

Fig. 6.8 The proportion of premium income in the insurance market of the GBA in the total premium income of China (*Source* China Banking and Insurance Regulatory Commission)

Catering to the strong demand for insurance in the GBA, the insurance companies in the GBA can design and launch innovative insurance products according to the differences in insurance industry systems, policies, products and services. They can take GBA as the "experimental field" to test the innovative products in the Bay Area, so as to meet the cross-border insurance renewal and claim settlement needs of mainland insurance customers as well as the demand for the subdivision insurance such as cross border motor vehicle insurance of Hong Kong and Macao working groups in the mainland. The insurance regulatory authorities of Guangdong, Hong Kong and Macao can strengthen the coordination and mutual recognition of regulatory rules, and enhance the influence and discourse power of the GBA in the international insurance market on the basis of safeguarding the common interests of the three parties. On this basis, the GBA can strengthen the reinsurance market system construction through further improvement of the innovation model of cross-border RMB reinsurance business.

6.3.4.3 Building an Interconnection and Mutual Recognition Mechanism for Green Financial Products

The *Outline Development Plan for the Guangdong-Hong Kong-Macao Greater Bay Area* proposes to continue to improve the green financial system of the GBA and strive to build Hong Kong into a green financial center for the development of the GBA. GBA has a good foundation in developing green finance. First of all, as a pilot green finance reform zone, Guangzhou takes the lead in exploring the development mode of green finance, and plays a demonstration role for other cities in the GBA to develop green finance. Secondly, as an international financial center, Hong Kong has helped to attract more international capital for the development of green finance in the GBA. Next, we will discuss the development of green finance in the GBA from aspects of green bonds, green funds, green credit, green insurance and carbon market.

First, green bonds. According to statistics, by June 2019, 76 green bonds had been issued in the GBA, with the issuance volume exceeding 62 billion yuan, accounting for 5.4% of the nation's total issuance. The issuance of green bonds in GBA has been growing in recent years, with an average annual growth rate of more than 70% since 2017. As shown in Fig. 6.9, in 2016, enterprises in the GBA issued a total amount of 2 billion yuan of green bonds, which continued to grow largely in 2017 and 2018. In the first half of 2019, the amount of green bonds issued reached 29.133 billion yuan, 1.5 times that of the whole year of 2018.

Second, green funds. The GBA plays a strong leading role in the construction of ESG (environment, society and governance) theme funds. Under the background of accelerating the construction of green finance and promoting sustainable development, ESG investment concept is becoming more and more popular. Since 2016, ASSET Management Association of China has encouraged the development of ESG in the mainland fund industry by carrying out relevant forums and organizing research projects. As early as 2013, Hong Kong began to pay attention to issues related to ESG

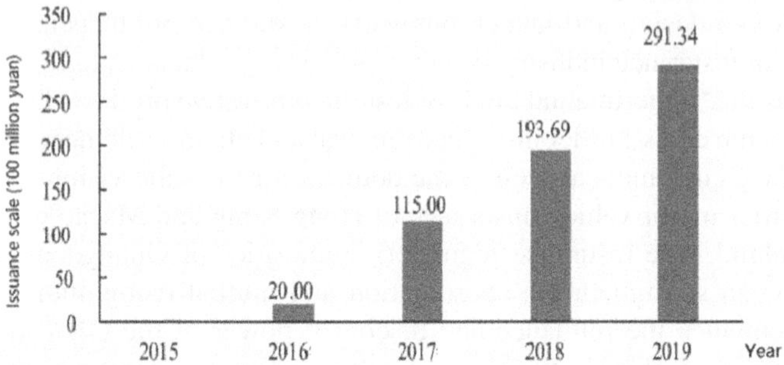

Fig. 6.9 The annual issuance scale of green bonds in the GBA (*Source* Tonghuashun, an analysis software of stock exchange)

information disclosure and investment. In 2016, HKEX issued *Guidelines on Environment, Society and Governance Reporting* to further improve the environmental regulatory system for listed companies.

Third, green credit. Data disclosed by China Banking Regulatory Commission (CIRC) shows that by June 2019, the balance of green loans of Chinese-funded banking institutions in Guangzhou accounted for more than 50% of the total scale of the province. Meanwhile, it also actively carried out green finance related innovation and issued the first asset-backed bill with green subjects, green fund uses and green assets in the mainland. Hong Kong launched its "Green Finance Certification Scheme" in March 2018, and green credit and other green financial products and services are also being improved. In the context of the deepening of green development in GBA, green credit has also been greatly developed and improved in product innovation and authentication mechanism.

Fourth, green insurance. Green insurance is mainly divided into green insurance products, green insurance services and the green application of insurance funds, etc. Due to its special location and policy advantages, the GBA can effectively attract more insurance funds into the green industry. Guangzhou area gives full play to the role of a "leader", constantly promote the implementation of environmental pollution liability insurance, and is also expected to carry out the innovation of insurance products with green characteristics such as the "vegetable rainfall meteorological index insurance", etc.. Shenzhen has launched a series of mandatory environmental liability insurance trials since 2017.

Fifth, the carbon market. By the end of June 2019, Shenzhen's carbon emission pilot project has achieved a quota of 25,919,500 tons and the trading volume has reached 719 million yuan, which was in the leading position in China. With the value of carbon emissions being created by carbon trading, relevant enterprises and investors demand more and more carbon financial products. We can meet the financing needs of the market by innovating carbon quota mortgage financing, hedge carbon market risk by means of carbon emission rights forward trading, and enable enterprises to manage their carbon assets efficiently through services like carbon emission quota trusteeship, etc..

6.3.5 Green Finance Cooperation in the GBA

The integration of regional finance is often promoted from multiple aspects and levels. The process involves the exchange and communication of talents, the agreement and cooperation among organizations and the cross-border circulation of products. The green finance cooperation in the GBA also strives to further improve the cooperation quality of green finance in terms of personnel exchange and sharing, organizational cooperation and research and development of innovative financial products.

In April 2018, Shenzhen Qianhai Administration Bureau and Hong Kong Quality Assurance Bureau signed the *Shenzhen-Hong Kong Green Finance Cooperation Memorandum*. Shenzhen and Hong Kong joined hands to promote the growth of green finance and related industries in Shenzhen and Hong Kong, and raised the development level of green finance in the GBA. In July 2019, the local financial supervision institutions of Shenzhen and Macao signed a memorandum of the training and exchange of financial talents at the ninth meeting of the Symposium on Financial Cooperation and Innovation among Shenzhen, Hong Kong and Macao. Shenzhen and Macao will carry out cooperation in talents, capital and projects in green finance, fintech and other industries, so as to provide guarantee for the high-quality construction of the GBA.

In terms of issuance quota, in 2015, domestic entities issued a total of 8.84 billion yuan of green bonds overseas, which reached 50.994 billion yuan in 2017. In the past five years, only in 2017 and 2018, the GBA enterprises issued green bonds overseas for financing, with an average annual issuance of about 47.1 billion yuan, accounting for about 20% of the national issuance in that year (see Fig. 6.10). With the continuous development and improvement of the green bond market and the increasing attraction of enterprises in GBA for overseas investment institutions, more and more domestic entities are expected to participate in the overseas green bond market.

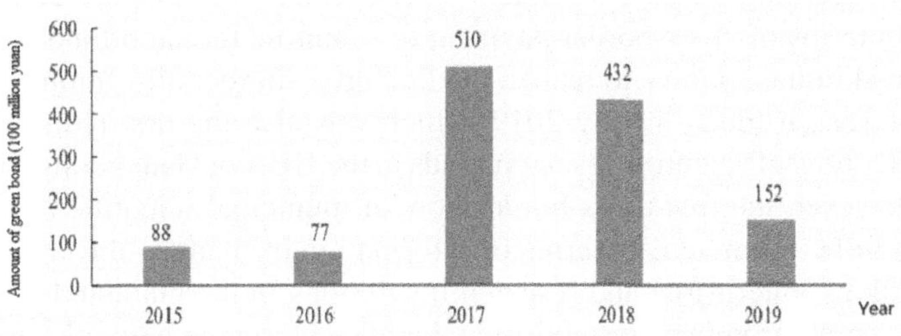

Fig. 6.10 Statistics on the amount of overseas green bonds issued by domestic entities (*Source* China Finance Information Network)

The concept of green development is an important requirement for the further deepening of Ecological civilization construction in China and also conducive to the high-quality construction of the GBA. Therefore, the green finance industry has received a lot of policy support, such as encouraging banks and other financial institutions to actively make innovations in green finance, encouraging all units to develop green economy, and constantly improving the development system of green finance.

6.4 Conception of Science and Technology Innovation Synergyin the GBA

There are a number of universities, scientific research institutes, high-tech enterprises and national large-scale scientific projects in the GBA that have important influence in China and even in the world. At the same time, it has mature industrial clusters, complete industrial chain and rapid response manufacturing, and has the foundation to build an international scientific and technological innovation center with global influence. The key of these elements is to give full play to the advantages of scientific and technological research and industrial innovation of Guangdong, Hong Kong and Macao, and realize the cross-border flow and regional integration of talents, capital, information, technology and other innovative elements in the GBA. However, compared with the New York Bay area, San Francisco Bay area and Tokyo Bay area, as stated in the *Outline Development Planning of Guangdong-Hong Kong-Macao*, "*Guangdong, Hong Kong and Macao have different social systems and legal systems, and belong to different tariff areas. The level of market interconnection needs to be further improved, and the situation of efficient and convenient flow of production factors has not yet formed*". There are various obstacles in the cross-border flow of goods, talents, capital, information and technology in the GBA. In terms of talents exchange, the scientific research talents from the mainland still face restrictions on frequency and duration of stay in Hong Kong and Macao for exchange and cooperation. In terms of scientific research equipment, there is strong demand for further simplified import and export procedures and tariff reduction and exemption regarding R&D consumable parts, technology display equipment and samples. In terms of cross-border payment of scientific research funds, Guangdong took the lead in the country to realize the first cross-border allocation of provincial scientific research funds in July 2019, which was also the first realization of free cross-border flow of scientific research funds in the GBA of Guangdong-Hong Kong-Macao. However, the free cross-border flow of municipal scientific research funds still needs to be promoted. In terms of information exchange, universities, science and technology enterprises and research institutions in the mainland need to strive for greater breakthroughs in establishing dedicated research networks and realizing cross-border connectivity of scientific research data.

To this end, economists like Gu Shengzu (2018) suggested that GBA should break through the bottleneck within the region that hinders the rational flow of innovation elements, the innovation of rational resources allocation, and the complementary collaboration of innovation functions, so as to activate and mobilize the potential of various innovation and entrepreneurship entities. They suggested focus be put on the in-depth cooperation among industry, universities and research institutes, to facilitate the close integration of knowledge innovation and technological innovation, to promote the effective alignment of scientific and technological achievements with industrial needs, improve the conversion rate of technological achievements, and enhance the overall innovation efficiency and capacity of the region. They also suggested build an open regional innovation system, strengthen the introduction and application of domestic and foreign scientific research achievements, and set up a cross-regional innovation alliance and innovation collaboration center. They called for the full play of the leading role of large science and technology enterprises and internet platform enterprises in regional innovation cooperation, and encouraged key scientific research enterprises to drive collaborative innovation among small, medium and micro sized enterprises in the upstream and downstream of the industrial chain, in order to speed up the cultivation of core technologies, brand advantages and business models with global influence in the Bay Area. Finally, the free flow of innovation elements will be realized at and among the levels of knowledge exchange, technology development and achievement transformation.

6.4.1 Promoting the Flow of Innovation Elements at the Level of Scientific Research Knowledge Exchange

Scientific research knowledge exchange layer mainly refers to the global knowledge innovation network formed by universities, scientific research institutions and think tanks through academic journals, academic conferences and visits. Obviously, the innovation elements at this level are mainly researchers and knowledge flow. There are world-famous universities represented by the University of Hong Kong and the Hong Kong University of Science and Technology, as well as high-end think tanks such as China (Shenzhen) Institute of Comprehensive Development in the GBA (Table 6.10). In terms of the flow of innovation elements in the scientific research knowledge exchange layer of the GBA, the flow of innovation elements, the communication among researchers can be promoted and the synergy effect of innovation elements can be realized through regular professional meetings, lectures, mutual visits of researchers and cooperation of major project.

Table 6.10 GBA Universities' ranking in the world in 2020

Number	University	Region	2020	2019	2018	2017
1	Hong Kong University	Hong Kong	35	36	40	43
2	Hong Kong University of Science and Technology	Hong Kong	47	41	44	49
3	The Chinese University of Hong Kong	Hong Kong	57	53	58	76
4	City University of Hong Kong	Hong Kong	126	110	119	119
5	The Hong Kong Polytechnic University	Hong Kong	171	159	182	192
6	Sun Yat-sen University	the Mainland	251 ~ 300	301 ~ 350	351 ~ 400	401 ~ 500
7	Macau University of Science and Technology	Macao	251 ~ 300	—	—	—
8	Macau University	Macao	301 ~ 350	351 ~ 400	351 ~ 400	351 ~ 400
9	Southern University of Science and Technology	the Mainland	301 ~ 350	301 ~ 350	—	—
10	Hong Kong Baptist University	Hong Kong	401 ~ 500	401 ~ 500	401 ~ 500	351 ~ 400
11	South China University of Technology	the Mainland	501 ~ 600	501 ~ 600	501 ~ 600	601 ~ 800
12	Shenzhen University	the Mainland	601 ~ 800	601 ~ 800	—	—
13	Jinan University	the Mainland	801 ~ 1000	801 ~ 1000	801 ~ 1000	>800
14	Guangdong University of Technology	the Mainland	801 ~ 1000	—	—	—

(continued)

Table 6.10 (continued)

Number	University	Region	2020	2019	2018	2017
15	Southern Medical University	the Mainland	>1001	801 ~ 1000	—	—

Source Times Higher Education World University Ranking (2020), covering 1396 universities in 92 countries and areas

6.4.2 *Promoting the Flow of Innovation Elements at the Level of the Technological Development*

The technology development layer is mainly a global innovation service network formed by the support of innovation and entrepreneurship incubation and investment and financing platforms. It pays more attention to how the cutting-edge knowledge capital is combined with the market demand, and how the development of products is completed under the promotion of capital flow. The Shenzhen-Hong Kong Innovation Center and Entrepreneurship Park in Qianhai Free Trade Zone of Shenzhen city provides a typical sample for the flow of innovation elements at this level. The Shenzhen-Hong Kong Innovation Center and entrepreneurship Park make full use of the location and policy advantages of Qianhai FREE Trade Zone, establish cooperation with universities such as Hong Kong University of Science and Technology, actively develop knowledge capital and innovative products, and effectively promote the conversion of more scientific research achievements into actual products with the support of numerous venture capital.

In accordance with the data, from 2013 to 2017, the annual number of invention patents in the GBA increased from 71,073 to 258,009, showing a continuous rising trend. However, the annual growth rate fluctuated, with increases from 2013 to 2017 of 15.01%, 45.85%, 49.67%, 24.92% and 33.19%, respectively. From the analysis of average annual growth rate, the number of invention patents in the GBA increased by an average annual growth rate of 33.7% from 2013 to 2017, among which the highest growth rate was 49.67% in 2015. From the perspective of increment, in 2017, GBA reached the peak value from 2013 to 2017, with an increase of nearly 64,300 pieces (Fig. 6.11).

6.4.3 *Promoting the Flow of Innovative Elements at the Level of the Industrialization*

The industrialization layer mainly refers to the global development industrialization network formed by the direct upgrading of the global production network of multinational companies. The core cities of the GBA should actively embed themselves into the global production network and become the hub of the network. The main

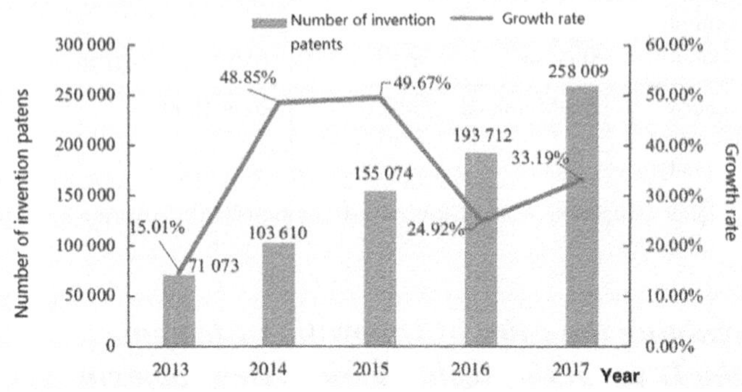

Fig. 6.11 The number and growth rate of invention patents in the GBA from 2013 to 2017 (*Source* The GBA Collaborative Innovation and Development Report [2018])

measures include improving the business environment, introducing the headquarters of scientific and technological enterprises and scientific research institutions, and creating industrial clusters of producer services. There are a large number of experienced entrepreneurs at the level of the industrialization. So a rich and diverse sharing and communication platform should be built to enhance communication and cooperation among each other and promote the flow of innovation elements within the level.

According to the industrial division of the national economy in the GBA *Collaborative Innovation And Development Report (2018)*, the statistics show that (see Table 6.11), among the 500 samples, the industry in which the innovation institutions are mostly established is the electrical machinery and equipment manufacturing industry with the largest number of 100 institutions, accounting for 20%, 2.55% lower than that in 2014–2016. It was followed by the computer, communication and other electronic equipment manufacturing industry, with 96 institutions accounting for 19.20%, 2.76% lower than that in 2014–2016. Both industries account for more than 10%, accounting for 39.20% in total, indicating that nearly 40% of the innovation institutions in the GBA belong to the electrical machinery and equipment manufacturing industry, as well as the computer, communication and other electronic equipment manufacturing industry. From 2015 to 2017, there were 238,227 patents in emerging industries. More than 50% of the total patents were concentrated in Shenzhen, a total of 121,699; which was followed by Foshan with 38,506 patents, accounting for 16.16%; then Dongguan (25,929 patents), Zhuhai (24,179 patents) and Huizhou (10,265 patents). In the past three years, there were 159,900 patents on the east coast of the Bay Area, of which 77.08% in Shenzhen; 77,400 patents on the west coast, nearly half of which in Foshan; 2,944 patents in Hong Kong and Macao, of which 98% are concentrated in Hong Kong (see Table 6.11 and Fig. 6.12).

Table 6.11 Industry distribution of innovation institutions

Industry classification	Quantity (unit)	Proportion (%)
Electrical machinery and equipment manufacturing industry	100	20.00
Computer, communication and other electronic equipment manufacturing industry	96	19.20
Scientific research and technology services	46	9.20
Institutions of higher learning	45	9.00
Information transmission, software and information technology services	30	6.00
Business services	27	5.40
Special equipment manufacturing industry	18	3.60
Chemical raw materials and chemical products manufacturing industry	18	3.60
General equipment manufacturing	18	3.60
Other manufacturing industries	17	3.40
Transportation manufacturing	16	3.20
Metal products industry	16	3.20
Production, heat supply	13	2.60%
Plastics and rubber	11	2.20
Medicine, medical research and manufacturing	8	1.60
Architectural decoration and other construction industries	7	1.40
Textile and clothing industry	6	1.20
Civil engineering construction industry	3	0.60%
Oil and gas production	2	0.40%
Agriculture, livestock and animal husbandry	2	0.40%
Real estate industry	1	0.20%

Source Report on Collaborative Innovation and Development of the GBA (2018)

6.4.4 *Promoting the Circulation of Innovation Elements at All Levels*

On the premise of sufficient circulation of innovation elements among the three levels of scientific research knowledge exchange, technology development and industrialization, it is the catalyst for innovation success to realize the circulation of innovation elements among different levels by breaking the boundaries among levels. Chen Jin and Zheng Gang (2013) put forward that the important factors for the success of innovation include the allocation of some key figures, good internal and external communication mechanism, and effective cross-functional connection. GBA is home

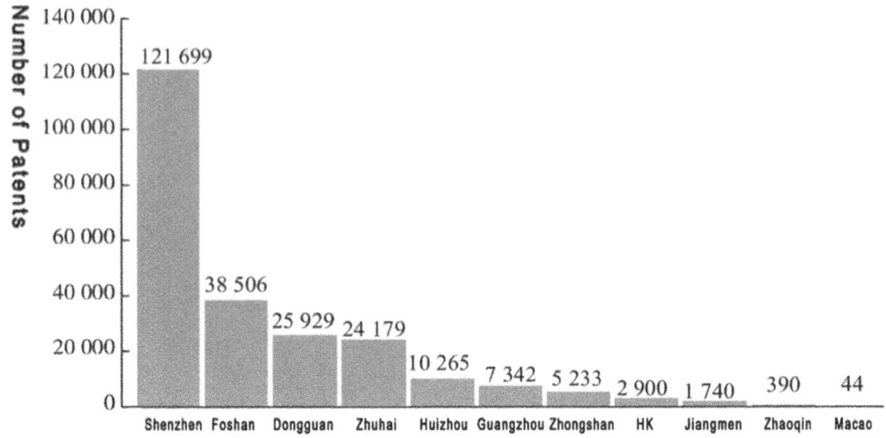

Fig. 6.12 The number of patents in emerging industries in the GBA of Guangdong-Hong Kong-Macao from 2015 to 2017 (*Source* Report on Collaborative Innovation and Development of the GBA [2018])

to many well-known universities, investment institutions and world-renowned enterprises, which have natural advantages in the coordination of scientific and technological innovation. On the one hand, the government can establish collaborative innovation centers and industrial incubation parks to guide the accumulation of talents and capital flows such as researchers, venture capital and entrepreneurs, and form a complete innovation network. On the other hand, we also need to improve the social security system, including housing, social security and communication and transportation infrastructure, so as to better support the innovation system to play its due role. In addition, government authorities can also appropriately encourage innovative entrepreneurs to set up association-like organizations, so as to strengthen their internal communication, cooperation and communication with the government.

6.5 Conception of the Systems Synergy in the GBA

6.5.1 Further Promoting the Facilitation of Customs Clearance

On the basis of summing up various opening-up and innovative measures of the pilot Free Trade Zone, we should fully learn from the experience of Hong Kong and Macao, promote the investment facilitation, trade liberalization, personnel and vehicle exchanges and customs clearance facilitation of the whole GBA, further deepen cooperation, further enhance the level of market integration. We should also explore and implement a more convenient and efficient supervision mode in the flow of people, logistics, capital and information to create a business environment with global competitiveness.

In terms of personnel freedom, with the connection of Hong Kong-Zhuhai-Macao Bridge and transportation infrastructure, the number of people passing through immigration control points in Hong Kong has shown an upward trend (Fig. 6.13 and Fig. 6.14). We should focus on the establishment of a more effective new mechanism for regional coordinated development, innovate the personnel exchange system in Guangdong, Hong Kong and Macao. We should also learn from the experience of Hong Kong and Macao, using electronic and information technology means to explore the simplification or cancellation of the pass for high-end talents in Guangdong, Hong Kong and Macao. It is also necessary to relax the employment restrictions for high-end talents, implement more open and convenient policies and measures in terms of personnel entry and exit, and establish a work permit system, a talent endorsement system, stay and residence policies and measures for foreigners in the GBA (Fig. 6.15).

In terms of investment freedom, we will carry out pilot reform of market access and regulatory system and mechanism, establish a more flexible prudential and inclusive regulatory system, and intensify opening up in key fields such as telecommunications, insurance, securities, scientific research and technical services, education, and health etc.. In addition to special fields, we will gradually explore ways to abolish the special management requirements for the operation period of foreign-invested enterprises, relax restrictions on registered capital and investment methods, and promote fair competition among various market entities. We should try out the registration and confirmation system for commercial subjects, respect the civil rights of market subjects, and conduct formal examination on the documents submitted by applicants.

In terms of trade freedom, customs supervision and facilitation measures are fully benchmarked against Hong Kong. We should abolish unnecessary trade supervision, licensing and procedural requirements, and implement a higher level of trade liberalization and facilitation policies and systems. For the goods arriving in and leaving GBA, we should explore and implement the supervision mode focusing on safety supervision, reflecting a higher level of trade liberalization and facilitation, and improve the efficiency of port supervision service. In total, we should fully implement the national policy on relaxing the access for foreign investment to financial and manufacturing industries, deepen the cooperation among Guangdong, Hong Kong and Macao in personnel training, mutual recognition of qualifications, standard setting and other service trade related fields, further optimize the institutional arrangements of mainland cities in the GBA in terms of market access, property rights protection, legal protection and government services, and improve the integrated online government service platform, focus on solving the pain points and difficulties for enterprises in the start-up and construction permission, improving the business environment of the GBA in an all-round way (Fig. 6.16).

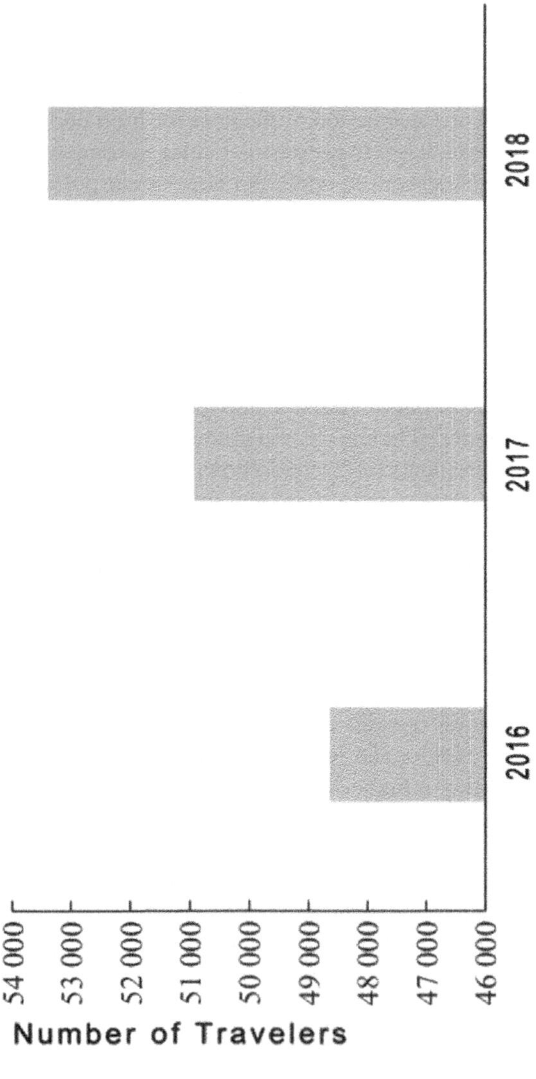

Fig. 6.13 Passenger numbers at Immigration Control Points, Hong Kong International Airport (*Source* Sorted by the authors)

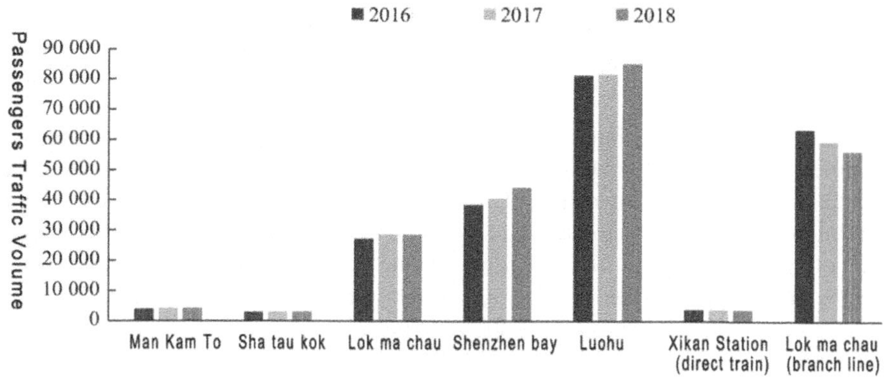

Fig. 6.14 Passenger flow at Immigration control points in Hong Kong (*Source* Sorted by the authors)

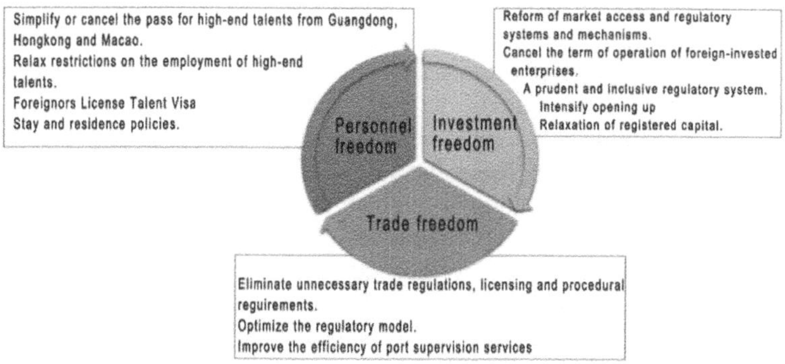

Fig. 6.15 Facilitating customs clearance in the GBA (*Source* Sorted by the authors)

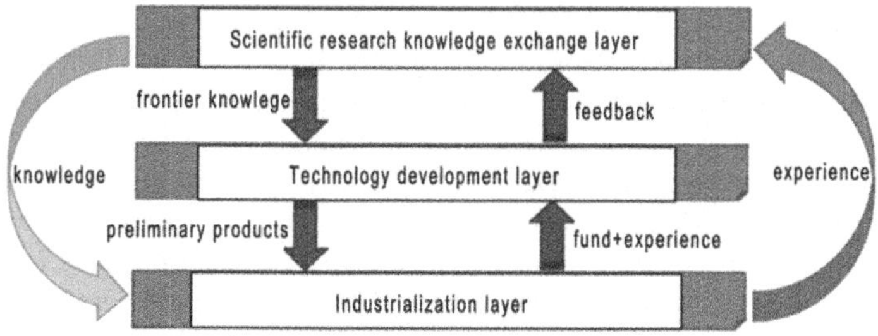

Fig. 6.16 The circulation of innovation elements among different levels (*Source* Sorted by the authors)

6.5.2 Gradually Promoting Financial Product Innovation and Regulatory Innovation

We should promote the interconnection of financial markets in the GBA, support qualified Hong Kong and Macao banks and insurance institutions to set up financial institutions in Qianhai, Shenzhen, Nansha, Guangzhou and Hengqin, Zhuhai. When conditions are ripe, we should gradually expand the mode to the whole bay area, promote the cooperation of Guangdong, Hong Kong and Macao Insurance Institutions in the development of innovative cross-border motor vehicle insurance and cross-border medical insurance products, and promote the joint settlement of cross-border electronic cheques. We will promote the innovation of financial services such as direct payment of cross-border electronic bills and cross-border use of payment instruments. We will gradually promote financial innovation and relax restrictions on financing freedom, exchange freedom, cross-border use of RMB and foreign exchange control, etc.

The financial market connectivity in the GBA has achieved good results and experience, including giving full play to the advantages of "one country, two systems" and the regional policy advantages under the framework of CEPA, exploring policy breakthroughs and pilot implementation, leading the bancassurance industry under jurisdiction to settle down in Hong Kong and Macao, acting on international convention, serving the mainland and radiating throughout the country, pioneering in the tryout, mutual benefit and achieving "the three innovations" in policy, product, service. In terms of policy innovation, we have carried out "four major policy innovations" including access threshold, layout mode, management mode and approval procedure, and achieved six "Number Ones" in China: the number of Hong Kong banking institutions in the jurisdiction area, the number of Macao banking institutions in the jurisdiction area, setting up the first branch of foreign bank that had been granted the approval to operate RMB business in the country, the first Chinese reinsurance institution dominated by social capital and the first mutual insurance institution.

In terms of product innovation, we rely on the innovative development of cross-border RMB business, docking enterprise on the "three big cross-border needs" including settlement, financing and asset transfer, taking the lead in "five cross-border product innovations" including the cross-border RMB settlement, cross-border RMB financing, pilot cross-border two-way RMB bonds, cross-border RMB pools as well as the cross-border transfer of financial assets, which further improved the integration of financial markets in Hong Kong and Macao. In terms of service innovation, we guide bancassurance under jurisdiction to actively mobilize the the advantages of Hong Kong and Macao in interconnected resources, focus on the people's livelihood service with active exploration and enthusiastic innovation. We took the lead in introducing "six characteristic services", namely, service characterized by banking-administration cooperation in commercial registration in the GBA, cross-border electronic direct payment, cross-border housing mortgage loan, joint settlement of electronic check, convenient cross-border remittance and cross-border auto insurance, to

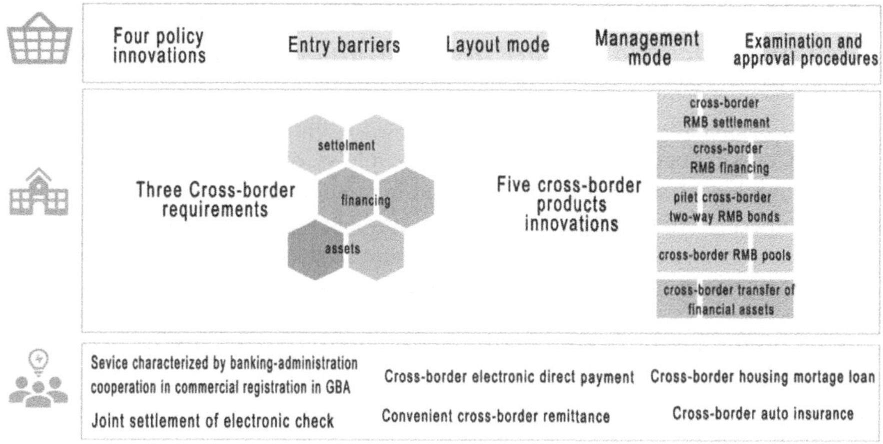

Fig. 6.17 Financial interconnection in the GBA (*Source* Sorted by the authors)

facilitate the connectivity of livelihood financial services in the GBA (Wang Xiaobo 2019) (see Fig. 6.17).

However, there are great differences between Hong Kong, Macao and PRD cities in terms of financial system and financial environment, which will bring new challenges to the existing system and mechanism under the background of improving financial connectivity in the GBA. This is mainly reflected in the increasingly prominent potential financial risks such as cross-border regulatory arbitrage of financial institutions, cross infection of cross-border financial risks and abnormal cross-border capital flows. At present, Guangdong, Hong Kong and Macao have not established a close and normalized regulatory coordination mechanism, which is not conducive to jointly preventing and dealing with systemic financial risks. Therefore, it is necessary for the country to support the pilot innovation of the comprehensive financial supervision mechanism in the GBA. We will support the pilot project of comprehensive financial supervision mechanism innovation in Guangdong, Hong Kong and Macao, and explore the innovation of comprehensive financial supervision, including the establishment of joint conference system of financial supervision in the GBA, the establishment of information sharing platform of financial supervision between Guangdong, Hong Kong and Macao, and the improvement of monitoring and analysis mechanism of cross-border capital flow. It is suggested that the national financial regulatory authorities delegate some of the regulatory functions that are close to the market and conducive to product innovation to the financial regulatory authorities and financial market organizations in Guangdong to strengthen the regulatory coordination and information sharing of financial business across departments, industries and markets (Wang Jingwu 2019).

6.5.3 *Learning from the Experience of Hong Kong and Macao to Explore the Innovation of Legal System*

In terms of legislative basis, we should strive for the legislation of the National People's Congress or Guangdong Provincial People's Congress as well as the suspension or abolition of some national laws and regulations and local regulations, and comprehensively stipulate the legal system arrangement in the "GBA" including investment system, customs system, management system, tax preference system and supervision system, and gradually promote the free circulation of personnel, funds and goods, etc.

We should strengthen the docking and cooperation with Hong Kong and Macao, speed up the creation of a legalized, internationalized and convenient business environment, and focus on "four steps further" (Fig. 6.18): the first step is to further promote the unification of commercial system rules, adhere to the principle of equal treatment, and encourage Hong Kong and Macao enterprises to actively participate in fair competition. The second is to further strengthen the protection and application of intellectual property rights, optimize the innovation environment of the GBA, build an innovation and development area with international competitiveness, and accelerate the development towards high quality. The third is to further improve the international commercial dispute settlement mechanism, accelerate the establishment of an international arbitration center, support the exchanges and cooperation among Guangdong, Hong Kong and Macao arbitration and mediation institutions, promote deep integration with the convergence of litigation protection rules, and enhance the competitiveness of the regional rule of law; explore the establishment of a mediation

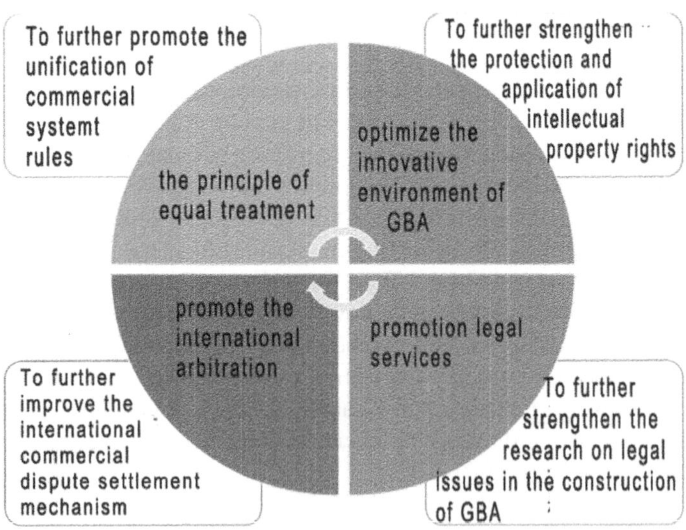

Fig. 6.18 Legal innovation of "four steps further" (*Source* Sorted by the authors)

system for lawyers of Hong Kong or other nationalities, and expand the application of relevant foreign laws, laws of Hong Kong and Macao regions or international conventions, international practices and general rules of mediation in accordance with civil and commercial contracts to facilitate the formation of a more international legal service market. Fourth, we shall further strengthen the research on legal issues in the construction of the GBA, timely summarize the advanced experience in promoting law services that safeguard the GBA, create a stable, fair, transparent and predictable law environment in the GBA, and promote the construction of the GBA to achieve tangible results (Peng Yong and Li Li 2019).

Qianhai's legal system innovation is at the forefront of the country. It has successively issued some major systems such as the *Outline of The Plan for Qianhai Demonstration Area of the construction of socialist legal system with Chinese characteristics* and *Action Plan for The Rule of Law for Qianhai's implementation of the ' Outline Development Plan for the Guangdong-Hong Kong-Macao Greater Bay Area'*, etc.. By the end of October 2019, Qianhai has made more than 90 original and advanced achievements in the rule of law construction, including the establishment of the first rule of law index evaluation system of China's free Trade Area; the national initiative system of "Hong Kong Mediator" and "Hong Kong Juror"; the first Guangdong-Hong Kong-Macao joint law firm; taking the lead in the reform of Guangdong-Hong Kong-Macao joint venture law firms; establishing the first in China Qianhai Bureau of Anti-corruption Supervision drawing on the system of the Hong Kong Independent Commission Against Corruption (ICAC), a new "five-in-one" system of supervision on honest and clean administration which integrates discipline inspection, supervision, procuratorial work, public security work and auditing; the first circuit court of the Supreme People's Court, the first international commercial court of the Supreme People's Court, and the "One Belt And One Road" economic dispute mediation center of the Supreme People's Court, symbolizing the judicial power of final adjudication in Qianhai; the establishment of Shenzhen Intellectual Property Court and Shenzhen Financial Court in Qianhai, which means the second instance of intellectual property cases and financial cases in Shenzhen shall be handled under the jurisdiction of Qianhai. The judicial adjudication power in Qianhai was landed in Qianhai; the intellectual property court of Shenzhen, Shenzhen Financial court was established in Qianhai, and the second instance of intellectual property and financial cases in the whole city were under the jurisdiction of Qianhai; the settlement of Shenzhen court of Guangzhou Maritime Court in Qianhai; Qianhai court's being designated by the Supreme People's court as a model court for comprehensive judicial system reform; Qianhai Shekou Procuratorate being the first procuratorate of the pilot Free Trade Zone in China; the completion of the civil and commercial rule of law maps for 64 countries (regions), providing strong legal advisory services for Chinese enterprises that want to "do their businesses abroad". By the end of October 2019, Qianhai has formed a unique layout of professional judicial institutions covering a complete range of fields including commerce, finance, intellectual property, maritime affairs, etc.

6.5.4 Reducing Tax and Promoting Tax System Coordination in the GBA

In terms of the construction goal of the GBA and the reality of "one country, two systems, and three customs", there are many tax coordination issues in the GBA, among which the personal income tax draws the most concern from the public.

Compared with the mainland, the personal income tax systems of Hong Kong and Macao are characterized by high threshold, low tax rate and large amount of allowance. Therefore, the tax cost is considered by talents from Hong Kong and Macao before they decide to work in Guangdong. To support the construction of the GBA, and to attract overseas high-end talents and talents in great demand to work in the GBA, in accordance with the unified arrangements of the CPC Central Committee and the State Council, the Ministry of Finance and the State Administration of Taxation issued "*Circular Regarding Preferential Policy for Personal Income Tax in the GBA*" (The Department of Taxation, Ministry of Finance [2019] No.31), which approves the subsidies to overseas high-end talents and talents in great demand working in the GBA in accordance with the difference between the mainland and the Hong Kong personal income tax bearing. And subsidies shall be exempted from personal income tax. The introduction of this policy has significantly reduced the actual tax burden on overseas talents working in the GBA, which will play a positive role in attracting talents to work in the GBA. However, the mode of "levy before subsidy" may bring about cumbersome application procedures and long processing time span. Therefore, specific implementation rules need to be stipulated to further optimize the application procedures and shorten the processing time. The Hengqin Free Trade Zone has fully implemented the policy of "Hong Kong Taxation for Hong Kong people and Macao Taxation for Macao people",[3] realizing that the actual personal income tax bearing of Hong Kong and Macao talents working in the GBA is basically equal to that of residents in Hong Kong and Macao. It is suggested that Hong Kong and Macao enterprises and foreign enterprises in the GBA that focus on developing high and new technology industries should be given tax preference such as extending tax holidays and reducing tax rates. We will relax the rules of origin for the import and export of scientific research materials and equipment among Hong Kong, Macao and the PRD, and gradually realize zero-tariff clearance of scientific research elements in the GBA.

In terms of tax administration, Hong Kong has formed a relatively complete credit service system. Nine mainland cities in the GBA can learn from Hong Kong's management experience and model to realize unified collection and systematic sharing of tax information. As for the introduction of new technologies, the Guangdong Provincial Taxation Bureau took the lead in launching the V-Tax remote visual self-service tax system in Hengqin, Zhuhai. Taxpayers can handle real estate transactions, deed tax preference, social security registration, tax withholding entrusted to the banks and other tax business without running across the border, which greatly

[3] http://ftz.hengqin.gov.cn/.

improves the efficiency and reduces the cost of taxpayers. Using the new virtual reality technology, Qianhai Tax Bureau of Shenzhen launched the smart VR Tax Bureau, providing a full range of tax bureau guidance, the whole process and the integration of "Internet +" innovative services. At the same time, services such as blockchain electronic invoice and online issuance of Certificate of Chinese Fiscal Resident, etc., so that taxpayers can handle cross-border taxation through channels such as electronic taxation bureau and WeChat public accounts, etc. whether they are at home or abroad. These advanced practices and experiences are worth studying and taking the lead in promoting in the GBA, so as to realize tax coordinated management in the GBA.

6.5.5 Strengthening Links Between Public Services and Social Security in the GBA

As stated in *Outline Development Plan for the Guangdong-Hong Kong-Macao Greater Bay Area*, "*We shall advance cooperation in social security. We will explore ways to ensure that Hong Kong and Macao residents working and living in Guangdong enjoy equal treatment with mainland residents in terms of people's livelihood such as education, medical care, old-age care, housing and transportation,* etc." At the same time, "*we will strengthen the connection between cross-border public services and social security, explore the use of Macao social insurance in the GBA, and improve the pension portability for the elderly in Hong Kong*". Specifically, it is necessary to actively study the cross-regional connection between the social security system and public services in the GBA, so as to achieve equal treatment in fields such as education, medical care and housing between the floating population and the permanent population in the region. It is also necessary to strengthen cross-regional medical cooperation and encourage social forces to develop high-quality medical institutions, so as to facilitate the development of Hong Kong-funded and Macao-funded medical institutions. It is highly suggested to make full use of high-quality medical resources in Hong Kong and Macao to upgrade medical services in the Mainland; in addition, it is also suggested to establish standards for medical personnel training and hospital accreditation in line with international standards, relax restrictions on overseas doctors practicing in the mainland, and take the lead in testing cutting-edge international medical technologies. We will deepen cooperation in old-age services and support Hong Kong and Macao investors in setting up social service institutions for the elderly in nine cities of the PRD in the form of sole proprietorship, joint venture or cooperation in accordance with regulations, so as to create convenient conditions for pension services in Guangdong for Hong Kong and Macao residents. We will encourage greater cooperation in the social welfare sectors among Hong Kong, Macao and the mainland, promote mutual recognition of vocational qualifications in the field of social work, and strengthen professional training exchanges of social workers among Guangdong, Hong Kong and Macao. We will strengthen cooperation in education within urban clusters, make further reforms and innovations in the areas of independent enrollment and interview enrollment, and encourage students from Hong Kong and Macao to study in universities in the GBA. At the same time, we will support the exchange of teachers in the GBA to improve the quality of education services in the mainland.

6.5.6 Establishing Comprehensive Risk Management System and Integrated Information Management Service Platform

We will comprehensively improve the risk prevention and safety supervision level of the GBA, taking risk prevention and control as the bottom line and having classified supervision, collaborative supervision and intelligent supervision as the foundation. We shall also establish high-standard intelligent regulatory infrastructure to achieve the interconnection, mutual recognition and sharing of regulatory information within the GBA. We shall draw on the experience of the Hong Kong, Macao and Shanghai Free Trade Zones to build up an integrated information management and service platform covering the GBA management agencies, industry authorities, enterprises in the area and relevant operating entities. We will strengthen the application of information technology in risk assessment, prevention and control, establish a mechanism for joint prevention and control, and exercise strict, precise and effective supervision. We will also build up accurate risk monitoring mechanisms in special areas such as quarantine, source areas, intellectual property rights, international conventions, cross-border funds, etc., to realize real-time risk monitoring and dynamic early warning management throughout the whole process. We shall improve the basic rules and standards of credit evaluation, implement the management of operators' suitability, and take credit rating as an important basis for enterprises to enjoy preferential policies and institutional convenience in accordance with the principle of "convenience for law abiders". We will establish a voluntary disclosure system and implement a system for disclosing trust-breaking names, banning market entry and withdrawing from the market.

6.6 Conception of Governance Synergy in the GBA

6.6.1 Speeding up the Establishment of a Cooperative Governance System in the GBA and Promoting the Integration of Social Security and Public Services

The *Outline Development Plan for the Guangdong-Hong Kong-Macao Greater Bay Area* calls for enhancing the "*convergence of cross-border public services and social security, and exploring ways to ensure that Hong Kong and Macao residents working and living in Guangdong enjoy the same treatment as their mainland counterparts in livelihood aspects such as education, medical care, elderly care, housing, transportation,* etc.". On November 6, 2019, GBA Construction Leadership Group Meeting launched 16 measures to benefit the people and facilitate the development of Hong Kong's professionals in the GBA. These measures not only facilitate Hong Kong residents to purchase housing in the GBA without residence and social security requirements, but also expand the scope of preferential policies for Hong Kong and Macao construction professionals to practice in the mainland, as well as supporting the construction of Shenzhen and Hong Kong science and technology innovation cooperation zone. After decades of development, the synergy of urban governance, public services and social security in Guangdong, Hong Kong and Macao has made steady progress (Fig. 6.19). However, due to differences in systems and development stages, education, medical care, housing, social security and other living facilities in Hong Kong and Macao have not been smoothly connected with other cities in the PRD, which impedes the rational allocation of resources within the GBA and the free flow of innovative elements. Considering the existing governance system of the

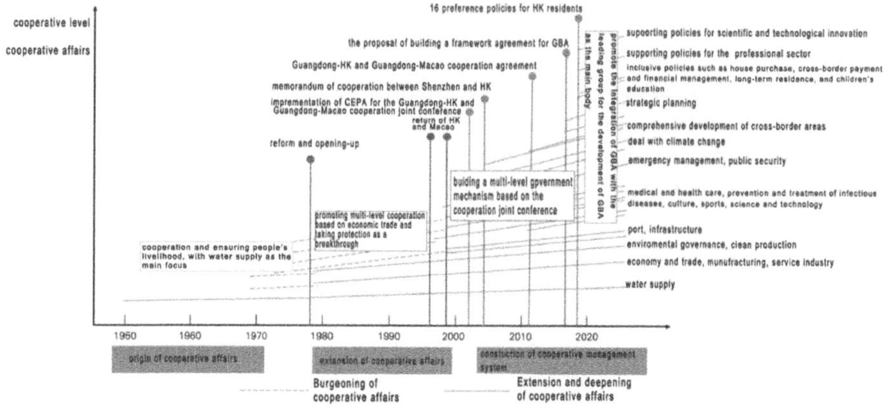

Fig. 6.19 Schematic diagram of the evolution of Guangdong-Hong Kong-Macao collaborative governance mechanism (*Source* Ernst & Young (EY), *GBA—Building an International Science and Technology Innovation Centre*)

GBA and the synergism goal of future governance, we shall focus on the integration of cross-border social security and public services, and accelerate the construction of a regional cooperative governance system based on crossing borders, urban clusters and urban–rural integration.

The first step is to strengthen the construction of the cross-border cooperative governance system of Guangdong, Hong Kong and Macao, and promote the collaborative governance of institutions. It is necessary to strive for all-round support from the central government to the local governments of Guangdong, Hong Kong and Macao, formulate the collaborative governance framework of Guangdong, Hong Kong and Macao under the basic national policy of "one country, two systems", and provide top-level collaborative governance solutions for the docking of basic public services such as education, medical care, housing security, etc., the construction of public service electronic platform, and ecological environment governance. It is also essential to establish a consultation and dialogue mechanism for Guangdong, Hong Kong and Macao under the guidance of the central government, through which consultations on a series of major issues in the field of public governance will be conducted. As a result, local proposals on giving priority to opening up some public resources will be studied and signed, and promote the implementation of the cooperative governance system in the GBA at the practical level as soon as possible.

Efforts should be made to give full play to the advantages of clean government in Hong Kong and Macao, promote the construction of clean government coordination mechanism, and promote the pilot of new clean government regulatory agencies. The joint efforts of Guangdong, Hong Kong and Macao in combating cross-border crimes and other major crimes should be strengthened.

The second step is to strengthen the construction of the "9+2" urban cluster cooperative governance system of Guangdong, Hong Kong and Macao, and promote the collaborative governance in the spatial dimension. In accordance with the standards of urban cluster, we will strictly promote the construction of the integrated governance system of Guangdong, Hong Kong and Macao. The top executive heads of 11 cities will take the lead to establish relevant deliberation agencies and jointly fund the public service fund of the GBA, so as to effectively promote regional collaborative governance through the dual integration of management and capital. We shall attach importance to the equalization of basic public services, establish a mechanism of counterpart cooperation and social assistance, and make up for the shortcomings of public services in weak areas. We will also explore the scheme of "one card universal" that covers public transport card, social security card and medical insurance card in the GBA, and carry out the pilot project of public service integration of transportation, medical insurance and social security in 11 cities.

The third step is to strengthen the construction of urban–rural integrated cooperative governance system in Guangdong, Hong Kong and Macao, and promote collaborative governance in the structural dimension. Supports will be given to the establishment of a GBA demonstration zone for urban–rural overall planning and standardization, and the acceleration of the orderly flow of high-quality public service elements to rural hinterland. Government, social and individual capital are welcome to participate in the construction of rural public service system, to promote the establishment of branches and sub-centers of high-quality public service institutions in medical care, education, pension, etc. in rural areas as well as to build a number of high-level public service institutions and facilities, in order to build a beautiful rural regional system in the PRD with the support of governance collaboration.

6.6.2 Promoting IT Application of Cross-Border Public Services and Establishing a National Public Service Platform in the GBA

The proximity of the three core metropolitan areas of Guangdong, Hong Kong and Macao determines the necessity of cross-border public information service informatization construction. With the help of information technology advantages of Guangdong, Hong Kong and Macao, we will accelerate the construction of world-class digital Bay area, promote the informatization construction of cross-border public services on the base of "Internet + government affairs services", and establish a national public service platform for Guangdong, Hong Kong and Macao Bay area.

Through the construction of electronic platform, multi-scene information flow resources such as medical treatment, education, public transportation, tourism and residents' administrative services can be integrated to facilitate different levels of governments, enterprises, social organizations and citizens in the GBA to obtain various kinds of effective information in a timely and rapid manner, ensuring the high-quality upgrading of public services, meeting the new demands of advancing the modernization of governance system and ability with informatization, and forming the collaborative governance community based on informatization platform.

In accordance with the requirements of General Secretary Xi Jinping in the Symposium on Network Security and Informatization, specific proposals are put forward towards three aspects. Firstly, measures should be taken to ensure the information resources sharing for GBA public services, and the open access mechanism among different regions. In order to break the barriers of cross-border public service information resource sharing, it is urgent to establish a global and open information resource sharing system in the GBA, and build a new model of cross-border public service information exchange and honest sharing. Secondly, efforts should be paid to strengthen the real-time supervision of public service information and establish a timely and efficient information feedback and problem-solving mechanism. Real time monitoring will be carried out in major areas such as cross-border transportation, logistics and personnel clearance to ensure the convenience of residents' life. Thirdly, we should promote the intelligent decision-making of public service system optimization, with the help of the accuracy of information resources, reasonably promote the scientific optimization and allocation of education, medical treatment and public transport systems in the GBA, and build an intelligent public service system in the bay area.

6.6.3 Supporting the Docking of High-Quality Health Education Resources Between Guangdong and Hong Kong and Macao to Create a High-Quality Life Circle in the GBA

We should reasonably promote the mutual overflow of high-quality public service resources among Guangdong, Hong Kong and Macao, deepen the cooperation in the field of social livelihood, support the docking of high-quality health education resources between Guangdong and Hong Kong and Macao, and advance the equalization of cross-border public services and the construction of high-quality life circle. We should also give full play to the advantages of efficient and perfect public services in Hong Kong and Macao, and provide experience and resource support for the optimization and improvement of public services in Guangdong. At the same time, we should tap the potential advantages of public service cultivation in Guangdong, build an overseas bearing place for public services in Hong Kong and Macao, and support Guangdong to build a high standard cross-border pension service institution.

On the one hand, we will encourage high-quality basic education institutions and medical institutions in Hong Kong and Macao to set up sub-centers or branches, to attract top talents in relevant fields to work in Guangdong through measures like platform construction, policy support, awards, etc., and jointly build international major medical centers and basic education centers. We should seize the opportunity of building the international education demonstration zone, further extend the exchange students and credit mutual recognition systems to the elementary education stage, and include the early childhood education sub-centers set up in Hong Kong and Macao in the scope of government subsidies. In combination with cross-border medical services, we will launch a series of financial guarantee measures including cross-border medical insurance, have been introduced to make it more convenient for residents of Guangdong, Hong Kong and Macao to seek medical treatment in other places. On the other hand, we will develop GBA Cross-border Health and Pension Service Demonstration Base, support the three regions in developing high-standard cross-border pension services through sole proprietorship, joint venture or cooperation, encourage Hong Kong and Macao residents to seek for pension services in Guangdong, and improve the retirement security system for Hong Kong and Macao residents living in Guangdong. We will promote short-term pension services in conjunction with industries such as the the medical and health care and convalescent real estate industries, and meet the needs of some Hong Kong and Macao residents for short-term pension services in Guangdong by means of market approaches.

6.6.4 Deepening Cooperation in Public Cultural Services and Building a Humanistic GBA

Guangdong, Hong Kong and Macao are close to each other and have a common cultural heritage. It is important to deepen cooperation in public cultural services and build a bay area of humanistic spirit and understanding among people from the three regions. It is suggested to build a unique landmark cultural complex in GBA, to display the common Lingnan culture for all residents of Guangdong, Hong Kong and Macao, and to form a landmark of memory and a common public cultural service place. The cultural center of the GBA can adopt the layout pattern of "one museum with multi-branches" to build up a central museum and several branches, among which the central hall will focus on the unique charm and humanistic spirit of Lingnan culture over thousands of years, reflecting important cultural features such as Cantonese opera, dragon boat, martial arts and lion dancing while the branch museums should focus on the internal area characteristics of Lingnan culture, and build characteristic venues in cities like Shenzhen, Zhuhai, etc. that reflect the cultural links between Shenzhen, Hong Kong, Zhuhai and Macao, undertake the historical task of maintaining a family on both sides of the Taiwan Strait, and make outstanding contributions to the promotion of the humanistic spirit of the GBA.

From the perspective of public cultural service cooperation as a whole, the GBA should take the lead in establishing a modern public cultural service system that covers both urban and rural areas, that is convenient and efficient and that ensures basic services and promotes fairness. As a world-class science and technology innovation Bay area, Guangdong, Hong Kong and Macao have the ability and responsibility to take the lead in building an inclusive, high-quality and sustainable cross-border public cultural service system, especially in the fields of equalization of public cultural services, promoting public cultural services via science and technology, internet + public cultural services, social participation and free or preferential opening, etc.. In terms of facility sharing, we shall promote the establishment of branch museums, cultural centers and art venues between Guangdong, Hong Kong and Macao will be promoted, and various cultural exhibitions for exchange will be held on a regular basis. In addition, it is suggested that GBA jointly hold brand-oriented cultural festivals to promote the core cultural brands of Guangdong, Hong Kong and Macao to the world and promote the internationalization of cultural public services.

6.6.5 Emphasizing the Joint Prevention and Control of Cross-Regional Environmental Governance in GBA and Carry Out the GBA Chief System on a Pilot Basis

We will establish a long-term mechanism for joint prevention and control of cross-regional environmental governance, and strengthen environmental protection and treatment of water, air, waste and soil, etc.. From the perspective of top-level mechanism design, it is suggested to carry out the "GBA Chief System" on a pilot basis, with the leading group for the development of the GBA as the principal person in charge, and the relevant departments of the three regions jointly set up a supervisory committee to focus on solving the problems of cross-border environmental pollution, and urge Guangdong, Hong Kong and Macao to carry out in-depth environmental governance in accordance with national environmental protection laws and regulations. In addition, we should combine the financial advantages of Shenzhen and Hong Kong and the green technology advantages of Guangdong, Hong Kong and Macao to develop the green financial system in an all-round way, so as to provide a monetary reference for the environmental transactions such as carbon trading and ecological compensation, etc. At the regional, national and even global level. Finally, with the market advantages, innovation advantages and trading advantages, we can effectively promote the marketization process of green development and the construction of science and technology support system, and achieve the goal of green interactive development (Fig. 6.20).

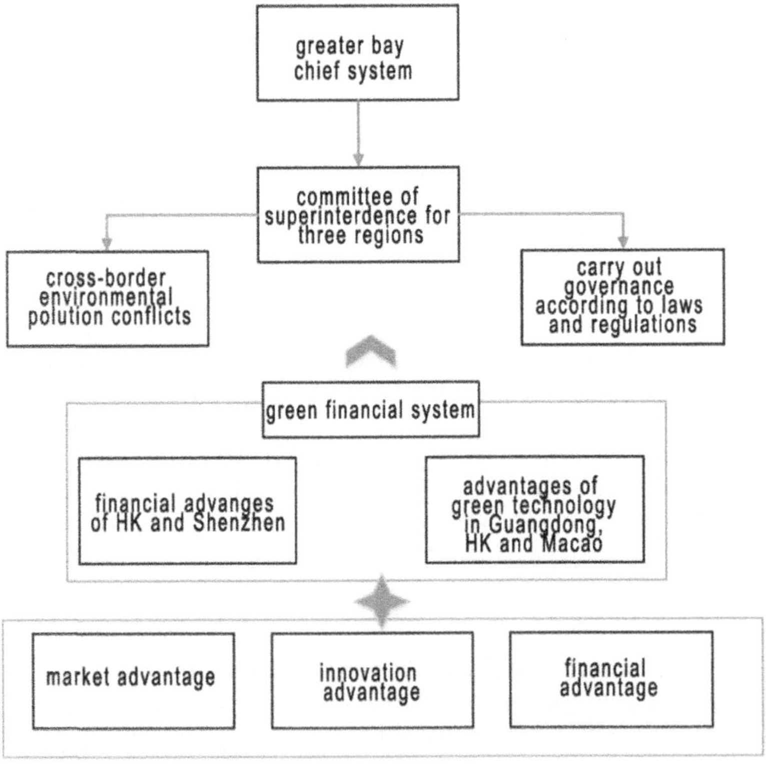

Fig. 6.20 The GBA Environmental Management System (*Source* Sorted by the authors)

In terms of specific management and control, we will firstly focus on strengthening ecological and environmental protection, governance and restoration in the Pearl River Estuary Basin and the South China Sea. We will carry out comprehensive promotion and tiered protection according to water function zoning, and conduct pilot construction of beautiful coastlines and clean bays at the national level. In addition, we shall also strengthen the ecological environment support and water conservation functions of the inland hinterland to maintain the comprehensive ecosystem functions of the Pearl River Basin. Secondly, we will put coordinated emission reduction plans into practice for a variety of air pollutants, implement emission reduction standards for major pollutants such as ozone (O3) and fine particulate matter (PM2.5), etc.. We will weed out backward industries and carry out industrial transformation and upgrading in strict accordance with the negative list for industrial access. Thirdly, we will vigorously carry out region-wide soil remediation projects, prevent and control agricultural non-point source pollution, and promote the building of a national green agricultural and sideline product supply base in GBA. Fourthly, we need to enhance the capacity for coordinated treatment of hazardous waste, implement comprehensive landfill treatment through research and development of the latest technologies, and give priority to in-depth treatment of typical landfill sites in Guangdong, Hong Kong and Macao.

6.7 Conception of Talents Synergy in the GBA

6.7.1 Establishing an Operational Mechanism for Integrating Talents in the GBA and Improving the Top-Level Design for Regional Talents Development

In the construction of the GBA, local governments take the talent policy as the propeller of talents flow and aggregation, establish the talents integration operation mechanism of the GBA and improve the top-level design of regional talents development, which is the fundamental guarantee for the active talents flow and coordinated development among cities in the GBA. In recent years, Guangdong Province has made a lot of attempts and achieved good results in the integration of talents and the policy support of talent policy and experience for the construction of the GBA, including exploring the reform of talent development system and mechanism in the GBA, optimizing the talent development environment for attracting and gathering high-level talents from abroad, and building a professional title system with Guangdong characteristics, as well as studying and formulating the policy of Preference Card for Talent, etc.. In addition, the free trade zone provides a "test field" for the talent system (Fig. 6.21).

In terms of talent development, the GBA enjoys the preferential treatment as a free trade zone. It enjoys the preferential treatment of talent policy innovation and trial in Nansha New District of Guangzhou, Shekou District of Qianhai in Shenzhen and

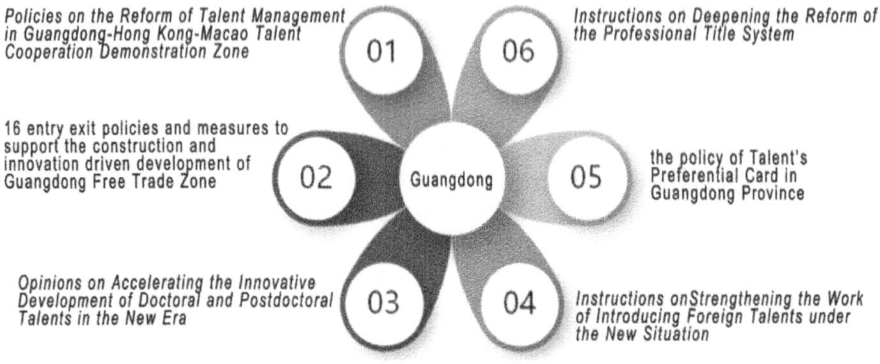

Fig. 6.21 Supporting Talent policy for Guangdong Province to promote the construction of the GBA (*Source* Guangdong Provincial People's Government Website)

Hengqin New District of Zhuhai[4] (Table 6.12). All these provide valuable experience for the top-level design of talent development in the GBA.

On this basis, since we want to realize the coordinated development of talents in the GBA, we need to further establish and improve the talent cooperation and coordination mechanism among the governments of Guangdong, Hong Kong and Macao. With reference to the Leading Group for the Development of the GBA, we will promote the establishment of a talent cooperation and coordination mechanism among the governments of Guangdong, Hong Kong and Macao, and we will build a talent cooperation mechanism featuring close connection, efficient communication and strong coordination among the three regions.

The GBA needs to establish a joint conference mechanism for talent collaboration. In addition to personnel service agencies and personnel departments of the "9+2" cities in the GBA, the members of the joint conference should also include social security, health, education and organization departments, so as to facilitate effective communication among the governments of the three regions in the process of talent cooperation development and enhance the integrity and coordination of policies. We will establish a system of talent introduction, evaluation and service based on mutual recognition, sharing and joint construction by promoting policies such as the "GBA Talents Card" and the "GBA Talents Plan", etc.. We will remove barriers in taxation, entry and exit, and professional qualification, and create an operational mechanism for a freer and more convenient flow of talents in the GBA.

We will cancel the travel permit for qualified personnel from Guangdong, Hong Kong and Macao in order to facilitate and liberalize the customs clearance for the flow of personnel among the three places. At present, the lack of convenience of entry and exit is one of the main factors hindering the talent exchange among Guangdong, Hong Kong and Macao. On the one hand, as most ports in the Bay Area and Hong Kong and Macao still adopt the mode of "handling the travelers' entry and exit procedures

[4] *Talent Development Report of the GBA (2018).*

Table 6.12 Highlights of talent policy in the three FTZs

Comparative item		Nansha New District	Shekou, Qianhai	Hengqin New District
Positioning		Talent Hub of the GBA, a "free port" for international talents	Special Features of Shenzhen-Hong Kong Cooperation, "Free Port" for International Talents	Hengqin-Macao Community of Shared Future, "International Talent Island"
Highlights of the innovations in the talent policy	Talent identification	Identification of high -end leading talents in Nansha District	Identification of overseas high-end talents and urgently-needed talents in Qianhai	Measures for the identification of Hong Kong, Macao and overseas high-level talents in Hengqin area
	Talent income tax preference	Key talents with annual taxable salary of more than 300,000 yuan (annual taxable salary of more than 200,000 yuan with scientific research institutions) will be rewarded 40% of their personal economic contribution. Hong Kong and Macao talents can choose to be rewarded according to the regional tax balance between the mainland and Hong Kong and Macao; foreign talents can choose to be rewarded more than 15% of the regional tax balance	15% preferential policy for individual tax subsidies: (1) high-end overseas talents and talents in short supply who meet Qianhai preferential industry direction can enjoy 15% preferential personal income tax; (2) for overseas high-end talents and talents in short supply who conform to the planned industrial direction of Qianhai, they will be temporarily subsidized by the Shenzhen Municipal Government in accordance with the individual income tax burden of the mainland and overseas, and will be exempted from individual income tax	1. Implementation of the policy of "Hong Kong tax for Hong Kong people, Macao tax for Macao people". Preferential individual income tax policy will be implemented for Hong Kong and Macao residents working in Hengqin, and full subsidy will be given according to the difference of individual income tax burden between Hong Kong, Macao and the mainland, and the scope of subsidy will include all 11 items of income under the mainland tax laws 2. Reward for special talents. The mainland and overseas talents who meet the "*Talent Development Catalogue of Hengqin New Area (2016–2020)*" and work in Hengqin will be given financial rewards based on 20%-40% of their personal direct economic contribution

(continued)

Table 6.12 (continued)

Comparative item		Nansha New District	Shekou, Qianhai	Hengqin New District
	Mutual recognition of talents' qualifications	1. It has been included in the pilot scope of mutual recognition of professional qualifications in Guangdong Province approved by the state, allowing professionals from Hong Kong and Macao to work in Nansha conveniently, and gradually expanding the scope of professional qualification recognition 2. Explore and carry out the pilot reform of the mode of "one test, three certificates" (one will obtain the international, Hong Kong, Macao and mainland vocational qualification certification by passing one examination) in Nansha	Promote mutual recognition of cross-border professional qualifications between Shenzhen and Hong Kong: at present, more than 10 types of talents such as Hong Kong certified tax agents, accountants, social workers and information technology talents can practice in Qianhai	To study the practice of construction engineering professionals, accountants, auditors and doctors from Hong Kong and Macao in Hengqin, and promote mutual recognition of the qualifications of relevant professionals

(continued)

Table 6.12 (continued)

Comparative item		Nansha New District	Shekou, Qianhai	Hengqin New District
	Talent flow	Promoting the facilitation of entry and exit and residence for foreign talents	Taking the lead in exploring and implementing 16 entry exit policies	1. Promote the household facilitation of industrial talents and create the household quota system for talents for major projects 2. Expand the scope of the "one visa-multiple entries" policy for talents traveling between Hong Kong and Macao 3. 24-h customs clearance at Hengqin port 4. Macao residents who have property or work in Hengqin can apply for motor vehicles to enter or leave Hengqin, and the application quota has been expanded from 100 to 800 5. Hengqin Port and Lianhua Port take the lead in starting the new operation mode of "reference and mutual recognition of inspection results of Guangdon-Macao passenger cars". Only one inspection *is needed at the two ports, which* reduces duplicate supervision and shortens the customs clearance time of about 15 min

(continued)

Table 6.12 (continued)

Comparative item		Nansha New District	Shekou, Qianhai	Hengqin New District
	Innovation of Talent Service	1. Implementing the treatment of talents: venture capital talents, market-oriented talents, professional and technical or skilled talents who meet the conditions can be directly registered; Hong Kong, Macao and foreign talents who have been registered in Nansha area of the free trade zone can directly apply for Guangzhou talent green card 2. For qualified talents, high-end talent cards are issued. Cardholders can enjoy 12 high-quality services, such as children's priority in choosing school, household registration for them and their family members, convenient customs clearance, priority in medical treatment, free physical examination and consumption discount 3. Priority should be given to the children of high-end leading talents. In particular, outstanding experts and excellent experts can choose a public school in the whole region to apply for admission of their children, and the children of young reserve talents and other talents can apply for admission to public schools	1. Exploring the establishment of a centralized and unified intellectual property law enforcement system; establishment of a fast IPR protection mechanism for key industries in Qianhai and Shekou Area; establishment of "South China High Technology and Intellectual Property Arbitration Center" 2. The establishment of Qianhai International Talent Service Center is based on the registration of enterprise legal person and the implementation of market-oriented operation and enterprise-oriented management. It is specifically responsible for the promotion and implementation of Qianhai talent policies, international talent introduction and contact services, talent recognition and acceptance, public services, talent exchange activities, etc. 3. Pilot free cruise for Guangdong-Hong Kong-Macao yachts	1. Establish a comprehensive legal service mechanism for intellectual property rights 2. Explore the cooperation with Macao SAR government to build "Macao New Community", and explore the extension of Macao's medical care, education, pension and other social welfare to Hengqin 3. Pilot free cruise for Guangdong-Hong Kong-Macao yachts

Source Sorted by the authors

respectively", the customs clearance procedures for residents from the mainland part of the Bay Area and Hong Kong and Macao are extremely cumbersome, such as security check, ticket buying, ticket collecting, real-name authentication, ticket checking, customs clearance and other procedures are quite time-consuming. In the security check of ticket purchase, "bilateral inspection and triple authentication" will be implemented. The time consuming of repeated certification has caused great inconvenience to various talents travelling to and from Guangdong, Hong Kong and Macao. On the other hand, mainland residents in the Bay Area are only allowed to visit Hong Kong and Macao twice at most (Shenzhen residents can travel once a week), and Macao only once every two months. Each time, they can stay in Hong Kong and Macao for no more than 7 days. With the increasing demand of residents in the Bay Area to travel to and from Hong Kong and Macao, the limited number of endorsements is difficult to meet the demand for frequent travel. In terms of business endorsement, applicants, especially small and medium-sized enterprises and personnel of science and innovation enterprises in the early stage of incubation and development, are limited in terms of enterprise filing, tax payment, foreign exchange earning and other conditions, and cannot smoothly carry out innovation and entrepreneurship activities at home and abroad (Xie Baojian and Hu Yijie 2019).

Therefore, in order to establish a more effective new mechanism for regional coordinated development, innovate the system of talent travel between Guangdong, Hong Kong and Macao, and explore the cancellation of the travel permit for high-end talents from Guangdong, Hong Kong and Macao, we need to take "three steps" to realize the talent travel between the three places "without a license" and "visa-free", and realize the rapid transit of "one inspection for customs clearance". The first step is to focus on facilitating customs clearance for high-end talents, promote the coordination and cooperation among relevant departments of Guangdong, Hong Kong and Macao from the upper level, and create a positive policy environment for the integration of customs clearance through data and terminals of the three places. The second step is to explore the establishment of "one inspection and clearance" information platform through the systemization of the new generation of information technology innovation achievements such as biometrics, big data and artificial intelligence, promote the transformation of "paper certificate" to "electronic certificate + biometrics" intelligent customs clearance mode, realize the rapid transit mode of "one inspection and clearance", and take the lead in popularizing among high-end talents. The third step is to cancel the certificate requirements for travel among three places for high-end talents and to open an express passage for high-end talents who meet the relevant policies so that they can go through the customs clearance by simple "face swiping" check-in.[5]

[5] Center for China and Globalization. Integration of talents from Guangdong, Hong Kong and Macao will contribute to the development of the GBA [J]. *International Talent Exchange*, 2019(3).

6.7.2 Promoting the System of Mutual Recognition of Professional Qualifications and Revitalizing the Professional Talent Resources in the GBA

The GBA is one of the most economically dynamic city clusters in China. Table 6.13 shows the top 10 positions and top 10 skills with the fastest growth rate of high-level talents in the GBA from 2014 to 2017. It can be seen from the table that the top ten positions involve many professional functions and fields, and most of them are middle and senior positions, indicating that the industrial development in Guangdong, Hong Kong and Macao is getting diversified, specialized and mature. At the same time, the demand for senior research talents has increased significantly, indicating the importance of research and development to the GBA. The top 10 skills that are growing the fastest are also obvious. Conference skills, such as public speaking and event planning, and digital skills, such as social media and social media marketing, have all increased significantly, showing the urgency of internal communication and external publicity in the GBA. The top ten positions with the highest demand intensity in different industries in the GBA are statistically analyzed, and the results are shown in Table 6.14. Table shows that there are obvious similarities and differences in job demands of various industries in the GBA. First of all, account manager, project manager and so on have entered the top ten in the demand of various industries, which shows that the industry has a great demand for general positions. Secondly, similar to the industry ranking of talents and skills, different industries have different emphasis on job requirements. Marketing and sales positions are in high demand in the consumer goods industry; the software and IT service industry has more demand for the positions of developers, R & D personnel and other technical personnel;

Table 6.13 Top 10 posts and skills with the fastest growth of high-level talents in the GBA

Ranking	Position	Skills
1	Investment manage	The data analysis
2	Director of marketing	Public speaking
3	Business Development Director	Social media
4	Office assistant	Event planning
5	The legal adviser	Communication
6	Postdoctoral Fellow	VBA
7	Marketing assistant	Social Media Marketing
8	Information Technology Director	Event management
9	Chief Operating Officer	Consulting
10	Business Development Manager	Editing

Source Tsinghua University & LinkedIn. Research Report on Digital Economy and Talent Development in the GBA

Table 6.14 The fastest growing job demand in major industries in the GBA

Ranking	Manufacturing	Consumer goods	Software and IT services	Computer networks and hardware	Banking	Company service
1	Key account manager	Customer manager	Mobile application developer	Application engineer	Senior financial adviser	Data advisor
2	Sales consultant	Marketing manager	Senior Account Manager	Sales manager	Fund accountant	Salesman
3	Salesman	Customer relationship management assistant	Business development director	Marketing manager	Underwriter	Human resource assistant
4	Business development manager	Purchasing assistant	Recruitment of HR	Director of sales	Financial services specialist	Project manager
5	Sales manager	Operating commissioner	R&D Scientist	Project manager	Customer manager	Recruitment consultant
6	Business commissioner	Acoustic engineer	Business Development Manager	R&D Engineer	Business commissioner	IT Consultant
7	Sales engineer	Information technology manager	Customer manager	Software engineer	Customer service specialist	Sales manager
8	Sales assistant	Sales manager	Human resources Business partners	Product manager	Product manager	Search consultant
9	Customer manager	Salesman	Product manager	Customer manager	Financial advisers	Customer manager
10	Product manager	Business commissioner	Software engineer	Brand strategy manager	Administrative assistant	Certified public accountant

Note The calculation formula of job demand intensity is: the number of the position in recruitment/the number of the position in employment
Source Tsinghua University & LinkedIn. Research Report on Digital Economy and Talent Development in the GBA

the computer network and hardware industry has a great demand for the positions of application engineers, research and development engineers; the financial industry has more demand for financial consultant, fund accountant and financial specialist; the company service has more demand for human resources and recruitment positions.

According to the above analysis, we can find that in the GBA, different industries have different demand for talents with different skills. Speeding up the promotion of mutual recognition of talents' professional qualifications in the GBA and promoting the flow of talents with different skills in the GBA will help to increase the employment rate of talents with relevant skills in the GBA, promote a virtuous circle of talents in various industries in the GBA, and play a vital role in the coordinated development of talents in the GBA. We will learn from the successful experience of mutual recognition of professional qualification between Guangdong pilot free trade zone and Hong Kong and Macao, and gradually copy this experience and extend it to other pilot areas of Guangdong, Hong Kong and Macao GBA, so as to realize mutual recognition of professional qualification in law, finance, education, health care, accounting and other professional fields in the GBA, and promote the construction of Hong Kong and Macao professional service cluster area. First, starting from the upper policy construction, we should break through the institutional barriers of mutual recognition of professional qualifications in Guangdong, Hong Kong and Macao, and work together with relevant government departments, professional associations and talents in Guangdong, Hong Kong and Macao to explore solutions. Second, according to the requirements of mutual recognition of different professional qualifications, different channels should be adopted to promote the implementation of mutual recognition of qualifications, such as applying for employment qualifications in the mainland through training and testing, direct mutual recognition of professional qualifications, equal treatment of employment experience in the three places, free employment of professional talents in the three places by joint ventures, etc.

6.7.3 Establishment of a Unified Employment Information Platform for the GBA

EU experience shows that the difficulty of obtaining employment information is an important factor affecting labor mobility. To this end, the European Union has set up a special employment information platform to help workers obtain the job demand information of various countries, such as EURES (European Employment Service). Therefore, the GBA should also establish a one-stop website to provide workers in Guangdong, Hong Kong and Macao with relevant information such as learning and training, job needs and ability certification, etc., focusing on the establishment and improvement of specific career information services for individuals, so as to help workers flow among regions. In addition, various activities will be held to provide workers with mobile information of jobs, training opportunities and job skills.

According to the data of talent concentration in Guangdong, Hong Kong and Macao (see Chapter 5), there is a great homogeneity of talents in various cities of Guangdong Province, but there are obvious talent disadvantages in the financial and education industries. Hong Kong has a very high talent concentration in industries such as the finance, education, corporate services, etc., while Macao has obvious advantages in the education, tourism and holiday industries, among which tourism and holiday industries are the most characteristic in Macao. Therefore, Hong Kong and Macao can form a good complementary advantage with the major cities in Guangdong in terms of talents, and the same employment information platform can lay a solid foundation for the flow of talents in various industries in GBA, so as to promote the formation of internal knowledge gathering effect and spillover effect in GBA, and realize the sound economic development of GBA.

6.7.4 Establishment of a GBA R & D Framework Plan to Support the Free Flow of Researchers

In terms of university cooperation, although the Chinese University of Hong Kong, Hong Kong University of science and technology, Hong Kong Polytechnic University, City University of Hong Kong and Hong Kong Baptist University have set up or will soon set up branches in Guangdong Province, the universities in Guangdong, Hong Kong and Macao have failed to play the role of collaborative development in talent training, sharing of science and education resources, integration of educational ideas, subject reference (introduction) or information exchange, etc., which is not conducive to the integration and international development of higher education in Guangdong, Hong Kong and Macao (Xian Xuelin, An Dongping 2017). In terms of industry-university-research cooperation, the bay area has failed to form an active innovation and technology ecosystem. Compared with the school- enterprise interaction in the three major Bay areas of the world, Hong Kong's universities and science and technology service institutions have less cooperation and interaction with the mainland region in the bay area, less tight linkage with the enterprises in the bay area, especially those in the PRD, and the collaborative innovation of industry university research institute needs to be strengthened. In addition, at present, the tax system conflicts among Guangdong, Hong Kong and Macao are obvious, which also inhibits the enthusiasm of talent flow. Compared with the tax system of Hong Kong and Macao, the mainland is still a high tax area, and there is also the problem of Double Taxation (Table 6.15). Hong Kong and Macao have similar tax burden on enterprise income and personal income, which is far lower than that of the mainland, and they do not levy tariff and value-added tax. Although there are some tax incentives in Guangdong, Hong Kong and Macao, the mainland is still a high tax area compared with Hong Kong and Macao. In recent years, the relationship between the mainland and Hong Kong has become increasingly close. Due to the differences in the tax systems between the two places, double taxation has occurred in some areas. According to the principle of local source taxation in Hong Kong, the income of Hong Kong companies from countries and regions outside Hong Kong is not subject to taxation in Hong Kong. If an income is taxable in addition to Hong Kong and is subject to turnover tax outside Hong Kong at the same time, the foreign tax levied will be allowed to be deducted as expenses in calculating the tax payable on the income according to the Hong Kong tax law. In addition, in order to avoid double taxation, Hong Kong, China has signed double taxation agreements with many countries and

Table 6.15 List of double taxation exemption concessions in Hong Kong

Type	Scope of duty-free	Signatory country
Agreement on the Comprehensive Avoidance of Double Taxation	Dividends, royalties, interest and technical expenses	Since 2004, it has signed agreements with 30 countries or regions
Incomplete Avoidance of Double Taxation Agreement	Shipping income and air transport income are exempt from taxation in the Contracting States	USA, Canada, Germany, Israel, South Korea, Mauritius, Netherlands, New Zealand, UK
Income tax is exempt from double taxation	It involves cross-border transportation, personal income tax and other aspects	Agreement with mainland China in 1998

Source Guangdong Academy of Social Sciences, 2018

regions in the world. The shortage of the mainland in this respect has greatly affected the inflow of talents.

Looking at foreign experience, we find that since 1984, the EU has invested nearly 10 billion euros in the implementation of the *EU R & D framework plan*. The plan is jointly funded by EU Member States. All countries submit the R & D projects to the *R & D framework plan*, and then attract top talents from all countries to participate through high subsidies. The countries that contribute scientific research achievements can share them.

The program not only promotes exchanges and cooperation among researchers of various countries to avoid duplication of research, but also strengthens cooperation and exchanges between advanced and backward regions in science and technology, so as to improve the academic level of backward regions. GBA can learn from the European Union's practice of concentrating on scientific research. The three governments should take the lead to set up a number of major scientific research exchange and cooperation projects every year, promote the cooperation among scientific researchers, universities and enterprises in the three regions, and attract a number of foreign experts to serve China, so as to solve the problem of difficult introduction of international talents. In addition, we will support domestic and foreign investors to set up joint innovation funds in the GBA, carry out cooperation on major scientific research projects, and allow relevant funds to be freely used in the GBA.

6.7.5 Implementation of the Talent Flow Plan of GBA and Enhancement of the Exchange and Cooperation of Talent Resources in the GBA

According to the analysis of the high-level talent flow among the major cities in the GBA, it can be found that Guangzhou and Shenzhen have the closest talent exchanges with other cities, accounting for more than 50% or even as high as 80% of the total talent flow of other cities. Compared with Guangzhou, Shenzhen has a lower proportion in the source of talent inflow in other cities, but a higher proportion in the destination of talent outflow, reflecting the different positions of Shenzhen and Guangzhou in the talent flow of Guangdong, Hong Kong and Macao. Huizhou and Macao have the least talent exchanges with other cities, and their talent attraction is not high enough. Zhuhai is the most closely connected city with Macao. It is not only the main source of talents in Macao, but also the main outflow place of talents in Macao. Hong Kong has the closest ties with Shenzhen, with more than 50% of the talents in the bay area coming from Shenzhen and going to Shenzhen. It is the core interface for Hong Kong to integrate into the mainland. On the whole, the talent flow of Guangdong, Hong Kong and Macao is still mainly limited in the PRD. The talent flow between Hong Kong and Macao and between Hong Kong, Macao and the mainland is very limited, which limits the coordinated development of talents in Guangdong, Hong Kong and Macao.

According to the current situation of talent flow among the major cities in GBA, we must implement the development plan of GBA, strengthen the talent interconnection among the three areas, innovate the talent flow plan of GBA, and effectively improve the current situation of talent flow. The first is to summarize the successful experience of Shenzhen Hong Kong (Qianhai) public officials exchange program, copy and promote it to other areas of Guangdong pilot Free Trade Zone, so as to realize the first trial of temporary training of public officials in the three places, and promote regional talents to participate in decision-making. Second, relying on Guangdong, Hong Kong and Macao Youth Innovation and entrepreneurship platform, postdoctoral exchange station and other platforms, we will carry out normalization cooperation of urgently needed professionals and projects in the three places, promote joint tackling of key problems by professionals and in-depth cooperation of industrial projects in the three places, and realize the sharing and co-construction of human resources in the three places (Zhong Feijian et al. 2019).

6.7.6 Promoting University and Key Research Platform Construction with Concerted Efforts for the Development of Young Talents and Communication of Researchers in the GBA

In view of the problems of insufficient talents, low originality and low conversion rate in high-end scientific research field in GBA, it is suggested that under the framework of "one country, two systems", the governments of Guangdong, Hong Kong and Macao should jointly fund to rapidly promote the implementation of "Guangdong, Hong Kong and Macao University" and undertake the demonstration and guidance function of science and technology, education and humanities cooperation in the bay area. Through the establishment of the GBA University, the imbalance in the development of higher education in the GBA has been overcome. There are few cooperation and exchanges among universities, teachers and students at all levels, and there are institutional barriers to cooperation, so as to promote the coordinated development of higher education in the GBA. It is suggested that the education departments of the three places should consult with each other to select a suitable place to set up the school, such as Qianhai in Shenzhen, the Shenzhen-Hong Kong boundary bend area, Hengqin in Zhuhai or Nansha in Guangzhou, etc., and choose one place to build the physical campus and set up the coordination agency of the three places. Referring to the school running mode of Westlake University, the main body responsible for the operation of the University, "GBA Education Development Foundation" will be established, which will be jointly funded by the three places, and will be authorized to be fully responsible for the construction, operation, management and financing of the university. Priority will be given to postgraduate education and university recruitment in the GBA to promote student exchange and common development in the area.

We will set up a number of innovation centers, science and technology industrial parks, innovation institutes and innovation workshops in the Bay Area, aiming at projects at the forefront of the new round of scientific and industrial revolution. We will accelerate the construction of the Guangzhou-Shenzhen-Hong Kong Innovation Corridor and actively promote the joint construction of high-tech industrial parks among cities of the three regions. We will give full play to the coordinating and leading role of central government departments to establish state key laboratories and partner laboratories of state key project platforms in Hong Kong, Macao and mainland cities. Based on platforms such as Guangdong, Hong Kong and Macao Youth Innovation and Entrepreneurship Platform and Postdoctoral Research Workstation, we will carry out regular cooperation on urgently needed professionals and projects of the three regions, promote joint tackling of regional professionals and in-depth cooperation on industrial projects, so as to share, integrate and build human resources of the three regions.

All in all, it may be difficult to realize the free flow of talents in all fields in the bay area in the short term. It is suggested to focus on the core high-end talents catering to the need of "building Guangzhou-Shenzhen-Hong Kong-Macao science and technology innovation corridor and building GBA international science and technology innovation center", and give these talents at home and abroad and their family members convenient measures, such as the most reasonable cost-effective accommodation and the lowest personal income tax rate in the GBA, high-quality education and medical resources, and special arrangements for free access to the three places, are taken to attract these talents. After the demonstration is mature, we can choose more fields to expand gradually, so as to attract top talents from many fields at home and abroad to gather in the GBA, and finally promote the construction of a world-class bay area.

References

Chen J, Zheng G (2013) Innovation management: gaining the sustainable competitive advantage (2nd ed). Beijing University Press

Gu SZ (2018) Establishing the Guangdong-Hong Kong-Macao Greater Bay Area as a highland for core technological innovation. China Daily, 2019-06-28, 03

Li X et al. (2018) Understanding the Guangdong-Hong Kong-Macao Greater Bay Area from the perspective of mega-city region 37(12):1609–1622

Peng Y, Li L (2019) Forum on legal environment of business in Guangdong, Hong Kong and Macao Greater Bay Area held in Guangzhou. ZAKER, 2019-05-15

Wang JW (2019) NPC deputy Wang Jingwu: establishing a coordination mechanism for financial supervision in the Greater Bay Area of Guangdong, Hong Kong and Macau. Financial News, 2019-03-11, 006

Wang XB (2019) Searching the outline of the Greater Bay Area development plan: promoting financial interconnection in the Greater Bay Area. https://sohu.com/a/298333327_618588

Xian XL, An DP (2017) Discussion on the current situation and cooperation mode of higher education in the GBA. J Shenzhen Inst Inf Technol 15(4):7–11

Xie BJ, Hu JY (2019) Study on the development of Hong Kong and Macao youth in the Greater Bay Area of Guangdong, Hong Kong and Macao. Youth Exproationm 219(1):7–16

Yao JC, Chi BC, Liu ZY et al (2018) Planning governance and coordination strategy of the GBA. Planner 34(268):14–20

Zhang GQ (2019) Study on the optimal and coordinated development of port clusters in the Greater Bay Area of Guangdong-Hong Kong-Macao. Integr Transp 41(1):1–6

Zhong FJ et al (2019) Learning from experience and taking the initiative to build a highland of talent in Guangdong, Hong Kong and Macau's Greater Bay Area. Foshan Daily, 2019-04-08, F02

Chapter 7
Value Simulation Analysis of the Combined Free Trade Ports of the GBA

Referring to the research progress of factors, subsystems and regulatory pathways involved in regional collaborative development at home and abroad, we can see that the GBA is a complex system integrated by economic, social, environmental and other factors, and its regional collaborative development is comprehensively affected by multiple factors. Therefore, the main purpose of this chapter is to predict the future collaborative development trend and key controlling factors of the GBA based on the unique advantages of system dynamics in the study of complex system problems, and take the free trade port system scenario as the regulatory variable to optimize the best model suitable for future sustainable development. Specifically, the system dynamics modeling method will be used to simulate and analyze the economic value and social value brought by the combined free trade ports for GBA through the integration of simulation real scene, and quantitatively calculate the key variables and corresponding parameters that need to be adjusted and controlled. Based on this, some suggestions for the coordinated development of Guangdong, Hong Kong and Macao Bay area will be put forward.

7.1 System Dynamics Model of Value Simulation of Combined Free Trade Ports of the GBA

7.1.1 Model Boundary and Feedback Structure

System Dynamics Model for Free Trade Port Value Simulation (FTPSD) is the core model of value simulation, which mainly integrates the economic and social aspects of Guangdong, Hong Kong and Macao free trade ports, and involves the key subsystems of trade growth, scientific and technological innovation, economic and fiscal growth, population growth, public service level and environmental quality. Referring to the economic spillover system dynamics model in Shanghai Free Trade Zone

© Xiamen University Press 2022

S. Ba et al., *Collaborative Innovation Mechanism of GBA in China*,
https://doi.org/10.1007/978-981-19-2251-0_7

established by Zhao Jing (2016), according to the research focus and the development basis of combined free trade ports in Guangdong, Hong Kong and Macao Bay area, the variables included in the model boundary are: increase in import and export trade, level of scientific and technological innovation, permanent population, economic scale, attraction of talents and labor force, fiscal revenue, financial security level of environmental regulation, and the scale of traditional manufacturing industry, per capita disposable income, etc. Determining the model boundary is the basis of modeling, and the system dynamics model of free trade portfolio port value simulation is established within the above boundary.

There are complex feedback relationships among different subsystems. From the perspective of effects, the construction of free trade ports may have significant impacts on the economy and society, but the direction and intensity of the impacts are different in different regions, which can be roughly divided into four categories: positive impacts, negative impacts, both positive and negative impacts and no impacts (Zhao Liang, 2015). Based on the analysis of factor feedback logic, free trade ports mainly influence economic and social development through three ways: increasing the volume of trade and investment, economic scale and improving social well-being (Yang and Martinez-Zarzoso, 2014; Zhao Liang, 2015; Zong Huiming and Zheng Lili, 2017; Qian Jin, 2019). Referring to the development practice of the GBA, adding the variable of scientific and technological innovation, it is considered that it will play an important role in the future development of the combined free trade ports. The volume of trade and investment is mainly represented by the volume of import and export, which has a significant impact on economic growth. Social well-being is mainly influenced by the superposition of economic growth and population inflow, forming a complex cascading effect of mutual game (Fig. 7.1).

In the specific model expression, the feedback relationship includes: (1) the positive cascade effect of the collaborative construction policy of combined free trade ports on import and export, economic scale and economic development level, that is, the collaborative construction policy of combined free trade ports.

$\xrightarrow{+}$ the increase of import and export trade $\xrightarrow{+}$ the total export trade $\xrightarrow{+}$ the economic scale development level $\xrightarrow{+}$ the per capita disposable income; (2) the positive promoting effect of coordinated construction policy of combined free trade ports on scientific and technological innovation, and the negative cascade effect of the scale of traditional industries on environmental quality, namely, the collaborative construction policy of the combined free trade ports $\xrightarrow{+}$ the level of scientific and technological innovation $\xrightarrow{+}$ the scale of traditional manufacturing industry $\xrightarrow{-}$ the level of environmental quality; (3) the positive promotion effect of the collaborative construction policy of free trade port on the permanent residents, as well as the complex cascade effect on the level of medical and educational services, that is, the collaborative construction policy of free trade port $\xrightarrow{+}$ the attraction to talents and labor force $\xrightarrow{+}$ the increase of the permanent residents population $\xrightarrow{-}$ the level of medical services / the level of higher education.

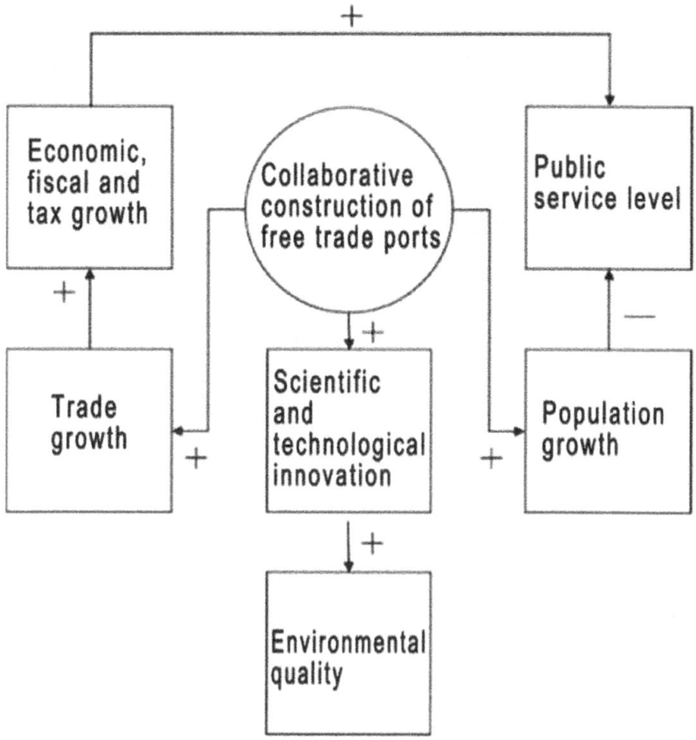

Fig. 7.1 Basic structure of dynamic model of value simulation system of combined free trade ports

The dynamic model of the value simulation system of the combined free trade ports has the following functions:

The first is to predict the development trend of key economic and social variables in GBA.

The second is to simulate the economic and social value of the GBA under the policy context.

7.1.2 Model Subsystem and Variable Equation

The dynamic model of the value simulation system of the combined ports of free trade is roughly divided into key subsystems such as policy variables, trade economy, scientific and technological innovation, population, public service and environmental quality (Table 7.1). Due to the difference in statistical diameter of data between Hong Kong and Macao, we focus on simulating the economic and social impact of the FTA combined ports in the nine cities of Guangdong in GBA. The variable equations of each subsystem are simulated through repeated training of the SD parameter learning

Table 7.1 Key variables and representation indicators

	Variable type	Indicators of representation
Total import and export trade volume of the GBA	Horizontal variable	Total amount of import and export trade, converted according to the average annual exchange rate of RMB to US dollar
Increase in import and export trade in the GBA	Auxiliary variable	–
Growth rate of import and export trade in the GBA	Auxiliary variable	–
The opening up level of the GBA	Auxiliary variable	Economic externality
Economic scale of the GBA	Auxiliary variable	Regional GDP
Economic development level of the GBA	Auxiliary variable	GDP per capita
Financial revenue of the GBA	Auxiliary variable	Local general public budget revenue
Proportion of fiscal revenue in GDP in the GBA	Auxiliary variable	–
Per capita disposable income in the GBA	Auxiliary variable	Per capita disposable income of permanent residents
Level of scientific and technological innovation in the GBA	Auxiliary variable	Proportion of R&D expenditure in GDP
Scale of traditional manufacturing industry in the GBA	Auxiliary variable	Significant relevance with the added value of the secondary industry
Proportion of traditional manufacturing industry in the GBA	Auxiliary variable	–
Population of permanent residents in the GBA	Horizontal variable	Population of permanent residents
Increase of the population of permanent residents in the GBA	Auxiliary variable	–
Growth rate of the population of permanent residents in the GBA	Auxiliary variable	–
Scale of medical services in the GBA	Auxiliary variable	Health workers
Medical service level in the GBA	Auxiliary variable	Number of health workers per 10,000 people
The scale of higher education in the GBA	Auxiliary variable	Number of students in Colleges and Universities
Higher education level in the GBA	Auxiliary variable	Number of students in Colleges and universities per 10,000 people

(continued)

Table 7.1 (continued)

	Variable type	Indicators of representation
Financial support level of environmental regulation in the GBA	Auxiliary variable	Significant relevance with the local general public budget revenue
Environmental quality level of Guangdong, Hong Kong and Macao	Auxiliary variable	Adoption of the comprehensive air quality index issued by the Department of Environmental Protection of Guangdong Province, with a comprehensive consideration of 6 pollutants including SO2, NO2, PM10, PM2.5, Co, O3, etc.. The bigger the index is, the higher the comprehensive pollution degree is

algorithm, and the parameters of the equation are finally determined, which include: arithmetic mean method, reference value calculation based on historical data and relevant standard; trend calculation method in accordance to the data trend recursion; table function method through the establishment of VENSIM table function to control the situation; linear regression method, supported by SPSS 19.0 and Urban and Regional Planning Model System (URMS), which adopts unary or multiple linear regression models to determine parameters (Cui Xuegang, 2019).

First, policy variable subsystem. It mainly represents the changes in the total value of import and export trade, the level of scientific and technological innovation, and the attractiveness of talents and labor under the policy context of the collaborative construction of combined free trade ports. The parameter of the table function is set as 1 in the initial state. The equation of policy variables is as follows:

The collaborative construction policy of combined free trade ports (CP)
= WITH LOOKUP(Time,([(0,0)-(2 035,10)],(2 000,1),(2 017,1),(2 035,1)))

Second, trade economy subsystem. It mainly represents the positive promotion effect of the collaborative construction policy on import and export trade of the combined free trade ports, economic development level, fiscal revenue and per capita disposable income. The main variable equations are as follows:

Total volume of import and export trade of the GBA = INTEG(increase in import and export trade of the GBA, 13 173),
Increase in import and export trade of the GBA = total volume import and export trade of the GBA × (the collaborative construction policy on import and export trade of the combined free trade ports -1) + total volume of import and export trade of the GBA × growth rate of import and export trade of the GBA,
Growth rate of import and export trade in the GBA = -0.05 × ln(time-199) + 0.197
Opening-up level of the GBA = Total volume of import and export trade of the GBA/Economic Size of the GBA

Economic Size of the GBA.

= (0.014 4 × total import and export trade volume of Guangdong-Hong Kong-Macao $^{1.4}$)$^{\text{1n (technological innovation level of Guangdong, Hong Kong and Macao} + 0.971) + 1}$

Economic development level of the GBA = 10 000 × economic size of the GBA/GBA

The population of permanent residents

Fiscal revenue of the GBA = Proportion of fiscal revenue in GDP of the GBA × the economic size of the GBA

Ratio of fiscal revenue in GDP of the GBA = 3.139 × 1n(Time)-23.789

Per capita disposable income of the GBA = 0.006 35 × economic development level of the GBA $^{1.34}$

Third, scientific and technological innovation subsystem. It mainly reflects the effect of promotion of the policy of the cooperative construction of the combined free trade ports to the scientific and technological innovation and how it further affects the proportion of traditional manufacturing. The main variable equation is as follows:

The scientific and technological innovation level of the GBA = WITH LOOKUP (the collaborative construction policy on import and export trade of the combined free trade ports, ([(0,0)-(10,10)],(1,0.029),(1.015,0.035)))

Traditional manufacturing scale of the GBA = the economic size of the GBA × the proportion of traditional manufacturing in the GBA

The proportion of traditional manufacturing in GBA = 0.029 × (-6.515 × 1n(Time) + 50)/ the level of scientific and technological innovation in the GBA

Fourth, population subsystem. It mainly reflects the population attraction of the coordinated construction policy of combined free trade ports and the changing trend of the permanent resident population. The main variable equation is as follows:

GBA's attraction to talents and labors

= the collaborative construction policy on import and export trade of the CP, [(0,0)-(10,10)],(1,0),(1.015,0.005))

Population of permanent residents in the GBA = INTEG (increase in the population of permanent residents in the GBA, 4 290)

Increase in the population of permanent residents in the GBA = population of permanent residents in the GBA × attraction to talents and labors in the GBA + population of permanent residents in the GBA × population of permanent residents growth rate in the GBA

The permanent resident population growth rate of the GBA = -0.084 × 1n(Time) + 0.66

Fifth, public service subsystem. It mainly reflects the influence of the policy of collaborative construction of combined free trade ports on the level of public services such as medical care and higher education, which is also influenced by the interaction of population growth and service scale growth. The main variable equation is as follows:

Medical service scale of the GBA = 0.285 $\times$ fiscal revenue of the GBA$^{0.59}$
Medical service level in the GBA = 10 000 $\times$ medical service scale in the GBA/GBA
Population of permanent residents in the GBA
The scale of higher education in the GBA = 1.88 $\times$ the financial revenue of the GBA$^{0.51}$
The level of higher education in the GBA = 10 000 $\times$ the scale of higher education in the GBA/population of permanent residents in the GBA

Sixth, environmental quality subsystem. It mainly represents the impact of the policy on environmental quality of the combined construction of free trade ports, which can be used as an important variable to investigate social well-being. The main variable equation is as follows:

Financial security level of environmental regulation in the GBA = 0.103 7 $\times$ economic scale of the GBA -627.41
Environmental quality level of the GBA = 1.6 $\times$ 1n (scale of traditional manufacturing in GBA)-1.39 $\times$ 1n (guarantee level of environmental regulation and financial resources in GBA)-1.31 $\times$ technological innovation level of the GBAss

7.1.3 *Model Visualization*

Through the variable decomposition of the model subsystem in Fig. 7.1, the dynamic model of free trade portfolio port value simulation system is constructed, and the visual expression and simulation operation are realized with the help of Vensim PLE platform (Fig. 7.2). The time boundary is set as 2000–2035, that is, in the model

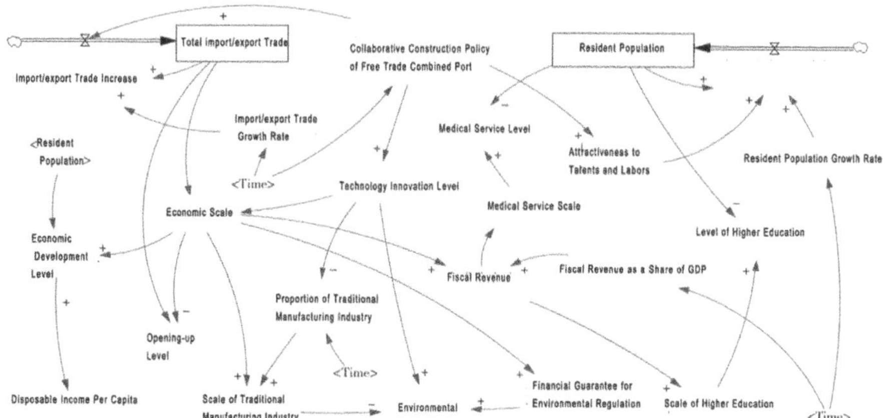

Fig. 7.2 Dynamic model of value simulation system of combined free trade ports based on Vensim PLE platform

system, units is year, final time = 2 035, initial time = 2 000.

7.1.4 *Model Test and Analysis*

7.1.4.1 Model Authenticity Test

In order to test the authenticity of the simulation results of SD model, firstly, the historical year data from 2000 to 2014 are input into Vensim PLE system for simulation operation; secondly, the simulated values from 2015 to 2017 are output and compared with the actual values for error comparison; thirdly, through repeated debugging of equation parameters, the convergence of simulation results is ensured and the good fidelity of SD model is guaranteed (Fang et al, 2019). As shown in Table 7.2, the absolute value of the relative error between the actual value and the simulated value from 2015 to 2017 is generally less than 5%, indicating that the model has been verified.

Table 7.2 Test results of system storage and flow

Year	Variable	Total amount of import and export trade (100 million yuan)	Gross Regional Product (100 million yuan)	Permanent population (10,000 people)	Local general public budget revenue (100 million yuan)	Ambient air comprehensive quality index
2015	Actual value	60 755	63 382	5 874	6 392	4.05
	Simulation value	57 611	66 538	5 879	6 234	4.23
	Error rate	−5.2%	5.0%	0.1%	−2.5%	4.5%
2016	Actual value	60 436	69 070	5 998	6 924	3.99
	Simulation value	60 974	72 038	6 002	6 861	4.23
	Error rate	0.9%	4.3%	0.1%	−0.9%	6.0%
2017	Actual value	64 883	75 710	6 151	7 456	4.25
	Simulation value	64 348	77 680	6 127	7 520	4.22
	Error rate	−0.8%	2.6%	−0.4%	0.9%	−0.7%

Table 7.3 Part of conclusions on the promotion of trade growth by the construction of domestic free trade zones

Case object	Policy context	Trade growth rate (according to low expectations)	Reference
China-Japan-Korea Trade	Establishment of a China-Japan-ROK Free Trade Area	3.36%	Kuang Zengjie (2015)
China-India Trade	Establishment of a China-India Free Trade Area	1.02%	Yu Zhen et al. (2014)
Guangdong Province	Establishment of a Guangdong Free Trade Area	1%–2% (replaced by quarterly GDP growth rate)	Ying Wangjiang and Fan Bowen (2018)

Note Unary linear regression test shows that there is a significant positive correlation between GDP (independent variable X) and import and export trade volume (dependent variable Y) of the GBA, that is, $Y = 0.118 \times X + 2\,450$, $R2 = 0.84$. Therefore, GDP growth rate can represent the growth rate of import and export trade to a higher extent

7.1.4.2 Model Context Parameter Setting

Setting up a comprehensive development scenario is the key to compare the data differences between the initial state and the policy context, and measure the economic and social value of the free trade combination port. According to the above analysis on the dynamic mechanism of the economic and social impact of the construction of the free trade zone, combined with the development practice GBA, we can focus on the three aspects of coordinated economic growth, scientific and technological innovation, and talent and labor inflow to describe the context.

Context of Coordinated Economic Growth

Although empirical studies on different international free trade zones have found that the economic growth effect of free trade zone construction is uncertain, some domestic research conclusions can be summarized as follows: free trade zone construction can promote trade growth by 1.0–3.4 percentage points (Table 7.3), thus promoting coordinated economic growth among regions. Given the fact that GBA is one of the most developed areas in the pan-PRD core area and even in China's foreign trade, based on simulation in free trade zone construction situation, according to the median value principle, we assume that would promote the import and export trade volume increases by 1.5%, which will be considered as the scenario of coordinated economic growth of combined free trade ports. Due to the long-term nature of the collaborative construction of the free trade zone, it is set to start from the initial state and reach the regulatory target in 2035.

Context of Scientific and Technological Innovation Synergy

Due to the lack of quantitative expression basis for the relationship between the free trade zone and scientific and technological innovation, the cooperative situation of scientific and technological innovation under the policy of collaborative construction of combined free trade ports was formulated by setting regulatory targets based on the current situation. It can be seen that the average intensity of R&D investment in the nine cities of Guangdong Province in GBA was 2.9% in 2017 based on the proportion of R&D investment in GDP of the whole society, among which Shenzhen's investment has the highest intensity, up to 4.3%; other cities' are basically between 1.0% and 2.5%. According to the goals set out in the *Outline Development Plan for the Guangdong-Hong Kong-Macao Greater Bay Area*, an open regional collaborative innovation community will be built in the GBA, which requires cities to promote the free and orderly exchange of resources. It is expected that the gap between the other cities and Shenzhen, the benchmark city of science and technology innovation, will be narrowed. Taking into account the international experience that the R&D investment intensity of post-industrialized countries generally reaches 2.5% to 3.0%, we set that from now to 2035, the average R&D investment intensity of the nine cities in Guangdong Province in GBA will gradually reach 3.5%, an overall increase of about 0.6%.

Context of Talent and Labor Flow

The coordinated construction of the combined free trade ports of GBA will likely drive a large inflow of external talent and labor force, thus expanding the size of the permanent resident population in the region. At the same time, the carrying capacity of sources such as medical and higher education in the GBA is also facing great challenges, which is in urgent need to match with the economic development and public service construction in the GBA. Under the interaction of population and economic growth, the trend of changes in the level of public services and social security in the GBA will be explored. Combined with other domestic collaborative development scenarios, 0.5% can be taken as a regulatory parameter and it is assumed that the population growth rate will gradually increase by 0.5% from now to 2035 (Fang et al., 2019).

Based on the above assumptions about regulation and control, the regulation and control table of policy parameters of combined free trade ports collaborative construction scenario is generated (Table 7.4).

Table 7.4 The regulation and control table of policy parameters of combined free trade ports collaborative construction scenario

Name of scenario	Policy implementation scenario		Policy non-implementation scenario	
	Expectation of policy effect	Regulation and control of variable parameter	Expectation of policy effect	Regulation and control of variable parameter
Coordinated economic growth	Import and export trade growth	Increase by 1.5% by 2035	Initial state	Maintenance of the historical trend
Synergy of scientific and technological innovation	Increase in the R & D funds	3.5%	Initial state	2.9%
Talent and labor inflow	Growth in the permanent resident population	Increase 0.5% by 2035	Initial state	Maintenance of the historical trend

7.2 Simulation Analysis of Economic Value

7.2.1 *Analysis of the Economic Value of GBA Combined Ports*

7.2.1.1 Free Flow of Production Factors

Under the premise of controllable risk, we explore to build a more open, fair, transparent and efficient management system for entry-exit, finance, investment, trade and foreign exchange, so as to promote the free and convenient flow of elements such as logistics, flow of people, capital and information, as well as the high-quality economic development, all of which will be completed by means of developing onshore trading and settlement center for RMB offshore business, offshore trade, entrepot trade, cross-border e-commerce and international trade "single window", etc..

7.2.1.2 Expanding Hong Kong's Development Space and Activating Its Leverage Role

We should consolidate and enhance the status of Hong Kong as an international financial center, trade center and shipping center, by means of exploring the mode and path of co-building Shenzhen-Hong Kong free trade port, realize mutual support and complementarity between Shenzhen and Hong Kong, and achieve differentiated construction and development along with Shanghai and other places, so as to enrich the practice of exploring the construction of a free trade port in China.

7.2.1.3 Forming an International Port Chain

We will promote the establishment of an international port chain in Shenzhen. We will actively carry out port cultural exchange activities, and enhance the international influence and popularity of the Shenzhen International Logistics and Supply Chain Fair (CILF), the Trans-Pacific Maritime Asia Conference, and the 21st Century Maritime Silk Road International Cooperation Port Forum. We will study the preparation of a Shenzhen Port Maritime Silk Road International Port and Shipping Training Base, and actively carry out cooperation in training seafarers from countries and regions along the Maritime Silk Road. Shenzhen Port shall accelerate the establishment of a global friendship port network in an all-round and multi-channel manner, expand the areas of exchange and cooperation, encourage the port and shipping industry to "go abroad", deeply integrate into the global industrial chain and value chain, enhance the Port's status as an "international port", and promote the formation of an international port chain combined free trade ports can play an irreplaceable key role in promoting China's opening-up, enhancing the momentum of outward economic development, and promoting the adjustment and change of the world economic pattern (Li Shanzhong, 2019).

7.2.1.4 Reducing the Trade Costs of Enterprises and Building Fast Customs Clearance Channels for Some Goods

A new model will be adopted to speed up customs clearance and reduce trade costs for enterprises. Specifically, we can actively promote the construction of a China (Shenzhen) "Single Window" for international trade, so as to realize "information exchange, mutual recognition of supervision and mutual assistance of law enforcement" among relevant departments of port management; to promote new customs clearance models such as "joint inspection and one-time release", and comprehensively promote "one-stop operation"; to promote the "integration of multiple certificates" for the filing of inspection and quarantine enterprises and commercial records, and promote the mode of "integration of zones and ports" and "pre-clearance"; to forge ahead the construction of the "Intelligent Inspection Port" platform, and promote step by step the information exchange and mutual recognition of inspection and certification bodies at home and abroad, and build fast customs clearance channels for some goods.[1]

---

[1] Wang Liying. The preliminary establishment of free trade port at the end of 2020 [N]. Shenzhen Special Zone Daily, 2018-06-21.

7.2.2 *The Theoretical Connotation of Economic Value of Combined Free Trade Ports*

7.2.2.1 The Relationship Between Free Trade and Economic Value

The promoting effect of import and export trade on a country's economic growth has always been one of the hot topics of academic discussion. From a theoretical perspective, the economic value of the development of free trade can be analyzed from the dimension of the effective allocation of world resources (Rodrik, 1992). Specifically, domestic and foreign scholars have demonstrated the economic value of free trade from the perspective of regional comparative advantage. The theory of regional comparative advantage is developed on the base of the theory of comparative cost of British economist David Ricardo, in combination with the theory of factor endowment (Ruffin, 2002). The basic viewpoint of the theory of regional comparative advantage is that regional comparative advantage is formed due to the significant difference of resource endowment in different regions. This theory mainly explains the influence of the comparative advantages of different regions on the allocation of resources. According to the theory of regional comparative advantage, each region has different comparative advantages, so each region should make use of its comparative advantages to rationally allocate resources and realize sustainable development through complementary advantages (Xing Jie, 2013). Due to various factors such as geography, resource endowment and policy, the key industries and service objects of different free trade ports will show certain differences. Taking Shanghai port and Ningbo Zhoushan port as an example, as early as 2005, Xi Jinping, then Secretary of the Zhejiang Provincial Committee, pointed out that "Zhoushan port is not only a part of Shanghai international shipping center, but also part of the integration of Ningbo and Zhoushan port". After the two centers came together, it has also become a centre, a "typhoon eye". New York - New Jersey ports in the United States are combined ports. Shanghai port is mainly for middle and high-end while Ningbo-Zhoushan ports are mainly for middle and low-end, which is featured by complementary functions and dislocation development, and should come into being combined ports in the future (Li Shanzhong, 2019). The construction of FTA combined ports can realize the differentiation positioning of different FTA ports, maximize their advantages, avoid detours, give full play to the synergistic effect, and enhance the competitiveness of China's FTA ports in the world.

7.2.2.2 The Relationship Between Scientific and Technological Innovation and Economic Value

With the deepening of economic globalization, scientific and technological innovation plays an important role in promoting national economic growth, and plays an important role in promoting a country's regional industrial upgrading and import and export trade level. In the literature related to scientific and technological innovation and import and export trade, R. M. Solow Growth Model shows that technological progress also plays an important role in economic growth, in addition to the three factors of capital growth rate, labor growth rate and the weight of the relative effects of capital and labor on income growth. Patick et al. (1989) analyzed the impact of resource endowment, technology and economies of scale on the international competitiveness of OECD member states, and found that technology-intensive industries are largely dependent on R&D. Anderton (1999) analyzed the relationship between Australia's R&D input in intensive industries and trade import and export through empirical research, and found that the increase of R&D expenditure had a promoting effect on the level of import and export. At the same time, the rapid development of scientific and technological innovation will drive the development of high-tech industrial sectors, thus changing the product structure of trade. Zhao Jingmin (2009) discussed the relationship between scientific and technological innovation and foreign trade growth in Jiangsu Province, and found that the R&D expenses of scientific and technological innovation were highly correlated with export trade. Huang Zhifei (2016) made an empirical econometric analysis of the relationship between the agglomeration of scientific and technological innovation elements and foreign trade and economic growth in Guangdong from the dimensions of economic scale and structure, and found that scientific and technological innovation elements played a promoting role in the expansion of foreign trade scale and structural adjustment at the same time.

7.2.2.3 Adequate Circulation of Production Factors

Factors that play an important role in innovation include the allocation of some key people, good internal and external communication mechanism, effective cross-functional connection, etc. By setting up a combination of free trade ports and through exchanges and cooperation among different free trade ports, we should build a collaborative innovation center to guide the aggregation of technologies, capital and talents, and form a complete and efficient innovation network, so as to further promote innovation and support high-quality economic development.

7.2.2.4 Efficiency of Cargo Clearance

The efficiency of customs clearance plays an important role in reducing the trade cost of enterprises. Taking Shenzhen Port as an example, international transit business is one of its key functions, and its core elements are closely related to the efficiency of customs clearance. By giving the free trade port more autonomy in reform, simplifying the cargo clearance procedures and improving the efficiency of cargo clearance under the premise of controllable risks, the trade cost of enterprises can be effectively reduced, and the rapid development of the free trade port area can be realized while supporting the growth of enterprises.

7.2.3 *The Economic Value Simulation Analysis of the Combined Ports*

As shown in Fig. 7.3, the SD equation modeling and parameter regulation indicate that the implementation of the policy of coordinated construction of combined free trade ports will have cumulative amplification effects on variables such as import and export trade and economic scale. According to the prediction of the current development model, by 2035, the total import and export trade of the nine cities of Guangdong Province will reach 11,764.2 billion yuan, with an annual growth rate of 3.36% compared with 6,488.3 billion yuan in 2017, and the implementation of the coordinated construction policy of combined free trade ports will eventually increase by 1,545.6 billion yuan. By 2035, the GDP of the nine municipalities of Guangdong Province will reach RMB 18,077.9 billion, with an annual growth rate of 4.95% compared with RMB 7,571 billion in 2017 (calculated at current prices), and the implementation of the policy of coordinated construction of combined free trade ports will eventually increase by RMB 5,048.2 billion. Although the scale of foreign trade can be expanded, scientific and technological innovation also increases the endogenous impetus for economic growth, leading to a steady decline in the level of opening to the outside world, which finally stabilizes at 57%, reducing the risk of economic dependence on the outside world to a certain extent. This also verifies to some extent that the synergistic construction of free trade zones and foreign trade dependence do not always promote each other, which can also have an inhibiting effect (Liao Liangmei et al., 2019). However, this does not mean that the coordinated

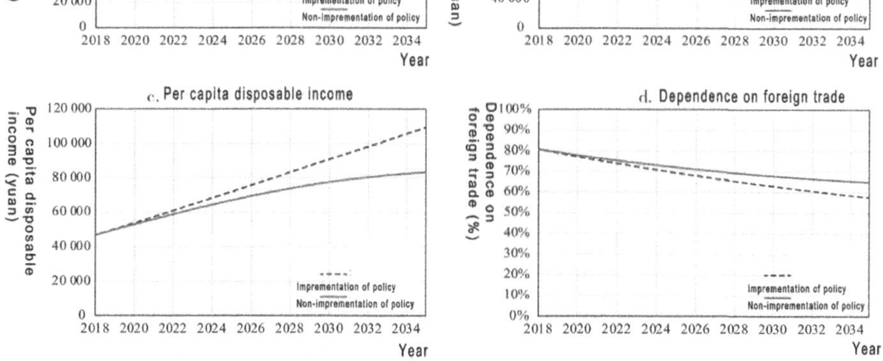

Fig. 7.3 Simulation results of economic value of combined free trade ports

construction of free trade zones may also lead to a decline in the level of economic openness. Instead, it should be viewed dialectically from the aspects of promoting endogenous growth and high-quality outward development.

7.3 Simulation Analysis of Social Value

7.3.1 Analysis of the Current Social Value of the Combined Ports of the GBA

7.3.1.1 Upgrading Urbanization and Creating a Sound Business Environment

Urbanization has been further enhanced. China's urbanization level has reached 59.58%, not far from 70%. But to be precise, a large number of people live in towns or outer suburbs and do not enjoy high level of urban public services. The urbanization in the next stage should be transferred from towns to cities. The GBA has pioneered a high level of urbanization. Hong Kong and Macao are already close to 100% urbanized. In 2018, the urbanization rate of the nine cities in Guangdong Province in the GBA was 69.85%, much higher than the national average, with Shenzhen's urbanization rate of permanent residents exceeding 90%.

The key to a good employment environment is to create a sound business environment. The business environment is the productivity, but also the vitality. Cities in the GBA attach importance to improving their business environment. It is included in *The Opinions of Shenzhen Municipal People's Government on Accelerating the Development of Shenzhen Port* that by reviewing and standardizing service charges related to business operations, suspending the entry-exit inspection and quarantine fees, and by measures such as lowering quarantine charges, we will create a world-class business environment and further reduce the proportion of inspection of import and export goods and the institutional cost of customs clearance. Moreover, we will, on a pilot basis, purchase services from the government to bear the costs of recruiting auxiliary personnel for investigation, optimize customs clearance services, in order to build a world-class port with "*the fastest speed, the lowest cost, the best facilities and the best service*", and establish a stable, fair, transparent and predictable business environment in line with the prevailing rules of international trade. We will continue to improve the credit-based supervision system during and after the event, and give full play to the role of social supervision and intermediary agencies. We will make every effort to promote "Internet + Government administration" services to enable government departments to share information and comprehensively enforce law. The functions of the three internet platforms, namely, the online government affairs hall, public credit information service, and supervision information during and after the event, have been continuously improved, and the implementation has achieved remarkable results. We will relax the threshold for access to international capital markets and reduce prior approval. We will vigorously improve the management of "national treatment before admission + negative list management", shifting the examination and approval system for foreign investment outside the negative list to a record system, and achieve key reforms in the foreign investment management system. We will also actively accelerate the reform of modern commercial system such as "separation of business license and operation permit", "integration of three licenses", "one license and one code" (Peng Lan and Zhao Wenyu, 2018).

7.3.1.2 Perfecting Infrastructure for the Construction of an International Shipping Hub

Under the guidance of the principle of "one country, two systems" and based on the platform of Qianhai Shekou Free Trade Zone, we will further reform the procedures for facilitating customs clearance in the Shenzhen-Hong Kong port area, implement the pilot "Shenzhen-Hong Kong Free Trade Link", open up a direct logistics corridor between Qianhai and Hong Kong, explore the joint construction of Shenzhen-Hong Kong composite port, and build an integrated logistics service system in the port area. Through in-depth docking and integration with Hong Kong, we will realize the comprehensive docking of port and shipping policies and standards, optimize the pilotage service at the boundary between Guangdong and Hong Kong, deepen the division of labor and cooperation between Shenzhen and Hong Kong, extend the value chain of Shenzhen Hong Kong port shipping cooperation, enhance the value-added service capacity of Shenzhen Hong Kong port and shipping, and promote closer cooperation between Shenzhen and Hong Kong in the trade of goods and services, modern shipping service industry and "going abroad" to build an international shipping center with lower cost and higher efficiency. The Shenzhen municipal government also vigorously provides financial support. For example, it established the Shenzhen port and shipping development industry sub fund by means of the government guidance fund; gave priority to projects related to green collection and distribution; supported international shipping projects and operational projects such as cruise routes, cruise passengers and water passenger transport routes.[2]

7.3.1.3 Forming a High-Quality Living Circle

Quality educational resources in the GBA have begun to flow. The GBA has excellent educational resources. All parts of the GBA have been making great efforts in recent years to access the educational resources and realize the flow of high-quality educational resources. Higher education resources have become the driving force for sustainable economic development under the new normal. Shenzhen has cooperated with the University of Hong Kong, the Chinese University of Hong Kong

[2] Wang Liying. Shenzhen's Plan to promote the construction of free trade port [N]. China Ocean News, June 26, 2018.

and the Hong Kong University of Science and Technology to establish the Shenzhen Graduate School of the University of Hong Kong, the Chinese University of Hong Kong (Shenzhen) and the Shenzhen Research Institute of the Hong Kong University of Science and Technology respectively. Guangzhou municipal government plans to cooperate with Hong Kong University of Science and Technology to set up a campus of Hong Kong University of Science and Technology in Nansha. In addition to higher education, different regions in the GBA are also cooperating on basic education. There are 54 international schools in Hong Kong, where there is mature school-running and strong international atmosphere. Guangzhou, Shenzhen and other places have made great efforts to introduce high-quality international school resources from Hong Kong to carry out cooperation in running schools. It is a trend to integrate online and offline high-quality basic education resources by using Internet technology for the integrated development of basic education in the GBA. New Oriental, the leading enterprise, is cooperating with schools in Hong Kong to introduce high-quality education resources and education management system, or taking a stake in international schools in Hong Kong to deliver high-quality education resources to New Oriental schools in Shenzhen, Zhuhai, Zhongshan, Huizhou, Dongguan and Guangzhou.

Medical resources began to flow across the border. The medical level of Hong Kong is at the forefront of the world, and that of Guangzhou is also at the forefront of China. Medical resources in other areas of the GBA are relatively poor. In recent years, Shenzhen, Zhuhai, Foshan, Dongguan, Zhongshan, Huizhou and other cities have sought cooperation with Hong Kong and Guangzhou to introduce high-quality medical resources. First-class hospitals in Guangzhou have set up branches or cooperative hospitals in Shenzhen, Zhuhai, Huizhou, Zhongshan and Foshan. In cooperation with the University of Hong Kong, Shenzhen established the Hong Kong University Hospital in Shenzhen.

7.3.2 *The Theoretical Connotation of Social Value of Combined Ports*

7.3.2.1 The Relationship Between Free Trade and Human Capital

Human capital is an important resource for national economic development and also an endogenous factor to realize social value. Though Marx's theory of labor value can be regarded as a manifestation of human capital, it did not have a clear definition, hence the role of material capital was emphasized during the period of classical political economics. With the progress of science and technology and the development of social productivity, the research of human capital theory reached its peak in the 1950s and 1960s. Prominent among them are the American economists T.W. Schultz and Gary S. Becker. They analyzed the promoting effect of human capital investment on economic growth from macro and micro perspectives respectively (Becker,

1962; Schultz, 1961). Edward Denison (1962) explored the effect of human capital factors on economic development with the method of econometric analysis, and the results showed that high-tech talents were a powerful driving force for economic growth and development. After the 1980s, the "new economic growth theory" based on the "knowledge economy" began to take shape, and further expounded the role of human capital and education level as endogenous variables on economic growth with mathematical thought. In the research related to the development of free trade and human capital factors, Zhao Jingmin (2006) found that scientific and technological personnel had a significant impact on export trade, and the correlation was the highest. Lin Wen et al. (2019) found in an empirical study on the impact of high-tech talents in Taiwan on trade growth that during 2008–2017, the introduction of high-tech talents was on the rise, and at the same time, it also played a significant role in promoting trade and economic growth. However, in reverse, the research on the impact of trade liberalization on human capital is relatively less extensive. On the theoretical research, the new model based on the factor endowment theory elaborates the impact of trade liberalization on human capital. Wood et al. (1999) explored the relationship between free trade and human capital accumulation and found that free trade has a positive promoting effect on human capital accumulation in developed countries. Acemoglu (2003) analyzed from the perspective of trade liberalization and wage gap of labor force with different skills, and showed that developing countries accelerated the accumulation of human capital in the process of trade liberalization.

7.3.2.2 The Relationship Between Free Trade and Environmental Effect

With the rapid growth of the world economic integration brought about by the liberalization of global trade, all countries, especially the developing countries, pay more and more attention to the ecological and environmental problems. At present, the impact of free trade on environment has become one of the hot topics discussed by scholars at home and abroad. Some scholars believe that free trade will have a negative impact on the environment, and the improvement of trade openness will aggravate the environmental pollution problem in developing countries (Lau et al., 2014; Kanjilal and Ghosh, 2013; Esty and Dua, 1997; Rock, 1996). But other scholars hold that in the long run, trade liberalization will help reduce environmental pollution and have a positive effect. Grossman and Krueger (1991) used the panel data of 42 countries to analyze the relationship between per capita income and ambient air quality, and found that there was an inverted U-shaped relationship between ambient air quality and per capita income, in view of the impact of North American free trade on environmental effects. Panayotou (1997) called this inverted U-shaped relationship the Environmental Kuznets Curve (EKC). Jalil and Mahmud (2009) investigated the impact of trade liberalization on China's per capita carbon dioxide emissions during 1975–2005 based on the EKC model, and concluded that free trade was conducive to environmental pollution reduction. Baghdadi et al. (2013) used the panel data of 182 countries from 1980 to 2008 to analyze the relationship between free trade and ambient air quality, and found that there was a negative effect between the two.

Shahbaz et al. (2015, 2017) analyzed the impact of free trade on carbon dioxide emissions in China and India from 1970 to 2012, and found that the relationship between free trade and carbon emission levels in China was consistent with EKC, while the relationship between free trade and carbon emissions in India was just the opposite.

7.3.2.3 High Urbanization and Optimal Business Environment

It is necessary for free trade port to achieve high urbanization. The urban system with reasonable division of labor and the equal development of urban and rural areas are the embodiment of high urbanization. The institutional environment of combined free trade ports will help to break the dual structure of urban and rural areas and establish a unified land and other social systems between urban and rural areas.

To achieve the optimal business environment is the inevitable requirement of free trade port combined free trade ports are a special regulatory area which is obviously different from other regions in terms of various policies. It achieves unification in currency system, customs system and tax system, and achieves a high level of comprehensive opening to the outside world. The combined ports will realize the freedom of investment, trade, capital, transportation and personnel. In terms of supervision, we should build a highly open system and strengthen the streamlining of administration and decentralization. In terms of supervision, we should build a highly open institutional system and strengthen the efforts to streamline administration and delegate power. Without specific legal provisions, the government usually only supervises a few matters such as dangerous goods and contraband.[3] In terms of customs clearance, it will change the current customs clearance methods and concepts to achieve international standards; in terms of taxation, we will unify the tax systems within the GBA and bring them in line with international standards.

7.3.2.4 Infrastructure Interconnection

Free trade port is not only a harbor and port in a narrow sense, but also a convenient transportation hub integrating customs clearance and goods circulation in a broad sense, including harbor, inland waterway transportation, airport and various transportation lines connecting the harbor and airport. In the future, the development of free trade port should integrate Hong Kong port, Shenzhen port and Guangzhou port, enhance the radiation and driving role of other ports in the Pearl River Estuary to form a world-class ports group, and make full use of the advantages of airports group, high-speed rail network and expressway network in the PRD, so as to promote the integration of large shipping system in Guangdong, Hong Kong and Macao Bay area.

---

[3] Xia Xutian, Liu Yang, Zhong Hua. Heating-up Race among Free Trade Ports– Which Regions Are Expected to Take the Lead in 2018? [N] twenty-first century economic report, January 8, 2018.

At the same time, through the pilot reform of one-time declaration, one-time inspection and one-time release of multimodal transport from Zhongshan and Dongguan to Shenzhen, we will strengthen the business ties between Shenzhen port and Guangdong, Hong Kong and Macao Bay area and surrounding ports, and steadily realize the integration of Guangdong, Hong Kong and Macao port customs clearance. Through the construction of free trade combination port, we can further improve the transportation system of Guangdong, Hong Kong and Macao, and promote the smooth flow of goods.

7.3.2.5 A Quality Living Circle Suitable for Living and Traveling

Education highland is an important requirement for the construction of free trade composite port. China's economy has entered a stage driven by innovation at the source. The most fundamental driving force of source innovation lies in the quality education system. The establishment of an education system that includes high-quality basic education, higher education and vocational education will be a requirement and an important result of the construction of the combined port of free trade. It is an important requirement for the construction of combined free trade ports to promote the aggregation and flow of talents. A number of high-quality universities and colleges have been established in cities in the GBA such as Hong Kong, Macao, Shenzhen, Guangzhou, Zhongshan etc. The construction of combined free trade ports can build a bridge for talent exchange and training, and provide excellent opportunities for the flow of intellectual capital in the GBA. In addition, by optimizing the cross-border endorsement process, it will facilitate the endorsement process and promote the further flow of talents.

Gathering and providing high quality medical resources is also an important requirement for the construction of combined free trade ports. The improvement of medical level is the main force to prolong human life and improve the quality of human life. With the progress of science and technology, human resources will be the most important strategic resources in the future. Both the government and enterprises have attached more and more importance to the "people-centered" strategy, and the actions taken have achieved their goals by directly or indirectly affecting people and groups. In order to improve the quality and quantity of human resources, high-quality medical resources are an important starting point. A key to the success of the construction of combined free trade ports is to gather and create high-quality medical resources and high-quality human resources.

7.3.3 *Simulation Analysis of Social Value of Combined Ports*

According to the simulation results of system dynamics, as shown in Fig. 7.4, the implementation of the policy scenario of collaborative construction of combined free trade ports will promote the inflow of external talents and labor force, and at the

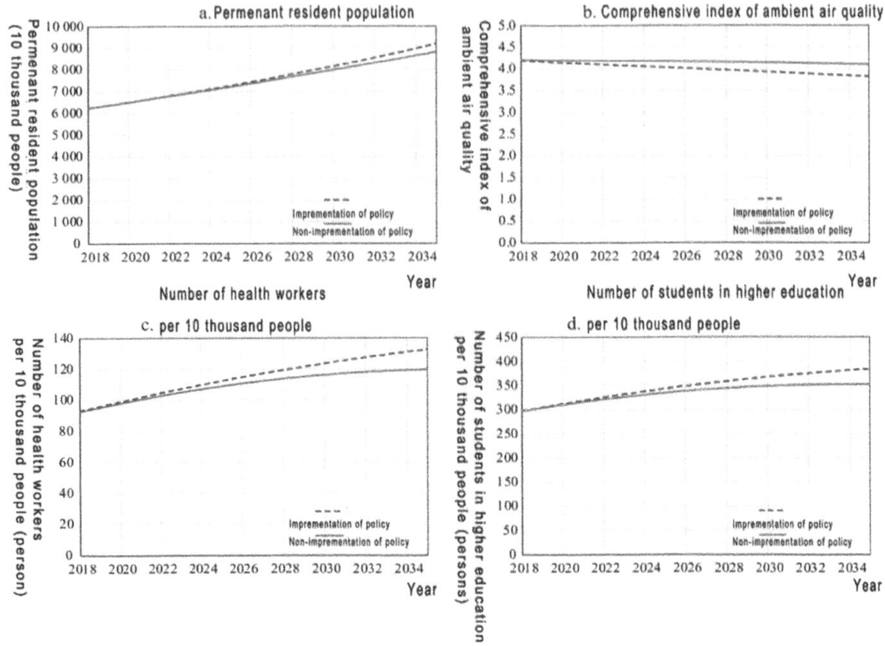

Fig. 7.4 Simulation results of social value of combined free trade ports

same time promote the significant improvement of medical care and higher education level through economic development. According to the current population trend, the permanent population of the nine cities in Guangdong will reach 88.22 million by 2035, an annual growth rate of 2% compared with 61.51 million in 2017. According to the statistics released by the Guangdong Statistics Information Network, the average annual growth rate of the permanent resident population in nine cities of Guangdong Province was 2% from 2000 to 2017, and it even climbed to 2.45% in 2018 (the statistical results of *Analysis of Guangdong Population Development Status in 2018*), which further enhanced the population attraction. Prediction results show that the population of attraction will gradually stabilize, which, through the implementation of combined free trade ports, collaborative construction policy, will attract more talent and labor from outside and the Bay Area population agglomeration effect will be further strengthened. According to the prediction, the population of permanent residents will be 91.97 million as of 2035, 3.75 million more than without the free trade port policy, and the number of health workers per 10,000 people and the number of students in institutions of higher learning per 10,000 people will reach 133 and 385 respectively. In addition, the implementation of the policy of coordinated construction of combined free trade ports can also have a positive impact on environmental quality control, which is mainly due to the synergistic improvement of scientific and technological innovation, the decline of the proportion of traditional manufacturing, and the increase of environmental protection input, so as to promote high-quality and green economic development. By 2035, the Ambient Air Quality Composite Index (AQI) will drop to 3.83, 1.26% lower than without the free trade policy, which indicates that the concentration of major pollutants such as SO2, NO2, PM10, PM2.5, CO, O3 will be further reduced.

7.4 Simulation Analysis of Strategic Value

7.4.1 Analysis of Current Strategic Value of the Combined Ports

7.4.1.1 World-Class City Cluster

Relying on the advantages of Hong Kong and Macao as the free and open economy and Guangdong as the leader in reform and opening up, we will continue to deepen reform and expand the opening-up. We will take the lead in building a system and mechanism for high-quality economic development, play a leading role in demonstration, accelerate institutional innovation and advance test, build a modern economic system, better integrate into the global market system, and build a world emerging economy, advanced manufacturing and modern service industry base as well as a world-class city cluster.

7.4.1.2 International Science and Technology Innovation Hub

We should focus on the frontiers of global science, technology and industry development, strengthen the building of innovation platforms, vigorously develop new technologies, new industries, new forms of business and new models, and accelerate the formation of an economic system with innovation as the main driving force and support. We will take solid steps to carry out comprehensive innovation and reform trials, give full play to the strengths of Guangdong, Hong Kong and Macao in scientific research and development and industrial innovation, remove constraints on the free flow of factors of innovation, further stimulate the vitality of all types of innovation entities, and build Guangdong, Hong Kong and Macao into a global hub for scientific and technological innovation and a major source of emerging industries.

7.4.1.3 Construction of the OBOR

We need to better play the role of function and Hong Kong and Macao in the country opening to the outside world, improve the level of economic development in the nine cities in the PRD, promote the international and domestic markets and the effective docking of two resources, participate in international economic cooperation and competition at a higher level, and build an international transportation and logistics hub and international cultural exchange center with important influence.

7.4.1.4 Demonstration Zone for In-Depth Cooperation Between the Mainland and Hong Kong and Macao

We should rely on the good foundation of cooperation between Guangdong, Hong Kong and Macao, give full play to the role of major cooperation platforms such as Qianhai in Shenzhen, Nansha in Guangzhou, and Hengqin in Zhuhai, explore a new mode of coordinated development, deepen the comprehensive and pragmatic cooperation between the nine cities in the PRD and Hong Kong and Macao, promote the convenient and orderly flow of personnel, materials, funds and information, provide new momentum for the development of Guangdong, Hong Kong and Macao, and provide a demonstration for closer cooperation between the mainland and Hong Kong and Macao.

7.4.1.5 Quality Living Circle

A quality living circle that is suitable for living, industry and tourism will be built. We adhere to the people-centered development idea, practice the concept of ecological civilization, make full use of modern information technology, realize the intelligent management of city cluster, give priority to the development of livelihood projects, improve the convenience level of people's life in the GBA, improve the life quality of residents, and provide learning, employment and innovation opportunities for Hong Kong and Macao residents. We should provide more convenient conditions for Industry and life, strengthen multi-cultural exchanges and integration, and build a beautiful bay area with ecological security, beautiful environment, social stability and cultural prosperity.[4]

7.4.2 Theoretical Connotation of Strategic Value of the Combined Ports

7.4.2.1 The Strategic Value of Innovation-Driven Development

We will implement the strategy of innovation-driven development, improve the regional collaborative innovation system, pool international innovation resources, and build an internationally competitive region for innovation and development. We will comprehensively deepen reform, push for new breakthroughs in reform in key areas and key links, unleash the dividends of reform, and facilitate the flow

[4] Source: *Outline Development Plan for the GBA.*

and optimal allocation of various factors of production in the GBA. We will fully implement the strategy of innovation-driven development, deepen innovation cooperation between Guangdong, Hong Kong and Macao, build a regional community of collaborative innovation that is open and integrated for development, pool international innovation resources, improve innovation institutions and policy environment, enhance our ability to commercialize scientific and technological achievements, and build ourselves into a global leader in scientific and technological innovation and a major source of emerging industries. We will steadily carry out experiments in comprehensive innovation and reform in Guangdong, and speed up the building of a national independent innovation demonstration zone. Guangdong, Hong Kong and Macao have outstanding capabilities in scientific and technological research and transformation. There are a number of universities, research institutes, high-tech enterprises and national big science projects that are of national and even global influence in these cities. They have strong attraction for innovation factors and a sound foundation for building themselves into an international scientific and technological innovation center.

We will strengthen cooperation in science, technology and innovation. We will give better play to the role of the Hong Kong and Macao Science and Technology Cooperation Committee between the mainland, Hong Kong and Macao, and encourage Hong Kong and Macao to integrate into the national innovation system and play a more important role. We should give full play to the technological and industrial advantages of Guangdong, Hong Kong and Macao, actively attract and align global innovation resources, and build an open, interconnected and rationally distributed regional innovation system. We will advance the building of the Guangzhou-Shenzhen-Hong Kong-Macao Science and Technology Innovation Corridor, explore policies and measures to facilitate the cross-border flow and regional integration of innovation factors such as talent, capital, information and technology, and jointly build a big data center and an international innovation platform in GBA. We will speed up the development of national innovation demonstration zones, national demonstration bases for entrepreneurship and innovation, and makerspaces, support them in establishing mechanisms of exchange for innovation and entrepreneurship with Hong Kong and Macao, share innovation and entrepreneurship resources, and work together to improve the innovation and entrepreneurship ecosystem, so as to provide more opportunities and better conditions for young people in Hong Kong and Macao to make innovation and entrepreneurship. We will encourage enterprises and research institutions in Guangdong, Hong Kong and Macao to participate in international cooperation in science and technology innovation, jointly organize science and technology innovation activities, support enterprises to set up R&D institutions and innovation incubation bases overseas, and encourage domestic and foreign investors to set up research and development institutions and innovation platforms in Guangdong, Hong Kong and Macao. We will support the establishment of the "One Belt And One Road" Life Science and Technology Promotion Alliance based on the Shenzhen National Gene Bank. We will encourage universities, research institutions and enterprises from other regions to participate in scientific and technological innovation activities in the GBA.

We will strengthen the construction of basic capacity for innovation. We will support the development of major scientific and technological infrastructure, major research institutions and major innovation platforms in the GBA. We will open in an orderly manner to Hong Kong and Macao the major national research infrastructure facilities and large-scale research equipment built in Guangdong. We will support relevant institutions in Guangdong, Hong Kong and Macao in taking an active part in national science and technology plans (special projects, funds, etc.). We will strengthen applied basic research and expand and implement major national science and technology projects. We will support measures taken by Guangdong, Hong Kong and Macao to deepen reform of their innovation systems and mechanisms as part of the pilot reform of comprehensive innovation.

We will strengthen the integration of enterprises, universities and research institutes. We will establish a technological innovation system featuring enterprises as the mainstay, the market as the orientation, and the deep integration of enterprises, universities and research institutes, support enterprises, universities and research institutes in Guangdong, Hong Kong and Macao to jointly build high-level collaborative innovation platforms, and promote the application of scientific and technological achievements. We will implement the Guangdong-Hong Kong-Macao Technology and Innovation Co-operation Development Plan and the Guangdong-Hong Kong Joint Innovation Funding Scheme, and support the establishment of a Guangdong-Hong Kong-Macao industry-university-research innovation alliance.[5]

7.4.2.2 The strategic Value of Regional Synergy Development

We will implement the strategy of coordinated development among regions, give full play to the comparative advantages of each region, strengthen policy coordination and planning coherence, optimize the distribution of regional functions, promote coordinated development between urban and rural areas in different regions, and make development more integrated.

The GBA ports, as the important hub of international integrated transport system, is an important support for building a national central city and a comprehensive gateway city, an important carrier for building an international shipping center, and a strategic gateway infrastructure for building a modern industrial system, promoting coordinated regional development, connecting the global economic and trade market and participating in the industrial system of economic globalization. Optimization of coordinated development of the GBA ports must be embedded into the national concept of the new development. We will implement the supply-side structural reform and integrate it into the modern power strategies such as national construction of traffic power, marine power, trading power, network power and the regional coordinated development strategy, etc., so as to contribute to building a well-off society in an all-round way and embarking on the new journey to fully build a modern socialist country.

[5] Source:*Outline Development Plan for the GBA*.

7.4.2.3 Strategic Value of High Quality Development

It is another important requirement for the coordination and optimization of the port groups in the PRD to promote the upgrading of the port industry, which is dominated by the construction of a complete industrial ecosystem, and realize the transformation of the port group from the extensive growth model based on speed to the high-quality development based on kinetic energy and efficiency.

In addition, theGBA should play an important role in the national BRI by actively participating in the construction of a new pattern of "One Core, One Belt and One Zone" based on national strategic needs. In particular, we will give full play to the role of Guangdong and Hong Kong as the core fulcrum and hub of internal and external linkage and coordination on land and sea. We will guide the coordinated opening-up of various areas in the region and enable Hong Kong to give full play to its economic and geographical advantages in promoting the OBOR construction. Imbalanced development between urban and rural areas is the biggest shortcoming in Guangdong's high-quality development. The development pattern of "One Core, One Belt and One Zone" is a major measure to implement the spirit of General Secretary Xi Jinping's important speech to Guangdong, and it is the general starting point for Guangdong to promote coordinated regional development at present and in the future. In accordance with the instructions and requirements of President Xi, we need to give full play to the leading role of the central cities of the GBA, fully implement the new regional development strategy with functional zones in the lead, and promote the implementation of the new regional development pattern of "One Core, One Belt and One Zone". We will strengthen the radiation-driving role of central cities. The core region of the PRD should seize the important strategic opportunity of the construction of the GBA, optimize and upgrade its central cities, take the four central cities of Hong Kong, Macao, Guangzhou and Shenzhen as the core engines of regional development, continue to give full play to its comparative advantages, and enhance its role in leading the Belt and Road Initiative and the One Area Initiative. We will build growth poles in the coastal economic belt. The coastal economic belt should rely on large projects and industrial parks to continuously expand the industrial scale, upgrade the industrial chain, and build a world-class coastal industrial belt. We will promote the construction of ecological protection areas in northern Guangdong, strengthening the role of "One Zone" as an ecological protective screen. Bearing deep in mind the development concept that "Clear waters and green mountains are as valuable as mountains of gold and silver", we shall improve relevant policies and mechanisms for the ecological development zone in northern Guangdong, which will be guided to follow the path of ecological and green development. We will improve systems and mechanisms for coordinated development and strengthen the concept of regarding "the development of the whole province as playing a chess game", and improve the provincial financial transfer payment system, regional ecological compensation mechanism, regional support and cooperation mechanism, infrastructure investment and financing system, and the mechanism for promoting equal access to basic public services.

7.4.3 Evaluation System of Strategic Value of the Combined Ports

As a pioneer of reform and opening up, Shenzhen proposes a statistical index evaluation system with five development concepts as the core for the construction of high-quality development framework. Adhering to quality-led and innovation-driven development, it takes the lead in quality-oriented growth and connotative development. Meanwhile, it carries out dynamic evaluation on the effectiveness of the implementation of the new development concepts on the base of the evaluation index system of the five development concepts.[6]

Specifically, the basic level of economic development can be represented by output benefit, structural optimization and economic security. Output benefits can be measured by per capita GDP, gross economic ecological product (GEEP), labor productivity of the whole society, asset contribution rate, industrial added value, total factor productivity and total factor energy efficiency, etc.. Structural optimization can be measured by comprehensive industrial capacity utilization, tax revenue, investment in fixed assets, added value of knowledge-intensive industries, household consumption expenditure, and contribution rate of scientific and technological progress, etc. And the economic security can be measured by the ratio of non-performing loans, the proportion of current account, the proportion of outstanding debts and the proportion of grain imports and exports.

The innovation-driven level is represented by human capital, research and development activities, scientific research achievements and innovation quality. Human capital can be represented by the number of new PhD graduates, the number of people who have received higher education, the number of people who have received college education or above and the full-time equivalent of research and development personnel. The situation of R&D activities can be represented by the proportion of R&D expenditure, the proportion of basic research expenditure, the number of enterprises implementing comprehensive innovation and the non-manufacturing R&D investment. Scientific research achievements are measured by the number of patented inventions, the number of patented inventions of high-tech enterprises, the rate of patent income, the per capita turnover of technology market and the conversion rate of scientific and technological achievements. The quality of innovation can

[6] Referring to the assessment method of economic development quality proposed in Quality Innovation and China's Economic Development (Cheng Hong, 2017), the evaluation index system is an important method to objectively measure the quality of economic development. The evaluation index system is an organic whole with internal structure which is composed of multiple indexes representing all aspects of the evaluation object and their interrelation. In view of the strategic value of the combined free trade ports, not any single index can make a comprehensive and accurate evaluation. In view of the strategic value of the free trade combined port, any single index can not make a comprehensive and accurate evaluation. We should build an evaluation index system to assess the strategic value of the combined free trade ports from perspectives of the requirements of the scientific outlook on development and the effectiveness, adequacy, coordination, innovation, stability and sustainability of the strategic development.

be represented by the efficiency of collaborative innovation, the integrated development index of informatization and industrialization, the proportion of middle and high-end manufacturing products, the qualified rate of product quality, the competitiveness index, the sales volume of new products, the dependence of core technology on foreign markets and the market share of independent brands can represent the innovation quality.

The level of synergy development can be measured from four dimensions: regional synergy, industrial synergy, urban–rural synergy and social synergy. Regional synergy can be measured from three aspects: difference index of economic development, service equalization and infrastructure accessibility. Industrial synergy can be represented by the proportion of added value of high-tech industry, added value of service industry and added value of modern service industry. Urban–rural synergy is measured by the income ratio of urban and rural residents, the proportion of urban population and the equalization of public services in urban and rural areas. The level of social synergy can be reflected by Gini coefficient, residents' per capita disposable income, deviation of industrial and employment structures, and basic public service expenditure.

The level of green development can be measured from three aspects: the economical and intensive use of land, environmental governance and ecological protection, the first of which can be represented by resource yield rate, energy consumption intensity, unit water consumption, unit construction land area, sewage utilization rate and probability of water supply, while the second of which can be measured by the total amount of pollutants discharged, the concentration of dust particles, the qualified rate of water, the rate of harmless treatment of domestic garbage, the rate of sewage treatment, the recycling rate of domestic garbage, the rate of green transportation and the rate of qualified green buildings. The level of ecological protection can be measured by the forest coverage rate, the proportion of blue and green spaces, the proportion of arable land area and the proportion of protected farmland.

The level of opening development can be measured mainly from three aspects: trade balance, structure of foreign capital and institutional opening, the first of which can be reflected by the proportion of total imports and exports, the proportion of import and export in general trade, the proportion of service trade, the proportion of high-tech products and the proportion of cross-border trade, while the structure of foreign capital can be represented by the actual utilization of it, and the institutional opening can be measured by the proportion of trade volume in the free trade zone, the excellence index of the free trade zone, the convenience of business environment, the proportion of foreign ownership in the financial industry, the convenience of cross-border transportation and the proportion of foreign tourists, etc..

The level of shared development can be measured by infrastructure and the better life. Infrastructure is mainly measured by the density of urban streets, the popularization rate of tap water in the rural area, the popularization rate of sanitary toilets in the rural area, the intelligent level of infrastructure, the broadband usage rate and the rate of the household settlement of cable radio and television. The better life can be reflected by per capita disposable income, the average life expectancy, the urban green coverage rate, the community living area coverage rate, the average years of education, the basic social security coverage rate, the area for public sports, the number of beds in the medical and health institution, the bus service coverage rate and the per capita area of emergency shelter(see Table 7.5).

7.5 Major Conclusion and Policy Implications

By comparing the implementation and non-implementation of combined free trade ports collaborative construction policy, this section discusses the evolution trend and differences of key economic and social variables, so as to judge the economic strategic value brought by the collaborative construction combined free trade ports in the GBA, and provide important policies references for regional collaborative development under the background of the construction of combined free trade ports.

7.5.1 Major Conclusions

The impact of the construction of the combined free trade ports of GBA on the value of the Bay Area is mainly reflected in three aspects: economic value, social value and strategic value (Table 7.6).

7.5.1.1 Economic Value

Through the simulation of the economic value of the cooperative construction of combined free trade ports, we found that the implementation of the cooperative construction of combined ports will greatly promote the regional import and export trade, and expand its trade scale and economic scale on the original basis. In this process, along with the continuous advancement of scientific and technological innovation, the endogenous driving force of economic growth will continue to be strengthened, thus bringing about a gradual decline in the level of foreign trade and finally stabilizing at a certain level, which reduces the risk of economic dependence on foreign countries to a certain extent. From another point of view, this also reflects that the cooperative construction of the free trade zone and the degree of regional dependence on foreign trade do not always promote each other, which will also have an inhibiting effect in the development process.

7.5.1.2 Social Value

In terms of social value, the implementation of the cooperative construction of combined free trade ports will, to a large extent, bring about an increase in the inflow of labor force and external talents. The aggregation of labor force will promote

Table 7.5 Evaluation indicator system of high quality development strategy

First level indicator	Secondary indicator	Third level indicator
Basic level of economic development	Output benefit	GDP: GDP per capita
		Gross economic ecological product: GEEP
		Labor productivity of the whole society
		Asset contribution ratio
		Industrial added value
		Total factor productivity
		Total factor energy efficiency
	Structure optimization	Comprehensive utilization of industrial production capacity
		Tax revenue
		Investment in fixed assets
		Value added of knowledge-intensive industries
		Household consumption expenditure
		Contribution of scientific and technological progress
	Economic security	Non-performing loan ratio
		The proportion of current projects
		The proportion of debt balance
		The proportion of grain imports and exports
Innovation driven level	Human capital	Number of new PhD graduates
		Number of people with higher education
		Number of people with college education or above
		Full time equivalent of R&D personnel
	Research and development activities	The proportion of R&D expenditure
		Proportion of funding for basic research
		The number of comprehensively innovating enterprises
		Non-manufacturing R&D investment
	Scientific research achievements	Number of patent inventions

(continued)

Table 7.5 (continued)

First level indicator	Secondary indicator	Third level indicator
		Number of patent inventions in high-tech enterprises
		Patent yield
		Per capita turnover of technology market
		Conversion rate of scientific and technological achievements
		Collaborative innovation efficiency
		Integration of the two development index
		The proportion of medium and high-end manufacturing products
	Innovation quality	Product quality pass rate
		Competitiveness index
		New product sales
		Dependence on external core technology
		Market share of independent brands
Coordinated development level	Regional coordination	Economic development difference index
		Service equalization
		Infrastructure accessibility
	Industrial coordination	Value-added of high and new technology industries
		Added value of service sector
		The proportion of added value in the modern service sector
	Coordination of urban and rural areas	Income ratio between urban and rural residents
		Proportion of urban population
		Equal access to public services in urban and rural areas
	Social coordination	The Gini coefficient
		Per capita disposable income of residents

(continued)

Table 7.5 (continued)

First level indicator	Secondary indicator	Third level indicator
		Industry-employment structure deviation degree
Green development level		Expenditure on basic public services
		Resource productivity
		Energy intensity
	The economical and intensive use of land	Unit water consumption
		Area per unit of construction land
		Rate of sewage utilization
		Rate of water supply security
		Total emission of pollutants
		Dust-particle concentration
	Environmental governance	Qualified rate of water
		Harmless disposal rate of household garbage
		The recovery rate on household waste
		Rate of utilization of green transportation
		Compliance rate of green buildings
		Forest coverage
		The proportion of blue and green space
	Ecological protection	The proportion of arable land
		The proportion of farmland protected area
		Proportion of total imports and exports
		General trade import and export ratio
Level of opening and development	The trade balance	Proportion of trade in services
		Proportion of export volume of high-tech products
		Cross-border trade
	The structure of foreign investment	Actual utilization of foreign capital
		The proportion of trade volume in FTA

(continued)

Table 7.5 (continued)

First level indicator	Secondary indicator	Third level indicator
		Free Trade Zone Excellence Index
	Open system	Ease of doing business
		Foreign shareholding ratio in the financial sector
		Cross-border transportation convenience
		The proportion of foreign tourists
Level of shared development	Infrastructure	Density of urban streets
		The popularization rate of tap water in the rural area
		The popularization rate of sanitary toilets in the rural area
		The intelligent level of infrastructure
		The broadband usage rate
		The rate of the household settlement of cable radio and television
		Per capita disposable income of residents
		Average life expectancy
		Urban green coverage
		Community living area coverage
		Average years of education
		Basic social security coverage
	Better life	Area of public sports land
		Number of beds in medical and health institutions
		Bus service coverage
		Per capita area of emergency shelters

economic development and further promote the continuous improvement of higher education and medical level in the region. At the same time, the implementation of the cooperative construction of the combined free trade ports will largely influence the government regulation of environmental quality, which mainly depends on the transformation of the industrial structure brought by the promotion of the scientific and technological innovation and collaboration. In the process of transformation,

Table 7.6 Overview of value simulation analysis of GBA combined ports

Category	Specific impact	Indicator changes (to 2035)
Economic value	The improvement in the import and export trade	An increase of 1545.6 billion yuan in the total of import and export trade
	The expansion of the scale of trade and economy	An increase of 504.82 million yuan in the regional GDP
Social value	Increase in the inflow of labor and external talents	An increase of 3.75 million people in the labor force
	Improvement of higher education and medical level	The increase of 31 and 13 respectively in the number of students in colleges and universities and the number of health workers per 10,000 people
Strategic value	Promoting the establishment of innovation collaboration system in FTZs and accelerating innovation driven development	
	Giving full play to regional comparative advantages and realizing regional coordinated development	
	Industrial innovation driven by institutional innovation to achieve high quality development of free trade zone	

the proportion of the output value of traditional manufacturing industry in the total output value keeps decreasing, while the proportion of the output value of high-tech industry keeps increasing, and the fiscal investment in environmental protection keeps increasing, which will finally realize the high-quality and green development of economy.

7.5.1.3 Strategic Value

The implementation of the cooperative construction of combined ports will promote regional coordination and innovation-driven development in the FTA to achieve high quality development. In terms of innovation-driven development, we need to build a collaborative innovation system in the free trade zone, collect domestic and international innovation resources, improve the basic ability of innovation by continuously promoting scientific and technological innovation cooperation, promote the in-depth integration of industry, education and research, and strive to build an innovative development region with international influence. In terms of regional coordinated development, it is necessary to give full play to the comparative advantages of different regions within the region, and on this basis, carry out planning and policy coordination, and continuously optimize the regional functional layout, so as to achieve regional coordination and overall development. In terms of high-quality development, we need to drive industrial innovation with institutional innovation, deepen financial cooperation to speed up the construction of free trade zone, build international transportation network, strengthen the linkage of Guangdong, Hong Kong and Macao, stimulate the industrial potential of the three places, build a modern industrial system, and strive to build GBA into an international emerging industrial base.

7.5.2 Policy Implications

The comparison of implementing and non-implementing the policy of the coordinated construction of combined free trade ports provides key policy implications for the development of regional coordinated development under the background of the construction of combined free trade ports.

Firstly, we shall expand the economic opening and development of the GBA and promote coordinated economic development within the area. The cooperative construction of combined free trade ports can promote the significant growth of import and export trade, break the trade barriers between regions, and thus promote the coordinated development of regional economy. From the perspective of quantitative analysis, in accordance with the current development model, it is predicted that by 2035, the total import and export trade and regional GDP of the nine cities in Guangdong Province will reach 11,764.2 billion yuan and 18,077.9 billion yuan respectively, with an average annual growth of 3.36% and 4.95% compared with 2017 (calculated at current prices). Provided that the policy of coordinated construction of combined free trade ports is implemented, by 2035, the total import and export trade and the gross regional product of the nine cities in Guangdong Province will increase by 1,545.6 billion yuan and 5,048.2 billion yuan respectively compared with the initial state, and the economic and trade strength will be significantly enhanced, so as to promote the construction of a world-class Bay Area more effectively.

Secondly, we shall encourage the development of an innovation network in the GBA and open up science and technology to each other. We shall promote the free flow of factors of scientific and technological innovation, which will not only effectively foster endogenous motives of economic growth, but also stimulate high-quality development in areas with weak scientific research, and ultimately achieve green and sustainable development in the whole area. According to the simulation results, if the collaborative investment level of scientific research in the nine cities of Guangdong Province increases to 3.5%, the comprehensive index of ambient air quality (which comprehensively reflects the pollution situation of six pollutants such as SO_2, NO_2, PM_{10}, $PM_{2.5}$, CO and O_3) will decrease steadily to 4.04 in 2025 and further to 3.83 in 2035, in other words, the environmental quality is expected to be significantly improved.

Thirdly, we shall guide the rational and orderly inflow of talents and labor from the outside. We learn from the simulation result of permanent residents population, according to the current trend of population change, that the permanent residents population of 9 cities in Guangdong Province will reach 88.22 million in 2035, indicating that the GBA will still have a strong attraction to migrants in the future, but the annual growth rate will gradually slow down to 2% compared with 2.45% in 2018. In order to attract more external talents and labor, the policy of coordinated construction of combined free trade ports can be implemented. By 2035, the permanent residents population of the nine cities in Guangdong Province will increase by 3.75 million, and the population agglomeration effect of the Bay Area will be strengthened. Based on the quantitative prediction results, although the influx of new population can provide sufficient talents and labor force, it will also pose great challenges to the capacity of public services such as medical care and education in the GBA. A step-by-step talent introduction mechanism should be implemented to ensure that talents and labor demand in the region can be effectively addressed and a talent highland can be formed. At the same time, great attention should be paid to the matching of basic public service resources when a large number of talents and labor force enter the region.

Fourthly, we shall multiply the channels for capital investment, building international high-level medical and higher education institutions. According to the feedback structure of the SD model, adequate financial security is the key variable to maintain high-level health care and higher education. According to the forecast results, by 2035, the implementation of the combined ports policy will promote the rapid economic development and significantly enhance the financial strength of the region, which will promote the number of students in colleges and universities and health workers to reach 385 and 133 per 10,000 people respectively. In the future, we should not only promote the development of education and healthcare through financial funds, but also take advantage of the cross-border advantages of the GBA and the opportunities of the coordinated development of the Free Trade Area to improve the level of regional social development through various funding channels.

References

Acemoglu D (2003) Patterns of skill premia. Rev of Econ Stud 70(2):199–230

Anderton R (1999) UK trade performance and the role of product quality, variety, innovation and hysteresis preliminary results. Scott J of Polit 46(5):570–595

Baghdadi L, Martinez-Zarzoso I, Zitouna H (2013) Are RTA agreements with environmental provisions reducing emissions? J of Int Econ 90(2):378–390

Becker G (1962) Investment in human capital a theoretical analysis. J of Polit Econ 70:9–49

Cheng H (2017) Quality Innovation and China's Economic Development, 39–42. Peking University Press

Cui XG (2019) Study on coupling simulation and regulation of urbanization and ecological environment in Beijing-Tianjin-Hebei city cluster. University of Chinese Academy of Sciences

Esty DC, Dua A (1997) Sustaining the Asia Pacific miracle: environmental protection and economic integration. Peterson Institute Press: All Books

Fang C, et al (2019) Modeling regional sustainable development scenarios using the urbanization and eco-environment coupler: case study of Beijing-Tianjin-Hebei city cluster. China. Sci of the Total Environ 689:820–830

Grossman GM, Krueger AB (1991) Environmental impacts of a North American free trade agreement (No. w3914). National Bureau of Economic Research

Huang ZF (2016) An empirical study on science and technology innovation factors and foreign trade economic growth in Guangdong. Guangdong University of Technology
Jalil A, Mahmud SF (2009) Environment Kuznets curve for CO2 emissions: a cointegration analysis for China. Energy Policy 37(12):5167–5172
Kanjilal K, Ghosh S (2013) Environmental Kuznet's curve for India: evidence from tests for cointegration with unknown structural breaks. Energy Policy 56:509–515
Kuang ZJ (2015) Reanalysis of economic effects of China-Japan-ROK Free Trade Zone: a study based on GTAP model. Explor of Econ Probl 3:170–175
Lau LS et al (2014) Investigation of the environmental Kuznets curve for carbon emissions in Malaysia: do foreign direct investment and trade matter? Energy Policy 68: 490–497
Liao LM, Lu TR, Lei YJ (2019) Free trade zone, foreign trade dependence and inland opening highlands. Spec Zone Econ 8:22–24
Li SZ (2019) Building the Zhejiang-Shanghai combined ports and explore the construction of free trade port to provide strong support for the high-quality development of the Yangtze River Economic Belt. China Water Transport 1:14–16
Lin W et al (2019) An empirical study on growth of trade in Taiwan's technological innovation ability—taking Hsinchu science park as an example. J of Fuqing Branch of Fujian Normal Univ (1):60–67
Panayotou T (1997) Demystifying the environmental Kuznets curve: turning a black box into a policy tool. Env and Dev Econ 2(4):465–484
Patick A et al (1989) Resistance to Theiler's murine encephalomyelitis virus (Tmev)-induced demyelination is inherited as a dominant trait in bio congenic mice. J of Neuropathol & Exp Neurol 48(3):120–123
Peng L, Zhao WY (2018) The evolution and development of China's free trade ports. Reg Econ Review 3:14–20
Qiu BX (2017) Preliminary Study on New Rationalism in Urban Planning: From the Perspective of Complex Adaptive System (CAS). Urban Dev Research 1:1–8
Qian J (2019) Study on trade growth effect of FTAAP with China as "wheel axis": based on extended gravity model. The Int Bus Research 40(1):51–59
Rock MT (1996) Pollution intensity of GDP and trade policy: can the World Bank be wrong? World Dev 24(3):471–479
Rodrik D (1992) The rush to free trade in the developing World: why so late? why now? will it last? NBER Working Paper No. w3947, Available at SSRN: https://ssrn.com/abstract=227366
Ruffin RJ (2002) David Ricardo's discovery of comparative advantage. Hist of Polit Econ 34:727–748
Schultz TW (1961) Investment in human capital. Am Econ Rev 51:1–17
Shahbaz M et al (2015) Does globalization impede environmental quality in India? Ecol Ind 52:379–393
Shahbaz M et al (2017) The impact of globalization on CO2 emissions in China. The Singap Econ Rev 62(04):929–957
Wood S (1999) Human resource management and performance. Int J Manag Rev (1):367–413
Xing J (2013) Research on development of "enclave economy" and policy support in Shandong Province. Shandong Normal University
Yang S, Martinez-Zarzoso I (2014) A panel data analysis of trade creation and trade diversion effects: the case of ASEAN-China Free Trade Area. China Econ Review 29:138–151
Ying WJ, Fan BW (2018) Do pilot free trade zones promote regional economic growth? : An empirical study based on four free trade zones in Shanghai, Tianjin, Fujian and Guangdong. East China Econ Mgmt 32(11):5–13
Yu Z, Shen M, Wang Q (2014) On the trade basis and economic effects of China-India FTA: An empirical analysis based on trade flows South Asian Stud (2): 12–27
Zhao JM (2009) A study on science and technology innovation and the change of foreign trade growth pattern: an empirical analysis based on Jiangsu data. China Manag Inform 12(4):75–78

Zhao L (2015) Research on the economic growth effect of China's free trade zone: theory and empirical study. Southeast University
Zhao J (2016) Economic Spillover effect of Shanghai free trade zone: a system dynamics approach. Int Bus Research 37(20):77–86
Zong HM, Zheng LL (2017) Analysis of trade pattern between China and South East Asian countries under the background of "One Belt And One Road." Econ Geogr 37(8):1–9

Chapter 8
Conclusion and Prospects

The development of the GBA has a long way to go. We need to fully draw on advanced experience at home and abroad and explore a development path with Chinese characteristics in light of the reality. This book creatively introduces the combined free trade ports model into the regional synergy development of the GBA, puts forward a new development idea for the construction of the GBA, and also provides a new research direction for academic circles to discuss regional synergy development, free trade port, GBA and other related fields.

8.1 Conclusion

8.1.1 Deepening Reform and Opening up as the Foundation for Building World-Class City Clusters in the GBA

The construction of the GBA is a national strategy planned, deployed and promoted by General Secretary Xi Jinping. It is not only a new practice to enrich the connotation of "one country, two systems" and maintain the long-term prosperity and stability of Hong Kong and Macao, but also an important measure for China to more actively participate in global competition and integrate into the global economic system at a higher level. On February 18, 2019, *Outline Development Plan for the Guangdong-Hong Kong-Macao Greater Bay Area* was officially issued, which sets out the strategic positioning and overall deployment for the two centenary development goals of the GBA, and points out the development direction for different fields in the area such as the science and technology, industry, ecology, institutions, etc.. In general, GBA enjoys unique geographical advantages, leading economic development level in China, complete industrial system, agglomeration of innovative elements and a high level of internationalization, which lays the foundation for building the GBA into an international first-class bay area and a world-class city

© Xiamen University Press 2022

S. Ba et al., *Collaborative Innovation Mechanism of GBA in China*,
https://doi.org/10.1007/978-981-19-2251-0_8

cluster. However, compared with the internationally famous bay areas, the development of the GBA still faces many challenges, such as lower institutional synergy, homogenized competition, unbalanced and mismatched supply and demand structure, unbalanced and unmatched supply and demand structure, production factors with poor flow, less number of innovation platform carriers, less international talents, and industrial structure which is in urgent need of upgrading. None of these challenges can be solved by one region's own efforts in a short period of time. Instead, Guangdong, Hong Kong and Macao need to deepen reform, expand opening-up, coordinate development and achieve mutual benefit under the unified leadership and deployment of the CPC Central Committee, with institutional innovation as the core. On the one hand, we should learn from the advanced international experience of the mature bay areas in regional planning, industrial upgrading and high-level opening up. On the other hand, we should combine the particularity and flexibility of "one country, two systems" in the GBA to explore a path of high-quality regional coordinated development that is different from other bay areas in the world.

8.1.2 Promoting Regional Synergy Development as the Key to Building a World-Class Bay Area

According to the report of the 19th National Congress of the Communist Party of China, regional coordinated development is one of the important strategies to build a modern economic system, and the construction of the GBA is further regarded as an important part of regional coordinated development. The development experience of the three bay areas in the world, the Beijing-Tianjin-Hebei region and the Yangtze River Delta city cluster in China shows that the key to improving the overall efficiency and international competitiveness of the region is to achieve unified planning, complementary advantages and coordinated development. First, a multi-level regional coordination mechanism with multi-party participation shall be established. In light of the international perspective, the regional collaborative development in the three bay areas is often jointly promoted by organizations of different natures, including government agencies (central or federal governments and local governments at all levels), non-governmental statutory agencies, public and private enterprises, and non-profit consulting agencies. In light of Chinese domestic experience, at the government level of the Yangtze River Delta city cluster, a three-level regional cooperation mechanism is implemented, including the main leaders' forum of the Yangtze River Delta region, the Yangtze River Delta Regional Cooperation and Development Joint Meeting and the key cooperation task group. Secondly, spatial synergy is an important factor in the regional collaborative development. On the one hand, it is not only essential to realize the regional transport infrastructure connectivity, but also necessary to optimize the layout of the transport network including the expressways, railways, urban rail and inland waterways.

On the other hand, the coordination of land use should be enhanced. Different optimization and adjustment strategies should be formulated in terms of controlling excessive investment in land area, improving environmental benefits, and strengthening regional spatial integration, etc.. Thirdly, industrial cooperation is an important way to promote the coordinated development of regional economy. Industrial synergy can promote the mutual supply, efficient integration and optimal allocation of production factors within the region, and help to stimulate the coupling induction of factors, technology ripple effect, industrial correlation effect and symbiotic economic effect in the process of industrial development. Tokyo established Keihin and Keiye Industrial areas in coastal areas in the Tokyo Bay, including industries such as steel, non-ferrous metallurgy, petrochemical, electronics, automobile, shipbuilding, modern logistics, etc., which were closely interacted with the functions of the hinterland of Tokyo including finance, corporate headquarters, research and development, energy, etc., and eventually developed into the world's largest, most advanced and most powerful new industrial zone. The city cluster in the Yangtze River Delta has also gradually established an industrial system with Shanghai as the leading city, with orderly and gradient internal structure, complementation, cooperation and effectiveness within the region. In addition, establishing regional collaborative development funds, jointly building regional large-scale projects, building talent exchange platforms, and connecting regional public services with social security are all advanced experiences in promoting regional collaborative development, which should be learned by GBA.

8.1.3 Free Ports Being the Key to the Formation of an Innovative Economic System and Development Model in the GBA

Free trade port, with the policy core of free investment, free trade, free capital, convenient personnel access and preferential tax, is a special economic functional zone with the highest level of openness in the world. It is also the development direction of the GBA's high-level opening to the outside world, high-quality participation in global competition and high-level participation in global governance. Hong Kong, Singapore and Dubai possess internationally recognized successful free trade ports. The successful experience of building free trade ports in the three places mainly includes the following aspects: in terms of investment freedom, there were no restrictions on the business term, business scope and shareholding ratio of foreign-invested enterprises except in some special fields; in terms of capital freedom, investment and financing exchange are relatively free, and capital flows across borders are free; in terms of trade freedom, the customs clearance of goods is convenient, the international trade settlement is free and the international shipping is free; in terms of tax preference, the policy of simple and low tax rate is implemented, with less tax categories and lower tax rate. Except for some special commodities such as tobacco and alcohol, general import or export goods are not charged with any tariff; in terms of customs clearance for personnel, the visitors and tourists engaged in business activities are provided with convenient entry and exit measures, and the flow of population and labor force enjoys a great extent of freedom and internationality.

8.1.4 Combined Ports Initiative Being the Core for Turning GBA into a World Benchmark

The essence of the combined free trade ports of GBA is to explore the introduction of the free trade port model to the GBA. The regional synergy development of the GBA is to explore a new mode of regional development, which is to introduce the free trade port mode into the regional development of the GBA, taking institutional synergy as the core, spatial synergy, industrial synergy, financial synergy, scientific innovation synergy, governance synergy and talent synergy as the focus, so as to promote the efficient and convenient flow of production factors in the region. Specifically, then GBA should make full use of the advantages of Hong Kong, draw on the development experience of Singapore and Dubai, learn from the advanced measures of regional coordination of the three international bay areas, and realize leap-forward development through a series of coordinated measures. In terms of institutional synergy, we will gradually explore synergy with Hong Kong and Macao in the fields of tax system, rule of law, currency system and customs system, etc. In terms of spatial synergy, a beaded pattern with an axial belt support and "one pole, three main areas and multiple targets" will be constructed, and a regional comprehensive transportation grid system integrating land, sea and air transport will be built. In terms of industrial synergy, a comprehensive industrial bay area featuring technological innovation industries, high-end manufacturing industries and modern service industries will be built, as well as an industrial cluster network and an industrial collaborative innovation ecosystem. In terms of financial synergy, the inter-connectivity of financial infrastructure, financial markets, financial institutions and financial products within the region should be realized to build a large ecosystem of coordinated financial development in the GBA. In terms of collaboration in science and innovation, cross-border flow and regional integration of innovative elements such as talents, capital, information and technology will be achieved in the GBA by means of facilitating customs clearance for talents, reducing and remitting tariffs on research equipment, building innovation platforms, establishing special research networks, and allowing cross-border allocation of research funds. In terms of governance coordination, the integration of urban governance, social security and public services among Hong Kong, Macao and nine cities of the mainland will be promoted. In terms of talent collaboration, through measures such as top-level design, mutual recognition of professional qualifications, unified employment information platform and joint talent training, etc., the free flow of talents in the GBA will be realized. The results of the value simulation analysis show that the implementation of the FTA combined ports collaborative policy will significantly enhance the economic, trade and financial strength of the GBA, strengthen the population agglomeration effect, and will also be helpful to improve the environment of the GBA, which will effectively promote the GBA to become the benchmark of the global bay areas.

8.2 Prospects

Based on the historical background and objective needs of the construction of the combined free trade ports of GBA, this book summarizes the systems, practice and development modes of the three globally recognized free trade ports and the three bay areas, and the practical experience of exploring free trade port (area) construction and regional coordination and integration development in China. On this basis, this book tries to introduce free trade port system into the regional coordinated development, in order to provide wisdom and plans for the construction of the GBA. However, compared with the pilot Free Trade Zone, the free trade port is still a new thing in the mainland of China, and the concept of combined free trade ports has been put forward for the first time. Owing to the uniqueness of "One country, Two systems", three tariff zones and three legal systems in the GBA, the construction of combined ports in the GBA is bound to be an extremely complex system engineering, which still needs to be improved in many ways. But this book does not demonstrate them in detail. I hope this book will attract people from all walks of life to study and pay more attention to institutional collaborative innovation, cross-border financial collaborative innovation, industrial collaborative innovation, technological collaborative innovation, legal collaborative innovation, etc., and contribute to the innovation and development of the GBA.

References

Agsgarwal A (2006) Special economic zones: revisiting the policy debate. Econ Polit Wkly 41(43/44):4533–4536

Chen C, Zhao M (2010) Rationality and alienation in the spatial development of central cities and outer regions: the surrounding aeas of Shanghai connecting with Shanghai. Urban Plann Review (12):42–50

Chen HZ, Meng GW, Gao YP, Yang S, et al (2015) Development and evolution, dynamic mechanism and enlightenment of Hong Kong free port model. Trop Geogr 35(1):70–80

Chen J, Wan Z, Zhang F, et al (2018) Evaluation and comparison of the development performances of typical free trade port zones in China. Transp Research Part Policy and Pract 118:506–526

Cheng MC, Wang D, Wang JJ (2018) A port-based evaluation framework of trade facilitation policies: case of Shenzhen and Hong Kong. Case Stud on Transp Policy 6(2):297–307

Cui X, Fang C, Liu H, et al (2019) Assessing sustainability of urbanization by a coordinated development index for an urbanization-resources-environment complex system: a case study of Jing-Jin-Ji region, China. Ecol Indic 96:383–391

Cui XG, Fang CL, Li J (2019) Research progress of dynamic simulation model of urbanization and ecological environment coupling. Geogr Sci Prog 38(1):111–125
Deng X, Wang Y, Yeo GT (2017) Enterprise perspective-based evaluation of free trade port areas in China. Marit Econo Logistics 19(3):451–473
Dou LC, Sun WCZ, Cheng GR (2019) Development status and cooperation path of high-tech industry in Beijing-Tianjin-Hebei Region. Shijiazhuang Univ J Chinese Med 21(4):53–58
Fang C, Yu D (2017) city cluster:an evolving concept of an emerging phenomenon. Landscape and urban Plan 162:126–136
Hamilton M, Lubell M (2018) Collaborative governance of climate change adaptation across spatial and institutional scales. Policy Stud J 46(2):222–247
Harrison M, Hong W, Lam S, et al (2019) The promise of China's free trade zones: the case of Hainan. Asian Educ and Dev Stud
Haynes KE, Fotheringham AS (1984) Gravity and spatial interaction models. Beverly Hills: Sage
Lin L, Xue J (2019) Reform approaches on tax preferential policies of Chinese free trade zones based on the comparative study on tax preferential policies of the global free trade zones. In 2nd International Conference on Economy, Management and Entrepreneurship (ICOEME 2019). Atlantis Press
Li JH, Li GP (2019) A new strategy model of western development based on generalized gradient theory. Dev Research (6):1–3
Li SZ (2019) Building the Zhejiang-Shanghai combined ports and explore the construction of free trade port to provide strong support for the high-quality development of the Yangtze River Economic Belt. China Water Transp 2019(1):14–16
Lin Y, Cai F, Li Z (1999) Comparative advantage and development strategy: a review of the East Asian Miracle. Chinese Soc Sci (5):4–20
Li Y, Wu F (2015 2017 2018) Understanding city-regionalism in China: regional cooperation in the Yangtze River Delta. Reg Stud 52(3):313–324. Association of Bay Area Governments. People, places, and prosperity. Metropolitan Transportation Commission. Plan Bay Area 2040. Sage Beverly Hills CA. OneNYC. New York
Lu DD, Lu WT, Dai C, Guo HC (2015) Land use scenario design and simulation based on Dyna-CLUE model in Dianchi Lake watershed. Geogr Research 34(9):1619–1629
Mishra P (2018) The rise of China and the fall of the free trade myth. The New York Times
Pan WD (2019) The integrated development of China's regional ports from the perspective of combined ports. Water Transp Manage (1):1–5, 12
Pan WD (2019) Differentiation analysis of port portfolio and port enterprise portfolio. J of Dalian Marit Univ (Soc Sci Edition) 18(2):59–64
Pan WD (2019) On the development mode of regional port integration. China Port 2019(5):1–5
Tang YL, Yu Y (2018) Active and connected regional cooperation: compound dynamics and mechanism innovation GBA for a new model of regional governance in the Yangtze River Delta. Theoretical Explor (1):28–35
Tian W, Xu Z, Yu M, et al (2018) China's free trade ports: effective action against the threat of de-globalization. China & World Econ 26(4):62–81
Wang S, Ma H, Zhao Y (2014) Exploring the relationship between urbanization and the eco-environment: a case study of Beijing-Tianjin-Hebei region. Ecol Ind 45:171–183
Ye C, Liu Z, Cai W, et al (2019) Spatial production and governance of city cluster in China 2000-2015: Yangtze River Delta as a case Sustain 11(5):13–433
Ye Y, Li S, Zhang H, et al (2018) Spatial-temporal dynamics of the economic efficiency of construction land in the PRD megalopolis from 1998 to 2012. Sustain 10(1):63
Zhang X, Guo QE, Cheung DMW, et al (2018) Evaluating the institutional performance of the PRD integration policy through intercity cooperation network analysis Cities 81:131–144
Zhang X, Sun Y (2019) Investigating institutional integration in the contexts of Chinese city regionalization: evidence from Shenzhen-Dongguan-Huizhou. Land Use Policy

The manufacturer's authorised representative in the EU is Springer Nature Customer Service Centre GmbH, Europaplatz 3, 69115 Heidelberg, Germany. If you have any concerns regarding our products, please contact ProductSafety@springernature.com

Printed and bound by CPI Group (UK) Ltd, Croydon, CR0 4YY
30/09/2026
02225234-0013